Guidelines for Investigating Chemical Process Incidents

Publications Available from the

CENTER FOR CHEMICAL PROCESS SAFETY
of the
AMERICAN INSTITUTE OF CHEMICAL ENGINEERS

Guidelines for Investigating Chemical Process Incidents

CENTER FOR CHEMICAL PROCESS SAFETY
of the
AMERICAN INSTITUTE OF CHEMICAL ENGINEERS
345 East 47th Street, New York, New York 10016

Library of Congress Cataloging-in-Publication Data

Guidelines for investigating chemical process incidents.

p. cm.

Includes bibliographical references and index.

ISBN 0–8169–0555–X

1. Chemical plants—Safety measures. I. American Institute of Chemical Engineers. Center for Chemical Process Safety.

TP155.5.G775 1992

660'.2804—dc20 92-9789

CIP

CONTENTS

PREFACE

The American Institute of Chemical Engineers (AIChE) has a 30-year history of involvement with process safety and loss control for chemical and petrochemical plants. Through its ties with process designers, builders and operators, safety professionals and academia, the AIChE has enhanced communications and fostered improvement in the high safety standards of the industry. Its publications and symposia have become an information resource for the chemical engineering profession on the causes of incidents and means of prevention.

The Center for Chemical Process Safety (CCPS), a directorate of AIChE, was established in 1985 to intensify development and dissemination of the latest scientific and engineering practices for prevention and mitigation of catastrophic incidents involving hazardous materials: advance the state-of-the-art of engineering practices through research: and develop and encourage the use of undergraduate curricula that will improve the safety knowledge and consciousness of engineers.

Over 80 corporations from all segments of the chemical and hydrocarbon process industries support the Center. They select CCPS's projects relevant to improved process safety, they furnish the professionals who give the Center's works technical direction and substance, and they help fund the Center. Since its founding, CCPS has cosponsored several international, technical symposia, developed training courses, undertaken research projects and published nine volumes in its *Guidelines* series, the proceedings of five technical meeting and teaching materials to help integrate process safety into undergraduate chemical engineering programs. CCPS research projects now in progress will yield new data for improved process safety.

Most CCPS books in print are written for engineers in plant design and operations and address scientific techniques and engineering practices. Some of the newer books embody the philosophy that successful process safety programs result from the committed and active participation of managers at all levels and a systematic approach to process safety that is an integral part of operations management. The first of these, *Guidelines for Technical Management of Chemical Process Safety*, is based on the best safety management systems in use within industry and was written for middle and top managers. It explains the twelve elements that must be considered in an effective program to manage chemical process safety. The next in this series of publications, *Plant Guidelines for Technical Management of Chemical Process Safety,* is designed to be used by plant managers and their staff, and it provides more detail and examples of useful management systems in these twelve elements.

One of the twelve elements in a process safety management program is the investigation of incidents, the subject of this book. The target audience for the book is a cross section of mid-level managers, engineering professionals, and production supervisors who will lead, manage, or participate on an investigation team. For them, this book in the *Guidelines* series presents techniques for investigating incidents of a serious nature, whether they result in accidents or not, whether they have in-plant or off-plant consequences, or whether they are characterized by actual or potential loss of life and/or property or damage to the environment. Guidance is also provided for initial establishment of an investigation team and establishment and evaluation of a management system for incident investigation. Lastly an annotated bibliography is included for safety professionals who may wish to refer to the many books available on incident investigation.

The major components in the investigation of an incident are

- Identify the root causes
- Determine recommendations necessary to prevent a recurrence
- Ensure that action is taken on these recommendations.

In many older approaches to investigation of a process incident, the investigation frequently ended when one or two direct or intermediate causes of an incident were identified. Newer technology has demonstrated that incidents and accidents are the end result of several failures which contribute to the event. The newer approaches have proven successful in their application and results. This book is based upon the new approaches and covers state-of-the-art technology and practices in use for thoroughly investigating an incident.

Consequently, the major principles around which this book was written include the following:

- **Every process incident is a symptom of a system failure.**
  Successful operation of a process plant results from multiple elements (process, equipment, employees, management practices, and policies) working together as a complete system. No process incident occurs as a result of any one cause, but is the result of a combination of features and/or failures of various system elements. To prevent accidents, we must, therefore, address system causes, not just direct or immediate causes of incidents.

- **Few, if any, process incidents occur as a result of a single cause.**

- **Process incident investigations should follow formal logical methodologies.**
  The reason for an investigation is to prevent another incident by taking steps to remedy all the system causes. An investigation is too important for hit-or-miss methods that may overlook significant causes or potential causes.

- **To prevent accidents all of the groups in the system (managers, designers, supervisors, maintainers, operators, engineers, etc.) have to work together as a team.**

The most significant concept in this book is that all groups involved with a process have a shared responsibility for success and failure in preventing a process incident. All groups must work together as a team throughout the life cycle of a plant to minimize incidents.

- **Communication of key learnings from process incident investigations is essential-** Sharing of lessons learned among plants, sites, and companies can help prevent recurrence of similar incidents. However, there can be legal difficulties in communicating the details of process incident investigations. Some groups are exploring means to work around these constraints and communicate necessary incident information.

This *Guidelines* book is an effort to present currently used state-of-the-art information on process incident investigation in a manner that would be most useful to managers and engineers in the chemical and hydrocarbon processing industries. We look forward to the day when there will be newer and even better investigation techniques and systems, and a second edition of the book will be a necessity.

Finally, the cornerstone of a successful investigation is the investigators' commitment to excellence. Excellence requires finding all the system causes, developing workable and innovative solutions to failures found and to problems encountered, testing new ideas, and continuing to look for better methods, techniques, and remedies. The reward of excellence is the prevention of accidents and better protection of employees, neighbors, and the environment.

ACKNOWLEDGMENTS

Guidelines for Investigating Chemical Process Incident was prepared by the Incident Investigation Subcommittee of the Center for Chemical Process Safety and HALLIBURTON NUS Environmental Corporation

The American Institute of Chemical Engineers wishes to thank the Center for Chemical Process Safety (CCPS) and those involved in its operation, including its many sponsors whose funding made this project possible; the members of its Technical Steering Committee who conceived of and supported this *Guidelines* project, and the members of its Incident Investigation Subcommittee for their dedicated efforts, technical contributions, and the guidance necessary for the preparation of this work.

The Chairman of the CCPS Incident Investigation Subcommittee was Patrick Ragan, Rhone-Poulenc. The Subcommittee members were Kenneth Austin, Chevron USA Incorporated; Arthur M. Dowell, III, Rohm and Haas Texas; Martin E. Gluckstein, Ethyl Corporation; Michael Kelyman, Dow Chemical Company; Eric Lenoir, Industrial Risk Insurers; Stephen Meszaros, American Cyanamid Company; and Donald E. Park, Ethyl Corporation. Thomas W. Carmody and Robert A. Schulze of the Center for Chemical Process Safety were responsible for the overall administration and coordination of this project.

The American Institute of Chemical Engineers thanks HALLIBURTON NUS Environmental Corporation for major contributions to the technological content, technical writing, and technical editing of this guidebook. Project manager and principal author was Jack Philley, CSP. HALLIBURTON NUS project team members included: Dan Rees, F. S. Dombek, B.O.Y. Lydell (primary author of Chapter 2), D. Franklin, M. Gelling, and B. Evans.

The CCPS Incident Investigation Subcommittee also wishes to thank the peer reviewers for their diligent perusal of this work and their thoughtful and detailed comments. The book is enhanced by their suggestions. Peer reviewers were C. Matthiessen (US EPA), R. Ormsby (Air Products and Chemicals), K. Turnbull (Texaco, Inc.), Dr. Harry West (Shawnee Engineers), W. "Skip" Early and M. Sherrod (Stone & Webster Engineering Corp.), D. Hendershot and S. Anderson (Rohm & Haas), J. Hoffmeister (Martin Marietta), D. Crowl (Wayne State University), D. Langlois (Langlois & Associates), and Ing. Sergio Riva Palacio (SEDUE, Mexico).

The members of the CCPS Incident Investigation Subcommittee also wish to thank their employers for providing time to participate in this project.

1

INTRODUCTION

Incident investigation is a well recognized and vital part of process safety management. The objective of this guidebook is to provide a technical foundation for systematic investigations in order to prevent recurrence of incidents. In the context of this book, *the term "incident" includes all accidents and all near-miss events* that did or could cause injury, or loss of or damage to property or the environment. By learning "what went wrong" and "why something went wrong" it is possible to prevent the same or a similar event from happening again through changes in operating procedures, facility design, or operator training. Some form of incident investigation has been an important part of established and evolving technologies for many years, resulting in valuable insights that could be applied to make new incident investigations more effective.

This introductory chapter covers:

- The relation of incident investigation to the total management of chemical process safety (Section 1.1)
- The need for and benefits of incidents investigation that can prevent recurrence (Section 1.2)
- The classification of incidents ranging from occupational injuries to major disasters, and the impact of investigation techniques required (Section 1.3)
- The concepts of problem solving and feedback as they apply to process incident investigation (Section 1.4)
- The objectives of this book (Section 1.5)
- The arrangement of this book to plan for, initiate, and carry out the various steps in an investigation (Section 1.6).

The objective of incident investigation is to prevent a recurrence

This is accomplished by establishing a management system that

- Identifies and evaluates causes (root causes and contributing causes).
- Identifies and evaluates recommended preventive measures that act to reduce the probability and/or consequence.
- Ensures effective follow-up action to complete and/or review all recommendations.

1.1. THE RELATION OF INCIDENT INVESTIGATION TO MANAGEMENT OF PROCESS SAFETY

In 1985, the American Institute of Chemical Engineers (AIChE) formed the Center for Chemical Process Safety (CCPS) to promote the improvement of process safety among those who handle, use, process, and store hazardous materials. Projects supported by CCPS have addressed technical and management approaches for the prevention of process-related incidents. This text is one in a series of technical guideline publications that deal with the common theme of prevention of episodic or catastrophic incidents within the chemical process industry. This guidebook builds on the basic principles already developed by the CCPS in its *Guidelines for Technical Management of Chemical Process Safety.*[1]

In this latter Guidelines book, CCPS has identified multiple components involved in successful management of process hazards and has grouped them into 12 elements with incident investigation listed as element 9. These components are highly interrelated and interdependent. The taxonomy of a process safety management system is illustrated in Table 1-1.

Process safety management (PSM) is "the application of management systems to the identification, understanding, and control of process hazards to prevent process-related injuries and incidents."[1] Process safety should be considered a dynamic system involving the technology, materials, people, and equipment that comprise a facility. The PSM program ensures that a properly designed facility is maintained and operated in a safe manner.

To be able to address, enhance, and control process safety, the analysts and engineers working on process hazard analysis studies such as HAZOP (Hazard and Operability Study) and QRA (Quantitative Risk Assessments), as well as plant management teams, need to have access to detailed and accurate information on a number of factors including the process, the materials involved, the plant as designed and built, operating procedures, maintenance regimes, and plant-specific and industry-wide operating experience. This operating experience includes equipment reliability data and insights from incident investigations. Together, the reliability data and the incident data form a "feedback loop" in the process safety management system. The feedback makes it possible to control and improve safety through better identification of process hazards; through application of effective changes in the process, plant equipment, and operating procedures; and through institution of operator training programs, all of which can prevent incidents.

Hence, this book provides a basis for successful incident investigation by defining its role in overall PSM and by providing investigation guidelines, concepts, and options. To date, CCPS has published books on topics including hazards identification, equipment reliability data, and process safety management. Although incident investigation has been addressed in some earlier books, this work has been developed to present techniques for more in-depth incident investigation and to provide guidance on how to establish an incident investigation system. This book is written for the

TABLE 1-1
CCPS ELEMENTS AND COMPONENTS OF PROCESS SAFETY MANAGEMENT

1. **Accountability: Objectives and Goals**
   Continuity of Operations
   Continuity of Systems (resources and funding)
   Continuity of Organizations
   Company Expectations (vision or master plan)
   Quality Process
   Control of Exceptions
   Alternative Methods (performance vs. specification)
   Management Accessibility
   Communications
2. **Process Knowledge and Documentation**
   Process Definition and Design Criteria
   Process and Equipment Design
   Company Memory (management information)
   Documentation of Risk Management Decisions
   Protective Systems
   Normal and Upset Conditions
   Chemical and Occupational Health Hazards
3. **Capital Project Review and Design Procedures (for new or existing plants, expansions, and acquisitions)**
   Appropriation Request Procedures
   Risk Assessment for Investment Purposes
   Hazards Review (including worst credible cases)
   Siting (relative to risk management)
   Plot Plan
   Process Design and Review Procedures
   Project Management Procedures
4. **Process Risk Management**
   Hazard Identification
   Risk Assessment of Existing Operations
   Reduction of Risk
   Residual Risk Management (in-plant emergency response and mitigation)
   Process Management during Emergencies
   Encouraging Client and Supplier Companies to Adopt Similar Risk Management Practices
   Selection of Businesses with Acceptable Risks
5. **Management of Change**
   Change of Technology
   Change of Facility
   Organizational Changes That May Have an Impact on Process Safety
   Variance Procedures
   Temporary Changes
   Permanent Changes
6. **Process and Equipment Integrity**
   Reliability Engineering
   Materials of Construction
   Fabrication and Inspection Procedures
   Installation Procedures
   Preventive Maintenance
   Process, Hardware, Systems Inspections, and Testing (pre-start-up safety review)
   Maintenance Procedures

(Continued on page 4)

TABLE 1.1 *(Continued)*

- Alarm and Instrument Management
- Demolition Procedures

7. **Human Factors**
   - Human Error Assessment
   - Operator/Process and Equipment Interfaces
   - Administrative Controls versus Hardware
8. **Training and Performance**
   - Definition of Skills and Knowledge
   - Training Programs (e.g., new employees, contractors, technical employees)
   - Design of Operating and Maintenance Procedures
   - Initial Qualification Assessment
   - Ongoing Performance and Refresher Training
   - Instructor Program
   - Records Management
9. **Incident Investigation**
   - Major Incidents
   - Near-Miss Reporting
   - Follow-Up and Resolution
   - Communication
   - Incident Recording
   - Third-Party Participation as Needed
10. **Standards, Codes, and Laws**
    - Internal Standards, Guidelines, and Practices (past history, flexible performance standards, amendments, and upgrades)
    - External Standards, Guidelines, and Practices
11. **Audits and Corrective Actions**
    - Process Safety Audits and Compliance Reviews
    - Resolutions and Close-Out Procedures
12. **Enhancement of Process Safety Knowledge**
    - Internal and External Research
    - Improved Predictive Systems
    - Process Safety Reference Library

technical professional or the middle level manager who will lead or contribute to an investigation team. The text also provides insights to engineers who are active in process hazards analysis activities. While the primary focus is on incidents with catastrophic potential, the concepts are equally applicable for investigating environmental incidents, minor injuries, less significant property damage events, or even near-misses.

1.2. THE NEED FOR AND BENEFITS OF INCIDENT INVESTIGATION

A process safety management (PSM) system should be simultaneously "retrospective" and "prospective"; that is, it needs to ensure that process safety lessons learned in the past can be utilized in day-to-day operations and when planning for new designs and construction projects. Incident investigation provides the important linkage between the lessons of past incidents and safer designs and operation in the future.

The connection between incident investigation and process safety management has been known to safety professionals for many years. Receptivity to the findings from investigation of major incidents have caused process safety management philosophies to evolve, advance, and recognize the need for even better incident investigation.

Incidents should be viewed as opportunities to improve management systems rather than as opportunities to assign blame.

Now, process safety guidelines are built on deeper insights and typically include special considerations and provisions for incident investigation. It is becoming common to find that process safety departments have clearly established roles for managing incident investigations which yield new insights that can make ongoing operations safer. Systematic techniques and tools have been developed that can structure investigative tasks for more thorough analysis—tools such as the MORT[2] (Management Oversight and Risk Tree) approach and the causal factors sequence diagrams used by the US National Transportation Safety Board and other organizations.

Chemical and hydrocarbon producers and users also benefit from other developments in process safety incident investigation (PSII) concepts, which can help reduce the recurrence of incidents and catastrophe accidents. The first of these deals with the actual objectives of PSII. The traditional view has been that once the investigation team submits its written report and recommendations, the investigation is complete. The newer and accepted approach extends the objectives to include the resolution and documentation of all recommendations, thus affording better protection against future incidents.

In a second development, the older and constraining concept of a single cause (formerly called "primary" cause) of an incident has been replaced by the concept of multiple root causes. By acknowledging that there may be multiple causes of an incident, investigators can develop multiple remedies and more comprehensive actions to improve plant process safety.

Lastly, previous approaches viewed investigation of process safety incidents as a special area of expertise outside of the duties of the line organization. Today it is recognized that operating, design, and maintenance engineers and managers all have roles in process safety and that they should have an appropriate role in incident investigations. Participation by many groups within an organization in a PSII involves them directly in reaching conclusions, developing recommendations that they may have to implement, and learning lessons that they may need in the future. This also serves to reinforce the concept that responsibility for PSM and incident prevention is shared by many departments and disciplines.

Fuller use of information and wider disseminating of lessons learned is an important factor in preventing future incidents and should be addressed during a PSII. To be considered complete, each incident investigation should identify items and findings that would be of value and should be disseminated to other company facilities, to company engineering, safety, training, research, development, and staff support groups and to trade organizations who might have a potential interest or application. It is important that the type of information to be divulged and means of dissemination be approved by relevant corporate groups.

A common finding from major incidents is the failure to adequately communicate lessons learned at one facility to another facility in the same company. Sometimes valuable insights are not captured, shared, or applied to the fullest extent possible, resulting in lost opportunities for preventing a repeat incident. The PSII provides the opportunity to have all departments, including those in similar company facilities that are involved in a PSM system, participate in the formation of a investigation plan. A company's process safety can directly benefit through plant interaction and exchange of ideas. Further, personnel from other facilities who become involved with incident investigations and process hazards identification may acquire useful insights from incidents at other locations.

A systematic investigation contains specific built-in feedback loops to ensure that opportunities to improve the operations can be identified and resolved to completion. These opportunities include internal communication between pertinent departments and related or similar units. Good internal communication is neither automatic nor easy, and requires consistent proactive measures. Figure 1-1 illustrates the feedback loop connecting the critique of the investigation with the planning activity, in order to capture and benefit from the lessons available for learning. Another opportunity to benefit from incident investigation is in the relationship between the management structure and organizational influences on process safety performance. Incident investigation techniques have been established which address organizational and human factors. These concepts are discussed in Chapter 2, 4, and 5 of these CCPS guidelines.

1.3. INCIDENT CLASSIFICATION AND DEFINITIONS

Various classification systems have been developed and applied, each specific to the needs of a particular organization. Perhaps the two most widely used in the United States are the Occupational Safety and Health Administration, U.S. Department of Labor (OSHA) *Recordkeeping Guideline* and the ANSI (American National Standards Institute) Z16.2 Standard, *Method of Recording Basic Facts Relating to the Nature and Occurrence of Work Injuries.* These two sources provide a foundation for many internal classification systems. Incidents can be analyzed in several ways: according to the causes and consequences, according to situations where they occurred, and according to system or process involved, etc. Additional information on incident classification is contained in Section 3.3

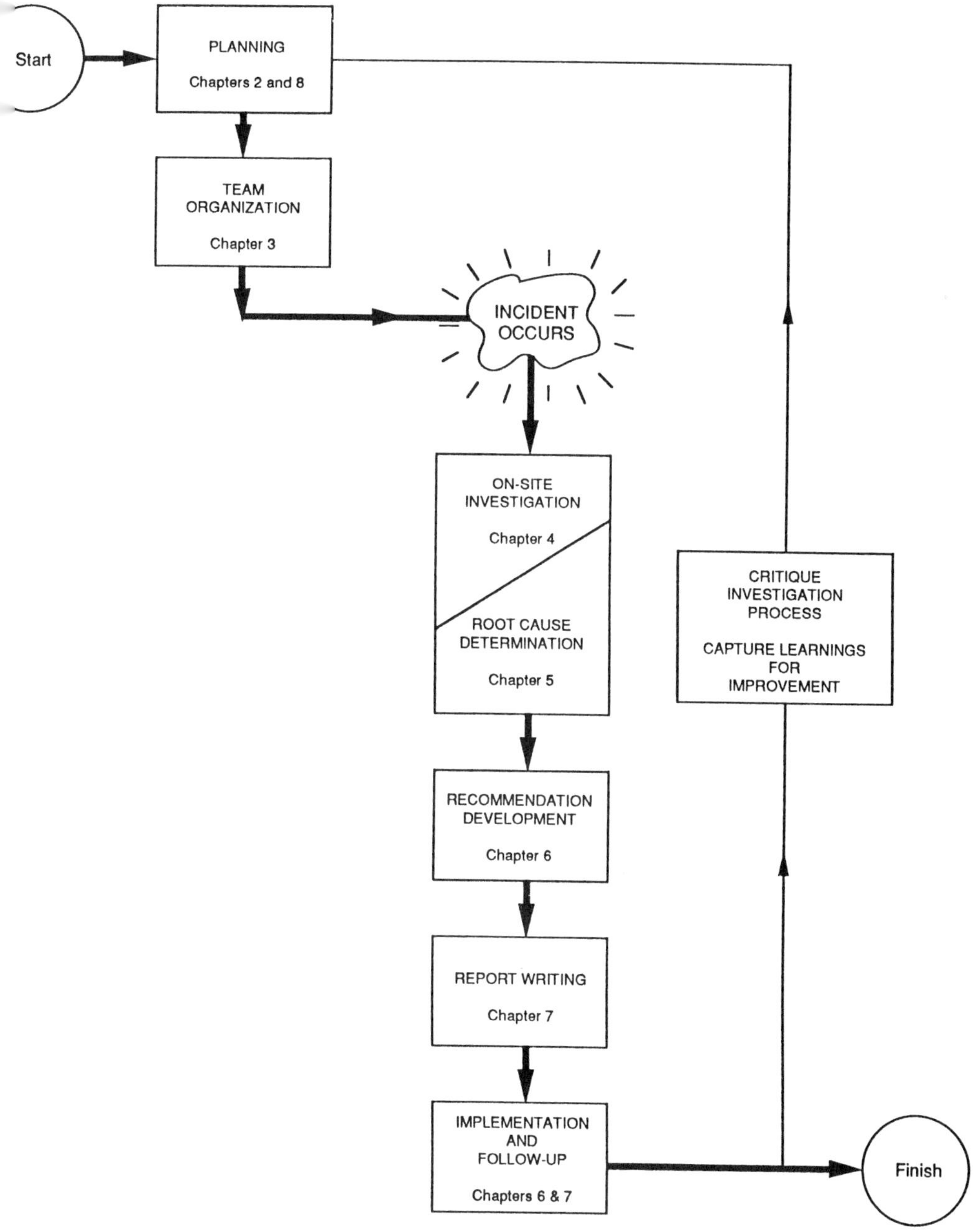

Figure 1-1. Flowchart—overview of incident investigation.

A full glossary appears at the beginning of this guidebook; however, the following terms have special significance and are highlighted in this section. The term **"accident" as used in this book** is defined as an *incident that is accompanied by actual negative consequences,* and the term "*incident*" is broadly defined as "an unplanned event with the potential for undesirable consequences." By definition, incidents **do include "near-miss" events**. In the context of process safety, incidents include events such as fires, explosions, releases of toxic or hazardous substances, excursions outside of critical operating limits, and sudden releases of energy. Such events can and sometimes actually do result in death, injury, adverse health effects, or damage to the environment or equipment. "Near-miss" incidents are extraordinary events that could, but actually do not, result in negative consequences.

There are two major conventions in defining the term "incident." This book uses the broader context where the category of incident includes both "near-misses" as well as events with actual negative consequences. The other convention limits the term "incident" to only those near-miss events that did not result in actual negative consequences.

The term "anomaly" is sometimes used as a separate subcategory of near-miss events. A working definition of anomaly is "an unusual set of circumstances which, left unrecognized or uncorrected, may result in an accident."

The discipline of incident investigation covers two primary branches, namely *process* and *occupational injury* incident investigation. The first branch is concerned with the process safety aspects (engineering and operational), whereas the latter concentrates on traditional personnel injuries. As previously stated, this particular guidebook can be used for either branch. In practice, their principles, objectives, and activities are comparable.

Additional definitions are listed below:

Incident Investigation: The process by which underlying causes of incidents are uncovered and steps are taken to prevent similar recurrences. In modern incident investigations, the use of analytical tools originally developed for process hazards analysis (e.g., HAZOP study techniques, fault tree techniques) and statistics on incidents, equipment faults, and human errors can support the determination of cause–consequence relationships. This approach is referred to as *systematic* or *analytical* incident investigation.

Cause: An event, situation, or condition that results directly or indirectly in an incident.

Root Causes: Prime reasons, such as failures of some management systems, that allow faulty design, inadequate training, or improper changes, which lead to an unsafe act or condition and result in an incident. Root causes are also known as underlying causes. If root causes were removed, the particular incident would not have occurred.

1.4. CONCEPTS FOR PROCESS INCIDENT INVESTIGATION

Incident investigation generally follows a problem-solving process that involves gathering information and evidence, analyzing the evidence, and summarizing the findings. The level of effort required for the performance of an investigation is usually a function of the type of incident and its potential consequences. An important basic concept is that the near-miss incident can be just as significant as a major accident, and equally challenging to analyze. A strong possibility exists that the near-miss event can be indicative of a trend that, if left uncorrected, could lead to a major accident.

Insights and results generated by the investigation team can provide essential feedback of information within an organization as well as among organizations. Depending on the root causes of an incident, the investigation results may relate to any of the 12 PSM elements listed in Table 1-1.

Figure 1-1 presents an overview of the steps in process incident investigation. This book generally follows the same logical development sequence. Planning begins with management, an understanding of the factors and causes of incidents, and the objectives of an investigation. From this base, an investigation system is created by assignment of responsibilities, preparation, and the organization of the investigation team. When an incident occurs, the on-site work is primarily directed toward evidence gathering and preliminary cause determination. The investigation team determines root causes and submits recommendations for corrective actions. Recommendations are reviewed, changes approved and implemented, and the entire proceedings documented. A feedback loop from an objective critique of the investigation completes the cycle. This review captures insights and lessons learned about the investigation itself that can promote continuous improvement of the incident investigation system.

Incident investigation techniques can be classified into three general approaches, as detailed in Chapter 2 (Sections 2.1 and 2.5) and summarized as follows:

THREE APPROACHES TO PSII

Type 1: Traditional, informal investigation carried on by immediate supervisor.

Type 2: Committee-based investigation using expert judgment to find a credible solution of cause and remedy.

Type 3: Multiple-cause, systems-oriented investigation that focuses on root cause determination, Integrated with an overall process safety management program.

The Type 3 multiple-cause, systems-oriented approach that is fully integrated with a process safety management program has evolved as the most organized, thorough, and probing approach. Since the typical process safety incident is a complex event, the systematic deductive method is best suited to yield successful results. The Type 3 approach also recognizes that most incidents have multiple underlying causes, and attempts to isolate the system-related causes. It provides a structure for developing preventive measures that can eliminate an exact recurrence and also help prevent similar events as well.

1.5. OBJECTIVES OF THIS BOOK

The primary focus of the book is on process-related incidents that have the potential for catastrophic consequences. The investigative techniques can be applied to events of less severe or even no consequences by reducing the scale of the investigation team activities. Not all activities addressed in this book are needed for every investigation.

The targeted users of this book are managers, engineers, and those technical professionals whose duties include responsibility for occasional contributions to or participation in formal incident investigations. Those who are involved with establishing a formal management system for incident investigation would also find this information helpful. This book is not intended to be a full-scope text for professional investigators. This book is designed to be equally applicable regardless of the size of the facility, size of the company organization, or severity of the consequences. Environmental excursions as well as operational upsets are within the scope of the incidents covered by this book. The objectives of this book are to provide:

- Principles and methodology for incident investigation
- Information for planning an incident investigation
- Steps for conducting an investigation
- An outline for timely reporting of incidents and remedial action
- A list of reference materials
- Examples of successful methods used in the chemical process industry

For the sake of completeness and comparison, the text gives an overview of incident investigation principles as implemented by other industries in the United States and other countries. Through an annotated bibliography, some of the current research and development issues are identified. Hence, this text is meant to be both a practical handbook and a resource document on incident investigation.

In its eight chapters and appendices, this book concentrates on the theory and practical guidance of incident investigation. The material aims to provide a basis for establishing a management system for investigation of episodic incidents that have potential for catastrophic consequences to human life, property, or the environment. This information can be used as a comprehensive, systematic, and generic model and attempts to provide a balance between theoretical and practical aspects.

1.6. ARRANGEMENT OF THIS BOOK

The sequence of activities for an investigation system is shown in Figure 1.1. The reader may refer to the listed chapters for information on each activity. Some material is repeated for the convenience of the reader.

This chapter is intended to establish the scope and objectives of the book.

Chapter 2 discusses basic principles of incident investigation and examines the available techniques. A large number of methods have been proposed over the years, many based on systematic approaches. The emphasis has been to provide tools to correctly identify root causes and cause–consequence relationships. Human factors and organizational issues can play dominant roles in "triggering" an incident. Chapter 2 elaborates on these issues. Finally, some guidelines are given regarding the effectiveness and range of applicability of the various investigative techniques, in order to assist in the selection of the suitable method for a particular incident.

Chapter 3 presents an overview of the management system for incident investigation. The basic premise is to prepare for the unexpected and to ensure that the present process safety management system recognizes the need for and benefits of systematic incident investigation.

In view of some of the fundamental considerations of Chapters 2 and 3, practical investigation considerations are addressed in Chapter 4. This chapter deals with how the investigation team is organized, what tools are needed, and what information is required. Because gathering and interpreting evidence can be difficult, numerous practical and useful suggestions are included.

Once the field operations have been completed (i.e., all of the evidence has been collected), the investigation team will have to identify the root causes. Chapter 5 explains the techniques for multiple cause determination, together with guidance on selection of the appropriate levels of detail for root cause analysis. Following the analysis of available facts, the investigation team is faced with the important task of generating preventive action recommendations and ensuring that these recommendations receive follow-through. These issues are developed in Chapter 6.

Chapter 7 provides advice on the preparation of investigation reports and communicating lessons learned.

Guidelines for initially establishing a management system for process incident investigation are illustrated in Chapter 8. This chapter can also be used to evaluate or revitalize an existing program.

1.7. REFERENCES

1. Center for Chemical Process Safety (CCPS), 1989. *Guidelines for Technical Management of Chemical Process Safety*. New York: American Institute of Chemical Engineers.
2. Johnson, W.G., 1973. *MORT—The Management Oversight and Risk Tree*, SAN 8-21-2. Albuquerque, NM: Sandia National Laboratories.
3. Rasmussen, J., 1981. *Human Factors in High Risk Technology*, N-2-81, Roskilde, Denmark: Electronics Department, Risø National Laboratory. Also in Green, E.A. (Ed.), 1981. *High Risk Safety Technology*. New York: John Wiley & Sons.
4. Peterson, D., 1989. *Techniques of Safety Management*, 3rd ed. Goshen, NY: Aloray, Inc.
5. Haastrup, P., 1984. *Design Error in the Chemical Industry*. Roskilde, Denmark: Risø National Laboratory.

2

BASIC INCIDENT INVESTIGATION TECHNIQUES

This chapter addresses three basic issues of systematic process safety incident investigation (PSII):

- The causes of an incident (Sections 2.2, 2.3, and 2.4)
- The available techniques for PSII (Section 2.5)
- The selection of a proper technique for PSII (Sections 2.5.2 through 2.5.4)

The presentation provides a summary of recognized incident theories and investigation techniques. The validity of the techniques for modern PSII is determined. It is also demonstrated that the analytical approaches to PSII and process hazards analysis (PHA), respectively, are very similar. Hence, the results and insights of the PSII support the PHA, and the techniques of PHA are used for the systematic PSII. The key difference between PSII and PHA is that PSII is applied after the fact, and PHA is applied *before* the fact. Aside from this difference, the same type of analytical reasoning is used.

Process safety incident investigation can benefit from the use of a systematic approach. As a rule, a structured approach to the PSII represents direct implementation of sound process safety management principles and assures consistency and accuracy in the investigative effort. To be most effective, the structured approach must recognize the basic concepts of incident causation and use tested PSII techniques.

Many theories of incident causation and related investigation techniques exist. None of the techniques is all-encompassing. The incident investigator must apply judgment and make adaptations to support a minor or major PSII effort and to contribute to the resolution of why and how an incident occurred.

2.1. PHILOSOPHY FOR PROCESS SAFETY INCIDENT INVESTIGATION

The investigation of incidents to reveal the root causes and then make recommendations can be as much an art as a science. The traditional (Type 1) PSII involved an informal investigation by the immediate supervisor with occasional participation by the injured or involved worker. In case of a more detailed (Type 2) investigation a committee was typically formed to reach consensus on the root cause and remedy through application of expert judgment.

THREE APPROACHES TO PSII

Type 1: Traditional, informal investigation performed by immediate supervisor.

Type 2: Committee-based investigation using expert judgment to find a credible solution of cause and remedy.

Type 3: Multiple-cause, systems-oriented investigation that focuses on root cause determination. Integrated with an overall process safety management program.

Recent years have seen efforts by the CPI to systematize the general PSII approach. The emphasis has been on implementation of techniques that use a multiple-cause and systems-oriented approach. This (Type 3) approach is effective for a broad variety of incidents since it specifically addresses the following issues:

- Quality of PSII by
  —Forcing the investigator to go beneath the surface to the underlying causes
  —Finding as many of the causes as practical
  —Improving documentation of the investigations
  —Increasing the utility for training and information sharing
- Uniformity of investigations by using the multiple-cause,systems-oriented approach
- Utility of recommended corrective actions

The following sections develop the basic principles of the Type 3 approach. The considerations that need to be acknowledged when implementing the systematic PSII techniques are presented.

2.2. ANATOMY OF THE PROCESS-RELATED INCIDENT

By a systematic analysis of historic incident data it has been possible to generate lessons learned and to identify incident stereotypes. This information has made it possible to develop a model, or "anatomy," of a process-related incident to provide a basis for understanding incident causation. Incident theories based on such an "anatomy" have evolved supporting the systematic PSII. A conceptual framework for the anatomy of an incident is given by Figure 2-1.

Whenever a system or process fails, it is not always easy to trace the reasons for its failure. Based on the available historic incident data we can determine that the anatomy of a major incident rarely is simple and seldom results from a single root cause. Serious incidents typically involve a complex sequence of events including

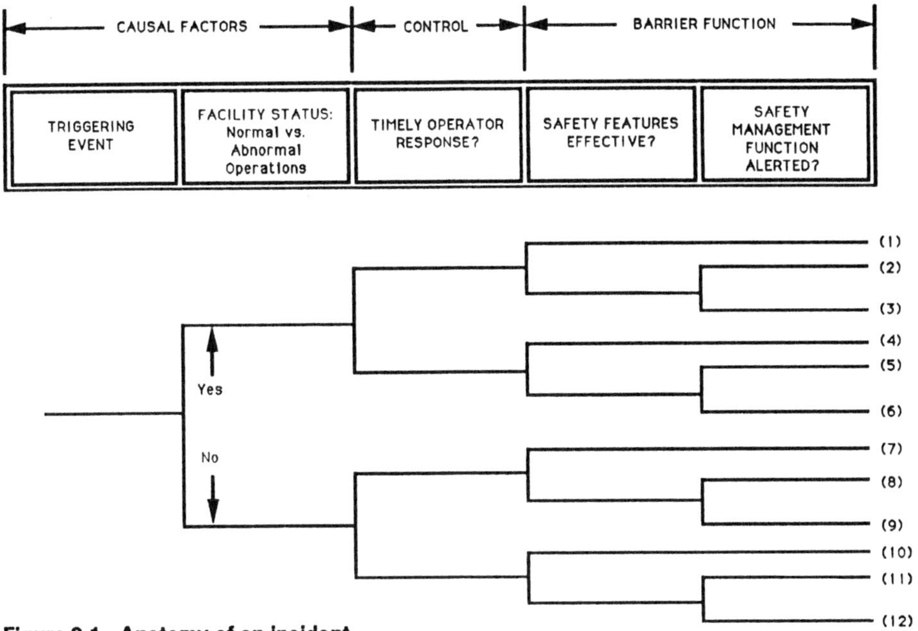

Figure 2-1. Anatomy of an incident.

equipment faults, latent unsafe conditions, as well as human mistakes and errors. Any process-related incident can be described by three different phases[1]:

- Change from normal operating state into a state of abnormal or "disturbed" operation
- Breakdown of the control of the abnormal operating phase
- Loss of control of energy accumulations

In all three phases the equipment and process systems, the human operator, and the organization are potential contributors to the incident cause. If during the incident the third phase is "challenged" and a breakdown of a barrier function (for example, shutdown valve, containment, procedure violation, communication system) occurs, the incident evolves from a near-miss event and becomes a minor or major incident. The potential consequence is a function of the following factors:

- *Inventory of hazardous material:* type and amount
- *Energy factor:* energy of chemical reaction or of material state
- *Time factor:* the rate of release and the warning time
- *Intensity–distance relation:* the distance over which the hazard may cause injury or damage
- *Exposure factor:* the people and/or property in the area affected by the incident.

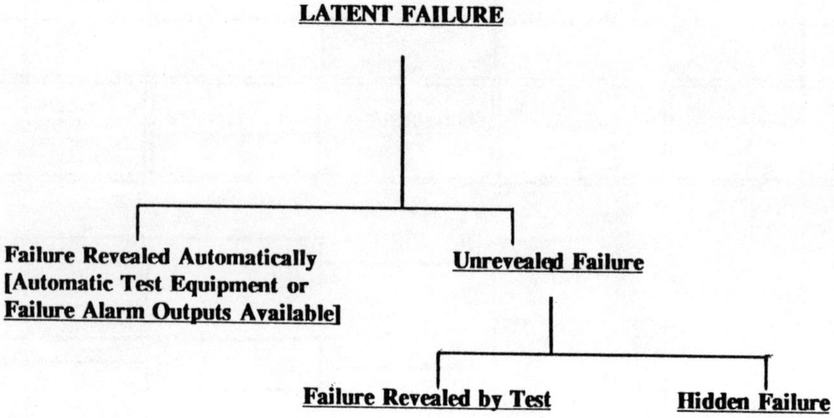

Figure 2-2. Latent (hidden) failure.

Historic incident data show that latent failures (or conditions) have played an important role in incident causation. Normally the latent failure is revealed either through testing or normal operations within the plant; see Figure 2-2. There is always a possibility, however, that a latent failure may remain hidden. The reason is that the failure is not activated by the test input used, not noticed by the test personnel, or because of miscommunication.

2.3. THEORIES OF INCIDENT CAUSATION

The theoretical incident models (or concepts) have evolved from the investigations into the "why" and "how" of case histories. The insights so gained have made it possible to better explain incident causation. These theories have encouraged development of techniques that support the systematic PSII effort.

According to the *incident proneness theory,*[2] incidents are a result of individual differences; for example, some people are consistently more incident prone than others. The theory has been subject to severe criticism, and is now viewed as obsolete. In the current thinking incidents are considered as mismatches between the human operator and the tasks/environment. It retains a valid application in certain cases involving personal injury repeaters. However, for PSII, this accident proneness theory has only limited value.

A classic incident theory is H. W. Heinrich's *theory of causation,*[3] which has had a significant influence on practical PSII. Many versions (or adaptations) of Heinrich's original proposal have been developed. Heinrich labeled his five dominoes:

1. Ancestry and social environment
2. Fault or person
3. Unsafe act
4. Unsafe condition
5. Injury

INCIDENT THEORIES—A SUMMARY

- Incident Proneness Theory by Greenwood and Woods.
- Heinrich's Domino Theory of Causation
  —Updated Domino Theory by Kuhlmann.
  —Seven-Domino Sequence by Marcum.
  —"Relabeled" Five-Domino Sequence by Bird.
  —Modified Domino by Weaver.
  —"Relabeled" Five-Domino Sequence by Adams.
- Process Theory; based on domino theory but includes time factor. Energy-Flow Theory by Gibson (1961); Haddon (1968); Kepner and Tregoe (1976); and Johnson (MORT).
- Multiple-Causation Theory. Incidents are caused by several factors, all coinciding (Peterson and Others).
- System Theory by Recht (1965).
- "Hazard-Carrier" Theory (Die Gefahren-tragertheorie) by Skiba (1973). A version of the "energy-flow" theory.

The domino theory has significant limitations. The basic assumption is that there is a linear relationship between causation and progression. In other words, one event follows another, ending in an incident. In the context of process-related incidents this assumption is not always valid. Often coincidental (parallel) events have resulted in an incident rather than sequential events. Nevertheless, the domino theory can provide a useful conceptual framework for occupational incidents or simple process-related incidents.

Today the most widely accepted and adapted incident theory relies on the system theory.[4] According to this theory an incident is seen as an abnormal effect of the technological or management system. System theory considers the structure and state of a physical (technological or human factors) system for its elements and their interdependencies. The theory, in a general sense, provides a framework for analyzing system requirements and constraints, detailed descriptions of component processes, and detailed descriptions of operational event sequences (including environmental conditions). It allows for development of models of complex engineering systems and management structures. These models can be analyzed for interrelationships between individual elements and the overall system function. Theoretically, there are as many causes of an incident as there are system components. The term "multiple-cause theory" is often used instead of "system theory." Dan Peterson espouses the multiple cause theory in his book *Techniques of Safety Management*, 2nd edition, 1978, McGraw-Hill.

The strength of system theory is its ability to provide descriptions of incidents that account for different hypotheses including multiple causes.[5] The same system that produces pounds of product and quality, produces performance and process incidents. If you want to change the outputs, you need to change the system.

One of several reasons the system theory has received broad recognition relative to PSII is that it builds directly on current, verified, and validated process safety principles. Any PSII based on the system theory concept can directly use proven techniques and tools originally developed for PHA. By using a structured approach to PSII that builds on proven and recognized techniques it becomes easier to communicate insights and results from investigations. The basic systematic PSII framework is represented by well defined, basic incident terminology, a recognized incident theory, and an incident classification scheme.

2.4. HUMAN FACTORS CONSIDERATIONS IN INCIDENT CAUSATION

A basic principle of modern PSII is always to look for the underlying causes behind an incident. As an example, whenever a human error has been identified the investigation must continue to find the root cause of the human error. It is an axiom of systematic incident investigation that human factors play an important role in incident causation.

Only the negative aspects of human factors are typically addressed during an investigation. It also should be acknowledged that human factors may play a positive role during the three phases of the process-related incident. The term "human factors" describes the specific elements of design, maintenance, operations, and management that influence the ability of humans to interact safely with their environment. Based on insights from case studies[6,7] it has been determined that human factors problems often are the root cause of human error. Conversely, whenever an investigation points to human error as part of the causation phase, the investigative process will have to search for underlying human factors deficiencies; that is, the reasons for human errors.

Human error can imply different facts about a process incident. The most obvious is operator error; for example, pumping product to the wrong tank or leaving equipment unavailable following maintenance or repair. Less obvious are the organizational errors. A typical organizational error can be failure to institute safe operating procedures including lack of verification and validation of written instructions, or improper training.

A NOTE ON "ORGANIZATIONAL ERRORS"

The term "organizational error" (OE) is relatively new and it refers to the root causes of human error that stem from management system breakdowns.

The reason for human error can be attributed to poor procedures, poor man–machine design, lack of training, etc. Thus, the root causes can be related to deficiencies in a management system. It is therefore important that the PSII always search for the underlying causes of human error and that the team members propose remedies that will improve the process safety management system.

From the point of PSII, we must have valid definitions of human error and organizational error that relate to human factors. Some recognized definitions are presented below.

The "Skills–Rules–Knowledge" (S–R–K) model[8,9] has been proposed as a framework for classifying human error. It divides mental processes in plant operation into three performance levels.

At the "lowest" level are routine skills of observation, hand–eye coordination, and control skills. **Skills** include pattern recognition and actions that are manual, well-trained, well-known, and practiced frequently. For example, these are the skills involved when an operator controls the pressure drop across a distillation column during a plant disturbance. This type of error is associated with skill-based performance and caused by slips and lapses. As an example, the operator may be distracted while controlling the pressure drop.

At the "second" level are **rules** such as "trained procedures," executed routinely. These typically correspond to written procedures learned in operation and maintenance classroom training. Mistakes are typically associated with the misclassification of situations leading to the application of the wrong rule or with the incorrect recall of procedures.

Finally, at the "highest" level are knowledge-based processes such as diagnosis, decision making, and planning. These all require **knowledge** about the plant and the processes, deductive, and inductive skills, as well as ability to decide and monitor results. Mistakes during attempts to find a solution to a disturbance can be associated with rule-based or knowledge-based performance. An example is the misinterpretation of alarms and indicators.

CASE STUDY INVOLVING HUMAN ERROR: AN OPERATOR CLOSES A VALVE AND CAUSES AN EXPLOSION

At Company ABC there were five reactors in parallel and two gas feed lines with cross connections between them. Oxygen was also fed to the reactors. At the time of the incident only two reactors (No. 1 and 4) were on line.

An operator thought valve B was open so he shut valve A. This stopped the flow of gas to reactor No. 1. The oxygen flow was controlled by a ratio controller, but it was out of zero, and a small flow of oxygen continued. When the operator realized his mistake and restored the gas flow, the reactor contained excess oxygen and an explosion occurred in the downstream waste heat boiler. Four men were killed.

A simple error by an operator produced serious consequences. The explosion was not, however, solely the operator's fault. The incident was also largely the result of poor design and lack of protective equipment.

[Courtesy of Taylor Associates ApS]

We must recognize that these types of mental processing continue in parallel, and often support each other. Each mental process can result in different types of error with different impacts on process equipment. One of the main successes of the S–R–K model was its prediction of hitherto unrecognized error types, in particular those involving a transfer to the "wrong" type of mental activity, or failure to make a transfer at all. The original S–R–K model has been modified and extended by several researchers[7,10] but remains a useful concept for relating human errors to potential root causes.

Having defined a conceptual framework (such as the S–R–K model) for human error, it is proper to turn to the underlying reasons behind an error. As is implied, errors associated with rule and knowledge performance are directly linked to root causes associated with organizational errors and human factors deficiencies. Design error can also contribute to human error.[11] A previously unrevealed design flaw can make it impossible for an operator to diagnose plant status correctly during a process upset. Design error can also be a direct result of an organizational error.

Frequently human errors are classified as *errors of omission* and *errors of commission*. No universally accepted definitions exist but the former class is typically described as tasks that are not performed because of a slip or a mistake. The error of commission usually refers to situations where an operator performs an action inappropriately because of a misperception of the actual process status. This separation into error of omission and error of commission is especially applicable to "dynamic" operator actions. Such actions involve detection, diagnosis, and decision making following an alarm in a control room.

An important distinction between the two classes of errors is given by the impact on process equipment. The error of commission not only can fail the function or action that it is meant to facilitate, it also can fail, or make unavailable, other equipment or functions needed to mitigate an incident. Also part of the "error of commission" class of human errors are any "extraneous actions" such as sabotage, procedure violation, etc. Peterson[5] elaborates on errors of commission and refers to the "logical decision to err" and the "subconscious desire to err." Experienced operators have been known to deviate deliberately from established procedures in cases where they (correctly or incorrectly) perceive the probability of adverse consequences to be low enough as to be acceptable.

The underlying causes of errors of omission and errors of commission can be very different. Hence, the root cause analysis of human error will have to acknowledge these differences. To perform such root cause analysis, the investigator must apply cognitive models of errors. This type of analysis is addressed in Chapter 5, "Root Cause Determination."

Practical analysis techniques have been developed from the theories for human factors and human and organizational errors. These techniques can support any PSII effort; they are addressed in Section 2.5.1.

2.5. TECHNIQUES FOR INCIDENT INVESTIGATION

This section describes the techniques for structured PSII. It starts with a general overview of philosophies behind the techniques. Following this overview, brief reviews of the key features of a selection of techniques are presented in Section 2.5.1. The review is not exhaustive but covers all the general types of techniques in current use. Next, Section 2.5.2 presents a discussion of the validity of available techniques relative to modern PSII. The key insights from the review of techniques are summarized in Section 2.5.3. Finally, recommendations on the practical application of PSII techniques are given in Section 2.5.4.

Based on the general incident anatomy, incident theory, human factors theory, and insights from practical PSII, several analytical techniques have been suggested, tested, and implemented in order to "streamline" the investigation process. All of the available techniques serve three purposes:

- They organize incident information once the evidence has been collected
- They help in describing incident causation and developing hypotheses for further examination by experts
- They help with the assessment of proposed corrective actions

Hence, the techniques can support an investigation and help focus on the important features of incident causation. Several, if not all, of the available techniques can provide useful frameworks for displaying and documenting the cause–consequence relationships. They can also be used to develop visual aids to better communicate the lessons learned.

When the selected PSII approach is based on system theory (that is, Type 3), many of the analytical techniques of PHA apply directly to the study of incident causation. This is an important observation, especially since most of the analytical techniques of PHA are tested and supported by user-friendly tools (for example, PC-based software). The CCPS publication, *Guidelines for Hazard Evaluation Procedures: Second Edition, with Worked Examples* is an excellent reference for process hazard analytical techniques. The same types of deductive or inductive reasoning for causal analysis apply in both cases. A potential limitation of techniques based on system theory is the emphasis on the structure of a technical system. In other words, if you have a P&ID it is quite simple to develop a causal tree through "mapping"; that is, a component on the drawing appears as an event in the causal tree. It is more challenging to explicitly represent physical processes such as heat-up or cool-down processes in the causal tree.

The principal concern of modern, Type 3, PSII is to find root causes by applying systematic methods for gaining information about causation. The information so gained is used for decisions on corrective action(s). There are three analytical approaches to the Type 3 investigation by which conclusions can be reached about an incident:

- Deductive approach
- Inductive approach
- Morphological approach

The **deductive** approach involves reasoning from the general to the specific. In the deductive analysis, it is postulated that a system or process has failed in a certain way. Next an attempt is made to determine what modes of system, component, operator, and organization behavior contribute to the failure. The word deductive originates from the word "deduct" (to take away from). A typical application of deductive reasoning is the incident investigation.[12] Starting with the facts, the analysis determines what failures (instrumental and/or human), contributed to the crash of a commercial airliner? Fault tree analysis (FTA) is an example of a deductive technique. The deductive approach starts at one point in time (the event) and looks backward in time to examine preceding events.

FAULT TREE ANALYSIS (FTA)

The fault trees are Boolean logic diagrams that show failure states. In order to visualize the causal relations between a component failure and system failure, standardized "building blocks" are used: gate symbols and event symbols. The gate symbols connect events according to their causal relations, and the event symbols are used to verbally describe the failure states of concern. The value of a fault tree can be summarized as follows:

- Directs the analysis to ferret out failures.
- Points out the aspects of the system important to the failure of interest.
- Provides a graphical aid in giving visibility to those in systems management who are removed from design changes.
- Provides options for qualitative and quantitative systems reliability analysis.
- Allows the analyst to concentrate on one particular system failure at a time.
- Provides an insight into system behavior.

[From: Fussell, J.B., 1976. Fault Tree Analysis: Concepts and Techniques. In *Generic Techniques in Reliability Analysis.* Noordhoff Publishing Co.]

The **inductive** approach involves reasoning from individual cases to a general conclusion. An inductive analysis is performed by postulating that a particular fault or initiating event has occurred. It is then determined what the effect of the fault or initiating event is on the system operation. Compared with the deductive approach, the inductive approach is an "overview" method. As such it brings an overall structure to the investigative process that is analogous to the previously discussed incident anatomy. To probe the details of the causal factors, control, and barrier functions, it is often necessary to apply deductive analysis. Many inductive techniques are in use in process safety. Examples include failure mode and effects analysis (FMEA), hazard and operability study (HAZOP), and event tree analysis (ETA).

Each of the deductive and inductive techniques has advantages and disadvantages from the perspective of ease-of-use, resource requirements, and range of validity. An alternative to the more traditional deductive and inductive techniques was proposed and tested in the mid to late 1960s. This technique, called cause–consequence diagram method (CCDM), uses a combination of deductive and inductive reasoning.[13] It has been subjected to substantial development and application (including application to incident investigation) primarily at Riso National Laboratory in Denmark throughout the 1970s. Although there have been many attempts at an international level to introduce this technique to analysts,[14] it is not as common as fault tree analysis or event tree analysis. The "cause portion" of the CCDM consists of fault trees. The "consequence portion" consists of a diagram illustrating the interrelationships among the incident outcomes and basic events (or root causes). The technique can be useful when analyzing an incident in which timing and sequencing of events are important.

Whether the deductive or inductive approach is taken in the PSII effort, the investigator needs to be aware of "inherent" problem areas (limitations). For the deductive or inductive approach to provide an accurate and complete account of a cause–consequence relationship, the investigator has to be unbiased and knowledgeable enough to recognize the inherent limitations of either approach and has to make appropriate "adjustments" as he or she proceeds. There will always be questions on the degree of completeness in the identification of failure modes using the deductive approach or of fault states using the inductive approach.[15] An important challenge facing the investigator is to decide when to stop the investigation. Judgment, based on insights from case studies, must be used when applying any of the analytical techniques, and this is discussed further in Chapter 5.

The charting of a cause–consequence relationship is a very effective communication tool. It can easily become cumbersome, however, when assembling the insights and results from the investigation of a complex sequence of events. Fortunately, some of the deductive and inductive approaches come with solution algorithms (or simplification algorithms). When applied to an incident causation chart, these solution algorithms help in focusing on the salient features of the incident. Do not expect charting always to be simple and straightforward.

We must recognize that deductive techniques can facilitate a comprehensive root cause analysis. The inductive techniques on the other hand are not intended for root cause analysis. They can, however, be effective in directing a root cause analysis.

The **morphological** approach to analytical incident investigation is based on the *structure* of the system being studied. The morphological approach focuses directly on potentially hazardous elements (for example, operations, situations). The deductive and inductive approaches are focused, directional approaches supported by formalism (symbology, rules) and solution algorithms. A morphological search is directed more by the form of the system and by experience from operating the system. The aim is to concentrate on the factors having the most significant influence on safety.

When performing a "morphological analysis," the analyst is primarily applying his or her past experience of incident investigation. Rather than looking at all possible deviations with and without a potential safety impact, the investigation focuses on known hazard sources (for example, concentrations of energy, or hazardous materials). Typically, the morphological approach is an adaptation of deductive or inductive approaches, but with its own guidelines.

2.5.1. Review of Analytical Techniques

This review focuses on 18 specific techniques for PSII. The selection of the review candidates resulted primarily from a literature survey. Hence, the selected techniques are described in publicly available documents (periodicals, technical reports, or textbooks). There is considerable overlap among the different techniques. Although some of the techniques were first developed to support the investigation of occupational incidents, they are nevertheless applicable to the PSII.

In the original descriptions of the incident investigation techniques there is seldom explicit recognition of the reliance on basic concepts from PHA. There is also a tendency not to acknowledge existing industry standards and guidelines for deductive and inductive approaches. As a result, there is evidence of semantic problems, inconsistencies, and even direct misunderstandings about the validity of investigation techniques.

Each technique is described for basic concepts, degree of recognition, and area(s) of application. The order in which the techniques appear in the text below is not indicative of implied or explicit validity and recognition. The Center for Chemical Process Safety does not specifically endorse any one particular technique.

2.5.1.1. DEDUCTIVE TECHNIQUES

The deductive approach is recognized as useful for PSII to meet the requirements of effective PSII. In most cases the deductive PSII techniques are adaptations of fault tree analysis. Hence, the strengths and weaknesses of fault tree analysis apply to these deductive PSII techniques. An important consideration of the deductive techniques is deciding when to stop the analysis. The "stopping rules" for deductive analysis are based on:

- Investigator's judgment of what is important
- Level of detail of available plant information (P&IDs, PFDs, written instructions, etc.)
- Need to classify failure events by type (e.g., latent failure, secondary failure, primary failure)
- Prior experience from applying deductive techniques
- Judgment that the investigation has identified a system cause and not just a symptom

The fault tree analysis technique has inspired the development of several PSII techniques. Hence, an overview of the fault tree analysis technique is given as introduction to the review. In addition to the fault tree analysis technique the following deductive PSII techniques are reviewed:

- Causal Tree Method (CTM)
- Management Oversight and Risk Tree (MORT)
- Multiple-Cause, Systems-Oriented Incident Investigation (MCSOII) Technique

Fault Tree Analysis (FTA): FTA provides a method for determining the causes of an incident.[16,17,60] The fault tree itself is a graphic model that displays the various combinations of equipment failures and human errors that can result in an incident. The solution of the fault tree is a list of the sets of equipment failures and/or human errors that are enough to cause the incident. The strength of FTA as a qualitative tool is its ability to break down an incident into root causes. This breaking down of the incident allows the investigator to focus preventive measures on these basic causes to reduce the likelihood of recurrence.

The undesired event appears as the top event. This event is linked to the basic failure events by logic gates and event statements. A gate symbol can have one or more inputs, but only one output. There are two basic logic gates: the AND-gate and the OR-gate. Event symbols are used to classify the events that contribute to the top event. A rectangular box denotes a "failure event" resulting from a combination of more basic events acting through logic gates. A circle designates a "basic event" that represents the limit of resolution of a fault tree. So, whenever a circle appears in the tree it means that the deductive analysis has stopped at that point. A summary of common fault tree symbols is given in Figure 2-3.

To solve the fault tree, the minimal cut sets (MCS) have to be determined.[18] By definition, a cut set is a group of basic events whose occurrence will cause the top event to occur. A cut set is minimal if it cannot be further reduced and still remain a cut set. Finding a minimal cut set can be the same as finding the root causes, assuming that the fault tree has been developed to sufficient level of detail; that is, each of the elements of a minimal cut set represents a root cause. Usually the qualitative fault tree solution is performed by manual application of the laws of Boolean algebra. For complex fault trees (many logic gates and basic events) the solution can become quite time consuming, and for this reason computer programs have been developed.

Causal Tree Method (CTM): The Causal Tree Method[19] was developed by Rhone-Poulenc in an effort to use the principles of deductive logic found in other methods such as Fault Tree but, make it more user friendly. Originally developed as an occupational incident investigation tool,[20] the techniques of CTM have been applied to process incidents and environmental incidents of varying sizes and levels of complexity.

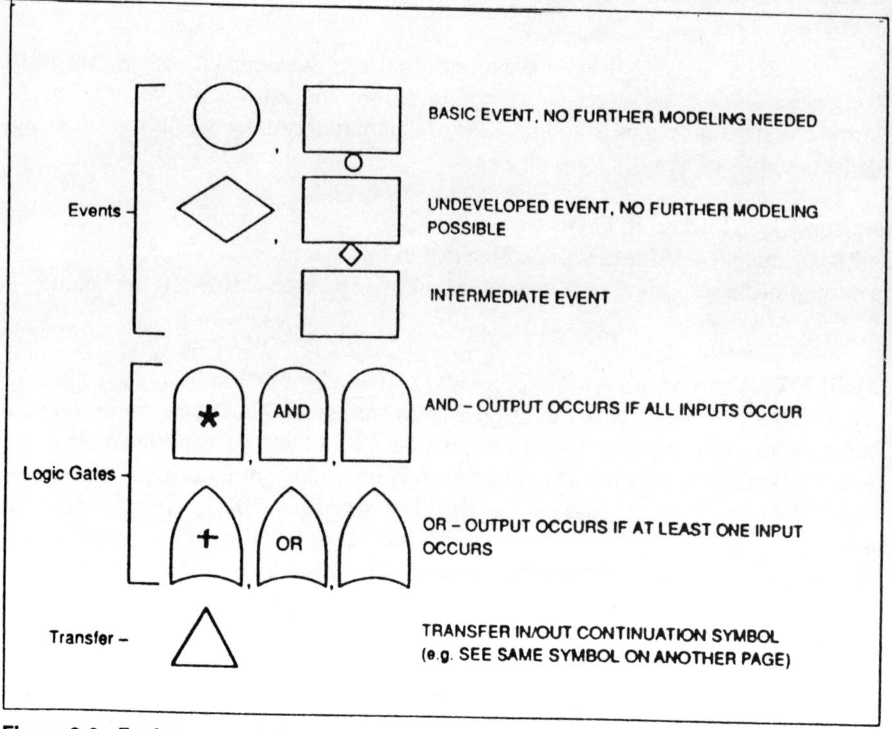

Figure 2-3. Fault tree symbols.

The method requires that the investigation team identify causal factors through interviews and site investigation. An emphasis is placed on striving to develop "factual" causal factors before they are placed into the structure of the logic diagram. This emphasis lets the facts dictate the logic of the incident diagram, and limits the influence of presupposed conclusions invariably drawn by investigators before all of the facts are identified and logically matched.

In its effort to be a broader-based more user-friendly system, causal tree uses a new set of logic connectors for the method. Three common words are used to develop the logic of an incident.

1. **RESULT:** The investigation team reviews its list of facts and asks, "What *result* is being analyzed?"
2. **NECESSARY:** The team then asks, "What was directly *necessary* to cause the result to have occurred?" The technique asks the investigation team to work one logic level at a time,including only those factors directly necessary to have caused the specific result to have occurred.
3. **SUFFICIENT:** After the *necessary* factors have been identified the team members then ask themselves, "Are these factors *sufficient* to have caused the *result*?" If

the answer is no they search out other factors that must be identified to complete the logic of the branch being developed. If the answer is yes the factors identified at this level of the tree become the next level of results to be analyzed for necessary and sufficient causal factors.

This structured logical development continues until each branch has reached a point the team agrees is the lowest level of evaluation that will be productive to consider for the specific incident. The theory of the method suggests that all causal factors of the logic diagram can be considered as issues to be corrected to prevent recurrence. But it charges the investigation team with the task of selecting some portion of the most effective target factors for which to develop corrective actions.

In identifying target factors and developing corrective actions, the CTM asks that a minimum of three factors be identified for each incident. It goes on to ask that at least one factor be identified in each of three broad categories of incident influencing groupings. Those categories are (1) organizational, (2) human, and (3) material categories of factors. This expectation further reduces the possibility that simple, single causes be accepted as complete definitions of the incident cause.

The Causal Tree Method suggests that when selecting causal factors to address with corrective actions that the closer to the end of the logic branch the targeted factor is the better the selection is. This is approaching the expectation of other methods to identify the "root cause" but allows for the philosophical expectation that all of the facts of an incident be considered as elements that could have prevented the incident. The investigators select those that are the most efficient and effective in preventing recurrence.

Rhône-Poulenc has expanded on the theories and methods of CTM and developed a proactive analytical method for evaluating unusual circumstances, referred to as anomalies, to determine their potential for resulting in incidents. The CTM enhancement has been named "Hunt for Anomalies" (H4A).

Primary advantages of the CTM and H4A method are that, while still requiring the user to adopt a new way of looking at incidents, it is simpler than other more strictly defined logic diagram development methods. Hence, these methods are more easily understood by a broader base of people.

The Causal Tree Method has been widely tested in Rhone-Poulenc with positive results. It is supported with a well-developed training package that utilizes a participatory training technique with game boards, overhead transparencies and a videotape. The H4A enhancement is also supported by a well-developed training tool and supervisor H4A cards to be used in hunting for anomalies in the workplace or process operation.

The disadvantages of the CTM are that it does not provide for a quantitative analysis of the impact of each causal factor of the incident. Also by simplifying the logic method of tree development some of the detail of the information conveyed by the logic tree is lost. CTM could be defined as a style of fault tree that only allows for the use of AND-gates. An example of a Causal Tree is shown in Figure 2-4.

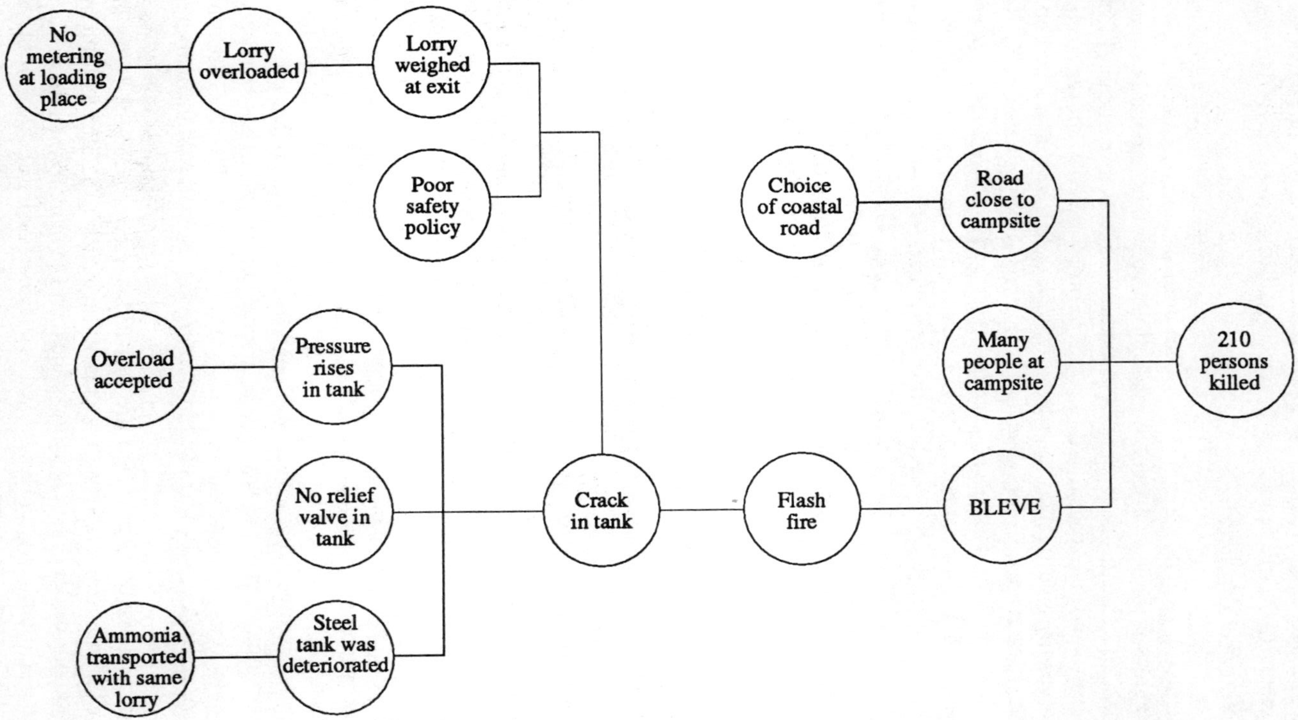

Figure 2-4. Example of a causal tree.

In conclusion, CTM is a good method to develop a sound logical description of an incident and obviously points to elements of the incident that must be further developed or should be further analyzed by other more specific methods. It is a good selection if a site wants to use one method for all types of incident investigations and are considering expanding their incident evaluation efforts to analyzing anomalies in the workplace and processes.

Management Oversight and Risk Tree (MORT): The MORT technique[1,21] was developed by the System Safety Development Center (SSDC) of the Department of Energy (DOE) for the investigation of occupational incidents at DOE sites. The technique is also intended to support safety audits and to solve management problems. The MORT diagram is the key to the investigation process, and is based on FTA (that is, MORT is a deductive technique); see Figure 2-5. Central to MORT are the energy flow and barrier concepts.

By definition, in MORT, an incident is an event for which a barrier to an unwanted energy flow is inadequate or fails without any loss or consequence occurring. An accident or a mishap is defined as the unwanted flow of energy or exposure to an environmental condition that results in adverse consequences. Wherever there is a chance that persons or objects may come in contact with an energy flow or an environmental condition that could cause harm to persons or hardware, it is necessary to isolate the energy flow or the environmental condition.

The basic MORT diagram consists of four elements. The first element (which is equivalent to the top event in FTA) defines the overall objective; that is, to investigate incidents one must first investigate the potential harmful energy flows (hazards) or environmental conditions. The second element consists of the people or objects (targets) of value that are vulnerable to an unwanted energy flow. The third element in an incident sequence is the failure or lack of barriers and controls that are designed to keep the potentially harmful energy away from the vulnerable people or objects. Finally, the fourth element in the analysis of an incident is the precursor events.

Application of the MORT technique is based on a ready-made (or generic) tree structure laid out vertically (top down). This tree structure should be viewed as a check list. Its structure is quite complex, and it is intended to be used as a reference or standard when investigating an incident. This generic tree contains approximately 100 problem areas and 1500 possible causes. The tree is based on historic case studies and on research performed by human factors specialists. A *MORT Tree User's Manual*[22] provides detailed instructions on how to use the generic tree. Lately, some enhancements have been added by the National Safety Council.

Because of the complexity of the MORT Tree, a technique called Mini-MORT has been developed.[23] It is primarily concerned with the preparation of oral and written reports related to a full MORT analysis. As is the case with most of the analytical techniques for incident investigation, MORT is usually not considered a field technique. It is viewed as a tool used to review and order evidence brought in from the site. Because the technique is based on FTA, there is the potential of loading the generic

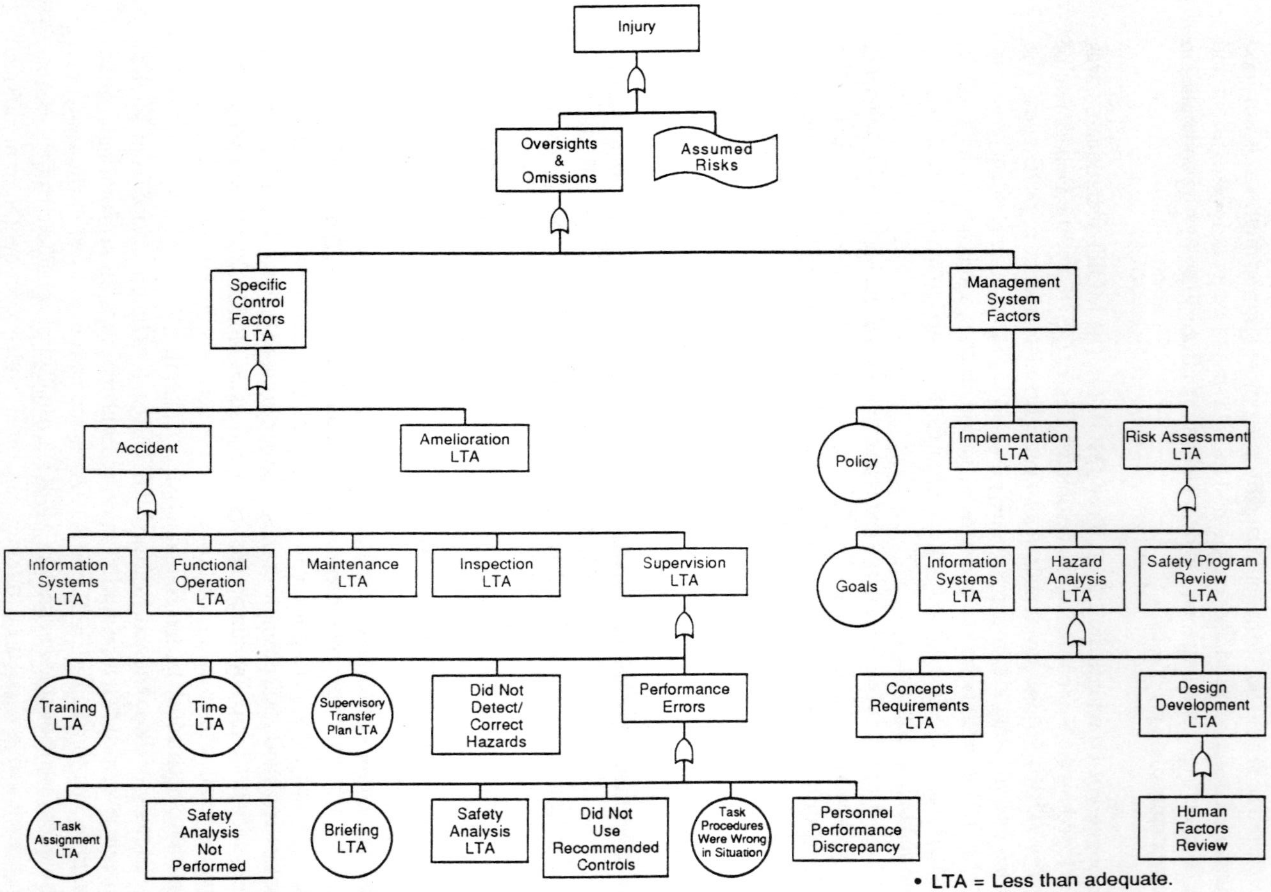

Figure 2-5. Top of a generic MORT diagram.

MORT Tree on a PC and using it as a convenient interactive tool during field investigations.

The MORT technique has received domestic and international recognition, and has been applied to a wide range of projects, from investigation of occupational incidents to hazards identification. It is supported by detailed documentation, and has been subjected to development efforts since it was originally introduced. On a regular basis the DOE organizes training seminars and workshops. Many of the analytical techniques reviewed in this section have been developed from basic MORT concepts.

Multiple-Cause, Systems-Oriented Incident Investigation (MCSOII) Technique: This technique (MCSOII, pronounced "mac-soy") was developed by Rohm and Haas in 1984[24,25] and is now in use in many locations as the site-required procedure for PSII (see Appendix C-1). The cause determination is a direct adaptation of the FTA with simplified use of symbols.

After the facts have been collected in the field, a multidisciplined team develops a sequence of events (chronology) for the incident. Like other techniques for PSII (e.g., MORT), a generic "top tree" structure (Figure 2-6) has been developed to facilitate practical development of the tree. The top event of the tree is the injury, damage, or environmental release. The generic "top tree" suggests three second-level events as a starting point to develop the incident tree:

1. The presence of the injured person or damaged equipment
2. The presence of the injuring substance or energy
3. A contact duration sufficient to cause the injury or damage.

For example, if the top event is "employee burned by fire," the second-level events could be "employee at vessel manway," "flame at vessel manway," and "employee exit blocked by temporary scaffolding."

Each of the second-level events is developed into a detailed tree by repeatedly asking the question, "Why did this event occur?" and drawing the events on a flip chart. For each new event added to the tree, the question, "Why?" is asked until the true system causes are shown as the bottom events on the tree. Some judgment is needed to determine the stopping point, and as in the FTA, one can always develop a more detailed subtree for any primal or basic event. An important characteristic of MCSOII is that system causes go beyond individual actions of personnel or equipment failures; system causes include the management systems that cause or make possible the personnel or equipment problems that led to the incident. For example, if an operations person makes the wrong response to an alarm, root system causes could include: "not trained," "no training system," "wrong (or no) information in training system," "culture to ignore alarm," "culture to try short cuts," etc.

After the tree is developed, the team is asked, "Are there other causes that you had in mind at the beginning of this meeting that are not included in the tree? Are there other causes that come to mind now that are not in the tree?" If additional causes are identified, the team adds them to the tree if the logic can support it.

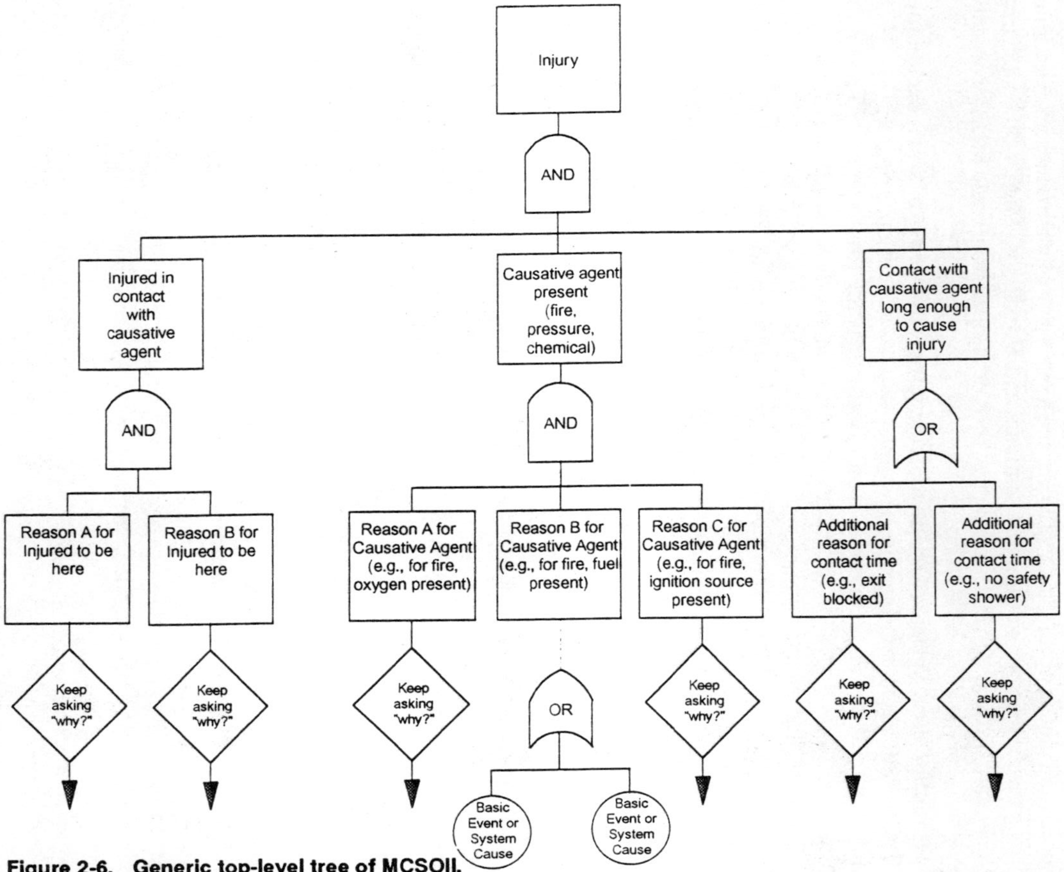

Figure 2-6. Generic top-level tree of MCSOII.

Recommendations for system improvements are made by examining each root cause and developing an action plan to prevent or mitigate that cause. The procedure requires a written report including the sequence of events, the tree, the recommendations, and a critique of the investigation process.

The MCSOII technique is intended to be used as part of a team approach to PSII. A PSII-facilitator, knowledgeable in the practical use of MCSOII, makes sure that team members stay on track and that the tree structures are technically sound. As the tree is developed, the basic concepts of causation and progression are included. The technique works well to highlight common cause events. The technique is applicable to occupational incidents as well as process-related incidents. Detailed user instructions and a training module exist.

2.5.1.2. INDUCTIVE TECHNIQUES

The inductive techniques are characterized as "forward search strategies" for identifying the impact of potential process deviations. They are as recognized as the deductive techniques. An important aspect of the inductive techniques is that they focus on the "big picture" rather than on root causes. Typical applications summarize the sequence(s) of events involved in an incident and give directions where the root cause analysis should begin. In the context of PSII, inductive techniques are combined with deductive techniques to provide comprehensive results. The following inductive techniques are reviewed:

- Accident Anatomy Method (AAM)
- Action Error Analysis (AEA)
- Cause–Effect Logic Diagram (CELD)
- Hazard and Operability (HAZOP) Analysis

It can be argued whether the "accident anatomy method" and "action error analysis" are pure inductive techniques. Regardless, in both cases the investigator starts by applying inductive reasoning. Once there is consensus on the overall nature of an incident a detailed root cause analysis based on deductive reasoning is pursued.

Accident Anatomy Method (AAM): The AAM technique was developed at the Riso National Laboratory in Denmark, and it uses the CCDM to address the three phases of the general incident anatomy.[26,27] It is a technique for process-related incidents as well as occupational incidents. A basic assumption is that any incident is the result of *multiple-causation*. Some of the basic concepts behind the AAM have been adapted directly from the MORT technique. There are two approaches to the application of the AAM technique:

- Based on available case histories, develop a generic AAM Tree, according to the MORT technique. This generic tree is used as a "template" during an investigation.
- Once the evidence has been collected, develop the AAM Tree according to the hypotheses that evolve as more information becomes available.

One difference between AAM and MORT is in the representation of incident information. While the AAM uses a combination of deductive and inductive approaches, MORT is based strictly on a deductive approach. As a result, the AAM can be a more flexible tool for organizing information from a complex event. Insights from practical applications[27] show that construction of the generic AAM Tree can be time consuming. The symbols used to develop AAM trees are shown in Figure 2-7, and an example AAM tree is shown in Figure 2-8.

The AAM has been subjected to development efforts ever since it was first proposed in the 1970s. The technique has been applied primarily on an exploratory basis by the Danish Labour Inspectorate. Some European research organizations have compared it against other techniques such as MORT. A Danish incident data base has been developed around the AAM.[28]

Action Error Analysis (AEA) Technique: The AEA technique[29] is a forward search (inductive) technique for identifying potential deviations in human performance. Conceptually, the AEA technique is similar to the Human Reliability Analysis Event Tree technique. It is to be used when determining potential problems with written

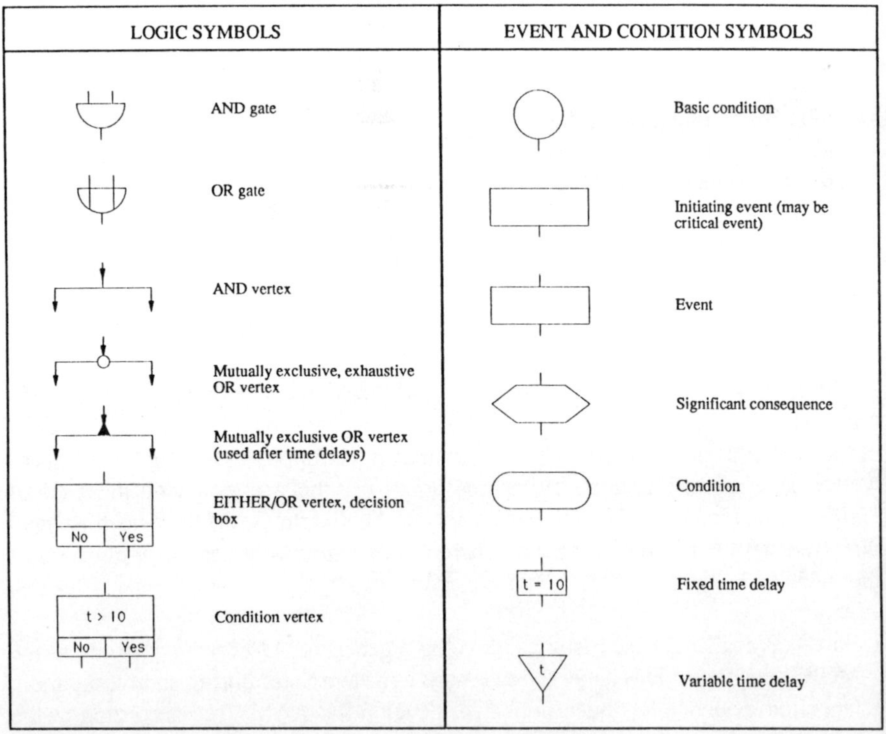

Figure 2-7. Symbols for construction of an AAM tree. Vertices are used to construct the consequences (i.e., inductive) portion of the diagram.

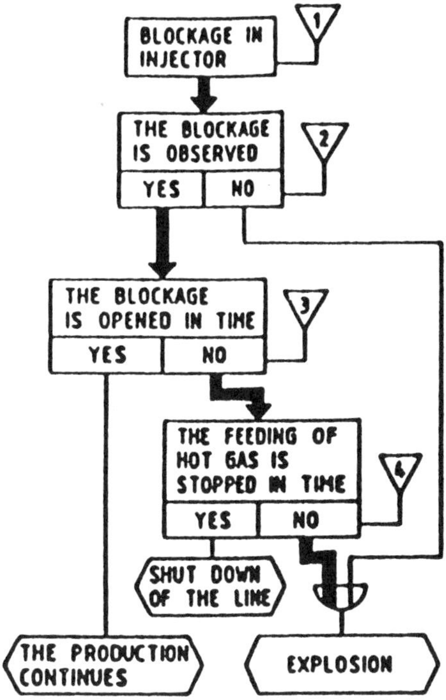

Figure 2-8. Sample AAM tree.

instructions. Human errors are addressed by applying the cause consequence diagram method.

The starting point is a listing of individual actions to be carried out on the process plant. These actions are drawn as a sequence, and for each action, the consequences of the action on the plant are noted; see Figure 2-9. The actions of concern are defined in terms of the possibilities of operating the plant, pushing buttons, opening valves, starting pumps, etc. Once the diagram has been developed in terms of correct operations (as defined by a written procedure), the effects of errors are added to the diagram.

It is possible to carry out such an analysis to include multiple combinations of human errors on a plant of moderate complexity, if safe states can be identified easily. The technique has been applied extensively in the context of PHA and supported by a development effort since its inception in the 1970s. Today PC-based analysis tools exist. The AAM discussed earlier builds on concepts of the AEA technique.

Cause–Effect Logic Diagram (CELD) Technique: This is a technique specifically developed for directing a root cause analysis. It has found use among reliability

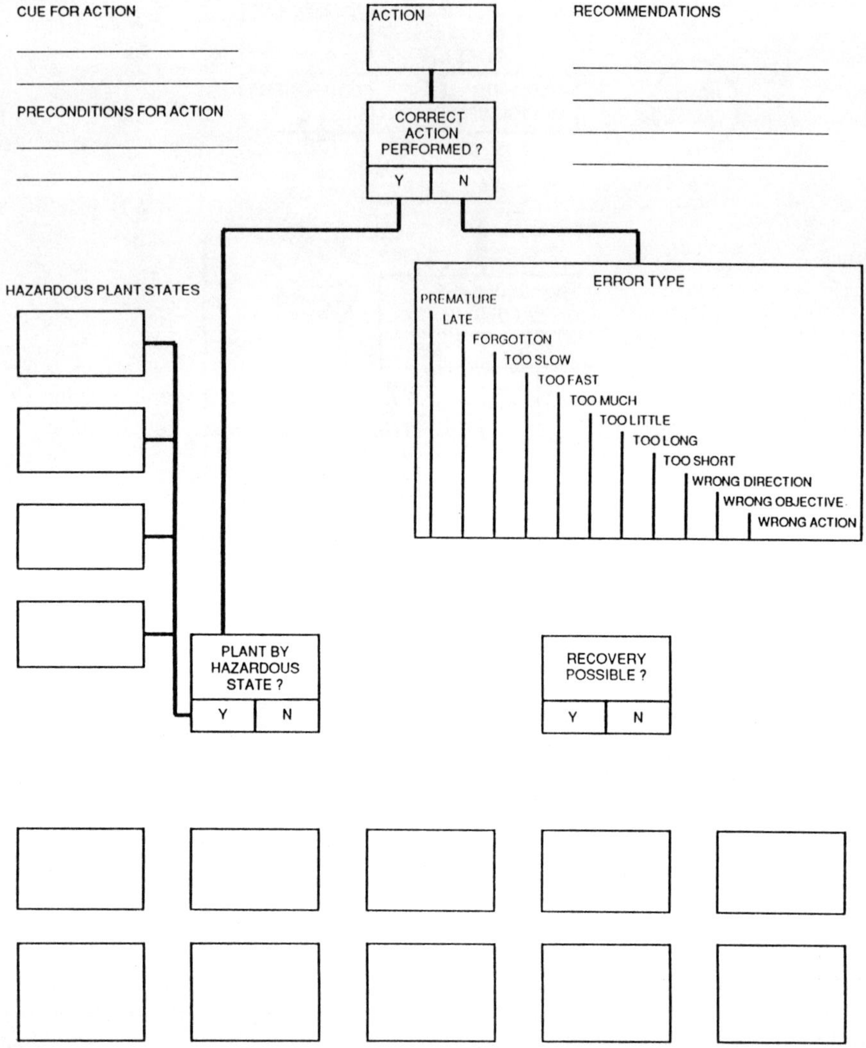

Figure 2-9. Sample work sheet for action error analysis. (Courtesy of Taylor Associates ApS.)

practitioners. The technique was developed by the Electric Power Research Institute (EPRI)[30] among others.

It portrays the interactions among root causes and component states in an event. Once the event scenario has been determined from a description of an incident, a diagram is drawn that shows the cause-and-effect relationship among various causes and component states; see Figure 2-10.

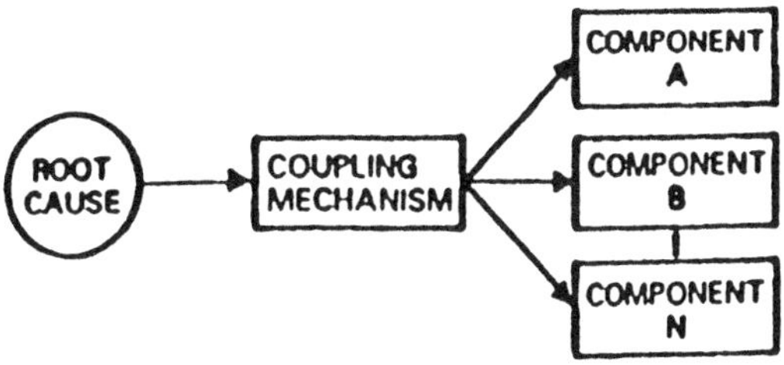

Figure 2-10. Sample CELD tree.

Using a set of standardized symbols, human errors, organizational errors, and hardware failures can be addressed. Special analysis work sheets have been developed together with check lists. The technique is useful for investigating near-miss events involving common cause failures. Thus far it has been used mostly by the nuclear industry.

Hazard and Operability (HAZOP) Analysis: The HAZOP Analysis technique[31] was developed to identify and evaluate safety and environmental hazards, and to identify operability problems which, although not hazardous, could compromise the plant's ability to achieve design productivity. In the HAZOP Analysis approach, an interdisciplinary team uses a structured, systematic brainstorming approach to identify hazards and operability problems that result from deviations from the process's design intent and that could lead to undesirable consequences.

The results of a HAZOP Analysis are the team's findings, which include identification of hazards and operating problems; recommendations for changes in design procedures, etc., to improve safety; and recommendations to conduct studies of areas where no conclusion was possible, due to a lack of information. The results of team discussions concerning the causes, effects, and safeguards for deviations for each study node or section of the process are recorded.

In the context of PSII the results from a HAZOP conducted prior to the incident can provide valuable supportive information. Hence, the HAZOP Analysis can be viewed as a "secondary" PSII technique. As such, the HAZOP is useful in evaluating the possible impacts of recommended preventive action items (see Chapter 6, "Recommendations and Follow Through").

2.5.1.3. MORPHOLOGICAL TECHNIQUES

These techniques use a structured analysis format directed by insights from historic events, and are not as rigorous as the deductive and inductive techniques. Hence, the morphological techniques represent simplifications and are often easier to apply and can be as comprehensive as any other structured technique for PSII. Whenever any of the formal deductive or inductive techniques are changed or simplified, they are converted to morphological techniques. Two techniques are addressed below, the Accident Evolution and Barrier technique and the Work Safety Analysis technique.

Accident Evolution and Barrier (AEB) Technique: The AEB technique remains in a developmental phase that is supported by the Swedish Nuclear Power Inspectorate.[3] It is based on the general concepts of incident causation and progression and on the specific concepts of the MORT technique. Specifically developed for investigation of near misses in the nuclear industry, it focuses on the interactions between the technical system and human factors. An application of the AEB technique consists of two main parts[33]:

- The modeling of the accident evolution (or progression) as an interaction between the human factors organizational systems and the technical systems
- A barrier function analysis.

To describe the accident evolution and associated barrier functions, the analyst develops a flow diagram that illustrates a series of failures, malfunctions, or errors that lead to an accident. In each sequence leading to an accident, it is assumed that there are barrier functions that can arrest the sequence and prevent the unwanted development of an accident.

For practical application, the flow diagram can be developed using preprinted forms with two columns of empty rectangles. The investigator fills in applicable text and connects the rectangles using arrows as appropriate. As an example, to the left of the two columns the analyst can fill in the clock time (start of the incidents to termination). To the right of the two columns the analyst can add free-format comments; see Figure 2-11.

Like MORT, the AEB technique is intended to be used as a tool to review and order evidence brought in from the site. To date AEB has been applied on an exploratory basis to the analysis of an incident at a nuclear power plant. An interesting feature of the technique is that it makes an explicit connection between results from PHA and the PSII. Thus, the technique supports the overall PSM concepts approach.

Work Safety Analysis (WSA): Work Safety Analysis is a systematic investigation of working methods, machines, and working environment to identify direct incident potentials.[34,35] The technique was developed by the Safety Engineering Department of the Technical Research Centre of Finland (VTT). It is a technique for occupational hazard identification and occupational incident investigation. A list of hazards and examples of their contributors is also presented to support the hazard identification (or root cause when applied to an incident investigation). The aim is to identify hazards and their contributors associated with a system.

Occasionally, WSA will miss some common hazards that are indirectly connected with the work steps under study. An example is the potential for contact with chemicals or excessive pressure caused by a release or an explosion *near* the process part under study. If a task is outside the "boundary" of the investigation it will not be addressed. This is an example of a limitation that can result in an important omission. Proper application of WSA requires careful planning.

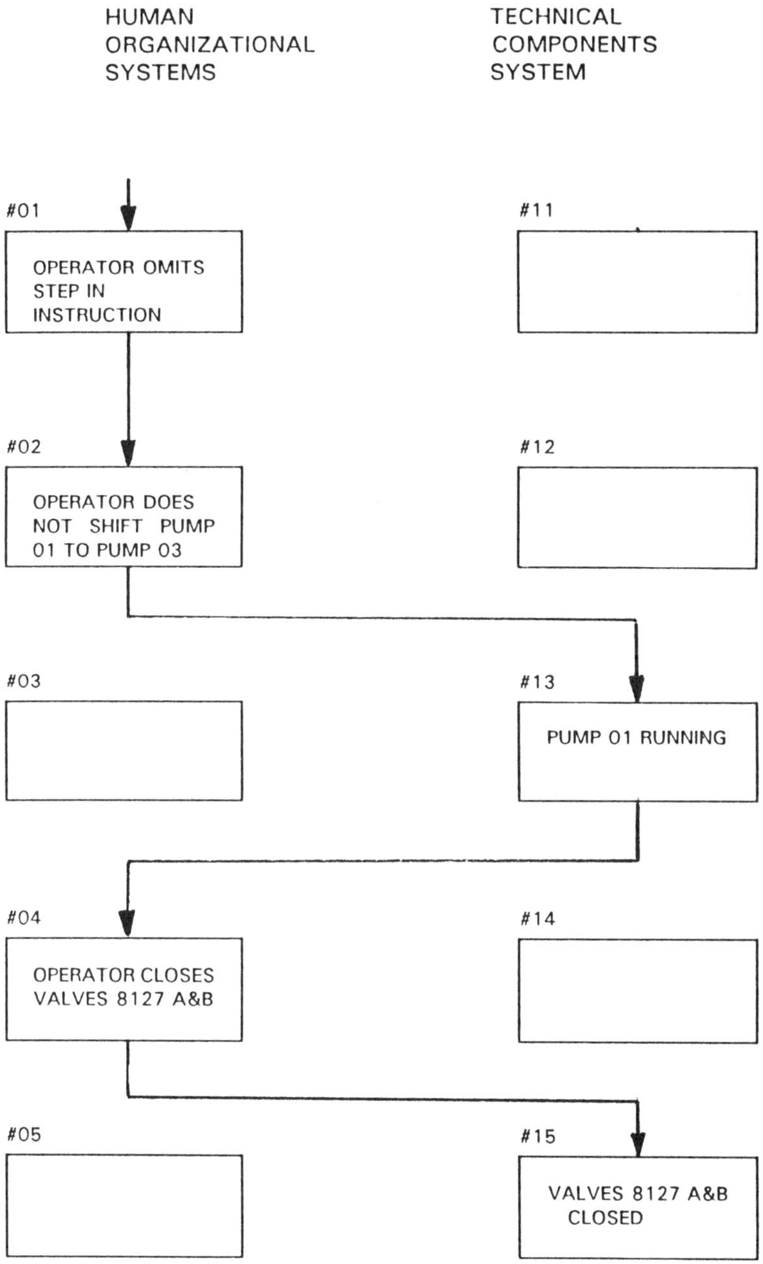

Figure 2-11. Sample AEB diagram. [After Svenson, O. 1991. The Accident Evolution and Barrier Function (AEB) Model Applied to Incident Analysis in the Processing Industries. *Risk Analysis: An International Journal* 11(3):499–507.]

The search for accident contributors is based on breaking a task down into a sequence of steps. The search begins with a consideration of known hazard types at each of the steps. Relevant contributors to the hazards and the contributors necessary to expose a worker to the hazards are then sought. The main emphasis is, however, on the search for hazard contributors. The factors contributing to a hazard, in particular are studied in greater detail by the methods employed with PHA.

All types of system functions and states should be critically considered, including "normal." The obvious result is that deviations and determining factors (barrier functions) are both included in the analysis. The main search for deviations and determining factors focuses on the physical and human subsystems. The "information" subsystem is partly reviewed and the management subsystem completely excluded. Hence, the WSA supplements other investigation techniques such as the MORT technique.

In its practical implementation, the WSA is similar to the line-by-line HAZOP. An example of a WSA work sheet is shown in Figure 2-12. Work Safety Analysis requires a team effort; a typical WSA team consists of members of the operations staff and a person with background in safety engineering and PHA. The strengths and weaknesses of WSA as a tool for hazards identification have been evaluated,[36] and WSA is not a general purpose technique. Work Safety Analysis is supported by a detailed user's manual.

2.5.1.4. OTHER NON–SYSTEMS-ORIENTED PSII TECHNIQUES

Many concepts exist for structured PSII that are not as comprehensive as the systems-oriented techniques described in Section 2.5.1.1 through 2.5.1.3. This section describes some of the Type 2 PSII techniques from which the multiple-cause, systems-oriented PSII techniques have evolved. The following techniques are reviewed:

- Change Evaluation/Analysis
- Human Performance Enhancement System (HPES)
- Human Reliability Analysis (HRA) Event Tree Technique
- Multilinear Events Sequencing (MES)
- Sequentially Timed Events Plot (STEP)
- Systematic Cause Analysis Technique (SCAT)
- TapRooT™ Incident Investigation System
- Technique of Operations Review (TOR)

Change Evaluation/Analysis (CE/A): A basic assumption in the CE/A technique is that change signals trouble. An operator being alert to a deviation in, say, process pressure can avoid a mishap from developing into a significant process upset. The basic CE/A as developed by Kepner and Tregoe,[37] is characterized by six investigative steps:

- Look at the mishap situation
- Consider a similar, but mishap-free situation
- Compare the two situations

CENTER FOR CHEMICAL PROCESS (CCPS) WORK SAFETY ANALYSIS		PLANT/SYSTEM: NDF Company, Georgetown PSII ID: ______		PAGE: 1 DATE: January 1, 1992 NAME: ______
WORK STEP SYSTEM/COMPONT AUXILIARY DEVICE	HAZARD	CAUSATIVE FACTORS	CLASSIFICATION		CORRECTIVE ACTIONS
			BEFORE[a]	AFTER[b]	

Notes: (a). Used to classify likelihood, consequence, relative safety ranking (similar to HAZOP); helps in assigning priorities.
(b). Used to estimate/classify impact of recommended action(s) on safety.

Figure 2-12. Example of a form used in Work Safety Analysis. [Based on Suokas, J. 1988. The Role of Safety analysis in Accident Prevention. *Accident Analysis & Prevention* 20(1):67–85.]

- Set down all differences among situations
- Analyze the differences for effect on producing the mishap
- Integrate the differences into mishap causal factors

The practical application of these basic ideas has been incorporated into a CE/A analysis work sheet. On the left column of the work sheet, 25 potential influencing factors are listed, and these are examined against the changes: "present situation," "prior comparable," "differences," and "affective changes." The work sheet is developed using a flip chart on which the input from the investigation team is documented. The PSII-team develops the work sheet with support from a facilitator.

Human Performance Enhancement System (HPES): The objective of HPES is to improve overall plant operations by reducing human error through correcting the conditions that cause the errors. The Human Performance Enhancement System represents a framework for multiple cause analysis (or root cause analysis) of human performance problems, and it involves the following analysis steps[38]:

- *Behavioral factor analysis:* Identification of factors that explain how the inappropriate action(s) occurred. The behavioral factors are indicators of applicable causal factors.
- *Causal factor analysis:* Identification of work situation deficiencies that combined to produce the behavioral factors.
- *Situational analysis:* Definition of "when, where, what, job category/ experience, shift schedule/work cycle" characteristics.
- *Normalization:* Determination of the effects of task frequency, task duration, sense of urgency associated with a task, and the overall level of activity going on in the plant on inappropriate action frequency

The detailed HPES methodology is documented in a procedure; HPES evaluations involve assessing the situation before and after an error, the human behavioral factors, and the work environment. The evaluations are structured around a set of check lists for the behavioral factors, causal factors, situational analysis, and normalization. Each cause is rated as "primary," "secondary," or "possible." The results of an application include

- Event reports for plant management
- Determination of human performance areas needing priority attention
- Exchange of human performance experience with other plants

The MORT technique was used as a basis for HPES, a methodology to identify, evaluate, and correct situations that cause human performance problems (for example, errors, near misses, potential problems). Other techniques have also influenced HPES, such as Change Evaluation/Analysis and Technique of Operations Review (TOR, discussed below).

In 1982 the Institute of Nuclear Power Operations (INPO) started a pilot program designed to identify and understand the real causes of human performance problems in nuclear utilities. Based on insights from the pilot program, an effort was made in 1986 to formalize HPES at the participating power stations. The Human Performance Enhancement System is now in place on a voluntary basis at about 40 U.S. utilities. Although it was originally designed for use at nuclear power plants, HPES is equally applicable to the CPI.

The applicable HPES analysis techniques and the HPES evaluation check lists support the information and fact gathering portion of the evaluation. Each utility that is applying HPES has an HPES coordinator who receives specialized training provided by INPO. From the participating utilities, INPO receives results from HPES-based investigations and provides feedback to industry on significant human performance issues.

Human Reliability Analysis (HRA) Event Tree Technique: Originally developed at Sandia National Laboratories[39,40,41] to support CPQRA, the HRA event tree technique also can support the PSII. It is a graphic method of presenting human errors that have been identified through a task analysis. The task analysis is an analytical process for determining the specific behaviors required of the human components in a man–machine system. As an example, the task analysis can be applied to a written maintenance procedure, and the result would be a listing of potential human errors. Each of the human errors is then entered as binary branches on the HRA event tree. The possible error events appear on the tree in the chronological order in which they might potentially occur.

Substantial user experience with HRA exists, and the technique is easy to apply, assuming that the investigation team is familiar with human factors issues. The technique focuses on human errors. It can be used to supplement other techniques, especially when applied to a major PSII.

Although the term "event tree" is used to characterize the technique, no formal event tree is developed. The tree structure should be characterized as a "fish bone" structure; see Figure 2-13. Any given task appears as a two-limb branch, with each left limb representing success and each right limb representing error. Once a task is diagrammed as having been completed successfully or unsuccessfully, another task is considered.

Multilinear Events Sequencing (MES): This is a charting technique developed by the National Transportation Safety Board.[42] The technique arranges events on a time-line basis by using the events and causal factors charting. An assumption in MES is that the success of the incident investigation depends on knowing precisely when the incident began and ended. The time line is a scale that parallels the sequences of events to show a time relationship of the events that happened. The first event that disrupted a stable situation sets the starting time of the incident, T_0. The ending time is called T_n. This time is viewed as the last consecutive harmful event connected

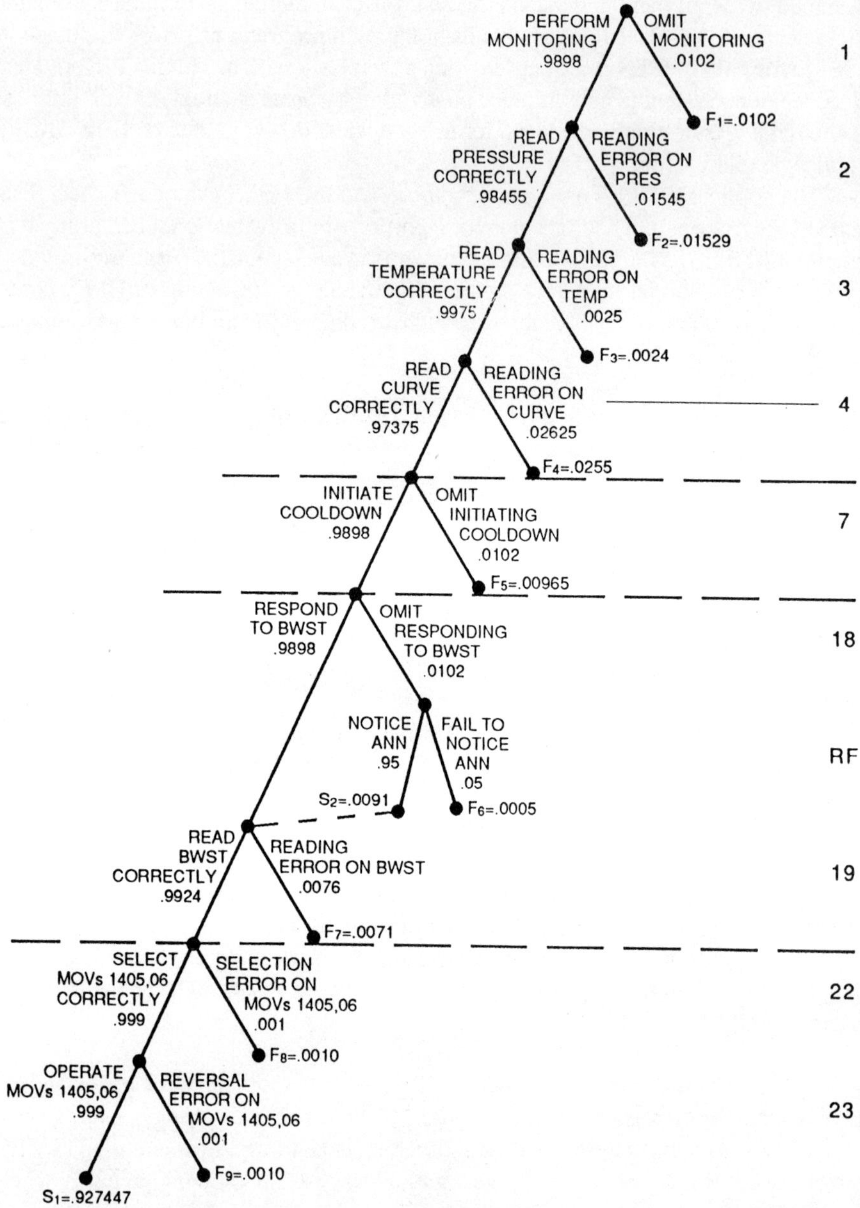

Figure 2-13. Example of an HRA event tree.

directly with the incident at the site where it occurred, and involving the people at the site.

The MES diagram is a block diagram with the events ordered in series/parallel according to the causation as determined by the investigator. The time line is placed underneath this block diagram. In the MES process the investigator must account for each action of every actor that brought about a change of state in the sequence. Thus each event is broken down until one event equals one actor and one action; the event is reduced to its simplest form. Events are posted in strict sequence so each action leads to the next, left to right in an inductive manner. If each event is not fully explained, it means there is a gap in the evidence, and further investigation is required.

Arrows are used for linking the events. According to the "arrow convention" in MES, arrows always flow from the earlier event to the later events, and from left to right. Practically, the MES diagram is developed on a board. The investigators use cards for recording the events, and these cards are placed on the board. As new information becomes available, the investigators simply replace the original card or insert a new card on the chart.

Sequentially Timed Events Plot (STEP): STEP[43] builds directly on MES. The main difference is that by utilizing insights and experience from application of MES, it has evolved into a more complete and practical framework for incident investigation. Special STEP work sheets have been developed to facilitate the investigation process.

Systematic Cause Analysis Technique (SCAT): SCAT was recently developed by the International Loss Control Institute (ILCI) for the support of occupational incident investigation.[44] The ILCI "Loss Causation Model" is the framework for the SCAT system. In this model an incident is viewed as the result of a domino involving:

- Lack of control
- Basic causes (personal factors or job factors)
- Immediate causes (substandard acts and conditions)
- Incident (contact with energy or substance)
- Loss (people, property, process)

The Systematic Cause Analysis Technique is a tool to aid an investigation and evaluation of incidents through the application of a SCAT chart. The chart acts as a check list or reference to ensure that an investigation has looked at all facets of an incident. There are five blocks on a SCAT chart. Each block corresponds to a block of "Loss Causation Model." Hence, the first block contains space to write a description of the incident. The second block lists the most common categories of contact that could have led to the incident under investigation. The third block lists the most common immediate causes, while the fourth block lists common basic causes. Finally, the bottom (fifth) block lists activities generally accepted as important for a successful loss control program. The technique is easy to apply and is supported by a training manual.

TapRooT™ Incident Investigation System: TapRooT™ is an integrated system that includes an investigation process, five root cause analysis techniques, and a computerized data base.[45,46] The method is specially designed to help investigators identify the causes of human performance problems. One of the TapRooT™ techniques contains a "paper-based" expert system with 14 key questions to help identify potential human performance problem areas. Hence, this aspect of TapRooT™ is similar to the HPES.

TapRooT™ is developed around "core techniques"and "optional techniques." The core techniques include the "Events and Causal Factors Charting" and the "Root Cause Tree™." The former builds on the principles of MES or STEP and is a graphic presentation of the sequence of events that led to an incident and the causal factors of those events. The Root Cause Tree™ represents a set of generic causal trees (or check lists) that is applied to each of the causal factors. The three optional techniques are Barrier Analysis, Change Analysis and Critical Human Action Profile (CHAP).

The overall technical approach of TapRooT™ is similar to the HPES, and can also be used for investigating equipment causes of incidents. The core techniques were first used together in 1985,and have gone through continued development and enhancement prior to publication of the TapRoot™ Incident Investigation Manual in October 1991. Implementation of TapRooT™ requires a licensing agreement with the developer, System Improvements, Inc. Such an agreement includes a user's manual that describes the use of core techniques and optional techniques.

Technique of Operations Review (TOR): TOR was developed by D.A.Weaver Safety Associates[47] as a diagnostic training and mishap prevention tool. It can also be used for incident investigation. Application of TOR requires a team effort with a group leader whose function is equivalent to that of the HAZOP leader. Once the team has been briefed on the key elements of the incident, the "Trace Step" commences using the TOR analysis sheet. This sheet centers on the management and supervisory factors in an operating system. The TOR analysis sheet displays an array of operational errors organized under eight headings:

- Training
- Responsibility
- Decision and Direction
- Supervision
- Work Groups
- Control
- Personal Traits

Associated with each array is a number, and the purpose of the team effort is to associate a prime error with responsible contributing factors to the incident. Starting with one prime cause the "Trace Step" produces a growing line of probable causative factors, each to be discussed and accepted or rejected. By drawing circles around the numbers on the TOR analysis sheet, the investigation team "traces" the root cause.

Technique of Operations Review comes with detailed instructions, and special training programs have been developed. It is simple to implement, and it can easily supplement other techniques to reach a consensus on causes and corrective actions. The technique has several features in common with the general-purpose methods of expert opinion solicitation and evaluation.[48]

2.5.2. Validity and User-Friendliness

Considerable synergism exists between analytical incident investigation and PHA. The analytical incident investigation provides insights and quantitative data that can be used to validate the assumptions and techniques of PHA. The formalism (including analytical techniques and solution algorithms) of PHA provides a structure that can raise the effectiveness of the investigative effort. In the long term, and as a result of the synergism, the current techniques for PSII will continue to evolve and mature.

Several of the investigation techniques reviewed in Section 2.5.1 are direct adaptations of techniques that have been in practical use by PHA practitioners for 20 years or more. Many of the adaptations to PSII are not yet fully developed, however, and the full analytical powers of individual techniques are not fully used. As an example, several of the deductive and inductive techniques were originally developed for computer implementation. In PSII the role of computers is still to be determined, although some steps have been taken to introduce concepts for computer-based PSII.[49,50]

Some of the investigation techniques are frameworks for systematic PSII, and require interpretation and adaptation on the part of the investigator. Typically there is large latitude in how the frameworks are applied. A few of the "techniques" reviewed provide only conceptual frameworks. Hence, investigation techniques range from detailed deductive/inductive approaches with step-by-step user instructions to broad conceptual frameworks.

Potentially, a PSII technique can have a wide range of validity, but its practical use can be very challenging and require substantial judgment. Hence, in a real application its level of validity can be limited. Conversely, a technique can have a narrow range of validity but be very easy to apply. It is recognized that *all* of the PSII techniques suffer from the same basic advantages and disadvantages as the PHA techniques. In the end the validity is determined by experience and judgment. Qualitatively, the validity of PSII techniques is determined by:

- Description of known limitations
- Completeness of user instruction
- Degree of joint recognition in the safety profession and risk assessment profession
- Acknowledgment of industry standards and guidelines
- Degree of user feedback
- Extent of development and user support
- Effectiveness in supporting the investigation of the minor incident versus the major incident

These characteristics are described below to give the basis of the framework that has been adopted for the examination of PSII techniques reviewed in Section 2.5.1.

Description of Known Limitations: This factor characterizes whether the technique is a general purpose technique or only focuses on specific aspects of an investigation. Further, it describes if the intended use is restricted to a minor incident or a major incident. Techniques supported by detailed user instructions are mature and limiting features are clearly identified.

Completeness of User Instruction: Where there are detailed user instructions, there is a basis for technology transfer. Also, detailed user instructions assure consistent and accurate applications. The degree of "completeness" is a direct function of how well all facets of a technique are addressed. It also addresses the availability of step-by-step guidance with necessary feedback loops. Proper use of work sheets and charts must be discussed, and the technique must fit into the overall PSII process. Resource requirements and team compositions must be clearly stated.

In general, techniques that are based on formal deductive/inductive approaches are also supported by step-by-step instructions. The conceptual frameworks (that is, Type 2 techniques and some Type 3 techniques) often require substantial support from an outside expert to ensure a consistent implementation.

Degree of Recognition: This factor is highly judgmental, but is intended to reflect the extent to which a technique is referenced, reviewed, and compared in professional journals. If a technique has been addressed in enough detail in a technical paper, this is often indicative of peer review.

Acknowledgment of Industry Standards and Guidelines: This element is coupled to "User Instruction." If a specific PSII technique is supported by detailed instructions, then the dependency on available standards and guidelines for development of a deductive/inductive incident chart, for example, is not critical. On the other hand, if there are few or no instructions or industry standards/guidelines, then there is reason for concern, because the technique might be applied in an inconsistent way.

Degree of User Feedback: This factor is coupled to "Known Limitations." Insights from practical PSII provide the basis for making modifications so an application is made easier. One of the roles of process safety management is to ensure that practical experience is given proper acknowledgment by maintaining preparedness and apply the lessons learned.

Extent of Development and User Support: Where there is active user support, there is also a higher likelihood of consistent and accurate implementation. Many of the PSII techniques reviewed in Section 2.5.1 were developed years ago and have not kept up with advancements in PHA. This can make implementation difficult. Most techniques are supported by training courses and formalized feedback of results through a clearinghouse. Users may also have access to a "hot line" service to help solve special problems associated with the implementation.

Effectiveness in Supporting Minor versus Major Incident Investigation: If a PSII technique was originally developed to support the investigation of occupational incidents, it might not be suited for the investigation of a major process incident. The purpose here is to rate any potential over- or understatement of the degree of applicability.

2.5.3. Some Observations

Table 2-1 summarizes the insights and results of the evaluation of PSII techniques about validity and user-friendliness. The discussion below focuses on the key observations. Sources of information about these techniques are listed in Appendix H.

There are limitations with all of the reviewed techniques. The most serious kind of limitation is one in which a technique is not suited for supporting the investigation of a major incident. Usually the techniques are flexible enough to allow for adaptation to circumvent a limiting feature. One technique can be combined with another to better support the investigative effort. Relative to their intended use, the reviewed PSII techniques fall into three categories:

- Techniques developed specifically for investigation of occupational incidents
- Techniques addressing the human/organizational error aspects of an incident
- General purpose PSII techniques

None of the techniques is rigorous from the point of how it is intended to be applied. It is assumed the investigator is experienced (either in solving process safety problems in general or in the application of PHA techniques) and can make appropriate judgments and adjustments so a technique meets the specific needs. Before choosing a new technique, PSII practitioners should be consulted. As a basic rule, it is not a good practice to apply a technique that is developmental and is not normally used in CPI application.

With regard to user instructions, two extremes are noted; the MORT technique and the AEB technique, respectively, represent the bounds for the evaluation. The MORT technique is supported by extensive and very detailed user instructions, as well as training programs. Department of Energy (DOE) has provided large funding for the development of MORT for a long time, and there is a library of MORT user instructions. The AEB technique, on the other hand, is still evolving. Detailed user instructions may not be available in the near future. Even with instructions, the safety engineer or loss prevention specialist may need the support of an outside consultant in order to apply AEB successfully.

An interesting approach worth special mention is that of the Institute of Nuclear Power Operations (INPO) for Human Performance Enhancement System (HPES)

TABLE 2-1
Overview of Techniques for Incident Investigation

INCIDENT INVESTIGATION TECHNIQUE	CATEGORY TYPE	LOGIC BASE: Deductive	LOGIC BASE: Inductive	LOGIC BASE: Morphologic	AVAILABLE TO PUBLIC OR PROPRIETARY	PRIMARY O SECONDAR METHOD
Accident Anatomy Method (AAM)[S]	3	X	X		Public	Primary
Action Error Analysis (AEA)	3			•	Public	Secondary
Accident Evolution and Barrier (AEB) Analysis[t]	—			•	Public	Secondary
Change Evaluation/Analysis (CE/A)	2				Public	Secondary
Cause–Effect Logic Diagram (CELD)	3		•		Public	Secondary
Causal Tree Method (CTM)	3	•			Proprietary	Primary
Fault Tree Analysis (FTA)	3	•			Public	Primary
Hazard and Operability Study (HAZOP)	3		•		Public	Secondary
Human Performance Enhancement System (HPES)[c]	2				Proprietary	Secondary
Human Reliability Analysis Event Tree (HRA-ET)[t]	—				Public	—
Multiple-Cause, Systems-Oriented Incident Investigation (MCSOII)	3	•			Public	Primary
Multilinear Events Sequencing (MES)	2				Public	Primary
Management Oversight Risk Tree (MORT)	3	•			Public	Secondary
Systematic Cause Analysis Technique (SCAT)[c]	2				Proprietary	Secondary
Sequentially Timed Events Plot (STEP)	2				Public	Primary
TapRoot™ Incident Investigation System[t,c]	—			•	Proprietary	Primary
Technique of Operations Review (TOR)	2				Proprietary	Secondary
Work Safety Analysis (WSA)	3			•	Public	Secondary

LEGENDS

X	=	Partially applicable.
•	=	Fully applicable
☐	=	Special care must be exercised in the implementation.
Morphologic	=	Morphologic approach—a combination of deductive and inductive. (See Section 2.5.)
Primary	=	Primary method; stand-alone technique.
Secondary	=	Secondary method. Provides special input to supplement another method.

FOOTNOTES

a This collection of information is not intended to be complete and is only provided as a general guide. It represents the judgment of the individuals working on this book and is based on available information sources. It is also recognized that many of these techniques are being revised and updated. No technique is recommended by CCPS; and incident investigators should complete their own evaluation of the techniques available, selecting those that best suit their needs.

b This heading indicates which category most closely matches the technique. The classification also reflects transparency and ease of use.

c Proprietary technique that requires a license agreement.
—HPES, avaliable only to members of the Institute fo Nuclear Power Operations (INPO)
—SCAT, single license available for $165 (11/91) and comes with instructor and student manual.
—TapRoot™, single license available of $140 (10/91) and excludes training

e CPI = Chemical Process Industries.

f TRANS = Transportation incidents: air, marine, rail, and other.

g NUCLEAR = Nuclear industries.

h OI = Occupational incidents: injuries, illnesses.

i HP = Human performance: human reliability or human error application.

j MATURITY = The degree of sophistication, experience, and expertise needed to apply the technique suc-

Table 2-1 *(Cont'd)*

ORIGIN AND/OR AREA OF RECOGNIZED SUCCESSFUL APPLICATION[d]					MATURITY[j]			TRAINING[n]			
I[e]	TRANS[f]	NUCLEAR[g]	OI[h]	HP[i]	EX[k]	SP[l]	EX[m]	IN[o]	TL[p]	TM[q]	N[r]
					•			=8	>8	>8	>8
				•	•	•		=8	>8	>8	>8
				•			•	—	—	—	—
			•	•		•		@8	<8	<8	<8
		•			•			=8	>8	<8	<8
			•			•		@8	<8	<8	<8
		•			•			=8	>8	>8	>8
						•		>8	<8	<8	<8
			•	•		•		@8	<8	<8	<8
				•	•			>8	>8	>8	@8
			•	•		•		@8	<8	<8	<8
	•					•		@8	<8	<8	<8
				•		•		=8	>8	>8	>8
			•			•		@8	<8	<8	<8
	•					•		@8	<8	<8	<8
				•		•		>8	>8	@8	<8
				•		•		>8	>8	@8	<8
			•			•		>8	>8	@8	<8

k EX = An "expert user" is needed as part of the investigation team. The term "expert" implies that the investigator has extensive experience in PHA *in addition* to prior incident investigation experience.

l SP = A "safety professional" with some prior training in PSII techniques is needed as part of the investigation team.

m EV = Evolving technique; that is, R&D is under way but pilot applications have not been pursued.

n TRAINING: Relates to the amount of time needed to becoem proficient, either as a leader or as a team member. The following rating is used:

- =8 Indicates either prior experience in PHA ***or*** at least 40 hours of formal classroom training.
- >8 Indicates that on the order of 1 week of classroom training is required.
- @8 Indicates a 1-day orientation including a workshop for hands-on problem solving.
- <8 Overview of technique, without hands-on training.

o IN = Instructor.

p TL = Team leader.

q TM = Team member.

r N = Novice team member.

s The AAM technique uses a combination of deductive and inductive logic, but in a less rigorous application.

t The AEB, HRA-ET, and TapRoot™ methods rank between a 2 and a 3 overall on the CCPS type categories.

applications. All the users of this technique are supported by a clearinghouse at INPO's Atlanta office. This clearinghouse provides customized training courses and written step-by-step instructions, and issues a newsletter that provides incident statistics, user feedback, and other information pertaining to the HPES. This approach is an example of "proactive" support.

Relative to recognition, it is apparent that the MORT technique has had a significant impact on the development of most of the other techniques. MORT has been reviewed, applied, and compared in numerous technical papers and research projects. By understanding the limitations of MORT, other techniques have evolved that have taken advantage of basic concepts and have improved user-friendliness.

Other techniques have received recognition but only within a narrow field of application, such as occupational incidents or transportation incidents. It is interesting to note that large R&D funding has been directed to occupational incident research for a long time. The problem of wide recognition is that the results of university research and development are seldom reported outside highly specialized scientific journals, for example, *Accident Analysis & Prevention, Journal of Occupational Psychology, Journal of Safety Research, Safety Science*, etc.

Except for MORT, AAM, and AEA, none of the reviewed techniques uses *standardized symbology* for the causal analysis. The symbols that are used are adaptations of established symbology. From the view point of PSII this is not a problem as long as the written instructions are descriptive enough to avoid misapplication/errors. On the other hand, use of nonstandard symbology means there can be ineffective communication of investigation insights and results. This could be pronounced when PHA practitioners are asked to assess the validity of recommended actions.

Ideally, the PSII practitioners should consult available standards and guidelines for deductive or inductive charting of cause–consequence relationships as a way of enhancing the investigative and communicative power of PSII techniques. There should also be some sort of coordination between PSII and PHA. With the possible exception of AEB and WSA, there is minimal reference made to PHA in the user instructions.

Recognizing the difficulty of assessing the degree of user feedback, it is acknowledged that increasing interest is directed to incident investigation. Systems like the European MARS (see Section 2.6) and HPES promote an exchange of incident information and user experience, and provide mechanisms by which practitioner scan get access to relevant information. Some of the reviewed techniques are proprietary and, hence, very difficult to assess. It is assumed, however, that users of proprietary techniques can get direct access to user feedback or can provide feedback through some form of user group forum.

The issue of user support is directly tied to user instructions and user feedback. A particular concern is the extent to which the techniques stay abreast with new process safety developments. Hence, the user support should be an active part of the overall process safety management approach.

Few of the techniques provide a structure for in-depth examination of human factors issues. Most of the techniques account for human factors issues, but there has been little or no developmental effort following the original development. In conclusion, the level of user support is limited, and it is expected that PSII practitioners will have to apply judgment and make modifications as required.

Process safety incident investigation techniques originally developed for major process incidents are also directly applicable to the minor occupational incident. The converse is not always valid. A technique like WSA would be ineffective in supporting the investigation of a major incident, and this is recognized by the developers of WSA. Several techniques were originally developed for incidents other than process incidents (for example, MES, STEP, TOR, CE/A). Although the basic principles of these techniques are based on the elements of the incident anatomy and associated theories, there is little confirmation that they can be applied effectively to process incidents. Hence, special care must be exercised when applying one of these techniques to process safety.

As explained earlier, there is a direct relationship between PSII and PHA. Where there is a strong PHA culture, the key elements of a structure for PSII are in place. It is fully appropriate to adapt HAZOP or standard FTA techniques, for instance, for PSII as long as the basic principles of the incident anatomy are adhered to. *The multiple-cause, systems-oriented principles must be acknowledged as well.*

Many examples exist within the CPI where the basic principles of PHA have been applied in the development of the specific procedures for PSII. To be effective investigation tools, these adaptations must be supplied with proper training and detailed instructions to assure consistency and accuracy. One potential drawback of the adaptations is that it can become more complex to communicate insights and results among users than when a better recognized technique is being used.

2.5.4. Application of PSII Techniques

The following recommendations relate to three issues: *(i)* approaches to adaptations of recognized PSII techniques, *(ii)* documentation of charts showing causation and progression, and *(iii)* use of the PC for structured PSII.

It is not a requirement to select a well-recognized PSII technique for the investigative effort to meet the defined objectives (that is, identification of root cause, development of recommended actions). The professional investigator has complete freedom to develop new techniques for PSII as long as the key principles of incident theory are acknowledged. Also the investigator must acknowledge the concept of continuous improvement resulting in continued evolution of the PSII management system.

The investigator is encouraged to extend the applications. To implement a new technique or adapt a recognized technique, a formal investigation procedure should be in place (see Chapter 3). The technique itself should be supported by verified and validated instructions. In addition, the technique to be used should, preferably, be acceptable to PHA practitioners, and consistent with management and operations expertise. If not, the performance of effective investigations can become difficult because of lack of communications.

Process safety incident investigation is not an exact science; it is a dynamic and interactive engineering framework that requires interpretation, judgment, flexibility, and inventiveness. Ideally, the technique used should be suited to or designed for specific processes and operations rather than relying on generic, published step-by-step instructions. The investigator must think through and fully understand the assumptions and implications of all aspects of the technique to be used.

All of the available, recognized techniques are intended to be used in a series of meetings, during which a multidisciplinary team methodically analyzes the incident following the structure provided by the PSII technique. To be effective, the use of a technique in a team effort should be planned. The roles and requirements of team members should be clearly identified (this is addressed in further detail in Chapters 3 and 8).

Several of the recognized PSII techniques, as well as the adaptations, use charts to visualize causation. A typical chart uses a logical tree structure such as fault tree or event tree. A PSII team effort can be greatly enhanced by using standardized work sheets for development of such charts. There are examples (e.g., MORT, MCSOII, and AAM) in which templates and/or generic tree structures have been developed for use as check lists during an actual PSII. To be effective, such templates should be developed on a process/technology-specific basis. Note that the MORT technique comes with an elaborate tree structure (fault tree) to be used as the basis for an investigation. It has to be realized, however, that this "generic" tree primarily relates issues of human and organizational error.

The implementation of the WSA technique builds on HAZOP-type principles, and conceptually this can be adapted to any type of PSII. Substantial development work may be required to define its practical ground rules (for example, deviations, guide words).

Based on available literature on incident investigation, only minor efforts have been directed to computer-based investigations. Conceptually, there are several applications that should be considered, especially when the investigative technique uses deductive/inductive approaches. As an example, instead of using flip charts to develop charts of causation and progression, a PC could be used. A practice similar to that of the PC-based HAZOP session is quite feasible. For example, the incident chart under development can be shown on a screen using a video display unit. This approach could make the analytical sessions more effective and also would facilitate high-quality documentation.

The PC also allows the data collected during an investigation to be tracked through all stages of an investigation. It is quite possible to design a user-friendly tracking system using available software products. The International Loss Control Institute (ILCI) offers the *Accident/Incident Investigation Module* as part of its Computer Assisted Loss Management System (CALMS).[49]

Advanced computer applications are being considered by using artificial intelligence concepts. The purpose is to develop expert systems to supplement the investigative effort and provide an overall framework for PSII.[50]

In conclusion, many PSII techniques have been proposed and applied. All the techniques require judgment, and changes can be made to fit specific investigation needs. Almost any of the recognized techniques can be helpful in organizing a systematic approach to PSII. To be successful in finding root causes and defining recommended actions, it is not an absolute requirement to adopt one of the reviewed techniques. The investigator first must ensure that a specific technique addresses issues of interest/importance. Next, modifications need to be made, and, finally, step-by-step instructions and training are required. Section 2.5.3 provides an overview of the limitations and applicability of the techniques discussed

2.6. INCIDENT DATA BASES

This section summarizes some of the available process-related incident data bases and examines the structure and applications. Many data bases on process incidents have been established for use as a process safety management tool. In most cases it is easy to access these data bases. Although there is often a discrepancy between the number of incidents that have actually happened and those that are recorded (that is, not all incidents are reported), a systematic use of available data can help in planning for incident investigation.

Most of the data bases have been developed by regulatory agencies or by national laboratories (public sources). Others are either commercial or proprietary data bases. New data bases are being developed at press time, and the reader should watch for those relevant to his or her industry.

2.6.1. Types and Sources of Historical Incident Data

A basic principle of loss prevention in the CPI is to learn from mistakes. To achieve this requires the reporting of incidents and the sharing of information. On the basis of such information, incident data can be compiled to determine the trend in safety performance. For a long time there has been a mostly unstructured system of:

- Incident reporting
- Incident investigation
- Incident data
- Incident case histories

Most of the incident data bases address major events or failures such as leaks of toxic materials, major fires or explosions. Also addressed are incidents causing fatalities or serious injuries. These kinds of events are sufficiently serious to be reported widely in publicly available sources such as reports by regulatory agencies, reports from research organizations, technical journals, and media reports. The historical incident data sources address major events or failures such as[51,52]:

- Leaks or toxic materials
- Major fires or explosions
- Pipeline leaks and ruptures
- Transportation accidents
- Accidents causing fatalities or serious injuries (any case)
- Near misses (with potential for serious consequence)

The incident information from these types of data sources can be grouped into at least six categories, which provide data on:

- Failure mechanisms and causes from mechanical or process factors
- Failure mechanisms and causes from human and organizational errors
- Latent failures; for example, numerous incidents occur because of an undetected fault in a system that remains undetected for a long time prior to an incident
- Consequence effects; for example, downwind concentrations, radiation levels, and toxic doses
- Frequencies of certain types of incidents
- Hazardous material and the process involved in incident.

Traditionally, the regulatory agencies have required that certain incidents be reported. In some cases the information from the reporting schemes has been summarized and made available to interested parties such as industry organizations, special interest groups, and the media. It is equally common that the incident information has been stored and remained unused. Many corporate safety groups have also promoted or required the reporting of incidents for internal use.

Table 2-2 presents a summary of incident data sources. Most are collections of data from industrial incidents around the world and from a wide range of sources. There is considerable overlap among the data bases; that is, a set of data appearing in one data base also appears in another data base. The most comprehensive data available often come from systems developed around a classification scheme that has been adopted by an industry; for example, nuclear industry, aerospace industry.

CHEMICAL MANUFACTURERS ASSOCIATION (CMA)
PROCESS SAFETY CODE, RESOURCE GUIDE, OCTOBER 1990

4.3 Communicate Lessons Learned

- Maintain an incident log and frequency monitoring system. Ensure that incident investigation reports become a part of the process hazards investigation package.
- Provide results and lessons learned to appropriate authorities and to other company divisions that could be affected (e.g., other company units with similar processes).
- Provide feedback from the investigation program on ways to improve company response to incidents. Periodically review the results from past investigations with new employees.

TABLE 2-2
Overview of Incident Data Bases

NAME	OPERATOR	AVAILABILITY	CONTENT
Major Hazard Incident Analysis System (MHIDAS)	Safety & Reliability Directorate (SRD) and the Health & Safety Executive (HSE), England. Phone No.: 011-44-(925)-31244, Ext. 7305	PC-based data base. Can be accessed by paying an annual fee.	Worldwide data base of incidents involving hazardous materials and with potential for offsite impact. Contains the British "contributions" to the MARS (see below).
Accident Prevention Advisory Unit (APAU) Data Base	Health & Safety Executive, London (England).	In the public domain.	Statistics on industrial incidents (primarily occupational) in the United Kingdom.
Failure and ACcident Technical Information System (FACTS)	TNO Division of Technology for Society, P.O. Box 342, NL-7300 AH Apeldoorn, The Netherlands. Phone No.: 011-31-55-49 3821 FAX No.: 011-31-55-49 3390	PC-based data base. Available by paying a fee; presently it is $3,750 as an empty shell plus cost of data. Information on specific subject(s) can also be obtained by paying a fee/record.	Worldwide data base of industrial incidents involving hazardous materials. The most recent version is called PC-FACTS; 2-day workshops are organized for the users.
OCcupational Accidents Analysis and Reporting (OCAAR)	Elf Aquitaine and Total-CFP, France.	Proprietary PC-based data base; for internal use only.	Occupational incident statistics and cause-consequence information involving petrochemical operations. The system provides data reported to local authorities.

TABLE 2-2 *(Cont'd)*

NAME	OPERATOR	AVAILABILITY	CONTENT
CONCAWE	The Oil Companies European Organization for Environmental and Health Protection, The Hague, Netherlands.	In the public domain.	Annual reports of leaks from oil industry cross-country pipelines in Western Europe.
World Offshore Accident Data (WOAD)	Veritec Offshore Technology and Services A/S, Høvik (Oslo), Norway. Phone No.: 011-47-(2)477250 FAX No.: 011-47-(2)-479871	Access to data base by paying an annual fee of $400.	Annual summary report of worldwide offshore incidents. Builds on publically available data sources. Contains 1800 'accident' and 4000 'incident' records.
Offshore Accident Data (OAD)	Mineral Management Services (MMS), Gulf of Mexico OCS Region, New Orleans (LA).	In the public domain; in the process of being computerized.	Data on offshore incidents in Gulf Coast area. PC-based system developed using dBase IV.
Human Performance Evaluation System (HPES).	Institute for Nuclear Power Operations (INPO), Atlanta (GA). Phone No.: (404) 953-3600 FAX No.: (404) 953-7549	Access limited to member organizations only. Annual summary reports published.	Focus on human factors issues in the nuclear power industry. Provides statistical data on HOEs and information on root cause analysis.

'100 Large Losses: A Thirty Year Review of Property Damage Losses in the Hydrocarbon Chemical Industries'	M&M Protection Consultants, Chicago.	Updated reports available from M&M Protection Consultants.	Includes 100 largest incidents; exceeding a minimum criterion of $10,000,000 of property damage.
Loss Prevention Bulletin	Institution of Chemical Engineers (IChemE), Rugby, England.	In the public domain; available through annual subscription.	Source of historical case study information provided by IChemE members.
Community Documentation Centre on Industrial Risk, CDCIR (Major Accident Reporting System, MARS)	Joint Research Centre, Ispra (Va), Italy. In the U.S.A., contact: European Community Information Service, Washington (DC). Phone No.: (202) 862-9500	Summary reports in the public domain. Full access to data base only granted the authorities supplying input data.	All industrial incidents involving hazardous material within the European Community. As of October 1990 a total of 97 incidents had been included in MARS.
Platform Data Bank	French Petroleum Institute (Institute Francais du Petrole), Paris, France.	In the public domain.	Worldwide offshore incident data; similar to WOAD. Over 850 records on incidents involving fixed and mobile drilling units.

TABLE 2-2 *(Cont'd)*

NAME	OPERATOR	AVAILABILITY	CONTENT
Pipeline Incident Data	Minerals Management Service (MMS), Gulf of Mexico OCS Region, New Orleans (LA).	In the public domain.	Data on pipeline leaks in the Gulf of Mexico.
Reportable Incidents for Natural Gas Transmisson and Gathering Lines, 1970-1984.	American Gas Association.	In the public domain.	Incident statistics on gas pipelines.
LNG Plant Failure Rate Data Base.	Gas Research Institute (GRI), Chicago.	In the public domain.	Compilation of failure rates and incident data associated with piping. Includes root cause analysis.
UKHSE, Contract Report No. 15/1989. Pipe Failures in Land Based Pipelines.	Study sponsored by the HSE in the UK with support from authorities in the Netherlands and Finland.	In the public domain.	Root cause analysis of reported incidents with special emphasis on the human error contribution.
Hydrocarbon Leak and Ignition Data Base	Exploration and Production (E&P) Forum, London (England).	In the public domain (report to be published in late 1991/early 1992).	Statistical data associated with offshore operations in the North Sea.

Lees, F.P., 1980. <u>Loss Prevention in the Process Industries. Hazard Identification, Assessment and Control</u>.	--	Published by Butterworth-(Publishers) Inc. Second edition in preparation.	Appendix 1, pp 863-881: Description of the major incident at Flixborough (UK) on June 1, 1974. Appendix 2, pp 883-885: Description of the major incident at Seveso (Italy) on July 10, 1976. Appendix 3, pp 887-927: Case histories of selected major incidents.
Ammonia Plant and Related Facilities Safety (formerly 'Safety in Air and Ammonia Plants')	Ammonia Committee of the American Institute of Chemical Engineers (AIChE), New York (NY)	Published by AIChE	This publication includes the proceedings of the annual symposium and contains descriptions of case histories.
IFP Databanks on Offshore Accidents	Division of Planning and Information, Institute Français du Pétrole, B.P. 311, F-92506 Rueil-Malmaison Cedex, France.	In the public domain.	Data base includes information on incidents involving carrier vessels, drilling vessels or offshore platforms. Only incidents resulting in spills of at least 500 metric tons are covered.
VARO	Finnish Technical Inspection Centre, Helsinki, Finland.	In the public domain.	Occupational and process incidents in Finland.

CONCLUSIONS ON INCIDENT INVESTIGATION AND REPORTING

18.43 I am convinced that learning from accidents and incidents is an important way of improving safety performance. That view is commonly held throughout the UK offshore industry. In relation to preventing incidents that cause hydrocarbon leaks that could lead to fires and explosions I consider it would be useful if there was a systematic means by which what could be learnt from such accidents and near misses was shared by all operators. The regulatory body should be responsible for maintaining a data base with regard to hydrocarbon leaks, spills, and ignitions in the industry and for the benefit of the industry. The regulatory body should

- discuss and agree with the industry the method of collection and use of the data;
- regularly assess the data to determine the existence of any trends and report to industry;
- provide operating companies with a means of obtaining access to the data, particularly for the purpose of carrying out quantified risk assessment.

From *The Public Inquiry into the Piper Alpha Disaster.* London: HMSO, 1990, p. 299.

The issue of completeness is a general problem associated with any data base. How can it be assured that all incidents, near-miss to major incident, actually get reported? There is no easy answer. All data bases have been struggling over this complex issue for a very long time. In 1973 the *Eu*ropean *Re*liability *Da*ta *A*ssociation (EuReDatA) was formed. Its mission was to promote uniformity and sharing of data and to establish practices and guidelines for collecting and analyzing equipment reliability data. This mission was soon expanded to encompass incident data for the CPI and non-CPI. Currently a project group on incident data[53] is addressing issues associated with user needs and applications of incident data bases.

Another general quality issue associated with incident data is the accuracy of information. Depending on the incident reporting scheme and requirements, there may or may not be any follow-up on the information entered into the data base. So, some of the information can represent the status prior to completion of the full PSII. In other cases, the information contained in the data base represents the post-PSII status. The MARS data base[54] acknowledges this issue and explicitly notes that a particular PSII has been completed or remains in progress. In summary, to attach any confidence to incident data there needs to be a mechanism for assuring completeness and accuracy.

2.6.2. General Considerations of Data Base Structures

Within the chemical process industry (CPI), two types of data bases have been developed:

- Compilations, computerized or not, of global and industry-wide incident information
- Structured and regionalized data bases tied to formal incident reporting schemes and requirements.

Examples of the first type of data base include the British *Loss Prevention Bulletin* issued by the Institution of Chemical Engineers (IChemE). It provides summaries of significant and/or interesting incidents with a bearing on process safety. Examples of the latter type are the Major Hazard Incident Data Service (MHIDAS) operated by the Safety and Reliability Directorate (SRD); the Health and Safety Executive (HSE) in England[55]; and FACTS operated by TNO in the Netherlands.[56,57] Both MHIDAS and FACTS are computerized and include worldwide information. Finally, the CDCIR[58] of the Joint Research Centre (JRC) at Ispra in Italy is an example of a structured and regionalized data base.

Jointly funded by the United Kingdom Atomic Energy Authority's (UKAEA's), SRD, and HSE set up an international incident data base (MHIDAS) in 1986. The original goal of MHIDAS was to establish a data base that could be used for validating assumptions and judgments in PHA. It was also intended to make the information available to safety professionals not associated with UKAEA. There are close ties between MHIDAS and the International Labour Office in Geneva, the World Health Organization, and the European Community (for example, MARS, operated by the JRC).

MHIDAS is a PC-based system developed around the dBase software package. The non-UKAEA affiliates can access data in MHIDAS by joining a user's group, or by paying for data as it is required, or by exchanging data. Originally MHIDAS could be accessed as follows:

- A single, annual payment plus a charge for each data entry found. This corresponds to being a member of the user's group. A newsletter provides general details of the information held in the data base and up-to-date details of the safety research conducted by the SRD.
- A payment for each request to interrogate MHIDAS plus a charge for each entry found.
- Arrangements to exchange information can be made with organizations who are in a position to supply information on major incidents. According to SRD and HSE, MHIDAS is operated on a commercial basis to recover the running costs of the data base and to conduct research on important past incidents.

A good example of a data base tied to a formal incident reporting scheme is the *M*ajor *A*ccident *R*eporting *S*ystem (MARS) operated by the JRC. This system builds on the requirements identified in the Seveso Directive[59] and the associated incident classification system. MARS is in the public domain and was set up to enable an exchange of incident information. Further, it was developed to extract important lessons on process safety management. Only the authorities supplying data to MARS

TABLE 2-3
MARS/CDCIR Incident Classification Appearing in Summary Reports

IV. INCIDENT CLASSIFICATION		
IV.1	Incident Classified by Substance Involved	
	IV.1.1	Ammonia
	IV.1.2	Chlorine
	IV.1.3	Fertilizers
	IV.1.4	Oxidizing substances
	IV.1.5	Phosgene
	IV.1.6	Pesticides
	IV.1.7	LPG
	IV.1.8	Other toxic substances
	IV.1.9	Other flammable or explosive substances
	IV.1.10	Substances capable of causing or undergoing run-away or decomposition reactions
	IV.1.11	Others
IV.2	Incident Classified by Installation Concerned	
	IV.2.1	Petroleum refining
	IV.2.2	Petrochemical industry
	IV.2.3	Gas processing
	IV.2.4	Coal industry
	IV.2.5	Carbon industry
	IV.2.6	Ceramic, cement, metal industry
	IV.2.7	Electrolytic industry
	IV.2.8	Glass industry
	IV.2.9	Halogen, alkali, phosphorus, sulphur and other inorganic industry
	IV.2.10	Pesticide industry
	IV.2.11	Pharmaceutical industry
	IV.2.12	Wood, pulp & paper
	IV.2.13	Surface coating and dyes
	IV.2.14	Food additives industry
	IV.2.15	Sugar, starch & fermentation
	IV.2.16	Soap & detergent industry
	IV.2.17	General chemical industry
	IV.2.18	Water industry
	IV.2.19	Waste treatment and disposal industry
	IV.2.20	Storage activities
	IV.2.21	Other industries
	IV.2.22	Maintenance and/or plant/process modifications incidents
IV.3	Others	

have full access to the information system, but annual summary reports are published by the JRC.[58] In the MARS summary reports, the incident information is classified as (see Table 2-3):

- Incidents classified by substance involved
- Incidents classified by the installation concerned

The Environmental Protection Agency maintains ERNS (Emergency Response Notification System) and ARIP (Accidental Release Information Program). The EPA has also been participating with the Organization for Economic Cooperation and Development (OECD) to exchange "accident histories" for construction of a system to foster lessons learned. The OECD system collects information from many countries.

2.7. REFERENCES

1. Department of Energy, 1985. *Accident/Incident Investigation Manual*, 2nd ed., DOE/SSDC 76-45/27. Idaho Falls, ID: System Safety Development Center, Idaho National Engineering Laboratory.
2. Greenwood, M. and H. M. Woods, 1919. "The Incidence of Industrial Accidents with Special Reference to Multiple Accidents." Ind. Fatigue Res. Board, Report 4. London: HMSO.
3. Heinrich, H. W., 1936. *Industrial Accident Prevention*. New York: McGraw-Hill.
4. Recht, I. L., 1965–66. System Safety Analysis—A Modern Approach to Safety Problems. *National Safety News*, December, February, April, June.
5. Peterson, D., 1984. *Human-Error Reduction and Safety Management*. Goshen, NY: Aloray Inc.
6. Kletz, T. A., 1991. *An Engineer's View of Human Error*, 2nd ed. Rugby (Warwickshire), England: The Institution of Chemical Engineers.
7. Reason, J., 1990. *Human Error*. Cambridge, England: Cambridge University Press.
8. Hollnagel, E., O. M. Pedersen, and J. Rasmussen, 1981. "Notes on Performance Analysis." Roskilde, Denmark: Riso National Laboratory.
9. Rasmussen, J., 1983. Skills, Rules, and Knowledge—Signals, Signs, and Symbols, and Other Distinctions in Human Performance Models. *IEEE Transactions on Systems, Man, and Cybernetics*, SMC-13(3):257–266.
10. Dougherty, E. M., Jr., and J. R. Fragola, 1988. *Human Reliability Analysis. A Systems Engineering Approach with Nuclear Power Plant Applications*. New York: John Wiley & Sons.
11. Haastrup, P., 1984. *Design Error in the Chemical Industry*. Roskilde, Denmark: Riso National Laboratory.
12. Roberts, N. H. et al., 1981. *Fault Tree Handbook*. NUREG-0492. Washington, DC: U.S. Nuclear Regulatory Commission.
13. Knecht, O. and H. Keil, 1968. Graphische Analyse vonReaktorstorfaallen (Graphical Analysis of Nuclear Reactor Incidents). *Atomund Strom*, 7/8:107–110. [In German.]
14. Burdick, G. R. and J. B. Fussell, 1976. On the Adaptation of Cause–Consequence Analysis to U.S. Nuclear Power Systems Reliability and Risk Assessment. In *A Collection of Methods for Reliability and Safety Engineering*, ANCR-1273. Idaho Falls, ID: Idaho National Engineering Laboratory.
15. Suokas, J. and V. Rouhiainen, 1989. Quality Control in Safety and Risk Analyses. *J. Loss Prev. Process Ind.*, 2:67–77.
16. Browning, R. L., 1975. Analyze Losses by Diagram. *Hydrocarbon Processing*, 54:253–257.
17. Arendt, J. S., 1983. A Chemical Plant Accident Investigation Using Fault Tree Analysis. Paper 11a, *Proceedings of 17th Annual Loss Prevention Symposium*. New York: American Institute of Chemical Engineers.
18. Center for Chemical Process Safety (CCPS), 1989. *Guidelines for Chemical Process Quantitative Risk Assessment*. New York: American Institute of Chemical Engineers. Pp. 509–518.
19. Boissieras, J., 1983. *Causal Tree. Description of the Method*. Princeton, NJ: Rhone-Poulenc. U.S. Contact: Corp. Safety Director, CN5266.

20. Leplat, J., 1978. Accident Analyses and Work Analyses. *Journal of Occupational Accidents*, 1:331–340.
21. Trost, W. A. and R. J. Nertney, 1985. *Barrier Analysis*, DOE 76-45/29. Idaho Falls, ID: System Safety Development Center, Idaho National Engineering Laboratory.
22. Buys, R. J., 1977. *Standardization Guide for Construction and Use of MORT-Type Analytical Trees*, ERDA 76-45/8. Idaho Falls, ID: System Safety Development Center, Idaho National Engineering Laboratory.
23. Ferry, T. S., 1988. *Modern Accident Investigation and Analysis*, 2nd ed. New York: John Wiley & Sons. Pp. 175–176.
24. Dowell, A. M., III, 1990. *Guidelines for Systems Oriented Multiple Cause Incident Investigations*, Version 3. 009. Rohm and Haas Texas Inc., Risk Analysis Department, P.O. Box 672, Deer Park, TX, 77536.
25. Anderson, S. E. and R. W. Skloss, 1991. "More Bang for the Buck: Getting the Most from an Accident Investigation." Paper presented at the Loss Prevention Symposium, American Institute of Chemical Engineers, New York.
26. Bruun, O., J. R. Taylor and A. Rasmussen, 1979. *Cause–Consequence Reporting for Accident Reduction*, Risø-M-2206. Roskilde, Denmark: Risø National Laboratory.
27. Keiding, J. T. and L. Skou, 1981. "Comparison of Two Methods for Analysis of Drilling Machine Accidents." SCRATCH Seminar 7. Methods for Risk and Safety Analysis, NORDFORSK, Stockholm (Sweden).
28. Taylor, J. R., 1991. Private communication. August 6, 1991.
29. Taylor, J. R., 1979. *A Background to Risk Analysis*, Vol. IV. Roskilde, Denmark: Risø National Laboratory. Pp. 777–793.
30. Mosleh, A. et al., 1988. *Procedures for Treating Common Cause Failures in Safety and Reliability Studies*, EPRI NP-5613. Palo Alto, CA: Electric Power Research Institute.
31. Center for Chemical Process Safety (*PS), 1992. Guidelines for Hazard Evaluation Procedures: Second Edition with Worked Examples.* New York: American Institute of Chemical Engineers. Sections 4.7 and 6.7.
32. Svenson, O., 1991. AEB Analysis of Incidents and Accidents in the Processing Industries. In Apostolakis, G. E. (Ed.). *Probabilistic Safety Assessment and Management*. New York: Elsevier. Pp. 271–276.
33. Svenson, O., 1991. The Accident Evolution and Barrier Function (AEB) Model Applied to Incident Analysis in the Processing Industries. *Risk Analysis: An International Journal*, 11(3):499–507.
34. Suokas, J., 1981. "Experiences of Work Safety Analysis" SCRATCH Seminar 7. Methods for Risk and Safety Analysis, NORDFORSK, Stockholm, Sweden.
35. Suokas, J. and Rouhiainen, 1984. *Work Safety Analysis. Method Description and User's Guide*, Research Reports No. 314. Espoo, Finland: Technical Research Centre of Finland.
36. Suokas, J., 1988. The Role of Safety Analysis in Accident Prevention. *Accident Analysis & Prevention*, 20(1):67–85.
37. Kepner, C. H. and B. B. Tregoe, 1976. *The Rational Manager*, 2nd ed. Princeton, NJ: Kepner-Tregoe, Inc.
38. Bishop, J. and R. LaRhette, 1988. Managing Human Performance—INPO's Human Performance Enhancement System. Conference Record for 1988 IEEE Fourth Conference on Human Factors and Power Plants, 88CH2576-7. New York: Institute of Electrical and Electronics Engineers. Pp. 471–474.

39. Bell. B. J. and A. D. Swain, 1983. *A Procedure for Conducting a Human Reliability Analysis for Nuclear Power Plants*, SAND81-1665 (NUREG/CR-2254). Albuquerque, NM: Sandia National Laboratories.
40. Swain, A. D. and H. E. Guttman, 1983. *Handbook of Human Reliability Analysis with Emphasis on Nuclear Power Plant Applications*, SAND80-0200 (NUREG/CR-1278). Albuquerque, NM: Sandia National Laboratories.
41. Lorenzo, D. K., 1990. *A Manager's Guide to Reducing Human Errors. Improving Human Performance in the Chemical Industry.* Washington, DC: Chemical Manufacturers Association.
42. Benner, L. Jr., 1975. Accident Investigation: Multilinear Events Sequencing Methods. *Journal of Safety Research*, 7(2):67–73.
43. Hendrick, K. and L. Benner, Jr., 1987. *Investigating Accidents with S-T-E-P.* New York: Marcel Dekker.
44. International Loss Control Institute, 1990. *SCAT—Systematic Cause Analysis Technique*, Loganville, GA.
45. Unger, L. and M. Paradise, 1992. "TapRooT™—A Systematic Approach for Investigating Incidents." Paper presented at the 1992 Process Plant Safety Symposium, Houston, TX, February 18–19.
46. Paradise, M., 1991. Root Cause Analysis and Human Factors. *Human Factors Bulletin*, 34(8):1–5.
47. Weaver, D. A., 1973. TOR Analysis: A Diagnostic Training Tool. *ASSE Journal*, June, pp. 24–29.
48. Seaver, D. A. and W. G. Stillwell, 1983. *Procedures for Using Expert Judgment to Estimate Human Error Probabilities in Nuclear Power Plant Operations*, NUREG/CR-2743 (SAND82-7054). Albuquerque, NM: Sandia National Laboratories.
49. International Loss Control Institute, 1991. Product Literature for CALMS —Computer Assisted Loss Management System. Loganville, GA.
50. Hale, A. R. et al., 1989. An Intelligent End-User Interface for the Collection and Processing of Accident Data. In Colombari, V. (Ed.). *Reliability Data Collection and Use in Risk and Availability Assessment.* New York: Springer-Verlag. Pp. 3
52. Kletz, T. A., 1988. *What Went Wrong? Case Histories of Process Plant Disasters*, 2nd ed. Houston: Gulf Publishing Company.
53. Amendola, A. and T. Luisi, 1989. Review of the EuReDatA Project Groups' Activities and Results. In Colombari, V. (Ed.). *Reliability Data Collection and Use in Risk and Availability Assessment*, New York: Springer-Verlag. Pp. 896–906.
54. Amendola, A., S. Contini, and P. Nichele, 1988. "MARS: The Major Accident Reporting System." *IChemE Symposium Series*, No. 110, pp. 445–458.
55. Systems Reliability Service, 1986. MHIDAS—Major Hazard Incident Data. *SRS Quarterly Digest*, November. Pp. 10–11.
56. Bockholts, P., 1983. "Collection and Application of Incident Data." *IChemE Symposium Series*, No. 80, pp. K11–21.
57. Koehorst, L. J. B. and P. Bockholts, 1991. FACTS: Most Comprehensive Information System for Industrial Safety. In Cannon, A. G. and A. Bendell (Eds.). *Reliability Data Banks*, New York: Elsevier. Pp. 53–80.
58. Gow, H. B. F. (Ed.), 1991. *Community Documentation Centre on Industrial Risk—Bulletin No. 4*, SP-I. 91. 09. Commission of the European Communities, Joint Research Centre, Ispra (Va), Italy.

59. Amendola, A., 1991. Major Hazards Regulation in the European Community. In Apostolakis, G. E. (Ed.). *Probabilistic Safety Assessment and Management.* New York: Elsevier. Pp. 229–232.
60. Vesely, W. E. et al., 1981. *Fault Tree Handbook*, NUREG-0492. Washington, DC: U.S. Government Printing Office.

3

SYSTEM FOR INVESTIGATING PROCESS SAFETY INCIDENTS

This chapter focuses on the *overall system* for investigating process safety incidents. Initial development and implementation guidelines for the material contained in this chapter are found in Chapter 8. It is an axiom of chemical process safety that "**process safety incidents are the result of management system failures.**"[1] The objective of incident investigation is to prevent recurrence. This is accomplished by establishing a management system for investigation that

- identifies and evaluates root system causes,
- identifies and evaluates recommended preventive measures that reduce probability of recurrence of and/or that mitigate potential consequences, and
- ensures effective follow-up action to complete and/or resolve all recommendations.

One of the goals of this chapter is to highlight management responsibilities and leadership. Another goal is to address the topic of incident category classification and the accompanying decision to activate a formal investigation team. Team composition, organization, leadership, and competencies are included. Guidelines for management, documentation, and reporting are presented. Details for gathering evidence (Chapter 4), identifying multiple system-related root causes (Chapter 5), recommendations (Chapter 6), and reports (Chapter 7) are covered elsewhere in this book and are not included in this chapter.

Figure 3-1 is a summary of the key elements of the management system for process safety incident investigation.

3.1. MANAGEMENT RESPONSIBILITIES

The process of incident investigation begins with management support, commitment, and action. Management should establish, communicate clearly, and *sustain* a consistent policy regarding incident reporting and investigation. This is most often expressed in a formal statement that fulfills the following requirements:

- Communicates management's commitment to prevent a recurrence by determining root causes, recommending preventive measures, and taking follow-up action.

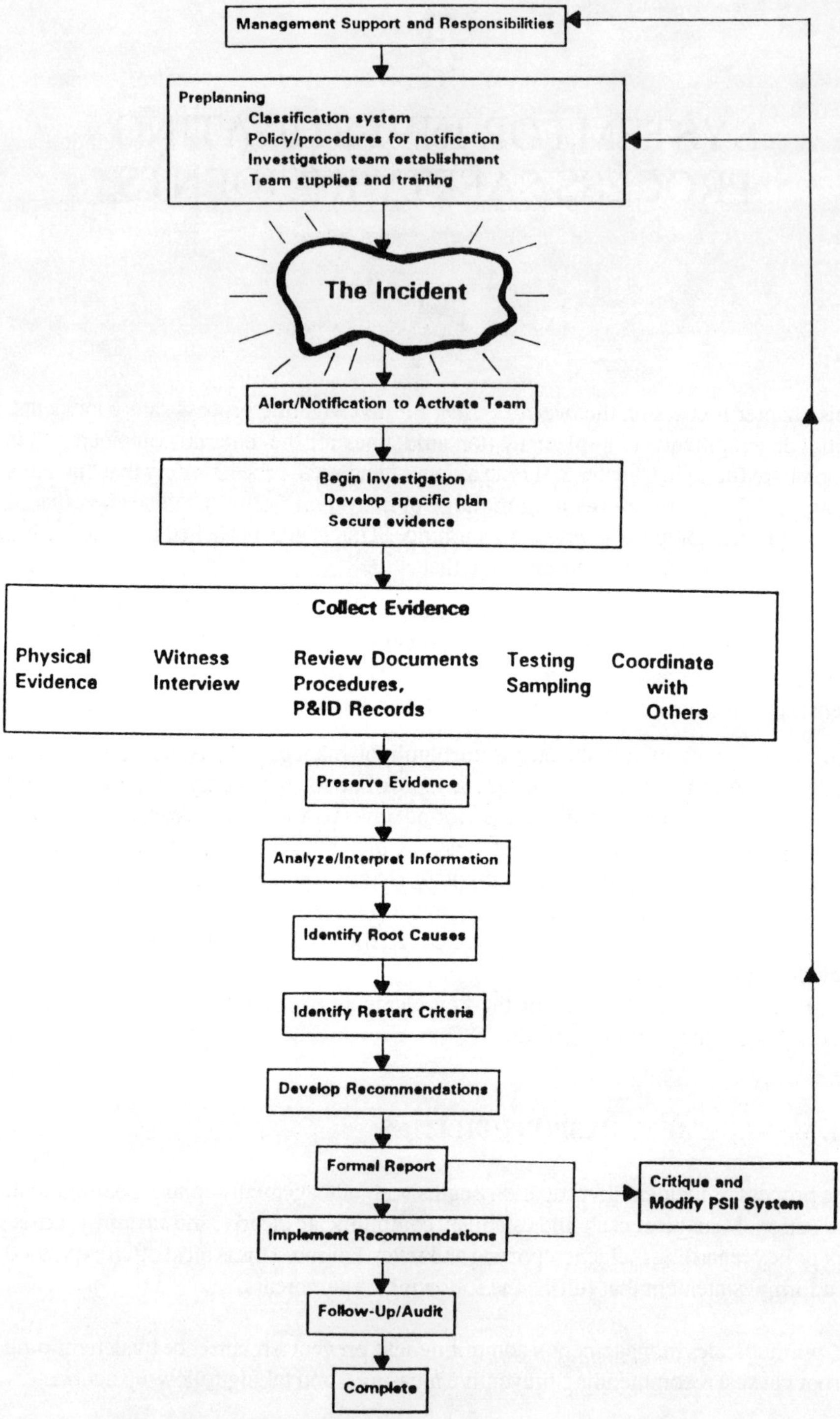

Figure 3-1. Management system for process safety incident investigation.

- Recognizes the importance of investigation as a primary hazard control mechanism.
- Focuses clearly the intention to "find cause" rather than "assign blame."
- Endorses sustained commitment of resources appropriate for the investigation and resolution of recommendations.
- Emphasizes the value and necessity of *communicating* and sharing the lessons learned from the investigation in a manner appropriate to all who may benefit.
- Implements a system to ensure all recommendations and findings are resolved to conclusion and documented.
- Strongly supports reporting and investigating near-miss incidents.

Management at all levels has the responsibility to create and maintain an atmosphere of trust and respect to encourage openness in reporting incidents and events. Failure to achieve this positive atmosphere may result in nonreporting of near-miss events. This may ultimately result in a catastrophic incident that could otherwise have been avoided. Near-miss reporting includes dealing with possibly sensitive information. The consequences of *not* reporting an incident should be known to all employees and should be applied in a consistent manner by those in supervisory positions.

Periodic reviews, audits, and reevaluations are necessary in order to ensure the process safety incident investigation (PSII) management system continues to function as originally intended and continues to achieve the desired results. This periodic review recognizes the fact that organizations are dynamic entities with constantly changing management. An obvious benefit of periodic reviews is verification that preventive action recommendations have been completed and documented. This follow-up is especially important for a recommendation that may have been rejected or modified.

Another management function is to establish an ongoing refresher training program for all levels of the corporation to ensure that the management system for investigation continues to achieve the intended result. Periodic refresher training gives further opportunity for management to exert leadership and reinforce commitment to the established policy and philosophy for incident reporting and investigation.

3.2. NEAR-MISS INCIDENTS

The near-miss deserves special attention in the investigation system. A **near-miss** is defined as **an extraordinary event that could reasonably have been expected to result in negative consequences, but actually did not.** A no-loss incident, such as an unignited vapor cloud, should be investigated with the same degree of vigor, diligence, and thoroughness as if it had actually ignited; and it merits the same degree of management attention. The same causes and modes of failure are present in major accidents as in near-misses. Near-miss reporting is necessary in order to decide if there should be a formal investigation. The decision to investigate a specific incident should be based on a realistic assessment of significant undesirable consequences.

Almost all serious accidents are preceded by numerous precursor events that give the opportunity to detect and eliminate potential hazards, thereby reducing risk (probability and/or consequences). Often these precursors may remain "masked" for an extended period of time. Some near-miss cases obviously deserve a full-scale investigation. Others are not so easily recognized and therefore go unreported. For example in a batch operation, operators learn to anticipate certain time patterns and rhythms. Deviations from normal system response (such as slight and/or gradual changes in temperature profiles) might be caused by an internal leak that could result in back flow or back mixing of ingredients. Some other near-miss incidents could generate unwanted publicity and may not be reported to avoid potential embarrassment.

Examples of typical near-miss incidents follow:

- Excursions of process parameters beyond preestablished "critical" control points.
- Activations of emergency shutdowns.
- Releases of material that are classified as environmentally reportable events.
- Activations of hazard control systems such as safety protective systems (e.g., relief valves, blowdown systems, fixed water-spray systems, and halon systems).

Many chemical plant operators are uncomfortable reporting an error of omission, such as forgetting to properly reset a double-block-and-bleed valve arrangement. The normal tendency would be to restore the valves to the proper position quickly and quietly. A near-miss of this type might normally go unreported, yet it may be a potential flag for discovering and eliminating a latent hazard. Perhaps such an omission occurs quite frequently or perhaps it has an underlying root cause in the physical arrangement, the sequence of operations, or a training system deficiency. The actual practices and attitudes toward open reporting and discussion of near-miss incidents are determined by the immediate supervisor of the group experiencing the event. Upper levels of corporate management can set general policy, but the actual performance in this area is *highly dependent* on local supervision. If local supervisors perceive rightly or wrongly that upper levels of management are not interested in near-misses, the near-misses will not be reported. Operations personnel are not likely to consistently report near-miss events in the absence of proactive and sustained support from management. Management must make a special effort to set a climate that will encourage reporting of undesirable events. The natural urge is to suppress embarrassing mistakes in order to avoid making the boss angry when he or she receives bad news.

A fragile balance exists between a manager's responsibility to achieve reporting of near-miss incidents and the responsibility to discipline nonperformance or inappropriate behavior. This issue is complex. Each case involving potential discipline must be handled on an individual basis, in which *all* the information is thoroughly assessed *before* a final decision is reached. Incident investigation techniques can be particularly fruitful when applied to such circumstances by helping to establish accurate information and underlying root causes. There will undoubtedly be some cases where the reporting of a near-miss does ultimately result in disciplinary action. These cases, however, are far outnumbered by the beneficial results gained by investigating the large number of near-misses where no discipline is exercised. A "two-edged credibility sword" figures prominently in this balance. Credibility is only achieved by a sustained and consistently applied policy. Months or even years of hard-won credibility can be erased by a single inappropriate management decision or response. It is often necessary to reaffirm repeatedly and publicly management's commitment to near-miss reporting and investigation in order to offset natural skepticism that can creep unnoticed into the attitudes of workers and lower level management. Management should constantly look for opportunities to reward near-miss reporting. A personal letter of commendation from a member of upper level supervision can be a powerful motivating tool in promoting near-miss reporting performance.

What is not reported cannot be investigated.
What is not investigated cannot be changed.
What is not changed cannot be improved.

The climate of trust and openness that comes into play when handling near-misses is one of the 14 quality management concepts expressed by W. E. Deming.[2] Eliminating fear is a prerequisite for improved quality and productivity. Examples of fear-producing behaviors include retaliation, loss of employment security, consistently receiving the worst job and task assignments, and withholding of discretionary privileges. Tom Peters presents strategies for dealing with this issue in his book *Thriving on Chaos.*[3]

Much has been written, debated, and contemplated regarding the relationship and ratio of near-miss events to incidents that do result in actual negative consequences. This ratio is often represented as a triangle (see Figure 3-2A).

Although the actual ratio does vary depending on the source of the data, there is general agreement on the concept. Reporting and investigating at the near-miss event level gives increased opportunities to detect and correct potential hazards. The successful result of investigating incidents is a decrease in the total number of incidents in the smaller triangle in Figure 3-2B.

If prevention efforts are aimed primarily at the upper two levels as is common in older approaches, then there will be fewer opportunities to detect and improve management systems. The result will be some decrease in incidence rate, but only on a sporadic basis. If, on the other hand, the thrust of the PSII effort is directed at the next two lower levels (minor injury and near-miss), there will be more opportunities to intervene to improve the management system.

3.3. CLASSIFICATION

This section presents a variety of incident categories that can be used to develop a classification system. The incident investigation system should include an easily

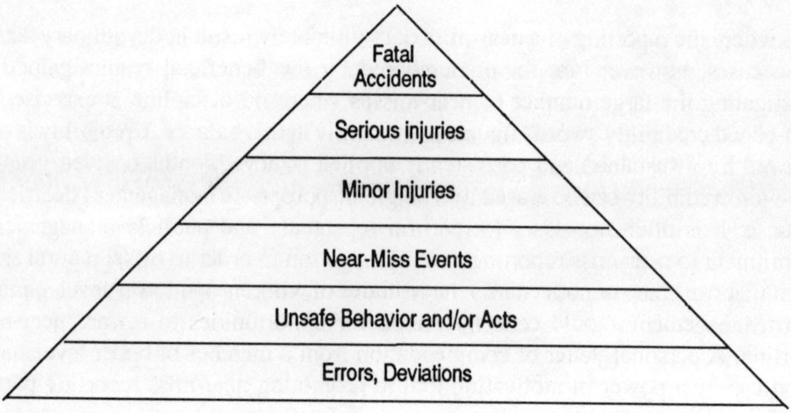

Figure 3-2A. Incident ratio triangle.

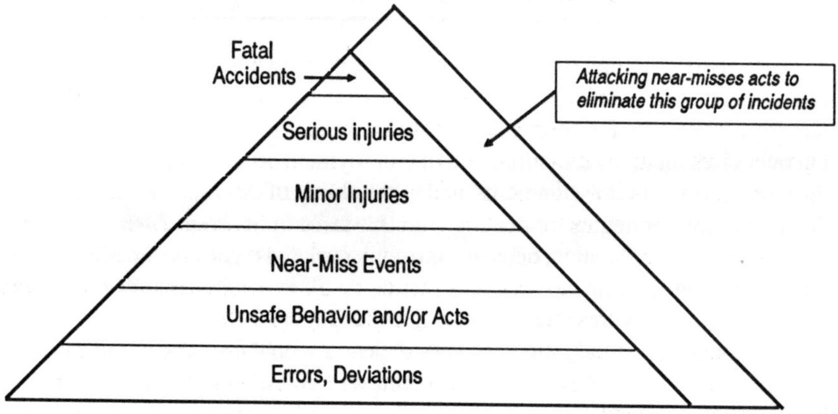

Figure 3.2B. Reduced incidents.

comprehended method for classifying events into discrete categories. It must include specific mechanisms that trigger the decision to activate a formal incident investigation team. The team activation mechanism requires corresponding internal and external notification procedures specifying who is to be notified, when, and by whom.

The classification system needs guidelines and examples for handling borderline cases and cases where the severity is initially not fully known. A general approach for doubtful cases is to include a default path in which an incident is initially classified as severe, and then subsequently downgraded if necessary. The system must contain a method for resolving genuine differences of opinion, and should specify the consequences of failing to report promptly and accurately.

Each classification system for incident categories will differ depending on the size and organization of the company, facility, division, or other business unit. While there is no perfect generic classification and reporting procedure, most systems will share some common terms:

Lost Workday Case—Days Away from Work[4] OSHA. This category includes those cases in which an employee would have worked, but was unable to do so owing to an occupational injury or illness. This category corresponds roughly to the old "Disabling Injury" from ANSI Z161.1[5] (American National Standards Institute, *Method for Recording Basic Facts Relating to the Nature and Occurrence of Work Injuries*). This category was also sometimes previously called "Lost Time Injury."

Lost Workday Case—Restricted Duty[4] OSHA. In simple terms, this category includes cases in which the employee was at work but was restricted in performing his or her duties owing to the injury or illness. Examples of such restrictions include temporary reassignment to another job, working at the regular job for a reduced period of time, or working at regular job but being unable to perform all normal duties.

Injury.[6] This category comprises cases of physical harm or damage to a person resulting from traumatic contact between the body and an outside agency or from exposure to environmental factors. **NOTE:** It is common practice for organizations to establish their own definition of the term "injury." Most of such definitions relate directly to the severity of the injury and/or the extent of treatment involved.

Incident. As defined previously by CCPS in its *Guidelines for Technical Management of Chemical Process Safety,*[1] the term "incident" is used in the broad context and includes events *with or without* actual undesirable consequences. Therefore, the term "incident" includes near-miss events and accidents. This is one of the two major conventions used to define the term "incident." The other convention considers an "incident" to be limited to those near-miss events that could have but actually did not result in negative consequences. In that convention, any event with a negative consequence is termed an "accident." Both conventions are in use in industry; therefore, it is important that company procedures clearly define which definition is to be applied. Furthermore, both definitions should be discussed to avoid potential confusion. One method would be to include the printed definitions on the internal investigation forms.

Near-Miss. This category consists of extraordinary events that could have reasonably resulted in harmful consequences but actually did not.[1] The classic near-miss example is the unignited vapor cloud. Minor or infrequent inadvertent releases of flammables usually dissipate harmlessly before finding an ignition source. A safety relief valve on a vessel may momentarily open and emit process material. In most all cases, this unusual event should be considered a near-miss incident. Another classic example would be the dropped tool that falls 100 ft (30.48 meters) from the top of a structure, yet does not hit anyone. Under slightly different circumstances, this incident could result in a fatal injury. Near-misses have also been referred to as "potential events."

Accident. An incident that does result in injury, illness, damage to equipment, release of material, or harm to the environment is defined as an accident.[1] According to the *Dictionary of Terms Used in the Safety Profession,*[6] the accident is an unplanned and sometimes injurious or damaging event that interrupts the normal progress of an activity and is invariably preceded by an unsafe act or unsafe condition or some combination thereof.

Recordable Injury[4] OSHA. Any injury such as a cut, fracture, sprain, or amputation that results from a work accident or from an exposure involving a single incident in the work environment and that requires medical treatment is a recordable injury. Conditions resulting from one-time exposures to chemicals are considered to be injuries. Also required to be recorded are loss-of-consciousness cases, restricted duty cases, and cases of transfer or active days off.

Recordable Illness[4] OSHA. This case category includes any abnormal condition or disorder, other than one resulting from an injury, caused by exposure to environmental factors associated with employment that requires medical treatment, results in restrictions, transfers, loss of work, or loss of consciousness. This includes acute or chronic illnesses or diseases that may be caused by inhalation, absorption, ingestion, or direct contact.

Medical Treatment[4] OSHA. For OSHA record keeping and classification purposes, the term "medical treatment" includes treatment (other than first aid) administered by a physician or by registered professional personnel under the standing orders of a physician.

Reportable Event OSHA. Although some injuries are required to be recorded on the OSHA 200 log, most incidents do not require a notification report to OSHA. The events that do require such a report (within 48 hours) include any hospitalization of five or more employees or any fatality.

Other Options for Establishing Classification Criteria. The amount of direct dollar damage is sometimes used as a sorting category. This is often some internally established limit related to insurance coverage deductibles or management financial authorization structure. Loss of production is another classification criterion. This criterion could be expressed in units of hours, days, or weeks of expected downtime.

A recent addition to category considerations is the relationship to external reporting. If a particular regulatory agency, such as EPA in the United States, is notified or becomes involved, then this report automatically triggers a certain specific corresponding internal action and requires specified internal notification.

3.4. ACTIVATING THE INVESTIGATION TEAM

The PSII team activation procedure should be keyed directly to the needs, size, and structure of the organization and to the type, size, consequences, and nature of the incident. Events can be loosely grouped into four general levels of severity. The lower and upper extremes (Levels 1 and 4) are easiest to decide regarding team activation. If there is a fatality, or the entire facility (or a major portion of it) is destroyed, the team will obviously be involved.

- **Level 1:** Very minor incidents and near-misses without catastrophic potential.
- **Level 2:** Limited impact incidents that can be handled locally.
- **Level 3:** Events that are less than catastrophic but more than minor.
- **Level 4:** Major catastrophes and the severe near-misses.

If a near-miss or minor incident occurs that has no potential for significant consequences, the local supervision normally handles the investigation without outside assistance. A typical example of a Level 1 event might be a sprained ankle caused by tripping over a hose left in a walkway. The PSII team clearly would not be needed in for such an incident.

Events of Level 2 severity have significant impact (or potential impact) but can be handled completely by on-site personnel. Team participation would be limited to providing selected assistance as requested by facility management. A typical example of this type of event would be an unignited vapor cloud or leak that did not have realistic probability of causing serious damage or injury owing to location (vent stack), quantity, and/or flow-rate of the leak. Another example would be a recognized and agreed on ultra-low-probability event (unforeseeable scenario). In these cases, the formal team activation typically would be requested by top facility management with the concurrence of the next level above and supporting off-site staff resource groups (corporate safety, for example).

Level 3 events are perhaps the most difficult regarding the decision to activate a team. Consequences of these events are more than minor but less than catastrophic, and in most (but not all) cases, the team will be formally activated. Representative of this category would be a fire that causes some downtime, a gas release or spill that results in off-site impact, or a serious injury. The key to success is prompt notification to initiate the deliberations and decision on how, when, and if the team will be mobilized. Notification procedures must be tailored to the facility and company organizational structure. The initial communication obviously must be made by on-site facility management and must progress upward through the organization until the official team activation decision level is reached. The decision to activate the team is normally made by the top level of management of the facility, accompanied by notification to upper levels of management located off the facility site.

Level 4 category incidents always warrant the formal PSII team, and decisions are usually easy to reach. Many organizations establish simultaneous communication (notification) requirements to the line organization and specified corporate staff groups.

Once a decision has taken to activate the PSII team, it should be mobilized as quickly as possible regardless of the level of the incident. The investigation should begin as soon as possible, before evidence is damaged or removed, and while memories are still fresh. A communication protocol to activate the PSII team should be developed for various incident levels and drilled periodically.

The management system for team activation should include requirements for documentation of the notification communications. The system should also include a provision for partial team activation, which may be appropriate in some incidents. The management system should be flexible regarding upgrading or downgrading of the severity level of incidents because of the often incomplete nature of communications regarding process incidents during the period immediately following the event. Any incident involving third parties or drawing media attention may require investigation, owing to potential liability issues and concerns over the accuracy of information provided to the public.

Many companies today are developing a crisis management program for truly major incidents (Level 4); a subset of the crisis management program is the incident investigation activity. In such an incident, the PSII team should not be burdened with many of the external and external communication needs in the early phases of the incident management. The PSII team must be allowed to perform the investigation in a timely manner with minimum disruption. Communication and hierarchy links should be established between the crisis management program and the PSII plan to meet these needs.

3.5. THE PROCESS SAFETY INCIDENT INVESTIGATION TEAM

Success of the PSII management system depends on many variables, including management involvement, support, and credibility; local and corporate culture (atmosphere); employee willingness to participate; and a history of correcting problems rather than pointing fingers of blame. Perhaps the most important variable is the performance of the investigation team. Poor performance by the PSII team may result in failure to detect and eliminate or control the hazard that caused the incident.

3.5.1. Purpose and General Concepts

The three primary objectives of the PSII team are as follows:

- Identify the system-related multiple root causes.
- Make recommendations to prevent recurrence of the incident.
- Implement and/or follow-up on the recommendations.

The team *does not* assign blame or dispense disciplinary action.

For maximum performance, the team should be as independent and autonomous as possible. The management level to which the team reports depends on the degree of severity (or potential severity) of the incident. Team autonomy helps to show to all who contribute to the investigation that significant efforts are being made to be impartial. If witnesses perceive (rightly or wrongly) that the team is in any way baised or intimidated, the quality and quantity of the information they provide will be adversely affected.

A major challenge facing any PSII team is to identify the underlying cause(s) of an incident and not to stop the discovery and analysis process prematurely. The traditional approach of simply identifying the unsafe act or condition can lead the PSII team merely to identify symptoms. This can often result in identical or nearly identical repeat incidents. The investigation must proceed to the actual *root causes*, sometimes called underlying causes. The team must keep this responsibility constantly in mind.

3.5.2. Team Leader

The person selected to be team leader must possess superior technical investigation skills as well as administrative and managerial skills. The majority of his or her activities will involve coordination and communication. The leader may be exposed to highly sensitive information with serious implications. The credibility and truthfulness of some discovered information may never be able to be determined completely. Often the leader will be faced with demands for release of findings prematurely from very strong and dominating personalities, and serious interpersonal conflicts can develop. Frequently the technical members are not accustomed to functioning as part of a close-knit team and may resent having their technical judgments questioned. This independence will create challenges for coordination and teamwork. The team leader also will need to deal with normal envy and resentment regarding work assignments among team members. The leader must constantly direct technical personnel in order to avoid duplicated work or omissions and to maintain investigative priorities.

The PSII management system should specify the responsibilities of the team leader, which may include the following:

- Direct and manage the team in its investigation and assure that objectives and schedules are met.
- Identify, control, and, if necessary, modify the restricted access zone.
- Serve as principal spokesperson for the team and as the point of contact with other organizations.
- Prepare status reports and other interim reports documenting significant team activities, findings, and concerns.

- Organize teamwork: establish schedule, plans, and meetings; make clearly defined work assignments for team members in accordance with their individual skills, knowledge, capabilities, and experience; set investigative priorities.
- Ensure that team members do not dilute their investigative commitments with any other work assignments, pressures, or conflicting priorities.
- Manage the team and procure resources necessary for the investigation team (assign accounting and record keeping responsibilities to one of the team members).
- Ensure safety at the incident scene.
- Arrange and preside over meetings.
- Ensure that the investigation team activities result in minimum disruption to the rest of the facility.
- Keep upper management advised of status, progress, and plans.
- Initiate formal requests for information, interviews with witnesses, laboratory tests, and technical or administrative support.
- Control and protect proprietary information and other sensitive information.

3.5.3. Team Composition

Team composition can vary considerably depending on the nature, type, and size of the incident. Typical team composition follows:

- Team leader
- Operations/manufacturing representative (or could be from sister unit or plant)
- Process engineer
- Safety department representative
- One operations supervisor from the unit experiencing the event
- One worker from the unit experiencing the event

At least one team member should have facilitator-level competence in the particular investigative methodology to be used by the team.

Depending on the nature of the incident and expertise needed, other participants from within or outside the company can be involved in a limited or consulting roles. These others may include:

- Chemist
- Industrial hygienist
- Maintenance engineer
- Materials engineer/metallurgist
- Process control (electrical/instrumentation) engineer
- Technicians—instrument, inspection, maintenance
- Recently retired employee with specific knowledge, skill, or experience
- Environmental
- Quality assurance

- Purchasing or stores
- Construction department
- Contractor participant—on-site contractor/outside specialist
- Collective bargaining unit participant
- In-house attorney
- Regulatory agency representative
- Civil/structural engineer
- Community representative
- Arson investigator—for fire burn expertise to help find probable point of origin, even if no malice is known, suspected, or involved
- OEM (Original Equipment Manufacturer)—representative factory or team services engineer
- Instrument designer
- Computer software programmer
- Insurance carrier representative
- Research technical personnel
- Fire chief
- Technical consultant

Team members can come from any part of the organization. A mix of outsiders and insiders is often ideal. Outsiders (company employees who do not work in the unit that experienced the incident) bring an unbiased, fresh, and less emotional perspective to the investigation, yet they understand general company policies, procedures, and approaches. Outside specialists can provide both assistance in fact finding and credibility to the investigation.

Recently adopted OSHA regulations (see Appendix E) address the team approach for investigations. These regulations contain nonmandatory guidelines attached as an appendix, which further discuss the multidisciplinary team, team selection, team training, and the need to include at least one person knowledgeable in the process involvement. The regulations contain a requirement to include a contract employee if the incident involved work of the contractor.

The team organization, size, sophistication, and skills need to suit the particular size and type of incident. The team leader should verify particular competencies for team members. Team members need the right and freedom to admit that they require help or that they do not have the particular competence needed. Since team members are not professional full-time forensic engineers, they should not be expected to perform as such. The team leader must exercise flexibility in making and modifying job assignments.

The team may also include participation by outside third parties. Typical examples are regulatory bodies such as OSHA, EPA, state regulatory agencies, LEPC (Local Emergency Planning Commission) representative, fire and municipal emergency response agencies, insurance representatives, manufacturers technical service personnel, and representatives of collective bargaining groups.

Invited third-party team members usually have no special vested interests and can weigh information without struggling to be completely objective. They can bring fresh perspectives and can increase credibility.

Following are example guidelines for team member selection.[7]

1. Desirable personal qualities
   —Open logical mind
   —Thoroughness
   —Ability to maintain independence and perspective
   —Special expertise or knowledge relative to the incident.
2 Consider the use of a member of upper level management to function as nominal and/or administrative team leader. This often results in faster response to requests, minimizes red tape, and sends clear strong message regarding the significance of the incident.
3. Consider the NASA approach of having one member as coordinator or representative of each area of interest, such as operations, maintenance, human factors, equipment faults, and control systems.
4. Some potential mistakes in team member selection to avoid:
   —Personnel with know-it-all, prima donna, or "expert" attitudes
   —Personnel too close to the incident who might be emotionally involved or biased
   —Using someone just because he or she happens to be available
   —Personnel who would have problems traveling away from home for the investigation activity
   —Persons who already "know" the causes of the incident, even before the team begins its investigation.

3.5.4. Development of Specific Plan for Investigating a Specific Incident

Because each incident has unique circumstances and conditions surrounding it, one of the first activities of the PSII team is to develop a specific plan for the incident. A check list for initiating this plan is shown in Figure 3-3. The plan addresses verification and restatement of priorities as follows:

- Rescue victims and provide medical treatment as necessary.
- Stabilize the incident to mitigate further consequences.
- Address environmental concerns—diking; drainage; runoff; and testing, verification, and neutralizing of hazardous materials (e.g., asbestos, PCBs).
- Secure the incident scene to preserve evidence.
- Collect evidence.
- Provide remediation and site clean-up.
- Rebuild–restart.

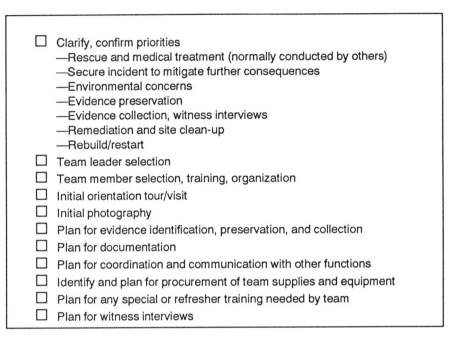

- ☐ Clarify, confirm priorities
  - —Rescue and medical treatment (normally conducted by others)
  - —Secure incident to mitigate further consequences
  - —Environmental concerns
  - —Evidence preservation
  - —Evidence collection, witness interviews
  - —Remediation and site clean-up
  - —Rebuild/restart
- ☐ Team leader selection
- ☐ Team member selection, training, organization
- ☐ Initial orientation tour/visit
- ☐ Initial photography
- ☐ Plan for evidence identification, preservation, and collection
- ☐ Plan for documentation
- ☐ Plan for coordination and communication with other functions
- ☐ Identify and plan for procurement of team supplies and equipment
- ☐ Plan for any special or refresher training needed by team
- ☐ Plan for witness interviews

Figure 3-3. Check list for specific plan development.

The specific plan should address the organization and composition of the team itself, identifying particular skills, training, and expertise needed, full-time and potential part-time members, and possible need for outside resources. Concurrent with the team designation, there should be a brief orientation visit made by the leader, and others, if available, to help develop expected needs and plan of action.

Immediate photography is one of the first planning tasks. In many cases of major process-related incidents, the use of a professional photographer is justified and should be arranged as one of the initial tasks. Photography is addressed in further detail in Section 4-9.

Evidence identification methods, evidence preservation measures, and evidence collection are critical activities that must be included in the specific plan. This may often involve arrangements for sampling and testing. Practical considerations for evidence handling are included in Chapter 4.

Another important planning activity involves coordinating and communicating with other groups, both on and off-site. Early establishment of communication channels and identified common responsibilities will minimize confusion and conflict. Documentation protocol should be established early and should be part of the specific plan.

Team supplies and equipment needs should be identified and a plan established for routine and for special procurement. Likewise, a plan should be established to locate needed experts, consultants, and other contract people, to transport them quickly to the site with required personal protective equipment, and to train them as required (see also Section 4.4), for a timely progression of the on-site investigation.

There should be an organized approach for witness interviews. Such items as identifying potential witnesses, designating team members who will conduct the interviews (train if needed), planning for the interview location and information documentation are important specific planning issues. The investigation is never a truly isolated activity. One important lesson learned from past major incidents is that important information was available yet never captured. The source of this valuable information may often be a person who is not regularly assigned to operating the unit in question. Examples of these unexpected witnesses are a tanker truck driver, a rail crew switchman, or a factory technical representative who worked in the plant three days before and who happened to see a crack beginning to develop in a sight glass. Such people may not recognize the significance of what they see or properly interpret it, yet their information may be valuable in resolving a missing or conflicting piece of data. Personnel who have been actively involved with the process or with previous incidents do not always get contacted, and thus valuable information is lost to the investigation. Some potential witnesses will "wait until asked," and will not come forward on their own initiative, yet want to cooperate fully once asked. Therefore, it is necessary to identify and seek out all known potential witnesses.

The specific plan should identify expected schedules, timetables, and milestone checkpoints.

3.5.5. Team Operations

The team leader is responsible for planning and directing the team activities, as addressed in Section 3.5.2. The specific plan for the team should include a designated mechanism for documenting the team activities, deliberations, decisions, communications, and a record of documents requested, received, and/or issued. A personal or portable computer is a valuable help to record and document the team's efforts. A single point of contact is recommended between the team and all other groups in order to minimize communication breakdowns, delays, and confusion. Outside groups need to know how, where, and whom to address when communicating with team.

The investigation discovery phase should follow a problem-solving process sequence. Investigation management activities are addressed in detail in Chapter 4 and include interface and coordination with other groups, evidence preservation, dismantling, evidence analysis, and resolution of conflicts and gaps in initial information received. Identification and analysis of root causes is presented in Chapter 5.

It is common for team members to disagree initially as to causes, remedies, probable sequence of events, scope of investigation activities, and sometimes on process technical concepts. The deliberations and exchange of ideas, opinions, and experience are critical to the function of the synergistic team approach. As the investigation develops, a series of team meetings is convened to resolve questions, update members on new information, report on subtasks, conduct preliminary analysis for causes and possible remedies, establish new items and questions for resolution, and generate short-term action plans.

As the discovery and analysis of underlying *root* causes concludes, the team begins to formulate and evaluate proposed recommendations. Details on these two activities are found in Chapters 5 and 6. The team has a serious responsibility to identify realistic recommendations that will not increase the risk, transfer the hazard, or create hazards not present before the original accident.

The final phase of the team's activities is preparation and presentation of the results, usually in the form of a written formal report, and follow-up. These two topics are addressed in detail in Chapter 7 ("Formal Reports and Communications Issues"). Actual implementation and follow-up on resolution of all recommendations is one of the three essential components of the PSII management system. The PSII system as written should specifically address the assignment of responsibility for follow-up. In some cases, the PSII team (or selected members of it) will retain responsibility *and* authority for the final resolution of the recommendations. In most cases, the primary responsibility will shift to a designated member of management. This member of management usually will not be a member of the PSII team. The team can be reconvened at a future date to audit, evaluate, and report on the actual implementation of the recommendations. This further capitalizes on the insights gained by the team during the investigation.

After each incident investigation, the team should critique its preparedness, thoroughness, and effectiveness, and the appropriateness of equipment and supplies.

Team readiness can include actual practice exercises in the activation, communications tests (with critique) and periodic check of team supplies and equipment.

3.5.6. Resumption of Normal Operation and Restart Criteria

Although the actual decision to restart is a line management decision, one of the most important responsibilities of the team is to identify recommended criteria and conditions for resuming operations. Restart is normally postponed until the PSII team specifies minimum criteria that are then acted on by line management. Restart must often be coordinated with other groups or third parties such as OSHA or other regulatory agency. Communications and notifications need to be precise, clear, and verified. This topic is addressed in more detail in Chapter 6.

3.5.7. Team Training

The PSII management system must be structured to provide for training, both initial and refresher, for three major groups. First, management must be familiar with the concepts, policies, extent of the company's commitment, and specific assignments of responsibility within PSII. The second group to be targeted for training is composed of employees, first-line supervision, and those auxiliary staff groups (e.g., technicians, engineers, middle-level management) not directly in the line organization. The third training group comprises the team members themselves. This group should be trained in the mechanics of investigation, techniques and documentation requirements. In addition to specific training in the investigative method to be used, team member training can include "role playing" for such activities as witness interviews, conflict resolution, and confidentiality issues. Team members should understand that they are not expected to perform at the level of full-time professional investigators. They must feel free to request help and/or training, especially at the early stages. Asking for help may be a challenge for some professional/technical personnel who are accustomed to solving problems individually.

3.6. DOCUMENTATION

The management system should be structured so as to clarify the need for and techniques for documentation. Several issues are obvious, such as witness interviews and physical evidence. Other important documentation required includes deliberations that address the technical basis for the team accepting or rejecting decisions, official notifications (especially to external agencies), methods for tracking documents (and evidence) requested, received, and/or issued by the team. Certain documents or evidence may need special attention owing to potential litigation, and a "chain-of-custody" record may be necessary.

3.7. CONTINUOUS IMPROVEMENT

A necessary element of the PSII management system is a mechanism for continuous improvement. Investigation programs that fail to prevent repeat incidents have frequent opportunities to exercise the investigation team. Highly successful programs, on the other hand, have progressively fewer opportunities. It is therefore important to include a mechanism for critiquing every team investigation to identify and understand lessons learned that can further refine the investigation program. It is also valuable to recognize and share the positive aspects of those investigation activities that were especially successful in a particular incident.

To ensure the management system continues to provide the intended results, periodic reviews and updates are necessary. This action is a recognition that organizations are dynamic and continuously evolving. Critique issues normally deal with the following questions:

- Did the investigation address all facets of the causes?
- Did the deliberations go deep enough to discover and analyze the root system causes?
- Is the internal (unpublished) team documentation adequate?
- Were the right skills available within the team?

- What other resources could be used next time?
- Were the corrective actions taken?
- Were the results communicated?

3.8. REGULATORY AND LEGAL CONSIDERATIONS

Regulatory and legal considerations should be included in the written management system. As a minimum, the legal department should be consulted at the beginning and the end of the investigation process. This section, perhaps above all others, needs to be flexible and responsive to constantly changing demands. OSHA and EPA regulations have steadily increased in the area of reporting, documentation, and investigation. The regulations for process safety management (OSHA 29 CFR 1910.119, Feb. 92) include specific standards relating to investigations of process-related incidents. The Federal Clean Air Act Amendment of 1990 also addresses investigations and calls for a special investigation board, similar to the NTSB (National Transportation Safety Board) that investigates aircraft crashes and other transportation incidents.

Legal considerations continue to evolve and profoundly affect cause determination, remedy implementation, communication, and documentation aspects of process incident investigations (see also Section 4.1). One issue common to both regulatory and legal concerns is use of information gained about the causes of an incident and its remedy. Failure to properly disseminate and use this knowledge may have significant legal and regulatory consequences.

The management system should address mechanisms and criteria for sharing the causes and lessons learned so that others can benefit. Since many chemical processes are generic and possess common inherent hazards, several facilities may benefit from the experience of others. However, in today's litigious environment, it is difficult to share many details of an investigation with those at similar facilities that might benefit. In addition, practical logistics can make it difficult to succeed consistently in communicating details and lessons learned to those who might benefit. These logistics are especially challenging in large corporations or even within a single large facility. Knowing who has a potential interest in the findings of an investigation can be a considerable challenge due to turnover of personnel and sheer size of the organization. Notwithstanding these challenges, broad communication of investigation findings is important to the overall reduction of incidents. One company's poor safety performance can affect the entire industry. Chapter 7 addresses specifics of communicating investigation findings to *all* potentially affected workers and to outside organizations.

3.9. INVESTIGATION AND DISCIPLINARY ACTIONS

The PSII team does not and should not have responsibility to determine the extent of any disciplinary action. The team may recommend that disciplinary action be considered by management, and it may forward specific information regarding employee, supervisor or management behavior as a basis for the recommendation. The team should not have the authority to grant limited immunity in order to elicit information. A witness who perceives (correctly or not) that the investigation interview is somehow a disciplinary hearing is likely to be less than candid during an interview. In addition to being counterproductive, wrong perceptions by the witness will hamper the research of the logic of events and facts before causes are established. Disciplinary actions, if taken, should be based on the facts of the incident, the employee's performance and how these were influenced by other employees, by supervisors and managers involved and by established company policy. These objectives should be clearly incorporated into the charter of the team, reinforced as part of team mobilization procedures, and explained to potential witnesses prior to any interview.

3.10. REFERENCES

1. Center for Chemical Process Safety (CCPS), 1989. *Guidelines for Technical Management of Chemical Process Safety*. New York: American Institute of Chemical Engineers. Chapter 11.
2. Deming, W.E., 1986. *Out of the Crisis*. Cambridge, MA: Center for Advanced Engineering Study, Massachusetts Institute of Technology.
3. Peters, T., 1987. *Thriving on Chaos*. New York: Harper & Row.
4. *A Brief Guide to Record Keeping Requirements for Occupational Injuries and Illnesses*. Publ. OMB No. 1220-0029. Washington, DC: U.S. Dept. of Labor, 1986.
5. *American National Standard Method of Recording Basic Facts Relating to the Nature and Occurrence of Work Injuries*. ANSI Z16.1. New York: American National Standards Institute, 1969.
6. *Dictionary of Terms Used in the Safety Profession*, 3rd ed. Des Plaines, IL: American Society of Safety Engineers, 1988.
7. *Accident/Incident Investigation Manual*, 2nd ed. Publ. DOE/SSDC 76-45/27. Washington, DC: U.S. Dept. of Energy, 1989.

4

PRACTICAL INVESTIGATION CONSIDERATIONS: GATHERING EVIDENCE

This chapter contains practical guidelines for investigation activities *in the field*. The chapter builds on principles established in Chapter 3 ("System for Investigating Process Safety Incidents") and discussed further in Chapter 8 ("Development and Implementation"). In particular it presumes that a process safety incident investigation (PSII) management system is in place and that team training and other preparations have been completed.

The chapter begins with a section on legal and credibility issues then gives an overview of field activities, reviews priorities for the PSII team, addresses the initial visit to the incident site, and finally discusses potential sources of information and useful tools and equipment.

Major emphasis is given to witness interviews and photography, since these are activities in which most PSII team members will be directly involved. The chapter concludes by addressing some special topics such as third-party information, aids and resources for studying evidence, and new technology challenges.

After completing the activities addressed in this chapter, the PSII team should have the information and evidence needed to proceed to the next step—systematic determination of the multiple root causes of the incident, as presented in Chapter 5 ("Multiple Cause Determination").

4.1. LEGAL AND CREDIBILITY CONCERNS

Legal concerns are now an integral part of every **major** incident or whenever a nonemployee is involved in an incident. In many states it is becoming easier and more common for employees to be litigants. Legal access to documentation of the PSII team deliberations and findings is becoming an increasingly complex issue. Traditional client–lawyer confidentiality is being continuously tested and explored in new ways. Since legal and liability issues can vary significantly among jurisdictions, particularly among the various states within the United States, legal advice should be sought when a PSII is undertaken.

Often the PSII team is placed in a position between two conflicting forces. The company's legal department may endorse a position of minimizing the retention of documents that have the potential to cause financial damage. Incident prevention specialists and process safety managers may, on the other hand, endorse a policy of thorough documentation and proactive sharing of lessons learned (including disclosure of actual specific causes of an incident). Each company will have to strike its own balance between these conflicting forces. The final official report from the PSII usually must be reviewed by the company legal department.

> It is important to consider and be sensitive to legal issues. However, both the PSII team and the legal group must remember that the objective is to prevent similar incidents. Documentation and communication must be adequate to inform others who may have similar hazards.

Credibility is a fragile achievement, taking years to establish. It can be destroyed by a single statement, action, decision, or event. The company should inform employees, contractors, neighbors, governmental agencies, trade associations, and the general public about the incident in an appropriate fashion and in the proper degree of detail. Most companies have abandoned the brusque "no-comment" response to the news media. The public is entitled to a certain reasonable amount of information, and the media will deliver a story regardless of whether the company cooperates.

Each company should have a communication plan and be ready to respond as soon as the first request for information is received from within or outside the company. Outgoing official communications such as statements, progress reports, initial/preliminary determinations and findings, and other communications should be developed carefully, cleared with relevant company departments according to the communications plan and delivered by the designated spokesperson. Team members must understand and cooperate with communications protocols. There is often an initial flood of requests and demands for information, followed by a short hiatus, which is in turn followed by renewed demands for the expected "answers" to what happened, why, and what will be done to prevent a recurrence. The company spokesperson, particularly if a member of the PSII team, should resist the temptation to offer possible conclusions before the investigation yields such conclusions. Credibility comes in question when the team keeps changing its conclusions. Having stated a preliminary conclusion can also bias the team toward that conclusion erroneously.

> "Communicating important process safety information to other companies may prevent accidents and save lives. Responsible sharing of information can be an important factor in maintaining credibility with the local government and communities surrounding a facility."
> From *CMA Responsible Care®—Resources Guide*

4.2. ON-SITE INVESTIGATION OVERVIEW

4.2.1. A Systematic Approach

The systematic investigation approach in Figure 1-1 shows the on-site team activities in the overall context of a management system. The specific objectives of on-site activities are to gather information used for determining root causes and to preserve appropriate evidence for possible future reference. There is no sharp demarcation between the end of evidence gathering activities and the onset of root cause determination. The majority of the evidence gathering and analysis is completed before cause determination begins, but evidence gathering and analysis can extend well into the investigation. The U.S. Department of Energy *Investigation Manual* recognizes this significant overlapping of the evidence gathering phase and the cause determination phase, as shown in Figure 4-1.[2] It is common to conduct follow-up interviews and additional special inspections to help clarify certain inconsistencies.

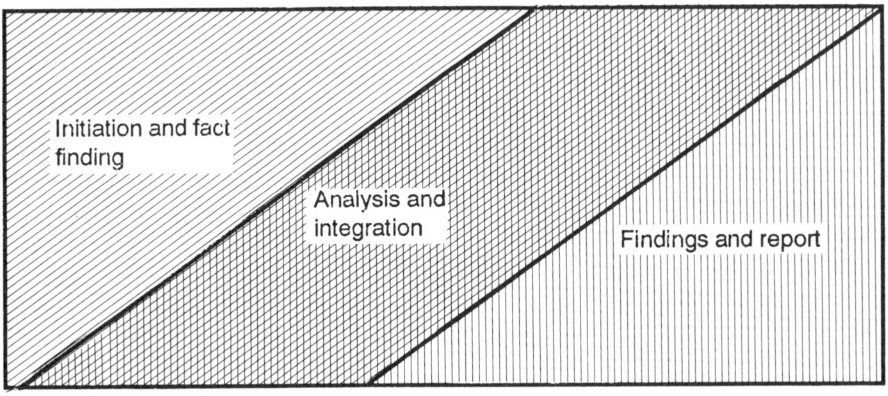

Figure 4-1. Overlap of evidence gathering and cause determination phases.

4.2.2. Specific Plan

Each PSII is a unique event and should be accompanied by a specific plan. The initial specific plan is continuously revised and updated as new priorities and concerns are identified during the normal course of the investigation. This specific plan builds on the general plan established as part of the PSII management system. The team leader can use a general check list as shown in Figure 3-3 (Chapter 3) to establish initial needs, action plans, and assignments. Some of the initial decisions address:

- Team member selection
- Team orientation
- Photography
- Evidence preservation
- Procurement of supplies and outside services

- Protocol for initial documentation
- Witness interviews
- Special training
- Coordination and communication with other functions and outside organizations

This initial plan is usually developed by the team leader after he or she has made a brief orientation visit and before the entire team has arrived. This visit is the first opportunity for the PSII team to establish the physical boundaries of the investigation. The team leader should ensure that access to the area is minimized as much as possible. In addition, he or she should verify that the personnel who do enter the incident area are aware of evidence preservation considerations.

The initial plan should include arrangements to locate needed team members, experts, consultants, and other contract people, to transport them quickly to the site with personal protective equipment, and to train them as required (see Section 4.4).

Identifying and selecting the actual team members for an actual investigation at a given time is one of the first and most important decisions for the team leader. Compromises are frequently necessary to match needs against available manpower. Because the time commitment for an investigation can be both long term and substantial. It can extend over many months and can require many hours each week. Each team member and their manager should understand the extent and be willing to make this commitment at the beginning. Changing team members causes inefficiencies and therefore should be minimized. A team member, highly skilled in a particular and required area of expertise, may not be able to make a full time commitment. A common alternative is to use this person in the role of a consultant.

One of the most critical issues is clearly establishing which groups have responsibility for which activities and areas. These responsibilities may not necessarily remain fixed for the duration of the investigation.

4.3. PRIORITIES FOR THE PSII TEAM

The PSII team has responsibilities for determining the root causes and therefore needs access to the incident scene and other sources of information. However, there are other overall priorities, especially in the early stages of the investigation.[3] Some of these priorities (such as medical treatment) are normally performed by other groups, but have an influence on the team's operation. In theory and in practice the evidence begins to degrade and change as soon as the incident sequence is over. Overall priorities can be expressed as follows:

- Rescue and give medical treatment to any victims.
- Decide if further on-site or off-site evacuation is needed.
- Secure the incident to mitigate any further consequences.
- Address environmental concerns (runoff, verification sampling for contamination from toxic and hazardous materials such as asbestos, PCBs, and other possible hazards).

- Notify agencies as required.
- Preserve physical evidence and secure the scene.
- Photograph evidence and the scene.
- Collect evidence.
- Remediate and clean-up the site.
- Repair or rebuild and restart.

An overriding mandate for the PSII team leader is to prevent injury to anyone on the team or anyone else due to activities of the team. Team members and auxiliary helpers could be exposed to some unusual hazards, such as unstable working/walking surfaces, sharp edges, partially collapsed structures of unverified integrity, unidentified chemicals, residual hazardous materials, and trapped latent energy. Sometimes investigators find stray electricity in a supposedly deenergized circuit even after all known sources are isolated, especially after an incident where short circuits or fire may have fused conductors or contacts. Double checking the actual circuit is always worth the additional effort; electrical lock-out, locks and tags are appropriate. It is not unusual for the team to work extended hours in whatever weather conditions prevail in order to minimize the downtime. The team leader should watch for signs of fatigue and burnout; either condition can affect the quality and safety of the PSII.

Team members should set a rigorous standard for consistent and proper use of personal protective equipment. They should approach each task with a questioning skeptical attitude to help prevent additional injuries and minimize unnecessary exposures. Regulatory authorities (such as OSHA or the EPA) will, in most instances, acknowledge that unusual conditions exist after an incident and that special measures are often appropriate. On the other hand they may deny access to the site until certain precautions are established or until certain tests are completed. One example of a special measure is extensive reliance on fall protection devices as a substitute for normal scaffolding. Insurance or legal representatives may also impose specific restrictions on the PSII team activities.

Pressures to resume production will eventually begin to increase, often at the same time as the rate of evidence gathering diminishes. The majority of process-related incident investigations will reach a point where the team leader must decide to release the incident scene back to the manufacturing management for repair and resumption of operations. Field evidence gathering cannot continue indefinitely. The decision to begin clean-up and rebuilding should be based on when it is safe to reenter the area. The decision to restart a process should be based on whether enough has been learned about the incident to prevent a recurrence.

4.4. INITIAL SITE VISIT

After the preliminary specific plan has been established, the next event is usually the initial visit by the investigation team. This is not intended to be an evidence gathering activity. It is, instead, a familiarization walk-through to establish perspective, relative distances, dimensions, orientations of equipment, scale or magnitude of damage, anticipated logistic challenges, and to start planning for initial photography/videotaping or sampling.

During this orientation tour, the team should use all the necessary safety precautions including appropriate personal protective equipment. If it is safe to do so, photography during this stage is normally quite productive; however, serious problems can be created if any physical evidence is disturbed in the slightest degree. Note taking and rough sketching are useful during this initial visit, again if no physical evidence is disturbed.

Since the initial team visit is done as soon as possible, the actual incident scene may still be under the control of the emergency response organization. Any restrictions established by the emergency response organization must be followed. It is common for the team to require an escort for this initial visit. An example of U.S. government rules is contained in 29 CFR 1910.120 OSHA regulations. Subpart q of these HAZWOPER (HAZardous Waste Operations and Emergency Response) regulations establishes specific requirements that apply to many PSII sites. Portions of the investigation area may remain under the administrative control of the emergency management organization for extended periods following the incident. If necessary, the investigation team can ask emergency responders to answer questions about the site, to take photos, or to collect evidence.

Immediately following this field tour, the team will begin to develop the detailed investigation plan, specifying action items and assigning responsibilities. This is the point in the investigation where the need for specialists is first identified and evaluated, and where plans are initiated to secure their services. One lesson learned from experienced investigation team leaders is not to assume that a particular skill or expertise is possessed by the team. Delayed discovery of a missing or incomplete team competence can lead to frustrating delays. Correspondingly, the individual members should know that it is acceptable not to claim to be an expert in everything. Individual team members should be encouraged and expected to decline assignments that are beyond their expertise.

The procedure for sharing documents and information among groups is critical and must be established very early in the investigation. This procedure should have a specific protocol for document control, thus establishing a clear record of which documents came and went from where and to whom. A document control procedure is especially important if regulatory agencies are involved with the investigation or its follow-up, or if litigation is anticipated.

4.5. SOURCES OF INFORMATION

Potential sources of information useful to the investigation team can extend far beyond the battery limits of the unit in which the event occurred, and the search for information may lead to obscure and nontraditional places. In some cases the type of incident has not occurred before, and the proper mix of backgrounds and experiences of the team members can help identify sources of information. In many cases, the incident is a repeat of another in the same or other place, and its investigation documents can lead to fruitful sources of information.

Hard-copy and electronically stored records usually provide the backbone for initial evidence collection. These records include: control instrumentation records (Distributive Control Systems—DCS data, strip and wheel charts), shift logs, maintenance records, run histories, batch sheets, raw material quality control records, retained samples, quality control (QC) lab logs, and emergency responder logs. These records are augmented by examining the actual field instrumentation devices such as pointer needles in locally mounted temperature, pressure, and flow devices.

A crucial item is the *"as found" position of every valve* related to the incident. Some valves will have been operated during emergency response or mitigation activities; thus, their position at the time of the incident may not be able to be determined with complete certainty. Electrical equipment status, in particular, any temporary or portable equipment and the position of switch devices, is always important evidence possibly relating to ignition sources. The condition of relief devices such as rupture disks can be vital in determining the actual incident sequence and cause. Determining which gaskets failed and their typical failure pressure can help define what was happening during an incident.

Residual liquid inventories and flame scorch marks are valuable information. Batch retained samples from shipments and samples of products or contents remaining in tanks can be analyzed for deviations. Analysis of the damage pattern can be useful in calculating the estimated blast energy from an explosion, and thus indicate the amount of material involved in a release. There are standard damage assessment references[4,5] for correlating the damage to conventional standard constructions to the corresponding overpressure wave experienced by that structure.

A process safety information package is now a required component of most process safety management programs including the EPA Clean Air Act (Section 304c and 112), OSHA regulations (29 CFR 1910.119), American Petroleum Institute (API Recommended Practice 750), the Chemical Manufacturers Association (CMA Responsible Care® Code), and the CCPS *Guidelines for Technical Management of Chemical Process Safety.*[6] This process safety information package is necessary for conducting a successful process hazard analysis and is uniquely valuable to the investigation team. Unfortunately, in some cases, much of this process safety information package may be damaged or even destroyed in the course of the incident itself.

One helpful practice for a PSII management system is to maintain a duplicate package in a less vulnerable location. Typical contents of a process safety information package that are helpful to PSII are shown in Figure 4-2. For incidents involving airborne emissions of possible harmful materials, meteorological records, dispersion calculations, and consequence analysis study results are needed.

Other sources of information for the investigation team include footage of news media videotapes, contacts with other manufacturers with similar processes, univer-

- P&IDs, and Detailed Instrument and Electrical Drawings
- Operating Procedures
- Training Manuals
- Design calculation bases
- Scenarios used for sizing overpressure relief, vent, and emergency systems
- Alarms and set points for trips
- Material safety data sheets (MSDs)
- Descriptions of normal and abnormal chemical reactions
- Records and reports of past incidents
- Control software logic
- Site maps and plot plans

Figure 4-2. Process safety information package contents.

sity research organizations, access to proprietary data bases (see Chapter 2, Section 2.6) such as those maintained by insurance carriers, government records accessed under the Freedom of Information Act, former employees of contract maintenance companies who have personal experience (but not necessarily any vested interest) in the unit of interest, and transcripts of police and other emergency service communications.

It is best in most cases for the team to make and work with reproductions of documents (recorder charts, alarm printouts, etc.) rather than with the actual documents in order not to damage or misplace the original evidence.

4.6. FIELD INVESTIGATION TOOLS/EQUIPMENT/SUPPLIES

The following equipment has been found useful for PSII. Not all is needed or appropriate for every investigation, but should be potentially available on short notice.

4.6.1. Personal Equipment

Personal equipment should be packed into a single soft pack container that can be carried with shoulder straps or attached around the waist, thus leaving both hands free.

- Good quality 35 mm camera, capable of taking sharply focused photos (both close-up and wide angle), flash, extra film, extra batteries
- Note pad, clipboard, pens, pencils
- Small plastic bags (sandwich size)

- Duct tape, string, several 2" (50 mm) nails, toothbrush (for cleaning soot/debris off selected evidence)
- Swiss-Army type knife (Phillips and regular screwdrivers, and scissors)
- Flashlight (explosion proof)
- Pocket extension mirror
- Magnifying glass
- Folding ruler or tape measure (6-ft, 1.8 m)
- Permanent marker
- Latex gloves and disposable wipes

4.6.2. Protective Gear

- Hard-hat, goggles, gloves (rubber and latex), rubber boots with steel shank and steel toe
- Extra pair of socks and gloves
- Respiratory protection
- Slicker suit
- Tie-off belt/harness

4.6.3. PSII Team Supplies

- Barrier tape
- Tags with plastic ties
- Plastic bags, self-closing (1-gallon, 3.8 liter)
- Small first aid kit
- Plastic jar with tightly closing cap (1-quart or 1-liter size)
- Level
- Video camera with extra battery pack and blank cassettes
- Pocket dictating recorder with extra batteries and blank cassette
- Pair of walkie-talkie radios with extra batteries
- Instant print camera and film
- Synthetic ⅜" (11 mm) rope for personnel fall protection tie off (100 ft, 30 m)
- Thermometer
- Compass
- Steel measuring tape (100 ft, 30 m)
- Paint stick markers, grease pencil (waterproof, indelible marking pens, dark and white)
- Small tool kit, spark resistant type tools (channel lock pliers, needle nose pliers, assortment of screwdrivers, adjustable wrenches, clamps, tie-wire, valve wrenches, micrometer, calipers)
- Large supply of duct tape; plastic drop cloth (100 ft^2, 9.2 m^2) for evidence preservation/protection
- PC—notebook or portable

4.7. WITNESS INTERVIEWS

4.7.1. Identifying Witnesses

Any person who has (or may possibly have) information relating to an incident should be considered a potential witness. This includes people who were not direct participants or eyewitnesses to the event. Valuable information is often contributed by "indirect" witnesses such as regularly assigned service personnel from maintenance, contract maintenance, laboratory, janitorial, and shipping groups. Occasionally delivery personnel who routinely visit the process unit are familiar with some aspects of what was normal routine and may have noticed some unusual condition, remark, or actions. These people should not be forgotten, since they have the potential to contribute valuable information and can help resolve mysteries that would otherwise remain hidden.

Indirect witnesses often contribute as much information as eyewitnesses. Off-shift personnel, previous shift personnel, or those who last ran the process should be contacted. Recently retired or transferred employees are a potential source of valuable information about the process dynamics, equipment, and systems involved. They often have unique knowledge based on many years of experience with the particular systems and equipment involved in the incident. Following are examples of potential contributions from former employees:

- Knowledge of actual operating practices or changes that are not always included in the formal written operating procedures.
- Insights on little known failure modes and anomalies in system behavior.
- Unique knowledge of process control system response to various upset conditions.
- Subtle changes in process variables.
- Unexpected relationships between certain parameters.
- Which instrumentation was considered undependable and which was considered consistently reliable.

If a similar incident occurred in the past, those witnesses involved in the previous incident should be reinterviewed and included in the investigation of the new incident.

4.7.2. Human Characteristics Related to Interviews

Eyewitness accounts should be considered as incomplete. Most of us have received little formal training in observation techniques. The common optical illusions in Figure 4-3 illustrate that our minds will often complete the expected or anticipated picture or image, even if it is not necessarily present. Another example of our usually adequate, but still imperfect, observation capabilities occurs in proofreading amusements and puzzles. These are crafted to look correct at first glance, yet are embarrassingly obvious once the error is noticed. Consider the text in Figure 4-3 below. Most people will miss the word that is repeated.

**A BIRD IN THE
THE HAND IS WORTHLESS.**

Figure 4-3. Illustrations of human observation limitations.

Take a second look at Figure 4-3

- Can you find the typographical error in the sentence? There is one that most of us naturally skip over.
- Look again at the triangle figure. It is an example of an illogical figure. It can be seen and interpreted in different ways.
- The figure in the center has become a classic in optical illusions. Is it silhouettes of two faces, or is it a vase?
- Study the three men. Are they the same size? Our brain interprets the image based on our previous experience with perspectives, depth perception, and background information clues. In this case, all three figures are the same size.

Although humans have a remarkable capacity to observe, interpret, accurately recall details, and then articulate information, they are not videotape recorders or computers. No single witness has a complete view or understanding of the entire event. Since each person experiences a unique perspective of the incident, discrepancies in descriptions of the incident may be due to different perspectives or different experiences of the individual witnesses. All incoming information is processed and "filtered" by the brain as part of the cognitive comprehension process. The information is again processed and "filtered" as it is articulated and transmitted to others.

A classic example of this "filtering" concept is the fable of the four blind men who encounter an elephant as they walk down the road together. Each blind man encounters a different part of the elephant and tries to communicate to his associates what he has found. The first man touches the trunk and believes they have met a boa constrictor. The second man grabs the tail and thinks it is a rope. A third who has encountered a leg begins to argue saying that both of his friends are wrong and that the thing is a tree trunk. The last man who has hit the side, insists they have hit a wall of some sort. Each blind man was basing his conclusion on the information available combined with his previous experience. The entire picture is not accurately interpreted until the composite information is assimilated.

Another human characteristic in interviews is that memory recall is not always in chronological order. Our replay mechanism does not function like a videotape player. This characteristic is one reason for using multiple attempts at remembering events. There is value in having the witness repeat portions of an interview after their memory has been stimulated by a review of their testimony.

Recollection is affected by emotions, by perceived "unfairness," by fear of embarrassment, by fear of becoming a scapegoat, and by preexisting motives, such as grudges and attitudes. Many people are so reluctant to be identified as different from their peer group that they may withhold information if they perceive the peer group would desire them to do so. The human characteristics such as those discussed are often at the root of apparent inconsistencies and conflicts generated by comparing witness testimony.

4.7.3. General Guidelines for Collecting Information from Witnesses

The accuracy and extent of information given by a witness is highly dependent on the performance of the interviewer and the rapport and atmosphere established during the interview.

Promptness in interviewing witnesses is a critical factor, which cannot be overemphasized. There are two general reasons for this. For most people, short-term memory for retaining and recollecting details degrades rapidly in a nonlinear fashion. This drop-off is dramatic and has actually been measured in various controlled studies. The second reason for promptness is that an "independent" recollection of events can be significantly affected by contact and communication with others. The interaction among witnesses blurs details and changes emphasis both consciously and unconsciously. Thus, it is best to prevent any exchange of information among witnesses where possible. In many cases complete isolation is not practical, so as a minimum the witnesses should be asked to refrain from discussing the incident with anyone until after they have been interviewed.

It is also a good practice to ask the witnesses to write down their observations and recollections in informal narrative statements separately and without discussion with other witnesses. The written statement helps the witness clarify and focus thoughts. However, some people do not like to write and may prefer to talk into a tape recorder for transcription later. The investigator needs to remember that most eyewitnesses are not trained nor accustomed to clearly writing such a document. Unclear and incomplete passages must be expected.

The initial interview with a direct witness is most often in the format of a narrative statement, *continuous and uninterrupted.* This is followed by questions specific to a particular topic of concern. The questions should be carefully worded to be as neutral, unbiased, and non-leading as possible. At least a common core group of questions should be asked of all witnesses to provide a control sample and to cross-confirm key information.

The interviewer must remain constantly aware of the potential influence he or she can have on the witness. Sometimes, there is a tendency for a witness to relay what he or she thinks the interviewer is expecting (wanting or waiting) to hear. There is also a corresponding possibility for the interviewer to "lead the witness" by sending various response signals. Sometimes the interviewer is not even aware of leading or steering the discussion.

4.7.4. Conducting the Interview

Some simple measures can be employed to maximize the quality and quantity of information gleaned from interviewing witnesses. The interview should not be mistaken for an interrogation. A location viewed as "neutral" will normally produce better results and should be used whenever the opportunity exist. Conducting the interview in the office of a high-level manager will unnecessarily increase the tension and stress on a worker from the front line ranks. The location should be as private as possible, thus reducing stress. Reasonable accommodations should also be made for witnesses who smoke.

Some planning can be extremely beneficial. Scheduling the sequence of the interviews can increase the productivity and can minimize the need for follow-up interviews. A brief list of questions/topics prepared before the interview will help reduce errors of omission. If the interviewer has some knowledge about the witness, such as the background, experience level, and nature of involvement in the incident, then the interviewer will be able to better interpret and understand the information being given by the witness. This small degree of insight can make a difference when interviewing a traumatized witness, one who is demonstrating an unusual degree of anxiety, or one who has an abnormal verbal communication style.

Minor arrangements can help to achieve a thorough, accurate, and useful interview. These include such items as arranging transportation home for the witness if he or she would miss a car pool, and providing overtime meals or refreshments.

The interview can in some ways be viewed as a two-way verbal communication event. The interviewer's role is more than that of merely recording, or of functioning as some type of human video camera. The interviewer must at times interact with and respond objectively to the information being given by the witness. A highly successful verbal communication technique is "reflective listening," sometimes called "active listening". In this technique, the interviewer periodically relates what he or she thinks the witness has said. This gives the witness a chance to correct any errors or misinterpretations or to add further details.

The best practice is to let the witness lead the exchange, but it is important for the interviewer to explore apparent paths of new information. More than one witness has claimed after the interview they knew a certain fact but did not mention it because the interviewer did not ask about it. The witness made a judgment that the information was not important or was not relevant.

One general interview style that has proven consistently successful contains four separate phases shown in Figure 4-4:

- Establishing initial **rapport**
- Witness gives **uninterrupted narrative** statement
- **Interactive** exchange phase, **dialogue**, questions and answers
- **Conclusion**, closure, and summary

The purpose of the initial phase is to establish a workable degree of trust and **rapport.** The interview can be a source of considerable stress, even if the witness is sincere, cooperative and not responsible for the incident. Each witness brings a unique collection of emotions (fears, anxieties), motives, attitudes, and expectations into the interview. On some occasions these emotions can include reactions to the death or serious injury to a friend or co-worker. A good way for the interviewer to begin most interviews is to explain the investigation process to the witness and to describe his or her role in the effort. A technique used successfully in the legal profession for witness depositions is to begin with intentionally bland, nonthreatening questions and topics. The main purpose is to help the witness overcome initial jitters.

This first phase may appear on the surface to be shallow chit-chat, yet it can determine the entire outcome of the interview! It provides an opportunity for the interviewer to explain the purpose, format, expectations, confidentiality, and to deal with any special concerns of the witness. Yet, the most beneficial aspect is the opportunity to establish a constructive atmosphere in which communication can begin.

A completely **uninterrupted narrative** statement by the witness is the next phase. Regardless of the urge to ask clarifying questions, it is critically important that the interviewer permit this initial monologue to be completed. The witness should be allowed as much time as he or she needs for pauses to recall and to find the best choice of words to express the information.

The third phase is the **interactive dialogue** which is the common image of an interview, as popularized by TV personalities. This is the phase in which specific objectively worded questions are asked of the witness. An example might be an attempt to pinpoint the exact time that an operator detected an upset condition and to learn the basis for his or her initial diagnosis of the situation. There is significant potential for the interviewer to influence the witness during this dialogue. This risk is constantly present and demands continuous recognition by the interviewers.

The **conclusion** phase contains significant potential benefits that are sometimes unappreciated and lost. During this concluding portion the interviewer should use "reflective listening" to summarize and play back to the witness what the interviewer heard during the interview session. It provides an opportunity to correct information that was incompletely or incorrectly captured and, secondly, to add additional information. Hearing the playback will often stimulate additional memory of details.

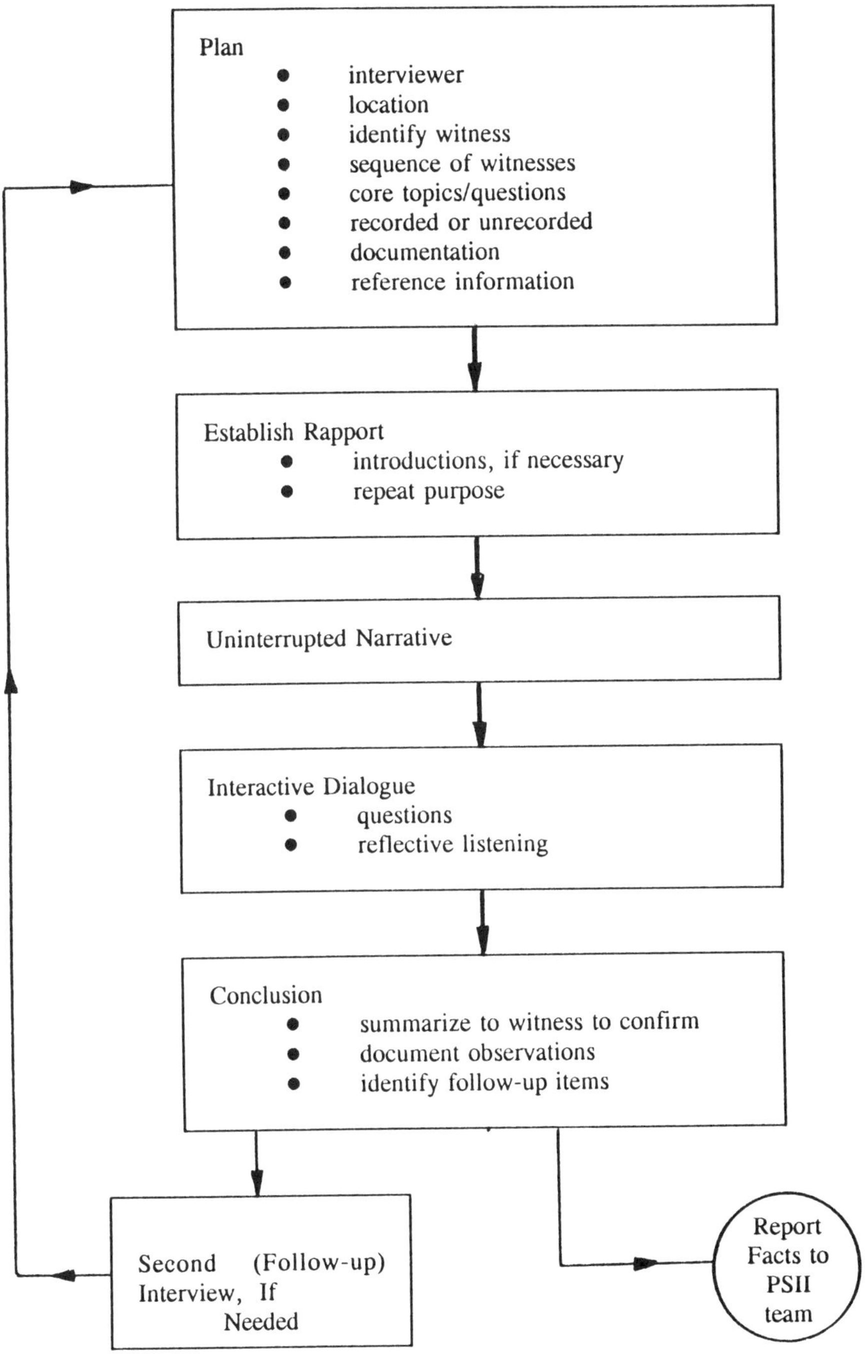

Figure 4-4. Flowchart typical interview sequence

Different people have different definitions in mind for the same word. Thus, it can be advantageous to ask questions to clarify the ideas expressed by the witness.[25]

- When a noun is used, the interviewer may use diplomatic words to ask, "*What*, exactly?" For example, a motor valve may be electric or air operated; the difference may be important to the investigation.
- When a verb is used, the interviewer may ask, "*How*, exactly?" For example, "shutting down the reactor" may mean "gradually reducing the feeds in normal shutdown mode" or it may mean "hitting the emergency stop button."
- Sometimes, rules or values may be mentioned, such as, "The outside operator should always close the drain valve." It may be helpful for the interviewer to ask, "What would happen if he did not?"
- A witness may make a generalization, such as, "all . . .," "always . . .," "everybody . . .," "never . . .," "they. . . ." The interviewer can *clarify these generalizations* by asking, "All?" "Always?" "Everybody?" "Never?" "Who are they?"
- Sometimes a witness may use a comparative without an antecedent, for example, "Pump A is better." The interviewer can clarify by asking, "Better than what?"

It is critical that the interviewer retain rapport with the witness; otherwise, the interview can take on the characteristics of an interrogation.

One valuable technique during the conclusion phase is the use of the pause. The witness is asked in as nonthreatening a manner as possible, "Is there anything else you want to add regardless of how unimportant you think it might be?" This question is then followed by an *extended* pause.

It is common for a witness to recall additional information after the interview is over. Astute investigators anticipate this and provide a clearly understood and easy method for the witness to recontact the interviewer. Always close an interview by inviting the witness to return if he or she remembers something else, or would like to modify or add to the interview.

Most of us constantly communicate by nonverbal means (body language) such as postures, crossed arms or legs, a sudden change in degree of body motion and eye contact, and facial expression. Interviewers who are alert to nonverbal signals can gain insights and better understanding of the information being offered by the witness. Interviewers should be careful, however, to avoid overzealous interpretations of body language.

Interviewers should also be aware of the need for "personal space." The witness will not benefit from the extra stress created by an enthusiastic or overly aggressive interviewer who encroaches on this personal space.

The interviewer should watch for sudden mood changes and note when they occur. The mood changes may reflect an unwillingness to discuss certain facts.[25]

Interviewers will always experience apparent inconsistencies while gathering information from interviews. All information from witnesses will not be actual fact, but may be perceived as fact by the person supplying the information. In most cases, it pays to delay judgment on the apparent inconsistencies. Just as the interviewer must avoid coming to conclusions on accident causes until the facts are fully developed, judgment should be delayed on these apparent inconsistencies. Often a scenario will emerge which reveals the conflicting items to be factual, but at different times during the incident sequence. Even if a statement is found to be wrong, the reason for the misinterpretation can frequently reveal other important information. At other times the source of the apparent inconsistencies can be traced to the interviewer, who inadvertently modified information from the witness based on what the interviewer knew to date about the incident.

On many occasions, the interview process deserves to be treated as confidential communication. The witness should be reassured before, during, and at the conclusion of the session that the interview is indeed confidential to the PSII team. In some rare circumstances. it may be desirable to extend anonymity to the witness. This situation sometimes arises if retaliation is a reasonable possibility. In such instances, the advice of legal counsel should be sought.

The issue of tape recording must be addressed by the PSII team. In some, but not all cases, it may be desirable and appropriate to audio or videotape the interview (or use a stenographer). Often the presence of a microphone creates an extra degree of stress for the witness. The interviewer needs to recognize when a witness might be inhibited by recording. The accuracy gained by recording the information may be offset by the decrease in participation by the witness. The decision to record depends on many variables, such as the nature and seriousness of the incident, the past and expected future relationship between the witness and the interviewer, and the climate of the work environment.

Immediately after the witness leaves the room, the interviewer should take the time to evaluate the interview, assess the quality and quantity of information received, identify any key points that confirm or conflict with previous information, and then record his or her findings **before doing anything else.** These would normally include such items as observations, specific insights, and items to be followed-up on in later interviews or investigation activity.

It is common to find that follow-up interviews are necessary. These are often very brief, focusing on only a few specific items that need to be verified or clarified.

Hand drawn sketches (regardless of the artistic quality) are a valuable tool in the interview process and should be encouraged by the interviewer. It is a good practice to have paper, flip charts, and pencils in the interview room. It is also helpful to have some documentary evidence (photographs, P&IDs, plot plans etc., process control data, DCS trend charts) available for use during the later stage of the interview. However, it must be remembered that premature use of photographs and documents can hamper information gathering by providing an opportunity for witnesses to lose their train of thought that is so valuable during the initial narration. Premature use of such documents can also lead to the witness becoming unsure or even confused. The confusion can lead to withholding information that would have otherwise been offered. On the other hand, use of these documents during the later stages of the interview is beneficial and encouraged.

4.7.5. Common Avoidable Mistakes

Inexperienced interviewers can improve results with these points:

- The interviewer must be constantly aware of the tendency to screen out incoming information that does not easily or comfortably fit into the desired or expected scenario. The interviewer must not project the direction in which he or she thinks or hopes the interview should go.
- The interviewer should resist the almost overpowering urge to interrupt the witness during the initial narrative statement.
- During the *initial* interview, careful consideration should be given to the number of people present in the room. Some investigators recommend the interview consist of one witness and two interviewers. Additional interviewers can decrease participation by the witness. Other investigators prefer limiting the initial interview to a one-on-one arrangement. The decision depends on the particular relationship between the witness and the interviewer, and on the nature of the incident.

For follow-up interviews and general information gathering (fact finding type meetings), the ratio of interviewees to interviewers is less critical. A group interview can be perceived as more open and honest, and less covert and intimidating than one-on-one or several-on-one interviews. A team atmosphere often can be created during a group interview.

- If two interviewers are present, one should lead the process and the witness should be made to feel as much a part of the team as possible.
- The interviewer should take time immediately after each interview to make notes, including observations, impressions, inconsistencies, specific key points, and items for follow-up action. The interviewer's overconfidence or overreliance on his or her ability to recall details can be very detrimental to the investigation. After several witnesses it can become very difficult to remember just who said what.
- It is normal and acceptable for apparent inconsistencies to be discovered during the initial interviews. Inconsistencies can usually be resolved later; identify them and try to remain focused on the present (i.e., what the witness is trying to tell you at this time). Accepting inconsistencies initially can help prevent the investigation team from jumping to premature conclusions.
- Interaction among witnesses which results in contamination and blending of information can be minimized if the interviews are scheduled promptly, and there is not a common waiting room.
- Conducting the interview in an intimidating location such as the plant manager's office is an avoidable mistake. Offices of senior management are often tempting potential locations, but the interviewer needs to be aware of the conscious and subconscious effect this location can have on many front line employees.

4.8. PHYSICAL EVIDENCE

4.8.1. General Considerations

Evidence collection actually begins even before the incident by incorporating certain evidence awareness and preservation concepts into such management systems as:

- PSII
- Emergency Response
- Management of Change
- Training Programs of operators, maintenance workers and contractors
- PSI (process safety information) package
- PHA (process hazard analysis)
- Documentation practices

By having these process safety management practices in place and functioning as desired, the quantity and quality of potential evidence will be enhanced. Non–PSII team workers may fail to recognize the significance of their well-intended efforts at prompt demolition and parts collection. However, if adequately trained, they can make positive contributions since they have the opportunity to notice items in or out of the incident zone that can be helpful to the PSII team. Figure 4-5 presents a summary check list for physical evidence considerations.

Not everything in the incident zone will be significant. The trick is to sort the "wheat" from the "chaff" quickly while causing minimum disturbance to the "wheat." The decisions made in this area are based on team members' experience and expertise. If at all possible, key physical items need to be photographed and tagged prior to any movement. A guiding rule for the decision on what to keep is "too much is better than too little." Any known or anticipated dismantling, disassembly, or opening of equipment should be planned and coordinated with the appropriate groups.

In addition to the PSII team, there will be others with vested interests in the evidence. Additional samples and copies of photographs will often be required.

It is important to document what is on top of what in the debris. Analyzing the layers is a valuable technique borrowed from archeology. It is most often necessary to perform partial and selective demolition in order to get to an area or item of possibly significant evidence.

INTERPRETING EVIDENCE
- What is on top of what?
- Which side was affected by the incident?
- How far did something go and in what direction?
- Which gaskets were blown and which were not?

Specific techniques for evidence analysis are beyond the scope of this book; however, some examples are highlighted in Section 4.11. Entire volumes have been written on specific issues such as the fracture patterns of alloys and the corresponding clues for

- ☐ Incorporate physical evidence preservation into planning, PSII team training, emergency responder procedures and training, and general concepts into employee and supervisor training.
- ☐ Coordinate with on-site emergency team
- ☐ Establish communications with external organizations (OSHA, EPA, Others)
- ☐ Identify and secure area of interest
- ☐ Secure hot work permit before using electronic camera, flash, motor drives, or video cameras
- ☐ Note, photograph, and/or document as-is layers
- ☐ Ensure all photographs are identified and documented, (date, time, and photographer)
- ☐ Establish missile mapping (or evidence of overpressure wave) if appropriate
- ☐ Promulgate chain-of-custody protocol
- ☐ Implement documentation control procedures
- ☐ Secure volatile electronic records data
- ☐ Take initial photographs
- ☐ Note "as found" position of all valves, switches, and control devices
- ☐ Draw residual samples
- ☐ Tag key items of evidence or photograph in place, if necessary before movement
- ☐ Arrange for necessary outside special services, metallurgists, labs, or other specialists
- ☐ Develop specific controls and procedures for investigative demolition if needed
- ☐ Arrange for long -term storage/preservation
- ☐ Identify recommended changes in PSII management systems and submit to management

Figure 4-5. Check list for Section 4.7, "Physical Evidence."

determining actual cause and mechanism for the failure. Suffice it to say that known specific materials and alloys perform and fail in consistent and predictable ways. This area of expertise is normally supplied to the PSII team through the use of part-time specialists, either from within the parent organization or from outside experts or labs engaged specifically for the task.

Fracture and metal failure analysis is almost always a very reliable and extensive aspect of investigations of major incidents. Macro evidence, such as indications of shear or brittle failure on fracture faces, lines showing detonation direction, and the chevron (herringbone) pattern all provide valuable clues to sequence, type, and cause of the failure.[7] Investigators can often distinguish among the ages of various segments of a crack in the metal. This age difference can often allow credible determination of whether the crack was present before the catastrophic incident. Metal fatigue and related failures are well-established phenomena. Two recommended references on metallurgy aspects of investigations are *Assessment of Fire and Explosion Damage to Chemical Plant Equipment/Analyzing Explosions and Pressure Vessel Ruptures*, by D. McIntyre,[8] and *Defects and Failures in Pressure Vessels and Piping* by H. Thielsch.[9] Elongations and evidence of twisting torque failure modes can be useful clues when analyzing failure mechanisms. Analysis of fractures in wood and plastic materials can also be conducted.

Examination of the tear pattern can often distinguish between deflagration events and detonation events. During deflagrations the pressure is uniform throughout the vessel; therefore, the failure occurs at the vessel's weakest point.[10] The damage is manifested as tears.

In piping systems, sometimes an event will initiate as a deflagration and then accelerate into a detonation. This change can often be determined by examination of the metal fragments. Detonations tend to produce shearing-type failures. In piping systems the damage is most pronounced at elbows or other constrictions such as valves. For detonations in piping systems, there is usually a distinctly different damage pattern downstream of the ignition source.

4.8.2. Preservation

There are two distinct phases of evidence preservation: the immediate and the long term. Some evidence will need to be retained for an indefinite period of time and will require special storage measures. A documented "chain of custody" has become more significant due to legal considerations. Provision must be made for long-term storage of large items in order to minimize effects of weather (especially ultraviolet light and rust). Items can easily become lost unless special measures are taken, such as a dedicated, fenced, locked, posted, and routinely inspected storage yard. Small items can present even greater challenges, since most facility warehouses do not normally have a special section that can be controlled and dedicated exclusively to this purpose. In process incidents, previous batch (raw material and finished goods) Quality Control results and retained samples should be secured and protected from degradation. If possible, postincident samples should be taken and similarly protected.

Short-term preservation (several weeks) can usually be successfully accomplished by generous application of polyethylene plastic wrap and duct tape. Even short-term preservation requires some control of access, chain of custody documentation and conspicuously posted signs. Many workers are genuinely curious to learn and see for themselves what the damaged or key evidence part actually looks like, and may unintentionally cause changes.

Preservation of paper printouts from instruments often requires some special attention, as does electronically stored data. Most process control computer systems are ultimately backed up by a battery system of finite duration. It is important to perform a data capture operation as soon as possible to maximize the quantity and quality of such information. For example, one investigator had to download the data within the preset file purge time of 8 hours.

Borrowing from lessons learned by law enforcement investigations, a generous supply of plastic bags in various sizes can be helpful in preserving evidence (provided the bag itself will not contaminate the chemical evidence).

4.8.3. Identification

Early in the investigation, and preferably before any field investigation activity is actually started, the PSII team must establish a protocol for systematically identifying all types of expected evidence. Some evidence will be easily handled (small parts of valves and instruments, personal protective equipment, and tools of injured workers), other items will be perishable (residual liquid and residue inventories for example), and still other evidence may be of interest to several groups including OSHA, EPA, the chemical safety and hazard investigation board (when established), insurer, fire departments, and representatives of potential plaintiffs. This variety of challenges requires a clearly understood, well-communicated, and publicized method for evidence identification.

Critical to success is a numbering system that can be applied to a wide variety of types of physical and documentary evidence. An up-to-date log of assigned numbers is necessary.

Color coding via tags or spray paint can be helpful to those engaged in moving or removing debris. One satisfactory method is for the demolition crew to move only material that has been clearly marked. The guiding rule is, "if it is inside the investigation zone and it is not marked, then it is to be left alone." Long intermittent runs of piping should be marked at regular intervals, especially where the piping passes across the boundary of the investigation zone.

Tag attachment can be best achieved using plastic twist ties. It is a good practice to also photograph the attached tag in place on key items. Logging of tagging should be coordinated with the evidence identification protocol.

In addition to the traditional photography, certain incidents, such as explosions, will require special mapping of missiles and fragments. By careful documentation, established at the onset of the investigation, it is possible to create an accurate diagram of where the various pieces of a vessel ended up after an explosion. Using this missile mapping data as a base, and knowing the weight of each fragment, an estimate of the initial energy release of the explosion can be calculated. The theoretical yield strength of the vessel can be calculated. The energy release value can sometimes be used to confirm or rule out some proposed scenarios for the cause or sequence of events. The

Pieterson (TNO) report on the Mexico City LPG terminal disaster is an excellent example of such a study.[12]

4.8.4. Document Control

Often the size and scope of the investigation will mandate a special document control procedure, in which each document is given a unique identification number, and records are maintained of which documents were issued to whom. A complete set of documents should be retained in order to minimize confusion. A special log can be useful in maintaining some control over the flow of paper documents. This is especially true when legal issues or regulatory agencies are involved. Some PSII teams find it helpful to procure their own copy machine.

Outside agencies can have a voracious appetite for documents. Often it will be necessary to dedicate one person full time to execute and manage this single area of the investigation in order to free up the other team members for actual investigation activities. In any case, it is a good idea to designate one person as document control officer who has sole authority, responsibility, and control over all documents that enter or leave the PSII location. That person should also have the responsibility of maintaining the official complete set of records and documents.

4.9. PHOTOGRAPHY

4.9.1. Overview

Treatment of injured personnel should always be top priority and should never be delayed due to photographic activity. Sometimes photographers have a tendency to lose sight of established priorities.

The term "photography" is used in this section in the *broadest* sense and includes videotape. Since the earliest days of image reproduction, investigators and documenters have applied this powerful tool in continuously creative ways[24]. Recent technological advances, resulting in size and price reductions of videotape devices, have created new horizons for capturing, preserving, and even presenting evidence.

Process safety incident investigation involves two practical levels of photographic expertise. For *most* incidents the team or a company employee can adequately meet the photographic needs. However, for some incidents, the services of a professional commercial photographer or other specialists are necessary and are justified. Examples would be:

- Microscopic analytical views
- Magnaflux
- X-rays
- Infrared

- Complex sequences
- Incidents with actual (or potential) serious consequences
- Extremely close-up views of machinery or equipment
- Nighttime shots

It is obviously desirable to photograph objects of interest before they are disturbed in any way, including moving, turning over, or even lifting to tag or affix an identification number. A thorough and up-to-date log is invaluable. To minimize movement of objects before photographing, evidence preservation procedures can and should be included in the initial and periodic refresher training on PSII given to all employees, supervision, and management. Photographic equipment containing electrical components should not be used in any location that has not been determined to be free of combustible concentrations of vapors. In short, get a hot work permit before taking pictures with an electric camera.

Whenever possible, identification of the evidence should be incorporated as part of the photograph itself.

The 35 millimeter camera is the standard tool. It is relatively simple and inexpensive to use, reasonably reliable, and can perform most tasks needed by the PSII team. Technological advances in semiautomatic modern SLR (single lens reflex) cameras enable amateurs and hobbyists to produce a high quality photograph that rivals commercial work for many applications. Even simpler autofocus compact "clam shell" 35 mm cameras are now available. Some are weatherproof; most have built-in flash; and almost all automatically set shutter speed and aperture. These small cameras can be used successfully by *any* team member and are easily carried.

Professional photographers will often use a 2¼" format. With the large negative, there is a considerable increase in image size (3266 mm^2 compared to the 864 mm^2 for the standard 35 mm format). The larger image results in clearer detail and less grain on enlarged prints. These extra benefits are desirable, but usually not necessary for most PSII work.

Additional lenses are sometimes useful. The wide angle lens can show relationships between equipment, and, for close up work (less than 3 ft or 1 m) a macro lens has great advantages.

The purpose of this section is *not* to provide a detailed tutorial on techniques of photography including depth of field, selection of film speeds and types, shutter speeds, filters, and F-stops. These are better addressed in photography primers and other publications. Suffice it to state that the higher the ASA film speed rating, the less natural light is needed. Some investigators have found ASA 200 and 400 speed to be good all around choices. The investigator should have some prior experience with the particular camera used in the investigation. An avoidable mistake is to use the camera for the first time during the actual investigation. Shooting several test rolls is a good investment.

Black and white photography still has its place, but has lost its previous price advantage. Black and white sometimes requires additional development time (except when used by professional photographers who develop their own exposures). Many fast photo labs do not have the capabilities to give 1 hour or even next day service on black and white exposures.

The normal practice is to designate a single person on the PSII team to be responsible for photography. This person works closely with the team member responsible for documentation/record keeping and coordinates with other groups outside the team.

An accurate, complete, and up-to-date log of photographs is a necessity. For most process safety related incidents, each photograph should be identified as follows:

- Date and time taken
- Key item of interest
- Reason for being viewed
- Direction looking toward the ? from the ?
- Identity of the person taking the photograph

The automatic date/time feature of some cameras is highly useful in major investigations, especially when investigative demolitions are being conducted. The investigation team should understand, however, that such camera imprinted date/time markings are generally ***not*** accepted in most courts unless auxiliary documentation is provided (e.g., log book). When using the date/time feature, the photographer should be aware of possible interference with the composition and background. Sometimes the date/stamp obscures or confuses the image of the object of interest.

Slides are an underused tool by many investigators. Any single 35 mm negative can be converted into a slide at any later date. Dual film (slide and print) is available and is a potential cost and time saver if the team knows that a particular series of shots will be needed for a presentation of the findings or for training.

Another highly useful application is the instant print camera. This is especially helpful during the first several days following a major incident when there is a high demand for initial information by outside parties. These prints should also be logged and identified. This method is relatively expensive when compared to 35 mm or videotape, but it does provide a unique resource to the team. These prints are especially useful when communicating to demolition workers who are assisting the PSII team.

The videotape camera, now often called camcorder, is emerging as one of the most powerful tools for visually recording evidence. Camcorders have become significantly easier to use, smaller, and less expensive than they were a few years ago. The VHS (2-hr full size) format is most common, followed by the 8 mm videotape cassette. Videotape in the 8 mm format is becoming the most common media for *compact* camcorders and is easily transcribed to VHS. For *compact* camcorders, 8 mm has the advantage of 2 hours recording time per cassette versus 40 minutes for compact VHS. One major advantage to videotape recording is the ability to have narration/commentary and otherwise record sounds at the scene. Another unique benefit is the capability to capture motion as an investigative action unfolds, such as the opening or disassembly of a particular piece of equipment. A common error in amateur videotaping is inadequate lead-in time before panning the camera. Allow a full 15 seconds at the beginning of each shot. This lead-in time is needed if the tape is later edited for reports or training. In major incidents, where media coverage is likely, it is a good practice to record newscasts that may show footage of the incident. Electronic clipping services can help fill this requirement.

For long-term storage, black and white photography is essentially permanent, whereas color prints, color negatives, and instant prints fade and lose detail with time. Avoid vinyl sleeves containing plastizers for storing color prints and color negatives. Kodachrome slide films have shown excellent long-term storage characteristics.

Electronic color video "photography" is coming into use. The technology allows easy transmission of photographs as data by phone. Some workers are using computer enhancement of electronic images from cameras or scanned conventional photographs.

A special application of photography is to record the view seen by a particular witness. At times this can enhance the testimony of a witness, help clarify apparent inconsistencies, and verify key items in question.

Medical and legal personnel may have need for photographic documentation of injuries. This area is usually best left to the medical and legal experts.

Before-the-event photographs will usually be extremely rare and difficult to find. One possible source is construction progress documentation shots. Company annual reports and advertising departments can sometimes produce a "before" picture that will be useful, although usually not of the exact view desired. Current and retired employees sometimes keep photographs of the areas in which they worked. Sometimes if the need or request is publicized in a productive and positive manner, illicitly taken "before" photographs will show up anonymously in the mail. If you do not now retain photographs of most portions of plants and major hazardous processes, it is a good practice to get started.

4.9.2. Guidelines for Maximum Results

1. Log and document every photograph.
2. Promptness is critical in order to minimize disturbing the evidence; however, in no case should emergency medical treatment or emergency response activity be delayed by any photographic activity.
3. Begin with overall views of the general area from multiple directions. This will help show perspective of distance and relative locations of items of interest.
4. Professional photographers often "bracket" their shots, intentionally under- and overexposing the same shot as well as correctly exposing it. Often, details revealed in one of these shots may not be apparent in another one, particularly if the shot contains both very bright areas and very dark ones. It is therefore wise to take multiple exposures of key shots from several angles at various settings.

5. Every shot should include an item of measurable scale as a size reference. It is common to include a ruler/scale or some other object of known size in any close up view (3 ft, 1 m, or less).
6. Flash units and motor drives are potential ignition sources. They deserve the same respect as if the photographer were holding an open flame. In many cases, a gas test and hot work permit will be required prior to using a flash unit, motor drive, or camcorder. *Each* specific use of flash devices may require authorization. When using a flash even with permission, it is a good practice to take the time to warn and alert *all* personnel who will see the flash (or could even possibly see the flash or a reflection of the flash). This will prevent "startle" response actions, and could prevent an injury (due to fall or other response).
7. When shooting outside, consider the location of the sun and the accompanying glare, reflections, and shadows generated. Sometimes a specially timed series of photographs is taken to document the approximate lighting conditions at the time of the incident. If more than several weeks have passed, the sun's relative position may have changed enough to make a significant difference.
8. One disadvantage of an autofocus camera is that the camera does not always focus on the desired object. If the object of interest to the photographer is in the background and another object in the foreground is in the focus beam, then the camera will select and focus on the closer object. A familiar example is the out-of-focus picture where the camera has focused on some background object in the gap between two people. Most autofocus cameras are now equipped with a selectable feature to overcome this limitation.
9. A common avoidable mistake is to expect the camera to duplicate the human eye in low light conditions such as dusk or heavy shade. The performance specifications for normally available 35 mm films represent a compromise among several factors. These include cost differences, expected lighting conditions, technical quality of the camera system, shelf life, and image resolution quality. Special low light level and extended wide range speed films are available at additional costs. The camera/film systems are designed to perform within a specific set of conditions. Operating near or beyond the edge of these conditions will produce poorer quality photographs.
10. Camera battery life can be unpredictable! A fresh and complete spare set is a necessity rather than a luxury. In many modern 35 mm camera systems, functioning batteries are required for a simple task such as loading film. If the camera is part of a seldom used supply kit, special attention is needed to ensure fresh *primary and spare* batteries are available and that the film has not passed its expiration date.
11. Some type of portable background is often desirable when shooting evidence in the field. A light colored pastel cloth will usually give better results than black or white.
12. When documenting a witness statement, the photograph should be taken from as close as possible to the actual viewpoint used by the witness.

13. Film (exposed or not), will be adversely affected by heat and moisture. The temperatures inside vehicles can easily exceed 100°F (40°C). Some protective lens coatings will melt and distort from the excess temperatures found inside closed vehicles. A common practice is to store film in a refrigerator. Be sure to rotate your stock of unused film to avoid the use of expired film.
14. The possible damage to underdeveloped film caused by airport security X-ray machines has been extensively debated. The Investigative Photography guide published by the Society of Fire Protection Engineers clearly states that *all* unexposed film *is* affected by these X-rays.[24] Each time the film goes through the machine, a light fog is deposited on the film. This can be significant for multiple passes. There is no easy solution, yet the degradation caused by a single pass through the machine is tolerable in almost all cases. High speed films are affected more by X-rays than lower speed films.
15. Backlighting can cause major problems, especially when using one of the newer automatic or semiautomatic exposure control cameras. Backlighting is the condition in which the subject of interest (in the foreground) is in relative darkness and is posed against a brighter background. The camera will sense the background and thus produce a photograph in which the object in the foreground is nearly a silhouette against the bright background. Examples of this occur often when shooting in an upward direction in an attempt to capture some detail on an overhead pipe rack. Most older (manual) cameras and many of the newer (automatic and semiautomatic) models have a feature that can be activated to help this situation.
16. A common mistake is to expect the camera to do the thinking for the investigator.[12] Some investigators have used the approach of taking a general barrage of pictures in the hope that somewhere in the large pile will be a "gold nugget" with the key to the investigation. Each shot should have an intended purpose. Planned shots have better results than random shots.
17. Professional photographers anticipate the instantaneous temporary shadow created by the flash itself and use various diffusers and backgrounds. For PSII, these devices are also helpful for inside bench/table top shots of evidence.

4.10. "THIRD-PARTY INFORMATION"

As discussed earlier in Section 4.7.1, not all information will originate from company employees who work in the immediate area. It is important to consider potential indirect witnesses such as contractors, retired employees, and workers who routinely visited the area such as laboratory technicians and delivery personnel. Equipment manufacturers' technical representatives often have an extensive intimate knowledge of the specific machinery or equipment involved in the incident. Contract workers who periodically work in the unit can gain a surprising degree of knowledge. For example, it is not unusual for the same outside contract machinist/millwright to work on the same compressor once a year for 5 or even 10 years during the annual "turn-around." This worker may only be in the plant for a few days each year, yet may provide unique knowledge helpful to the PSII team.

If approached properly, news media personnel will sometimes share their information with the investigation team and will try to screen out obviously untrue or unlikely reports. Media representatives often have aerial footage shots of the incident during its initial and most dramatic stages. They are usually interested in getting details of the incident and can therefore be in a cooperative mood. Each party, is therefore, in a position to bring something of value to the table for a potential win–win outcome.

Regulatory agencies will usually share general information gathered during their independent investigations, but are generally concerned about preserving the specific confidentiality of their witness interviews.

4.11. AIDS FOR STUDYING EVIDENCE

4.11.1. Sources of Information

The following discussions are intended as an introduction and illustrative examples of some special techniques used by professionals for technical analysis of evidence. The National Fire Protection Association (NFPA, Quincy, Massachusetts) has established a series of specialized guides for gathering and analyzing evidence. These include:

- NFPA 902M Field Incident Manual[13]
- NFPA 906M-7 Evidence[14]
- NFPA 906M-8 Photography[14]
- NFPA 906M-9 Sketches[14]
- NFPA 906M-11 Records/Documents[14]
- NFPA 906M-1 Fires[14]
- NFPA 907M Determination of Electrical Fire Causes[15]

Kuhlman in Chapter 10 of his publication, *Professional Accident Investigation*, presents some excellent information regarding failure modes of metals. These can be helpful in analyzing the physical evidence for determining sequence, mechanism, and reason for failure.

Fire investigators can reach remarkably quick and accurate determinations as to fire origin. Using carefully observed burn, char, melt, and damage patterns, the PSII team can gain a significant amount of information.[16] Even after a high energy event such as an explosion, examination of damage patterns can reveal sequences of events.

Melt and autoignition temperatures for many materials are known, as are normal flame temperatures. Table 4-1 gives selected temperatures of interest to many investigators. Soot will normally *not* affix itself to surfaces in excess of approximately

TABLE 4.1
Temperatures of interest to Process Safety Incident Investigation[17,19,20,21]

EFFECT	*°F*	*°C*
Paint begins to soften	400	204
Zinc primer paint discolors to tan	450	232
Zinc primer discolors to brown	500	260
Normal paints discolors	600	310
Zinc primer paint scorches to black	700	371
Lube oil auto-ignites	790	421
Stainless steel begins to discolor	800-900	427-482
Plywood auto-ignites	900	482
Vinyl coating on wire auto-ignites	900	482
Rubber hoses auto-ignite	950	510
Aluminum alloys melt	1125-1215	610-660
Glass melts	1400-1600	750-850
Brass melts (instrument gauges)	1650-1880	900-1025
Copper melts	1980	1083
Cast iron metals	2100-2200	1150-1250
Carbon steel melts	2760	1520
Stainless steel melts	2550-2790	1400-1532

700°F (371°C). Therefore, areas of high fire intensity may have little or no soot deposits. Flame temperatures are dependent on the amount and type of fuel and oxygen (air) present and whether these are pressurized or not. For example, normal flame temperatures (match, candle, methane/air) are in the range of 1000–2000°F (550–1100°C). Yet with pressurization and pure oxygen, a methane flame can approach 3000–5000°F (1650–2700°C).[17,18]

4.11.2. Analyzing Physical Evidence

When electrical conductors break while *not* carrying current, the break is different from the pattern shown when current is flowing. Thus, investigators can often determine if a particular device was actually energized at the time of the incident. One of the more elegant evidence analysis techniques was first developed by air crash investigators. It involves study of the surviving filaments from indicator light bulbs. Close examination can give fairly reliable information as to the condition of the bulb at the time of the incident. Bulbs that were lit (warm filaments) have a different shock loading failure pattern from those that were not lit (cool filaments).[27] If the filament was hot at the time of impact, it will stretch and distort substantially. If the filament was cold, it will break but will not distort or stretch from its original shape and pattern. This difference in failure modes may give valuable insight as to the signal being indicated by the bulb at the time of the incident.

Professional arson investigators have developed highly effective methods of deducing facts from a systematic study of burn, char, and melt patterns. Typical examples include the following measures:

- Most woods burn at a steady rate of 1.5 inches/hr (3.6 cm/hr).
- Hydraulic fluids usually exhibit a consistent response of smoke color, flame color, autoignition temperature, and a whitish residue.
- Glass breakage patterns and other damage can be used to estimate the overpressure wave, which in turn, can be used to estimate the energy released in an explosion. (See Table 2.13 in *Guidelines for Chemical Process Quantitative Risk Analysis*, New York: CCPS/AIChE, 1989.)

Not all evidence is simple to diagnose. Steel weakens at approximately 1100°F (575°C).[20] Steel exposed to 1500°F (816°C) for a short period can begin to fail and show the same degree of damage as steel exposed to a lower temperature for a longer period of time. Thus a sag pattern can be relatively reliable indicator that the steel was exposed to a temperature of *at least* 1100°F (575°C), but the maximum temperature above 1100°F (575°C) cannot be accurately determined without additional evidence.

Figures 4-6 and 4-7 illustrate use of evidence analysis. In this particular incident, an exploded pipe was laid out to identify the remaining pieces and to better understand the failure mode.

4.11.3. Laboratory Testing in Support of Failure Analysis

There are five testing techniques used to evaluate materials and components involved in an incident: visual examination, dimensional measurements, nondestructive evaluation, chemical analysis, and mechanical testing. Visual examination is always used in any failure analysis whereas the other techniques may or may not be required.[26] The PSII team should contact expert failure analysis personnel as soon after the failure as possible. Additional damage may occur to failed components if the analysis is delayed, making the analysis more difficult.

4.11.3.1. MACRO VISUAL EXAMINATION

Macro visual examination is done with the unaided eye or low power (up to 20X) magnification. Cleaning of the item to be examined may be required. Fracture origins and location of samples to be removed for further analysis are determined by macro visual examination. Nondestructive evaluation methods may assist macro visual examination in locating secondary cracks and other flaws.

1. N_2 Header in proper orientation looking north.

Figure 4-6. Explosion in a nitrogen pipe. An explosion occurred inside a nitrogen supply header due to a buildup of solid alkyl–lead–nitrogen compound. Here the investigation team has partially reassembled the all known fragments in an effort to determine the cause and location of the explosion. Chemical residue samples and metallurgical analysis were helpful in this case in identifying the root causes.

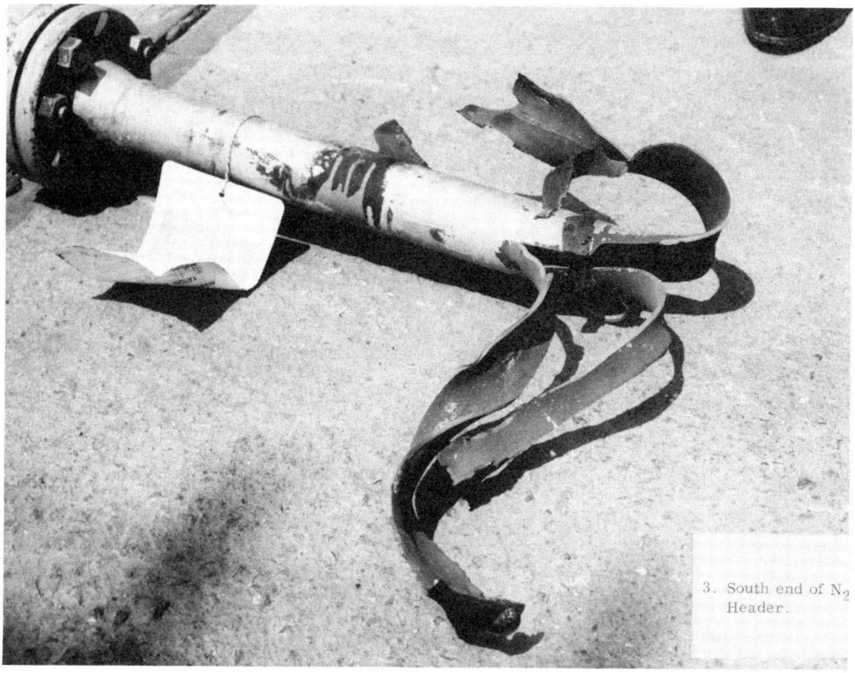

Figure 4-7. Closer up view of the pipe in Figure 4-6. Note the evidence preservation identification tag and identification of the photograph itself. This photograph was used in the final report to illustrate the extent of energy release.

4.11.3.2. MICROSCOPIC VISUAL EXAMINATION

Microscopic visual examination is done on mounted, polished, and etched samples prepared by metallographic (metals), petrographic (ceramics, glasses, and minerals) and resinographic (plastics and resins) techniques. The microstructure of the material and the nature of damage can be determined by microscopic visual examination. Reflected light microscopy is used with opaque materials. Transmitted light microscopy, often with polarized light, is used to examine transparent or translucent materials at magnifications up to 2000X. The scanning electron microscope (SEM) and transmitting electron microscope (TEM) are used for examination of specimens up to 150,000X magnification.

Fractography is the examination of fracture surfaces with no sample preparation other than cleaning to determine the fracture mechanism. The SEM at magnifications from 5X to 15,000X is the primary instrument for fractography due to the large depth of focus. Sometimes fractographic examination with the unaided eye or low power optical microscope (up to 100X) is conclusive. The TEM is used to examine replicas from fracture surfaces when magnification greater than 10,000X is necessary to characterize the fracture.

4.11.3.3. DIMENSIONAL MEASUREMENTS

The extent of corrosion or wear can be determined by measuring the remaining thickness and comparing it to the original thickness. The extent of distortion in deformed components and elongation of fractured components should be determined. Common machine shop measuring tools provide adequate accuracy.

4.11.3.4. NONDESTRUCTIVE EVALUATION (NDE)

Various NDE techniques are used to locate defects and flaws in the failed or similar equipment that may not be apparent during the macro visual inspection. An analysis of cracks and other damage during the initiation or progressive phases often provides more information regarding the failure mechanism(s) than the same analysis would at locations where complete failure occurred. Considerable secondary damage to a worn, fractured, or corroded surface may occur after failure. The most common methods of NDE are

- *Visual Examination*: With the unaided eye or assisted by borescopes, fiberscopes, television cameras, and magnifying systems.
- *Leak Testing*: Location of through wall defects and flaws while under pressure or vacuum. Various fluids and gases are used for pressure testing; several types of leak defects are used to locate a leak.
- *Liquid Penetrant Inspection*: Only useful to find surface discontinuities. Can be used with any material that has a reasonably smooth nonporous surface.
- *Magnetic Particle Inspection*: Only useful to find surface discontinuities and some discontinuities very near the surface in ferromagnetic materials. More sensitive than liquid penetrant inspection.
- *Eddy Current Inspection*: Eddy current inspection is the most widely used for several methods of discontinuity detection used with electrically conductive ferromagnetic and nonferromagnetic materials. Both surface and subsurface discontinuities can be detected.
- *Ultrasonic Inspection*: Ultrasonic inspection is used to detect surface and subsurface discontinuities in metals and sometimes other materials. Skilled inspectors are needed for ultrasonic testing.
- *Radiography*: Primarily used to detect subsurface discontinuities in metals by use of gamma or X-rays. Gamma or X-ray radiography can detect discontinuities in nonmetallic inorganic materials and the location of many metal components in an assembly. Neutron radiography is used to detect changes in density of organic materials.
- *Acoustic Emission Inspection*: Quite useful for locating defects in fiberglass and other composite materials. Considerable acoustic emission tests or metal components have been attempted, but these tests were not always successful. Once the location of a defect is determined, other NDE methods are used to determine its severity.
- *Other NDE Methods:* The following methods have limited applications: magnetic field testing, microwave inspection, thermal inspection, and halography.

4.11.4. Chemical Analysis

Chemical Analysis may be applied to a material in bulk usually to determine if it has met product specifications. Chemical analysis can be conducted on individual phases in a material, deposits on a surface, or wear particles. Most of the chemical analysis techniques are used to identify or quantify elements, ions, or functional groups. It is also very useful in many cases to identify and quantify compounds that are present.

4.11.4.1. BULK ANALYSIS METHODS

- *Atomic-Absorption Spectrometry*: Quantitative analysis of about 70 elements.
- *High Temperature Combustion*: Quantitative analysis of sulfur and carbon.
- *Elemental and Functional-Group Analysis*: Identification of organic compounds and determination of their empirical formulas.
- *Electrochemical*: Anions and cations in aqueous solutions.
- *Electron Spin Resonance*: Identification of transitional elements and their valence states.
- *Ion Chromatography*: Water soluble anions and some cations.
- *Inductively Coupled Plasma Atomic-Emission Spectroscopy*: Can do multi-element quantitative and qualitative analysis for about 70 elements simultaneously.
- *Inert-Gas Fusion*: Quantitative analysis of hydrogen, oxygen, and nitrogen in metals.
- *Infrared Spectroscopy*: Primarily used to determine organic compounds.
- *Liquid Chromatography*: Separation and quantitative analysis of soluble compounds.
- *Molecular Fluorescence Spectroscopy*: Analysis of fluorescent chemical species or species that can be coupled to a fluorescent chemical.
- *Neutron Activation Analysis*: Trace element assay.
- *Nuclear Magnetic-Resonance Spectroscopy*: Analysis of certain organic functional groups.
- *Optical Emission Spectroscopy*: Analysis of metallic elements in major and trace quantities.
- *Raman Spectroscopy*: Molecular analysis of bulk organic samples.
- *Spark-Source Mass Spectroscopy*: Analysis of inorganic and metallic materials.
- *Ultraviolet/Visible Absorption Spectroscopy*: Usually used for analysis of organic compounds.
- *Wet Chemical Analysis*: Numerous different techniques that can be used for most elements.
- *X-Ray Diffraction*: Identification of crystalline compounds.
- *X-Ray Spectrometry*: Suitable for all elements with atomic number greater than 5.

4.11.4.2 ANALYSIS OF SMALL AREAS, PARTICLES, AND SURFACES

Optical examination of etched polished surfaces or small particles can often identify compounds or different minerals by shape, color, optical properties, and the response to various etchants. A semiquantitative elemental analysis can be used for elements with atomic numbers greater than 4 by SEM equipped with X-ray fluorescence and various electron detectors. The electron probe microanalyzer and Auer microprobe also provides elemental analysis of small areas. The secondary ion mass spectroscopy, laser microprobe mass analyzer, and Raman microprobe analyzer can identify elements, compounds, and molecules. Electron diffraction patterns can be obtained with the TEM to determine which crystalline compounds are present. Ferrography is used for the identification of wear particles in lubricating oils.

4.11.5. Mechanical Testing

Mechanical testing to support failure analysis is conducted to determine if the failed component met original product specifications, to determine if changes have occurred in the component over time, and to determine if material exposed to simulated service conditions behaves similar to the failed component. The last reason for testing may take a considerable time to complete and can be fairly complex. Mechanical testing to determine if the material met specifications or if it changed over time should be conducted where possible, measuring against the requirements of the original product specification.

4.11.5.1 METALS

Tensile testing or a hardness test is a basic requirement of most metal specifications. Some product specifications also require impact testing, bend and other ductility tests, proof testing, flange or flare tests. The size of the sample may limit which test can be performed. Macro, superficial, and microhardness tests are routinely done in a failure analysis even if the original product specification did not require them.

4.11.5.2. CERAMICS, CONCRETE, GLASSES

The mechanical tests required by the original product specification should be conducted. Changes in the physical properties occur with many of these materials over time regardless of service.

4.11.5.3. PLASTICS, ELASTOMERS, RESINS

The requirements for mechanical testing called for by specification should be performed. Degradation of the physical properties of organic materials is the best indication of chemical, radiation, or thermal degradation. When organic materials are removed from contact with solvents and other chemicals the physical properties right after removal may be quite different than those measured several days later.

4.11.5.4. TESTING TO SIMULATE SERVICE CONDITIONS

No general outline can be given since such testing should be tailored for each case. Such tests may include corrosion testing, stress corrosion cracking tests, formability testing, fatigue testing, stress testing, creep testing, and some combination of these tests.

4.12. NEW CHALLENGES IN INTERPRETATION OF EVIDENCE

Technology advances in electronics such as process control instrumentation systems, computer capabilities, programmable logic controllers, and the use of independent personal computers at field locations for special dedicated functions present new challenges to PSII. Some of the advances are so rapid that the team may not have the internal expertise to adequately determine failure scenarios, sequences, and modes. The suppliers and manufacturers of these high tech devices are sometimes the only source of credible information on failure modes of these devices.

Sneak circuit analysis is one example of these new investigation challenges. A sneak circuit is an unwanted connection in an electric or electronic circuit, not caused by component failure, that leads to an undesirable circuit condition or that can inhibit a desired condition.[23] Sneak circuit analysis is a technique developed to identify such conditions.

Reliance on outside expertise may be the most feasible option for some of these issues. The PSII team may act as facilitators and advisors in a similar mode to a PHA study. The outside expert would supply the failure mode information on which possible failures are credible.

Another new challenge for PSII investigators is in capturing, preserving, and retrieving electronically stored data. As previously mentioned, electronic computer control systems are ultimately backed up by battery power. These battery systems have functional performance time limits that jeopardize accurate and complete data retrieval.

Multilevel computer security measures such as software and hardwired keyed systems can be a blessing or a headache for PSII investigators. If a well-designed and well-functioning management of change system is in place, then following the electronic trail can be greatly aided by rigorous security measures. On the other hand, an incomplete or inconsistent security system and management of change system can present impossible obstacles to determining the exact causes of a particular electronics event. The basis for certain decisions can be permanently lost if the management of change system is inadequate.

Lasers, radioactive devices, complex chemical reaction kinetics, fiberoptics, biomedical, biological hazards, and high tech laboratory devices represent additional unique technologies that are normally outside the PSII team skill level. For such investigations it is reasonable, appropriate, and cost effective to engage outside resources for selected tasks during the investigation.

4.13. REFERENCES

1. *A Resource Guide for Implementing the Process Safety Code of Management Practices.* Washington, DC: Chemical Manufacturers Association, 1990.
2. U.S. Department of Energy, 1985. *Accident/Incident Investigation Manual,* 2nd ed. DOE/SSDC 76-45/27. Washington, DC: U.S. Department of Energy.

3. Ferry, T. S. 1988. *Modern Accident Investigation and Analysis,* 2nd ed. New York: John Wiley.
4. Lees, F. P. 1980. *Loss Prevention in the Process Industries,* Vols I and II. Boston: Butterworths.
5. Stephens, M. M. 1970. *Minimizing Damage to Refineries.* Washington, DC: U.S. Department of Interior, Office of Oil and Gas.
6. *Guidelines for Technical Management of Chemical Process Safety,* 1989. New York: Center for Chemical Process Safety, American Institute of Chemical Engineers.
7. Bulkley, W. L., *Technical Investigation of Major Process-Industry Accidents.* AIChE Loss Prevention Series #0823. New York: American Institute of Chemical Engineers.
8. McIntyre, D., *Assessment of Fire and Explosion Damage to Chemical Plant Equipment/Analyzing Explosions and Pressure Vessel Ruptures,* Materials Technology Institute of the Chemical Process Industries, Publication #30, National Association of Corrosion Engineers.
9. Thielsch, H. *Defects and Failures in Pressure Vessels and Piping,* Malabar, Florida: R. E. Krieger Publishing.
10. Crowl, D. and J. Louvar, 1990. *Chemical Process Safety—Fundamentals with Applications.* Englewood Cliffs, NJ: Prentice Hall.
11. Pieterson, *Report TNO—Mexico City LPG Terminal Disaster.*
12. Kuhlman, R., *Professional Accident Investigation. Loganville, GA:* Institute Press—International Loss Control Institute.
13. NFPA 902M. *Fire Reporting Field Incident Manual.* Quincy, MA: National Fire Protection Association.
14. NFPA 906M. *Guide for Fire Incident Field Notes.* Quincy, MA: National Fire Protection Association.
15. NFPA 907M. *Investigation of Fires of Electrical Origin.* Quincy, MA: National Fire Protection Association.
16. *Fire Investigators Handbook.* 1980. Washington, D.C.: U.S. Department of Commerce, National Bureau of Standards.
17. Marks, L. S. and T. Baumeister. *Standard Handbook for Mechanical Engineers,* 7th ed. New York: McGraw-Hill.
18. Althouse, et al., 1980. *Modern Welding.* South Holland, IL: Goodheart-Willcox Co., Inc.
19. Perry, R., *Chemical Engineers Handbook,* 6th ed. New York: McGraw-Hill.
20. NFPA 422M. *Manual for Aircraft Fire and Explosion Investigators,* 1989. Quincy, MA: National Fire Protection Association.
21. Cote A.E., and J. L. Linville Eds. Fire Protection Handbook, NFPA, 17th ed. Quincy, MA: National Fire Protection Association.
22. Carper, K. 1989. *Forensic Engineering.* New York: Elsevier.
23. O'Connor, P. D. 1991. *Practical Reliability Engineering,* 3rd ed. New York: John Wiley.
24. Berrin, E. 1982. *Investigative Photography, Technology Report 83- 1.* Boston: Society of Fire Protection Engineers.
25. Laborde, G. Z. *Influencing with Integrity: Management Skills for Communications and Negotiation.* Palo Alto, CA: Syntony Publishing Co. Pp. 92–106.
26. Smallwood, R. E. 1991. *Laboratory Testing in Support of Failure Analysis.* Internal Report, American Cyanamid Company.
27. NFPA 422M, *Aircraft Fire and Explosion Investigations,* Section 5- 13. Quincy, MA: National Fire Protection Association.

5

MULTIPLE CAUSE DETERMINATION

Guidelines for identifying the multiple causes present in every process safety incident are presented in this chapter. These causes will become the foundation for the recommended preventive measures addressed in Chapter 6 ("Recommendations and Follow-Through"). As with preceding chapters, this chapter assumes a fully implemented management system is in place for investigating process safety incidents (see Chapter 3 and Chapter 8, "Development and Implementation.") This chapter also assumes that a trained investigation team has completed a large portion of the initial gathering of evidence and information (see Chapter 4).

This chapter is organized around a systematic approach as illustrated in the multiple cause determination flowchart (Figure 5-1). Multiple cause concepts are first developed by expanding on the principles established in Chapter 2. Next a collection of analytical techniques is presented. Special attention is given to human factors associated with incident causes. Use of a fact/hypothesis matrix is discussed. The flowchart is presented in a step-by-step approach, and finally, case history examples are used to illustrate application of the multiple-cause systems-oriented approach.

5.1. INTRODUCTION

5.1.1. Overview

If failure of an important piece of hardware occurs and no changes are made in the way it is operated or maintained, then the failure will very likely occur again. Many times, of course, something *is* done, yet the failure *still recurs*! Frequently, this is because the corrective actions address symptoms rather than causes.

The objective of incident investigation is to prevent a recurrence

That is accomplished by establishing a management system that:

- Identifies and evaluates causes (root causes and contributing causes).
- Identifies and evaluates recommended preventive measures that act to reduce the probability and/or consequence.
- Ensures effective implementation follow-up to complete and/or review all recommendations.

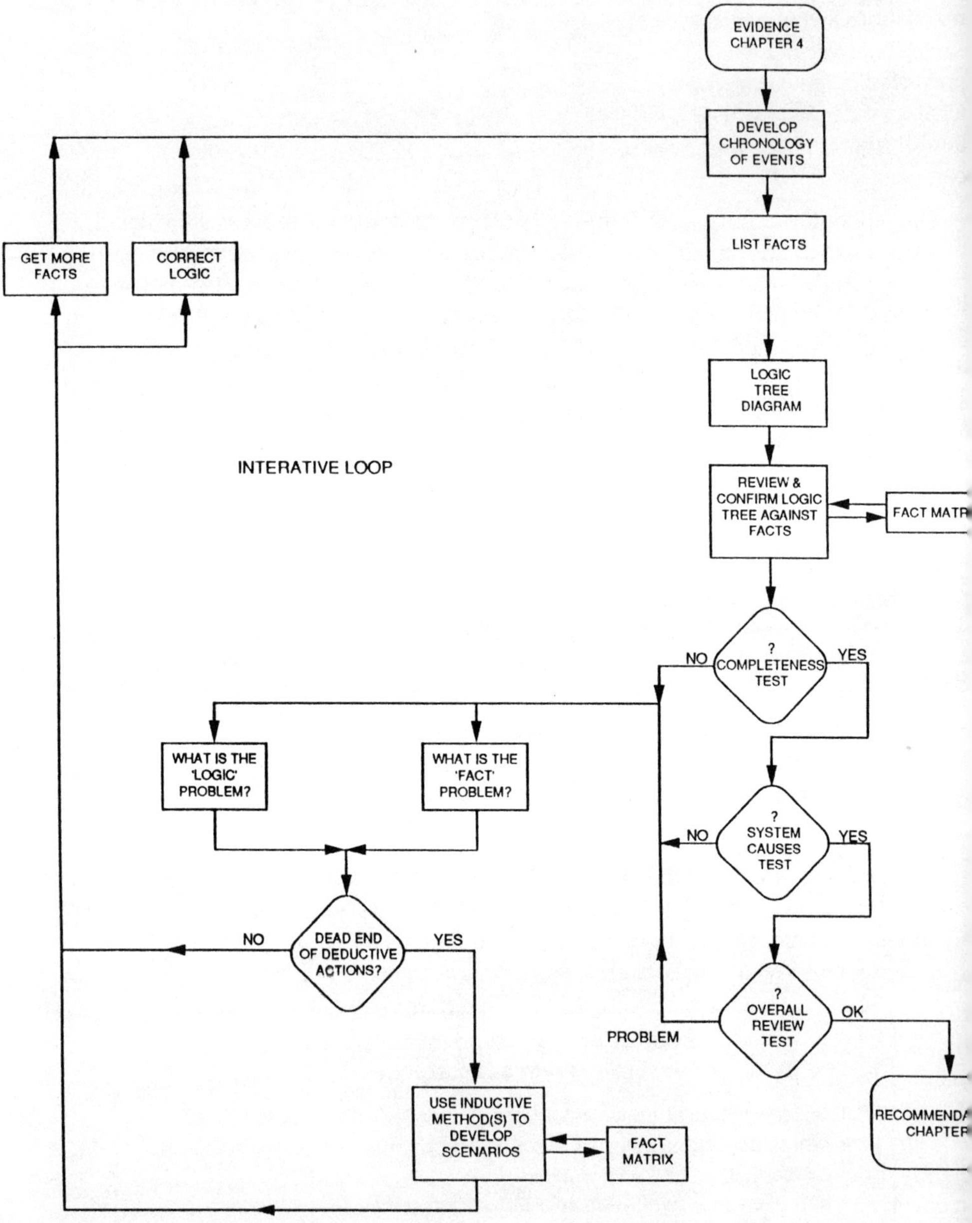

Figure 5-1: Flowchart showing multiple cause determination.

As established in Chapter 1, prevention of a repeat incident is achieved by completing three tasks. The first task is determining the causes, and it is a necessary precursor for the other two tasks. The other two tasks deal with identifying recommendations and implementing preventive action.

Figure 5-1 presents an overview of the approach for multiple cause analysis as presented in this chapter. The process begins by using the evidence gathered (see Chapter 4) to develop a chronology of events. The known facts are listed and a logic tree diagram is built using them. The logic tree is then reviewed and analyzed for completeness.

This completeness test is the first of three quality control measures. In most cases, the initial tree diagram will indicate missing facts, apparently contradicting facts, or incompletely developed logic branches. Therefore, the PSII team will use an iterative loop to resolve gaps, contradictions, or problems. If the deductive process approaches an apparent "dead-end," then one or more inductive methods can be applied to restart the process.

The second quality control test is a pause to verify that causes being identified are systems-related type causes. The third and final quality control test is a pause to look at the overall result to ensure that it is compatible with logic rules and to incorporate any information or concerns not yet addressed.

If this last review is acceptable, then the investigation has identified the multiple underlying causes, and the team is ready to proceed with recommendations. Section 5.3 of this chapter addresses each step of the flowchart in expanded detail.

> ....It is from identifying the underlying causes that the most benefit is gained. This is because by addressing the immediate cause, one only prevents the identical accident from occurring again; by addressing the underlying cause, one prevents numerous other similar incidents from occurring....
>
> [Source: *Guidelines for Technical Management of Chemical Process Safety*. New York: CCPS/AIChE, 1989.]

5.1.2. Concept of Multiple Causes

Process safety incidents are the result of multiple causes. The investigation team must therefore develop event scenarios supported by logical reconstruction of all the facts in order to determine the most likely scenario. In all cases, several causes act in conjunction to result in a particular incident. Singling out just one particular cause is of little value in preventing a repeat of a similar incident.

The term "root cause" has been used by investigation practitioners in several slightly different contexts. For the purpose of this book, root cause is taken to mean an underlying system-related prime (the most basic) reason why an incident occurred. Although there are alternate definitions, they are slightly different in focus and will not be used.

ROOT CAUSE:
An underlying prime reason why an incident occurred.

Another important term in PSII is "management system," which is defined as a structured, systematic method to implement an identifiable set of activities to achieve desired results. Management systems consist of many components; technology, process, plant equipment and other physical systems, employees, supervisors, managers, policies and procedures. The human is an integral portion of the system, and human reliability and human factors play important roles in management systems. Each person has an individual responsibility to perform within a preestablished framework. Individual managers have distinct roles and responsibilities in the overall management system. There is a shared responsibility to function as an interdependent team. Root causes are intimately interrelated to management systems. The majority of PSII recommendations will address modifications to management systems.

> ...experienced incident investigators know that such specific failures are but the immediate causes of an incident, and that underlying each such immediate cause is a management system failure, such as faulty design or inadequate training....
> [Source: *Guidelines for Technical Management of Chemical Process Safety.* New York: CCPS/AIChE, 1989.]

5.1.3. Multiple Cause Analysis

Finding multiple root causes is not always simple or straightforward. Multiple root cause analysis is approached from one of two fundamental perspectives: deductive or inductive. Deductive logic progresses from the general to the specific. With the major event or general concept at the top level, the logic progresses *backward* in time (sometimes called a "backward search") examining possible scenarios for the path to the top event. Fault tree analysis is one example of the deductive approach (see Section 2.5.1.1).

Inductive logic picks a starting event or set of facts and then moves *forward* in time, examining possible effects, results, outcomes, or consequences. It is sometimes called a "forward search." A deviation from normal operating conditions is chosen, then the study group proceeds to develop the reasonable outcome or effects of the deviation. The hazard and operability study (HAZOP) is one example of the inductive approach.

Multiple root-cause analysis involves a deductive search for all credible ways in which an event could occur. It can be viewed as an integrated method for systematically searching for all underlying root causes. The structured framework helps the investigator to keep on track, to reach sufficient depth, and not to stop at the symptoms or apparent causes.

As the analysis proceeds, certain findings will begin to emerge. A common intermediate level finding may be that "an operator failed to follow established sampling procedures for hazardous chemicals." The investigator could possibly stop at this point and state, "The cause of the incident was failure to follow established procedure." Then the investigator might proceed to evaluate how best to get the operator to follow the established procedure as a recommendation to prevent recurrence. Stopping at this point would be a mistake since, *failure to follow established procedure* is not necessarily a root cause.

A root cause approach would look further into the reason(s) for the operator failing to follow the procedure by considering such questions as:

1. Was a procedure used?
If not, does a procedure exist? Is one available? Is it reasonably convenient for use? Is it too difficult to use? Is the use not required or consistently enforced? Some issues involved in these questions might be policies, standards, administrative controls, supervisory practices, or training.

2. Was the procedure followed incorrectly?
If yes, was the format confusing? Were the instructions ambiguous? Were the limits, details or graphics less than adequate? Was the check-off misused?

3. Was the given procedure itself wrong?
If yes, was it a typographical error? Was the sequence or the facts wrong? Was the situation not covered? Was an out-of-date revision used?

5.1.4. Illustrative Case Histories

To give further insight into the distinction between multiple root causes and non–root causes, consider the following actual case histories.

FLIXBOROUGH
At Flixborough in the U.K. in 1974, 28 people died in an explosion resulting from a large release of cyclohexane.[1] The source of the hydrocarbon release was a failed expansion joint in a section of pipe 20 inches (508 mm) in diameter. Investigation revealed the pipe had been "designed" with little technical input as a temporary bypass for a reactor that had been removed after developing a crack.

The "apparent" cause was a failed expansion joint. Fixing or replacing the expansion joint was the apparent preventive remedy. However, a more thorough root-cause analysis looked deeper into the reasons why the joint failed. Here are some of the identified underlying root causes:

- The management system for reviewing, approving, and managing changes to process equipment was inadequate and needed substantial modification. Temporary modifications were not reviewed by the appropriate technical discipline.

- The reactor failed due to stress corrosion cracking from nitrates. The source of the nitrates was water sprayed from an external hose used for supplementary cooling. The inadequate cooling capacity was resolved with a less than adequate technical solution.

***CHALLENGER* SPACE SHUTTLE**

The *Challenger* space shuttle disaster (January 1986) was the culmination of a series of events each with its own root cause.

The actual recommendations submitted by the Presidential Commission focused on *root* causes, that is, changes in management systems that would not only fix the ring joint problem, as well as the systems, procedures, and overall approaches to identifying, evaluating, resolving, monitoring, and auditing safety related concerns.

The immediate cause was failure of the ring joint seal on the solid rocket booster. Yet a root-cause analysis revealed a much more complex scenario. According to information published after the investigation, postflight evidence from as far back as early 1984 showed that the joint seals were failing to meet design specifications. Engineers knew, almost 2 years before the incident, that holes were being blown in the putty that shielded the *primary* O-rings from hot gases. In addition, evidence from 1983 showed the *secondary* O-rings were experiencing problems due to joint rotation during launch conditions. The reduced flexibility of the O-rings at temperatures below 50°F was also known. In July 1985, the concerns had grown to the point that further launches were postponed until the problems with the joint were remedied. The *Challenger* space shuttle disaster is an excellent example for showing the principle that apparently simple mechanical problems are related to more complex underlying causes rooted in management systems.

PIPER ALPHA RIG DISASTER

The Piper Alpha oil rig disaster resulted in 167 fatalities in July 1988. The offshore processing platform in the North Sea was completely destroyed by fire and a series of explosions. The source of the initial fire was a leaking hydrocarbon pump. Operating personnel apparently tried to return the pump to service while repair work had not been completed. Initial emergency response was severely hampered by inadequately functioning fire protection systems. Multiple root-cause analysis identified needed improvements in the management systems for lock-out/tag-out, for auditing and ensuring fire protection reliability, and for design standards for crew quarters isolation.

5.1.5. Type 3 Approach

As previously addressed in Chapters 1 and 2, the Type 3 approach for investigating process incidents is based on multiple-cause and systems-oriented concepts. The focus of Type 1 investigations is often limited to determining the immediate specific remedies that would prevent an exact repeat of the incident circumstances. Type 2 investigations are broader in perspective and typically focus on effective barriers to reduce the probability or consequences. The Type 3 approach recognizes that incidents have multiple underlying causes. Type 3 investigations attempt to identify and implement system changes that will eliminate recurrence not only of the exact incident, but of similar events as well.

> ***THREE APPROACHES TO PSII***
>
> **Type 1:** Traditional, informal investigation performed by immediate supervisor.
>
> **Type 2:** Committee-based investigation using expert judgment to find a credible solution of cause and remedy.
>
> **Type 3:** Multiple-cause, systems-oriented investigation that focuses on root cause determination. Integrated with an overall process safety management program.

This Type 3 approach improves quality of investigations by directing the focus from the surface causes to the underlying causes and mandating a search for multiple causes. One strength of this systematic approach is that a complex incident can be separated into discrete small events and each piece can be examined individually.

It is not the intention of the CCPS to endorse one particular method, but to present guidance on the various options and applications available. However, a structured methodology that seeks out multiple underlying systems related causes of an incident is generally most useful in the broad spectrum of activities in the CPI.

> **SOME GUIDING QUESTIONS FOR MULTIPLE CAUSE DETERMINATION.**
>
> ***WHY? (Keep asking WHY? WHY?)***
>
> What was the underlying cause?
>
> Was there a system related deficiency (or weakness) that caused or allowed this condition to exist, or caused or allowed the event to proceed?

5.2. TOOL KIT FOR MULTIPLE CAUSE DETERMINATION

5.2.1. Logic Tree Diagram

The logic tree is a systematic mechanism for organizing and analyzing the elements of the incident scenario. Standard symbols from systems theory are used to construct the logic tree diagram. The diagram often takes the form of a qualitative fault tree, showing the incident as the top event and the various branches using conventional AND- and OR-gates. Some investigators have simplified development of the logic tree by using a universal gate (not distinguishing between AND-conditions and OR-conditions).

As detailed in Section 2.5.1.1, there are several deductive investigation techniques that use logic tree diagrams. A partial list of these proven methods includes management oversight and risk tree (MORT), fault tree analysis (FTA), causal tree method (CTM), multiple-cause systems-oriented incident investigation (MCSOII), and accident evolution and barrier technique (AEB). Table 2-1 presents a matrix of the various techniques, their characteristics, strengths, and limitations.

Logic tree diagrams are developed after the PSII team has assembled the initial facts and has established a preliminary starting point for the sequence of events, as shown in Figure 5-1. A highly simplified and generic logic tree for a fire incident is shown in Figure 5-2. The top event is defined as the unwanted fire, with fuel, oxygen, and ignition depicted in the three branch conditions leading to the top event. Each of the three branches would then be examined, developed, and expanded into further detail as the investigation progresses.

The diagram can be developed from the top downward and can model a system, a subsystem, or an individual component. For each level, a set of *necessary* and *sufficient* lower-order conditions or events is identified. During logic tree construction, the developers should ensure hierarchy and completeness. This is done by "looking" *upward* to indicate *why* the item must be achieved (is this necessary?) and by "looking" *downward* to indicate *how* the item is to be satisfied (is this complete?). If the section of the tree does not meet these tests, then the structure should be modified.

5.2.2. Fault Tree Analysis

Since FTA is the foundation for many of the more refined deductive techniques, an understanding of basic fault tree fundamentals is a valuable tool. Fault tree analysis has frequent application in process hazard analysis and is capable of being used in a

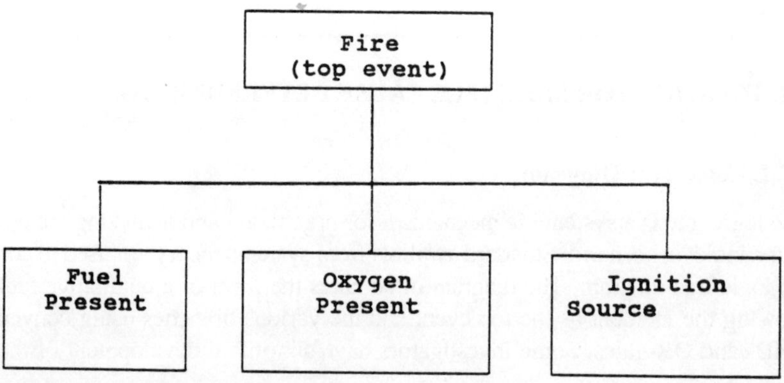

Figure 5-2: Simplified logic tree for a fire.

qualitative or quantitative application. The purpose of a FTA is to identify combinations of system failures (equipment, human, or material) that can result in an incident.

The investigation team starts by selecting a specifically defined top event (incident), postulating that the overall system has failed in a certain general way, then attempting (in a deductive way) to determine what modes of system, component, or human performance contributed to this failure. Thus, FTA focuses on one particular undesired event and provides a method for determining the multiple underlying causes for that event. A strength of FTA is its ability to break down an accident into basic equipment failures and human errors. This enables the investigator to develop preventive measures for several causes to reduce the likelihood of an incident.

FAULT TREE TERMINOLOGY

The system failure or incident of concern is called the *Top Event.* The failures described in a fault tree can be grouped into three classes:

Primary faults or failures that *cannot* be attributed to some external force or equipment.

Secondary faults and failures that occur in an environment for which the equipment was not intended. These kinds of faults can be attributed to some *external* force or equipment.

Command faults and failures occur when the component operates properly but at the wrong time or in the place. These kinds of faults can be attributed to the source of the incorrect command.

The above three groups are important when defining "stopping rules" for FTA, that is, how to know that a fault tree is sufficiently complete. The basis for fault tree construction lies in the application of logic gates (other fault tree symbols are used to explain the overall system structure and analysis boundaries). The most important logic gates are the OR-gate and the AND-gate (other gates are used occasionally).

The AND-gate is such that the *output fault occurs if all the input events occur.*

The OR-gate is such that the *output event occurs if one or more of the input events occur.*

Other frequently used fault tree symbols follow:

BASIC Event: The BASIC event represents a basic equipment fault or failure that requires no further development into more basic faults or failures.

INTERMEDIATE Event: The INTERMEDIATE event represents a fault event that results from the interactions of other fault events that are developed through logic gates such as those defined above.

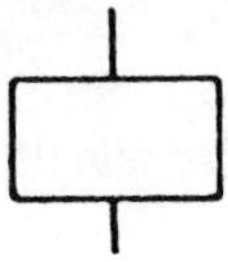

UNDEVELOPED Event: The UNDEVELOPED event represents a fault event that is not examined further because information is unavailable or because its consequence is insignificant.

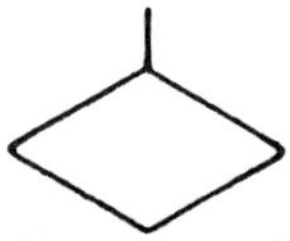

TRANSFER Symbol: The TRANSFER IN symbol indicates that the fault tree is developed further at the occurrence of the corresponding TRANSFER OUT symbol (e.g., on another page). The symbols are labeled using numbers or a code system to ensure that they can be differentiated.

IN OUT

EXTERNAL or HOUSE Event: The EXTERNAL or HOUSE event represents a condition or an event that is assumed to exist as a boundary condition for the fault tree.

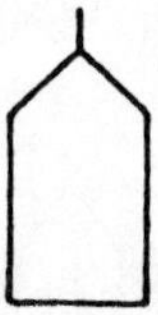

BASIC RULES FOR FAULT TREE CONSTRUCTION

- **Rule 1:** Write the statements that are entered in the rectangular event boxes as faults: State precisely what the fault is and when it occurs.
- **Rule 2:** Ask the question, "Can this fault consist of a component fault failure?"
  —If the answer is yes, then classify the event as *a state-of-component-fault*, and go to Rule 3.
  —If the answer is no, then classify the event as a *state-of-system-fault*, and go to Rule 4.
- **Rule 3:** If the event is a *state-of-component-fault* add an OR-gate below the event, then look for primary, secondary, and command modes.
- **Rule 4:** If the event is a *state-of-system-fault*, look for the minimum necessary and sufficient immediate cause or causes. This may require an AND-gate.

Using FTA convention, identical subbranches may appear in several branches. These duplicated structures are shown fully developed, usually only in one place on the tree, and then handled by transfer gates (a triangle with a reference identifier).

EXAMPLE OF SIMPLIFIED FAULT TREE

Referring to the fictitious case study incident contained in Appendix F, a major fire and explosion occurred in the catalyst area. One of the causes was rupture of a feed

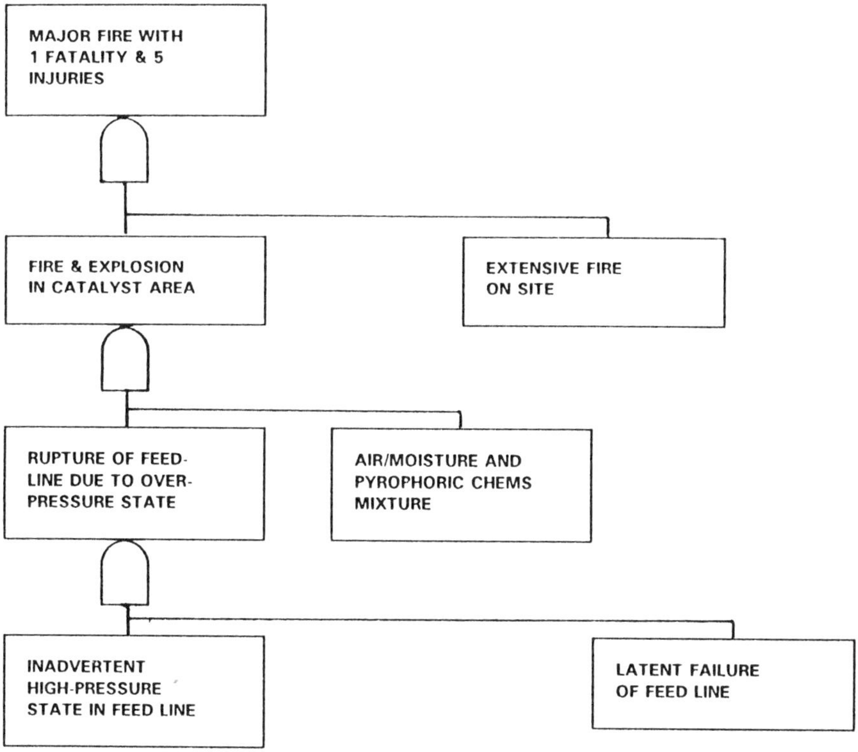

Figure 5-3: Partial fault tree—major fire.

line. The feed line overpressured due to inadvertent high pressure combined with a latent failure of the pipe system (AND-gate). These relationships are shown in Figure 5-3.

Each of these causes can then be further explored by asking the question "Why did this event occur?" The pipe failure branch of the tree might look like this, with an OR-gate structure. Either the corrosion control management system was less than adequate, or perhaps an improper choice of materials was made.

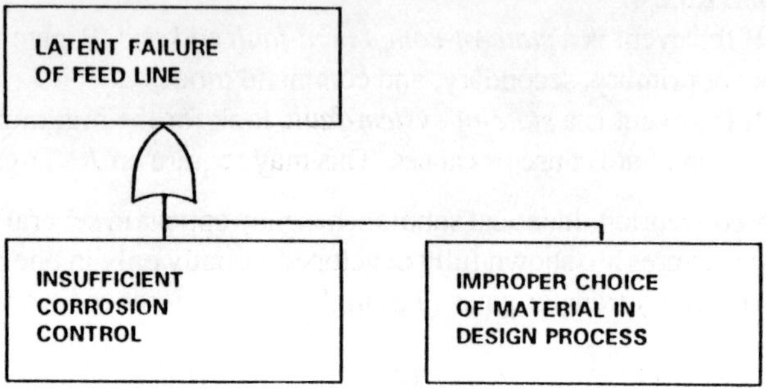

The high pressure branch can be further developed to:

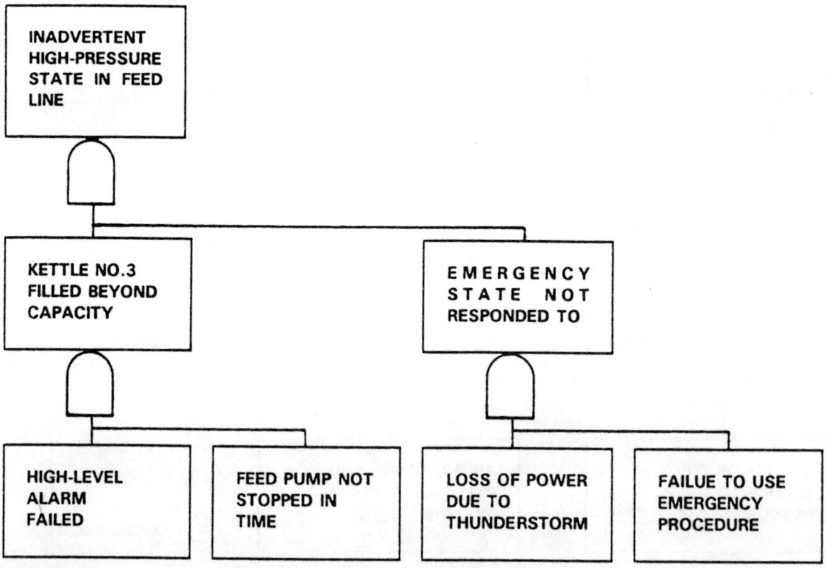

5.2.3. Guidelines for Stopping Tree Development

After the most likely scenario has been identified and the logic tree developed, the PSII team now reaches the stage of searching out the system-related multiple causes, with the accompanying challenge of deciding when to stop further tree development.

Application of "stopping rules" to multiple root-cause analysis has fundamental impact on the resources required and the final quality obtained for the completed tree. Normally the quality of a logic tree is a direct function of the level of detail of the tree structure. To achieve a detailed logic tree for multiple root-cause analysis, the investigator will have to consider *all* aspects of the incident, *regardless* of the perceived or known importance. A root cause is, by definition, an identified "prime" reason that caused the incident and normally requires a change in a management system in order to achieve prevention. Process safety incidents will in almost all cases have multiple causes.

An important aspect of root cause analysis is knowing when to stop the progression down the tree. While there is no easy or universal solution to this question, management system changes are a reliable indicator. If a management system requires a substantial change to correct a deficiency, then the item is a strong candidate for being a root cause. These deficiencies can include breakdowns, oversights, weakness, intolerance for reasonably anticipated variations, failure to audit periodically, or failure to incorporate changes caused by changes in other systems. Judgment is needed to determine a realistic stopping point for downward tree development. In the case of FTA and most other logic tree approaches, it is always theoretically possible to develop another lower level for any event.

Determining the appropriate "stopping place" is not an easy and straightforward activity. The general tendency is to stop the downward tree development of each branch when the first root cause is identified. Sometimes, however, it is desirable to continue the downward branch to identify additional causes for a management system breakdown. Usually the downward progression is stopped at the component level for devices supplied by outside manufacturers, unless the device is normally opened, repaired, calibrated, adjusted, or inspected by in-house personnel. Electronic black boxes (similar to those under the hood of our automobiles) are good examples. We as owners may have occasion to manipulate the connection points (wires, attachment, and securing brackets) but we do not open nor usually attempt to diagnose an internal malfunction of these devices. For work on our automobile electronics black boxes, we turn to experts who are specially trained and who have special equipment.

In a similar fashion, there are certain systems that are assembled and maintained by operators of chemical plants. For example, for a control valve system, various components may be purchased separately and then be assembled and configured by plant personnel. The PSII team would investigate possible accident causes associated with the methods of assembly, maintenance, inspection, and calibration of the control valve system. But if a malfunction of a factory-sealed subcomponent was involved, the PSII team would seek out the appropriate expertise. The team would *not* attempt to analyze any factory supplied components that normally remain sealed, without additional help. If the malfunction contributed to the incident, it should be investigated until it is understood, especially if similar components are in use elsewhere.

CASE STUDY—AN EMPLOYEE SLIPS AND FALLS

Recalling the three approaches to PSII, consider the following typical incident.

A worker was walking on a concrete walkway in the process unit. There was some lube oil on the pad. He stepped into the oil, slipped, and fell. It was a sunny day, the worker was not carrying anything, was not distracted, and was not doing any particularly urgent task.

A traditional (Type 1) investigation would identify the cause as "oil spilled on pad" and the proposed remedy would most likely be limited to cleaning up this one particular spill and admonishing the worker in some fashion. A more sophisticated investigation (Type 2) approach would attempt to determine the *source* of the oil and specific preventive measures to prevent spillage, such as an improved container. The investigation may be extended to search for similar hazards in the immediate and adjacent areas. This investigation certainly comes closer to achieving prevention of a repeat incident.

A multiple-cause system-oriented investigation (Type 3) would further explore the underlying causes and examine the systems and conditions involved in the incident. Some items that would be considered follow:

- How did the oil come to be on the pad in the first place? (Source, frequency, tasks involved.)
- Why did the oil remain on the pad? (How long had it been there? What is the "normal" condition for working/walking surfaces in that unit?)
- What influenced the employee to walk into the oil? (Did he notice it? Are there training or consistent enforcement aspects involved?)

Thus the top portion of the logic tree may look something like this:

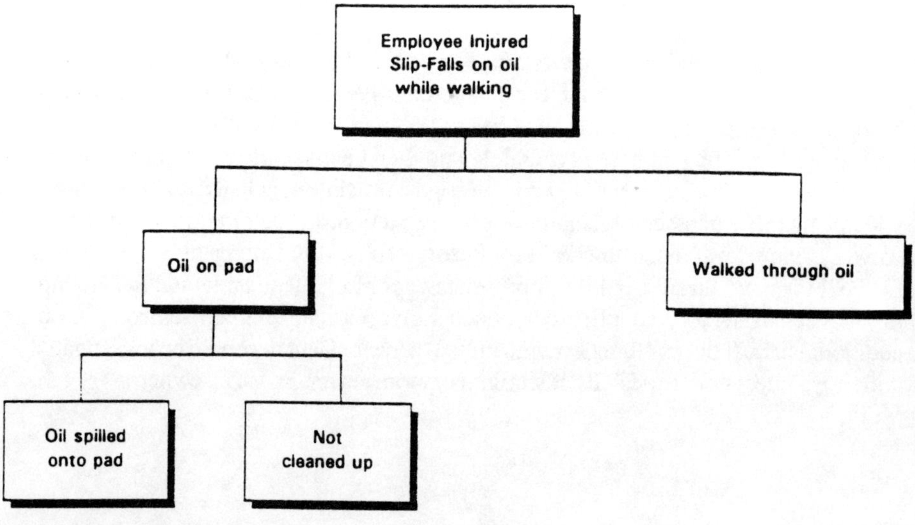

Each of the succeeding lower level events is further developed by repeatedly asking the question, "Why did this event occur?" Pursuing just one branch, for example the *Oil Spilled onto Pad* branch would lead to two possible sources: *Leak from Pipe* and/or *Hand Carried Containers.*

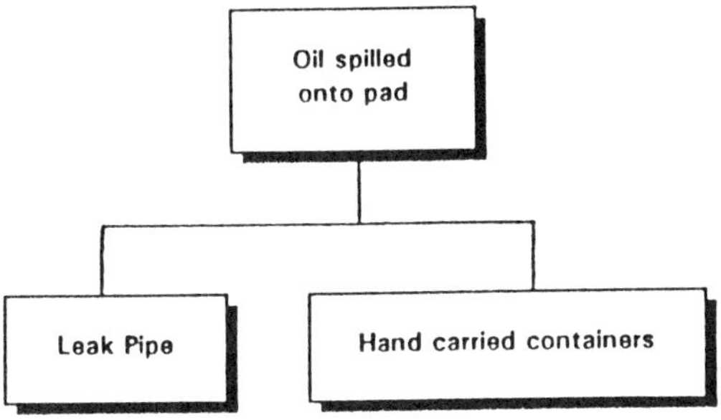

Further developing just one of these sources, hand carried containers, would yield additional subcategories.

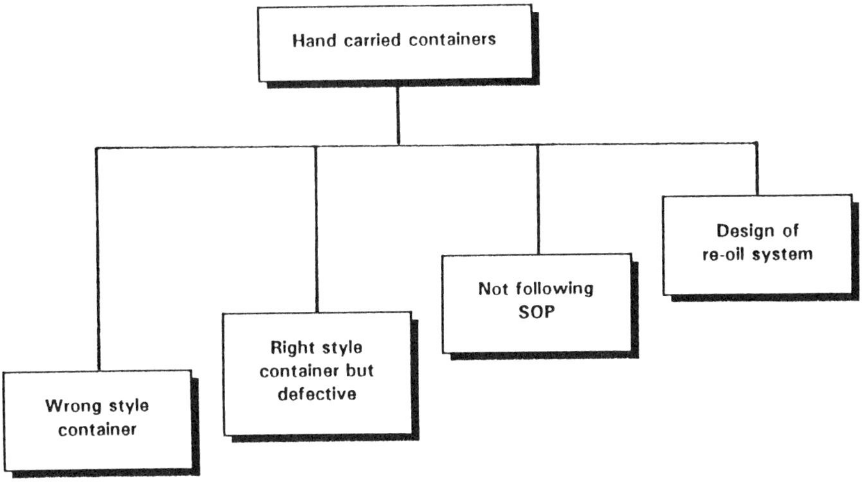

Each of these four subcategories can now be examined individually. Selecting one (*Right Style Container but Defective*) and returning to the concept of management systems leads to the following considerations.

- What is the management system involved in inspecting, repairing, or replacing the containers?
- Is the management system properly designed and arranged to achieve the desired output?
- Is the management system clearly understood and consistently enforced?

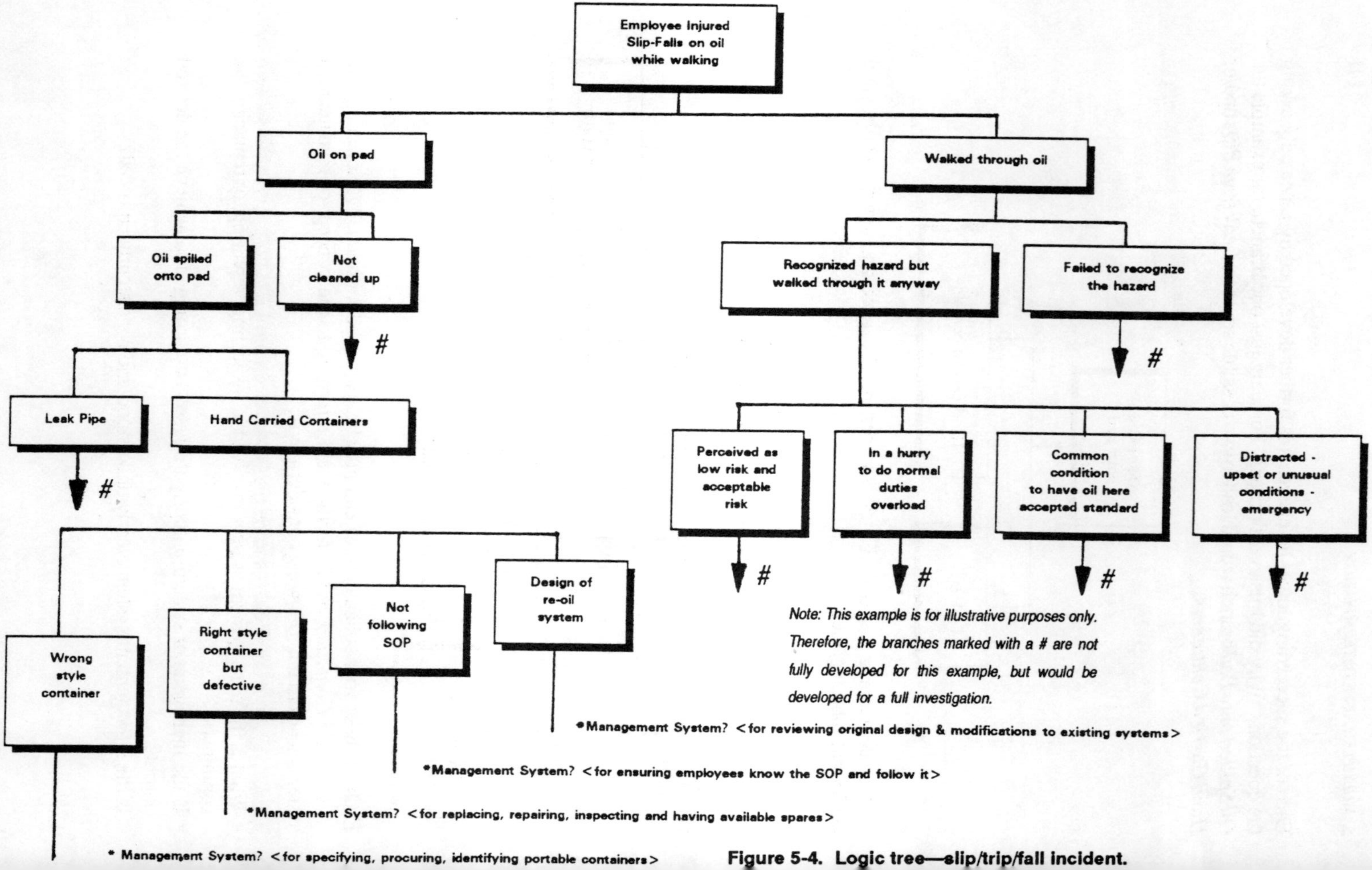

Figure 5-4. Logic tree—slip/trip/fall incident.

Figure 5-4 shows a partially developed logic tree for the issues just addressed.

Thus, in a systematic way, the logic tree provides a structure for thoroughly considering possible multiple causes. Each of the succeeding lower levels is developed by repeatedly asking "Why?" until a level is reached that allows examination of a management system or a small segment of it. The particular management system would then be scrutinized for deficiencies that caused or contributed to the incident. Identifying deficiencies provides foundation for recommended improvements and preventive action.

Another criteria for stopping the development of the tree relates to the ability to control the events, or ability to take preventive or even mitigating action. There are significant differences in the ability to control *internal* events as opposed to *external* events. Company A may experience a massive explosion and toxic vapor release that injures employees at the adjacent plant of Company B. Investigators and managers at Company B may not be able to change systems within Company A to prevent a repeat explosion and release. Therefore, Company B may have to limit the focus on those internal actions which they *can* undertake to mitigate the effects of the release. Such items as alerts, alarms, evacuations, training, personal protective equipment, or other emergency preparedness and emergency response actions all represent internal actions that Company B *can* address.

The guideline is to stop the development of the tree when the events become external to the point that they can no longer be controlled by your organization. The extreme case example is the airplane crash into the chemical plant, sometimes called the "747 Scenario." The chemical company would have control of the emergency response and damage mitigation aspects of the incident. The plant investigation team would start at the crash itself and look at how to reduce the *effects* of catastrophic collisions in the future. They would also look at how emergency systems responded. The owner of the aircraft would have control of the *crash prevention* investigation and remedies. Each side would stop its tree development at the point where it no longer had control of the events.

ASKING THE RIGHT QUESTIONS

At this point, the investigation process has identified the actual sequence of events that occurred. The next task is one of identifying why the event occurred. Not until the "why" has been truly answered can corrective or remedial actions can be employed.

Consider the case of a physical system component failure, such as a bolt or a gasket. When an unexpected failure occurs, it is because either (1) something changed while the component was operating and a increased load was imposed on the component or, (2) the strength of the component was degraded but had been undetected. Investigators would focus on issues such as:

- What was the management system involved in this failure?
- Why didn't the management system for plant surveillance, test, or inspection programs detect the incipient failure?

- Why didn't the plant preventive maintenance program prevent the failure?
- If the failure resulted directly from a human error, what was the underlying reason for this error?

5.2.4. Human Factors Applications

Investigators are discovering that increased opportunities to improve process safety management can be found in the area of human performance and human reliability. Technology advances have resulted in increasingly complex and highly automated processes. System designers are now considering the expectations placed on the operator. As previously defined in Chapter 2, "human factors" is a discipline concerned with matching the system to human capabilities and limitations. Uncorrected human performance deficiencies can result in duplicate incidents.

Example: *If a component fails as a result of a human error, "counseling" the worker may prevent him or her from performing the same error again, but what of the other members of the operating crew? Conditions that led up to the original failure remain, so other crew members are still prone to repeating the error! Many repeat events could be avoided if the correct information and reasons for them are uncovered by the investigatory team.*

Multiple root-cause analysis acts to uncover the base reasons for human error and as a result provide guidance on suitable corrective actions. Human error is discussed in Section 2.4. There are special analytical methods designed specifically to study human performance. Sanders and McCormic define human error as an inappropriate or undesirable human decision or behavior that reduces, or has the potential for reducing effectiveness, safety, or system performance.[5]

Four common classes of human errors are[6]

- Errors of omission
- Errors of commission
- Sequence errors
- Timing errors

Errors of omission are obviously defined by omission of a required, necessary, or appropriate action. *Errors of commission* include failing to act correctly, doing the wrong thing, or using the wrong procedure to attempt to do the right thing. *Sequence errors* are tasks that are done out of order, such as disconnecting a chemical transfer hose before de-pressuring it. Failure to execute a task within the proper time frame is an example of a *timing error,* doing something too quickly or too slowly. There are other types of human error that should be considered during the search for root causes. A partial list includes high-stress errors; low-stress errors; errors associated with information processing; errors in detecting, recognizing, and diagnosing deviations.

Traditional investigations (Type 1 and Type 2) have tended to stop once the topic of human error was identified. on the other hand, systematic multiple root cause investigations (Type 3) require that the underlying causes of the human errors be identified. The PSII team should attempt to determine what management systems improvements could be made to remedy the particular human error associated with the incident under investigation. **Oversimplification of the human error cause branch is an avoidable mistake for PSII.**

Designers and manufacturers of aircraft often use a "performance envelope" concept to summarize the expected and intended performance specifications of their product. If the limits of the envelope are approached or exceeded, reliable performance cannot be expected. In the same way, workers function best in a fairly well identified performance envelope of working conditions—temperature, lighting, reach limits, exertion limits, data input load limits, decision making burden limits, and many others. Exceeding these known limits will result in significantly reduced performance, and a resulting increase in human error. Investigators and designers should be constantly on the lookout for opportunities to make a system more reliable by making it less error prone and more error tolerant.

Some examples of commonly encountered human performance deficiencies include:

- Errors that resulted in the component being unavailable when needed: not restored to full operability following an earlier maintenance, test, or inspection activity (e.g., valves closed, actuation or protective systems not reconnected, slip-blinds left in the line, pump selector switches not being left in the standby autostart position).
- Maintenance errors that led to the component being left in a condition in which the likelihood of failure was increased: loose bolting, misaligned shafts and bearings, gaskets not sealed, internal clearances incorrect, foreign materials left in the component or system, etc.
- Operator errors that initiate process upsets due to valving errors, that is, closing the wrong valve, opening a bypass valve at the wrong time, lining up to pump from or to the wrong tank.

It is not uncommon for a cause analysis of human performance problems to be looked at as an add-on to an already completed incident investigation. This may occur because the analysis was originally limited to an incident report generated from a Type 2 investigation. However, the Type 3 multiple-cause systems-oriented investigation includes human performance considerations, and can be very successful in addressing human factors mismatches. Some of the available techniques come with extensive check lists and flowcharts that help the investigators address human performance problems or concerns. The investigator does not have to be a psychologist or an expert on human reliability analysis to do a reasonably competent job. Numerous "interface devices" have been developed that translate theoretical models of human error

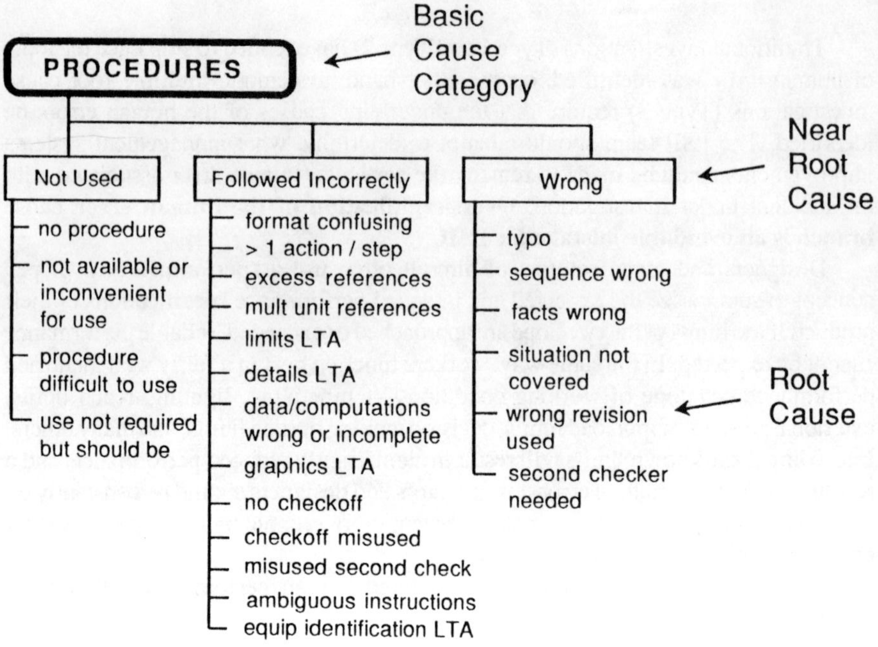

Figure 5-5. Example of hierarchical structure and root causes. LTA = Less than adequate. [From Paradies and Busch, 1990. Copyright 1990 by System Improvements, Inc., Knoxville, TN. Reprinted by permission.]

causation into easy-to-understand engineering terms.[7] Some of these devices are in the form of check lists or logic trees,[8] see Figures 5-5 and 5-6.

Incident investigators should be alert for human errors caused by a mismatch between the system design and reasonable expectations of human cognitive performance. Sometimes the designers of chemical processing systems fail to adequately consider reasonable human capability limits. The result can often be a system that promotes human errors rather than discouraging them. These mismatches are addressed in a comprehensive way in the book *The Psychology of Everyday Things*, by D. Norman.[9]

In almost every plant over 5 years old, a search would probably reveal a series of control circuits arranged in illogical sequence. The most common reason is that a minor modification was made, and the most convenient solution was to slightly rearrange the control switches. For example, four pumps in the field may be arranged from north-to-south, A-B-C-D. Yet in the control room the switches may now be configured as A-B-D-C sequence. For most operating conditions, the human operator can cope with the incremental additional mental load, but during emergencies or other high-stress periods each additional mental task will act to decrease the overall performance.

Did the incident involve. . . ?

- ☐ *Inadvertent Operation*
  - ☐ of electric switch or control device
    - ☐ access too difficult
    - ☐ not clearly labeled—ambiguous
    - ☐ arranged such that errors are more likely
- ☐ *Error in Executing Procedure*
  - ☐ Written procedure was not appropriate
    - ☐ system physical changes not incorporated into procedure
    - ☐ new method or sequence not used
    - ☐ original procedure overlooked a hazard
    - ☐ original procedure overlooked a precaution
    - ☐ original procedure was incomplete, overlooked a step
    - ☐ as written, the desired action is not clearly described
    - ☐ consequences of safety deviations not included
    - ☐ responsibility of tasks/assignments are unclear
  - ☐ Written procedure not understood
    - ☐ original training inadequate
    - ☐ refresher training not done
    - ☐ written procedure no longer matches the actual actions in the field
    - ☐ written procedure does not match physical equipment
  - ☐ Procedure written OK but not followed this time
    - ☐ inconsistent enforcement
    - ☐ worker knowingly deviated from SOP
      - ☐ in a hurry
      - ☐ perceived that the action he took was actually more appropriate than what written SOP states
      - ☐ temporary emotional state
      - ☐ response to peer pressure
      - ☐ response to perceived supervisor/managment expectations
    - ☐ communication breakdown

Figure 5.6. Sample check list for human performance factors.

Human performance can be enhanced by conforming to certain expected conventions. PSII teams should be alert for built-in design deviations from normal conventions which are an underlying cause for human error. We all expect the hot water tap to be on the left side and the cold water on the right side. Rising stem gate valves are expected to close if the handle is turned in a clockwise rotation. Deviating from these conventions can be an underlying cause of human error.

5.2.5. Fact/Hypothesis Matrix

A special matrix of facts against hypothesis is another tool available to the PSII team. It has application during the development of the sublevels of the logic tree structure (see Figure 5-1). The matrix can help clarify thinking and compare the known facts against the various hypothetical scenarios. It can be used in the deductive stage, or the inductive stage, if there is one.

Scenarios for many process safety incidents will often be rather complex. The fact/hypothesis matrix technique has proven useful in sorting, analyzing, and comparing information. One side of the matrix lists each plausible scenario, and the other side (usually across the top) lists the known facts, conditions, and stipulations. Each intersecting box is then examined for compatibility, known truthfulness (yes, no, or unknown), and fit into the particular scenario hypothesis. The degree of complexity of this matrix can vary depending on the nature of the incident, from a simple [YES/NO/?] to a variety of categories. A more complex set of matrix conditions might take the form

+ in view of the fact, this supports this scenario as likely or probable
O in view of the fact, this supports a possible, but unlikely scenario
— in view of the fact, this is an unlikely scenario
NA this fact apparently has no relation to this hypothesis
? not enough information is currently available to decide on this fact.

A sample appears in Figure 5-7 for a fictitious incident. Developing the matrix is not a one-time exercise, but is usually added to over a time period. Gradually, some hypothesis will emerge as more likely and others will become less probable.

APPLICATION OF FACT/HYPOTHESIS MATRIX

Example case: *Explosion and fire in anhydrous pachadermguanadiene reduction (APRG) unit.*

Background

- Tank blew up 3 hours after batch product transfer was made,
- Maintenance had recently replaced a gasket on the transfer pump,
- There was a power outage shortly before the incident.

Status

Investigation is incomplete. The PSII team is in second day of investigation, has accumulated some evidence, and has begun to compare known facts against possible scenarios.

The matrix in Figure 5-7 is the result of their initial deliberations and is being used to develop action items and priorities such as which direction the information gathering and cause analysis should proceed.

APRG Explosion

Fact or Condition / Hypothesis	Power Tripped Out 4:09 PM	Operator Added Component "A" To Batch At 10:30 PM	Storage Tank Transfer Made on Evening Shift 7:30 PM	Maintenance Changed Gasket P120B	Top of Tank Found On East Side of Warehouse	Lab Analysis Showed 0 Water in Residue
Contaminated Batch of Incoming Raw Materials	+	+	?	+	+	x
New SOP Not Followed	+	x	+	+	+	?
Engineering May Have Designed or Installed Wrong Pressure Rating for Flanges	+	+	+	x	+	x
Oxygen Entered Nitrogen Header from Back Flow-Preventer Device Failure	+	+	?	x	+	x

Figure 5-7. Example fact/hypothesis matrix. Legend: (+) compatible with hypothesis; (x) not likely, not compatible with hypothesis; (?) undetermined at this time.

5.2.6. Simulations and Re-Creations

Information gained from simulations and re-creations can reveal key insights that explain gaps or contradictions in information. For incidents of unexpected chemical reactions, it is common to attempt a lab scale re-creation of the conditions involved in the exotherm or explosion. Many chemical processes can be modeled and duplicated dynamically by computer algorithms. Accelerated rate calorimeters (ARC) have proven to be highly useful tools for studying exothermic or overpressure runaway reactions.

Two important concepts must be kept in mind when considering use of simulations or re-creations. First, top priority should be prevention of a second injury or incident, which may be caused by the simulation/re-creation activity. This classic error happens with surprising frequency when investigating partial amputations involving cycling of machinery. Considerations for a safer simulation or re-creations include the volume and concentration of reactants, amount and type of reaction initiator (catalysts, ignition source), and special barriers such as personnel protective equipment, overpressure relief devices (capacity, type, and discharge point).

Second, these simulations and re-creations only mimic and do not exactly duplicate the event. The information obtained can be useful, but it is narrow in scope and by nature is obtained under ideal and known conditions. Investigators should be mindful of the limitations and should use discretion when applying the data from these sources.

Investigations involving complex human performance problems can benefit from simulations. Process simulators are often used for operator training. In some cases these process simulators can be excellent tools for learning more about human error causation. The incident investigation team can expose operators to simulated process upsets and gain valuable insights into an operator's response in rapidly and accurately diagnosing the problem and in executing the proper action.

The talk-through exercise is a technique sometimes used by investigators to gain insight and to verify conclusions drawn from verbal testimony. The technique is similar in format to a talk-through emergency drill. To be effective, such exercises must be planned in advance by the investigator. The actual talk-through itself is seldom very time-consuming, but the burden is on the investigator to take good notes and observe any potential problem areas.

The talk-through is a commonly used technique that has particular application for learning more about specific tasks or events. The technique is often used by human reliability analysts. It is a method in which an operator describes the actions required in a task, explains why he or she is doing each action, and explains the associated mental processes. There is a normal protocol for how to organize the talk-through. If the performance is simulated, the operator touches the manual controls that would be operated and describes the control action required. The operator points to displays and states what reading would be expected. Any time delays and feedback signals are described, including any implications of an action to the process function.

A talk-through of control room operations can reveal previously undisclosed information. In a control room analysis, an operator and the investigator actually follow the path taken by the operators during the performance of the procedure being analyzed. When the procedures call for the manipulation of a specific control or for the monitoring of a specific set of displays, the operator and the investigator approach them at the control panels, and the operator points out the controls and displays in question.

5.2.7. Determining Conditions at the Time of Failure

Determining conditions at the time of the failure is an activity bridging the gap between evidence gathering and root cause determination. Failures rarely occur without some prior indication or precursor information. However, unless someone specifically is charged with looking for it, the information is frequently overlooked. A goal of the PSII team is to search back in time, find this information and correlate it with the failure event to confirm or refute a postulated failure hypotheses. This circumstantial evidence may be short term, that is, immediately preceding the failure, or may be long term and include anecdotal information from earlier failures or from previous operating experience.

The documents that are gathered as described in Chapter 4 will be most useful in accurately determining conditions at the time of the incident and immediately preceding it. These include

Plant status:
- Control room or operating log sheets showing the plant state prior to the failure
- Activities associated with the system in which the failure occurred, such as equipment being started or shut down
- Maintenance logs that define the extent of maintenance or testing activities going on
- Any process or procedural changes

Plant monitoring:
- Parameter traces or trend data that show the system or process conditions prior to the failure
- Any condition monitoring information that is maintained or taken on a continuous or periodic basis—vibration, temperature, pressure flow, fluid levels, etc.

Plant history:
- Incident reports from previous events
- Known changes in process equipment (expansions, reconfigurations, changes in sequences)
- Changes in raw material vendors, methods of delivery, concentrations of incoming ingredients

Operators and maintainers:

- Evidence of anomalies in behavior, such as noise, vibration, temperature, or unusual environmental conditions (heat, cold)
- Need for operation maintenance, such as filling oil reservoirs, adjusting cooling water flows, cleaning heat exchangers, adjusting controls
- Any observable trends or information that may, in *retrospect*, have been indicative of long-term degradation or changes in equipment behavior
- Any previous operational occurrences that, at the time, caused no problems, but could possibly have stressed the component—such as multiple attempts to start an electric motor, vibration or other trip-outs.

Analyzing evidence and determining conditions prior to the incident begin as parallel efforts, but converge as the investigation progresses. For the case of systems, the failure occurs when the imposed load exceeds the capability limits. This failure definition is just as valid for a hardware or piping system as it is for a human being.

The PSII team must look specifically for evidence that provides the point of initial failure, its progression path, and the preexisting conditions that led to the initiation. Having an understanding of a fundamental failure mode, the investigator should seek evidence that shows or confirms the actual failure mechanism. The PSII team could analyze to confirm material properties and examine the actual failure sites to identify the nature of the failure, such as fatigue, stress corrosion cracking, intergranular stress corrosion, or embrittlement.

5.2.8. Severity of Consequences

As the PSII team begins the process of multiple cause determination, it is important and appropriate to consider the question, "What could have happened?"

Sometimes when investigating a near-miss incident, there is a temptation not to pursue the cause analysis with the same vigor and to the same degree of detail as would be done for an incident with actual injury. Also, when dealing with a near-miss, there can be differences of opinions among the team members as to the credible negative consequences of the incident.

Team members should remember that
SEVERITY IS OFTEN A MATTER OF CHANCE

The PSII team must evaluate potential effects of an incident on

- employees
- community
- environment
- equipment
- operability of the process unit
- public perception

The team must also keep in mind the likelihood of the incident being repeated, which is the reason upper management is committed to pursuing near-miss incidents. This reminder should be given at the beginning of the multiple cause determination meeting.

5.3. FLOWCHART FOR MULTIPLE CAUSE DETERMINATION

5.3.1. Introduction

The following section presents an expanded discussion, step-by-step, of the concepts and actions shown in the flowchart for multiple cause analysis, Figure 5-1. The starting point for the flowchart is the accumulation of facts, information, observations, insights, questions, and preliminary speculations gained from the evidence collection activities described in Chapter 4.

5.3.2. Develop Chronology of Events

The first task is to develop a chronology of events based on the available known times and sequences. This document is sometimes referred to as a *time line*. Unconfirmed assumptions regarding chronology should be clearly identified as unconfirmed, and action should be initiated to verify the assumption.

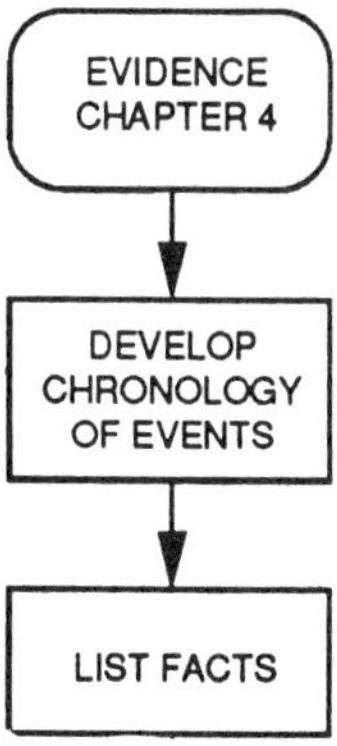

5.3.3. List Facts

The next step in the progression is a listing of all known facts, not only those relating to the incident sequence, but also all pertinent background data, specifications, and recent past and/or external events that could or did have an influence on the overall system.

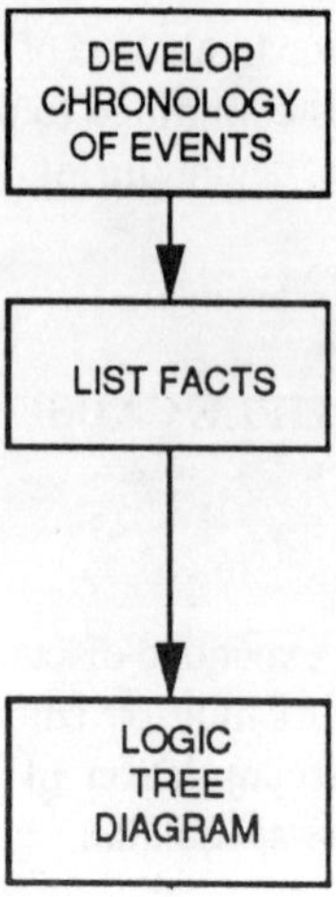

5.3.4. Develop Logic Tree

After the initial facts have been listed, construction begins on the logic tree diagram as discussed extensively in Section 5.1. The tree diagram is a dynamic document; it continues to expand and may even rearrange as additional information becomes available or when different information changes the understanding of the original facts.

At this juncture, all the minimum pieces are theoretically in place to confirm or refute the hypothesis. For many simple and straightforward failures, general knowledge of component failure mode behavior, used in conjunction with the specific information gathered for particular incident, may be sufficient to diagnose the cause. However, most process safety incidents are complex in nature and always have multiple underlying system causes. Therefore a systematic deductive approach is appropriate.

A Type 2 (brainstorming) investigation approach may provide bias and may direct the thinking toward incorrect conclusions. The team should look for multiple scenarios only when it has run out of facts and must develop new hypotheses. The goal of this task is to identify likely initiating failure events and be able to follow their progression to the experienced damage state. Look at each scenario, identify the evidence that would be available if it were the actual scenario, then compare this with the observed evidence. A match indicates that the scenario may have actually occurred, so at that point the cause of the failure can be identified. If a match cannot be made, then a search for more information is initiated. This concept is illustrated graphically in Figure 5-1.

The common format for this stage of the investigation is to conduct a multiple root-cause determination meeting. The participants should be the PSII team, unit management, operators, experts, employee unit representative, legal representative where needed, and regulatory agency where required. The meeting should be facilitated by the PSII team leader who should begin by setting the tone of the meeting and by confirming the purpose of the meeting with a reaffirmation of management's commitment to prevention. The meeting should be as open and honest as possible.

The facilitator should continue the opening segment by discussing the importance of and methods for choosing the top event and any pre-established and existing boundaries of the investigation. If multiple events are involved, it is best to start with the last event in the time sequence. It may be appropriate, depending on the nature of the event, to formally review the rules and symbols for logic tree or fault tree or whichever other formal method will be used.

At the end of this meeting, a formal critique should be considered to consolidate lessons learned for future meetings. The critique should consider what went well and what changes could be made to improve future meetings? It would also be appropriate at the conclusion of the session to thank the participants and to again restate the purpose of the meeting.

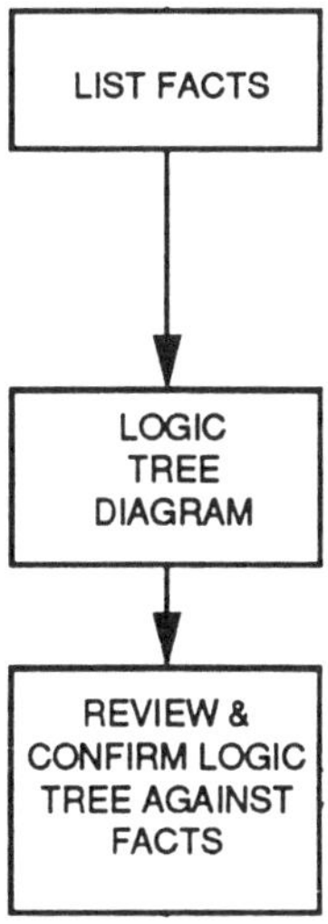

5.3.5. Review and Confirm Logic Against Facts

At this point, the logic tree structure is examined to ensure the tree is logically consistent and compatible with the known facts. In many instances, there will initially be apparent inconsistencies and application of the fact/hypothesis matrix will be appropriate. This powerful tool is described in Section 5.2.5. Inconsistencies will require further tree development or rearrangement.

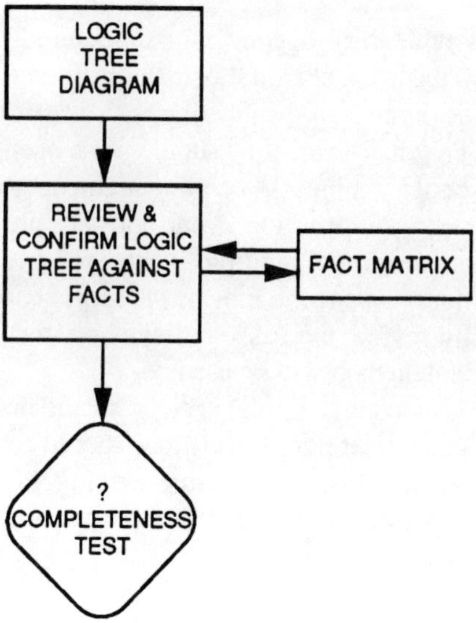

5.3.6. Completeness Test

Once the logic tree structure appears to be consistent, the first quality assurance test is applied by pausing and examining the overall logic tree structure for completeness. If the tree does appear to be complete, the next quality assurance test is exercised (see Section 5.3.7). If the tree is incomplete, then the *iterative loop* is activated (see Section 5.3.9)

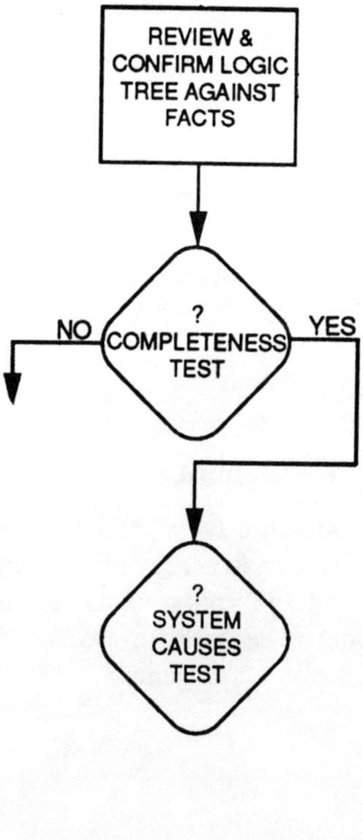

5.3.7. System Causes Test

If the logic tree appears to be complete, then the second quality control test is applied, by asking the question "Are the causes that have been identified actually related to systems?" If the answer is yes, then the investigation proceeds to the third quality control test, the final overall review (Section 5.3.8) If system causes have not been found, then the *iterative loop* is activated (per Section 5.3.9).

It is important to note that **not all system causes may be located at the extreme bottom points on the logic tree.** Some of the multiple-cause systems-related causes can be and often are located in the upper or middle portions of the logic tree diagram. Some causes can also be identified by the logic tree structure itself. For example, an overview of the entire tree structure may indicate significant gaps or overlaps in responsibilities, or it may disclose conflicting activities or procedures. These insights may be overlooked if the investigators limit their cause search to only the bottom level of the structure.

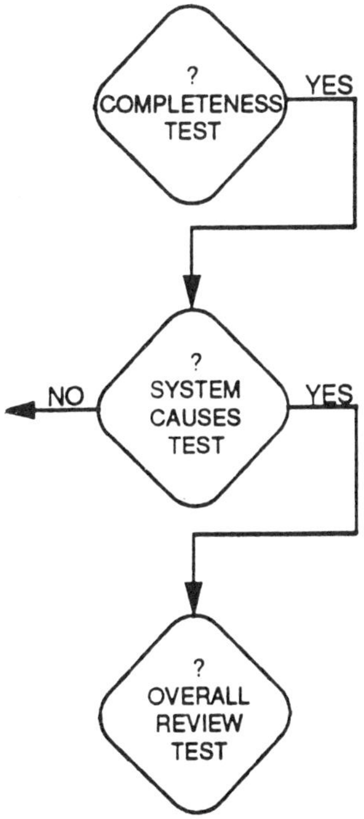

5.3.8. Overall Review Test

If the test for systems causes is satisfactory, then the third and final quality assurance test is applied. This is an overall review of the logic tree as a whole for both facts and logic. It is a pause to focus on the "entire forest" from an overall perspective, not just each tree. If the PSII team is satisfied with the causes identified, then the investigation proceeds to the recommendations stage which is addressed in Chapter 6. If a problem or some incompleteness is noted, then the iterative loop is activated.

After the tree is developed, and before moving on to the recommendations and deliberations, the team is asked, "Are there any *other* causes that you had in mind at the beginning of this meeting that are *not* included in the tree?" If additional causes are identified, the team adds them to the tree if the logic can support it. Some team members may have specific concerns that the logic tree has not adequately resolved. This is the point where these remaining issues are dealt with.

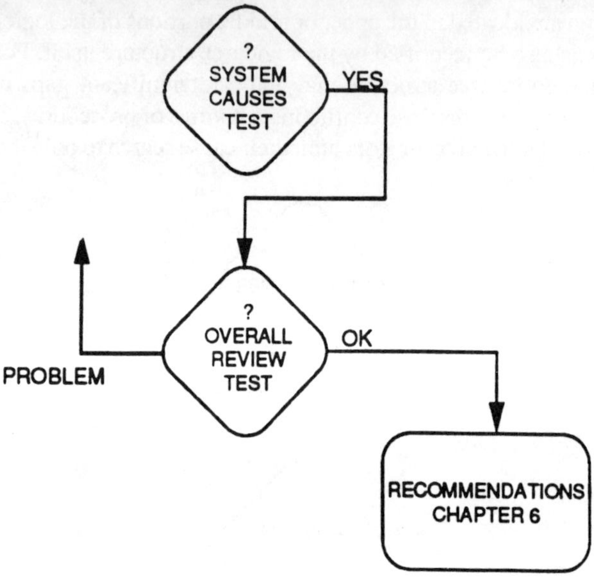

5.3.9. Iterative Loop

In the deductive process of identifying root causes, known facts are assembled and used to develop and test one or more possible scenarios. The process will normally require multiple iterations of the feedback loop until one or more plausible scenarios are identified that fit the known facts.

If the scenario is completely disproved by the known accepted facts, it is disregarded. If the scenario needs additional facts in order to be proven or disproved, then the *iterative loop* path is followed and additional information is gathered. Sometimes this new information is very specific, precise, and limited in scope. Follow-up witness interviews, revisiting or reexamining a certain area of the incident scene to verify the position of a valve handle, are examples of tasks initiated by the iterative loop (shown in the portion of Figure 5-8 enclosed within the dashed line).

The loop is entered from one of the three quality control checkpoints. The first segment of the loop deals with problems in logic or facts. The problem could be incompleteness or apparent inconsistencies.

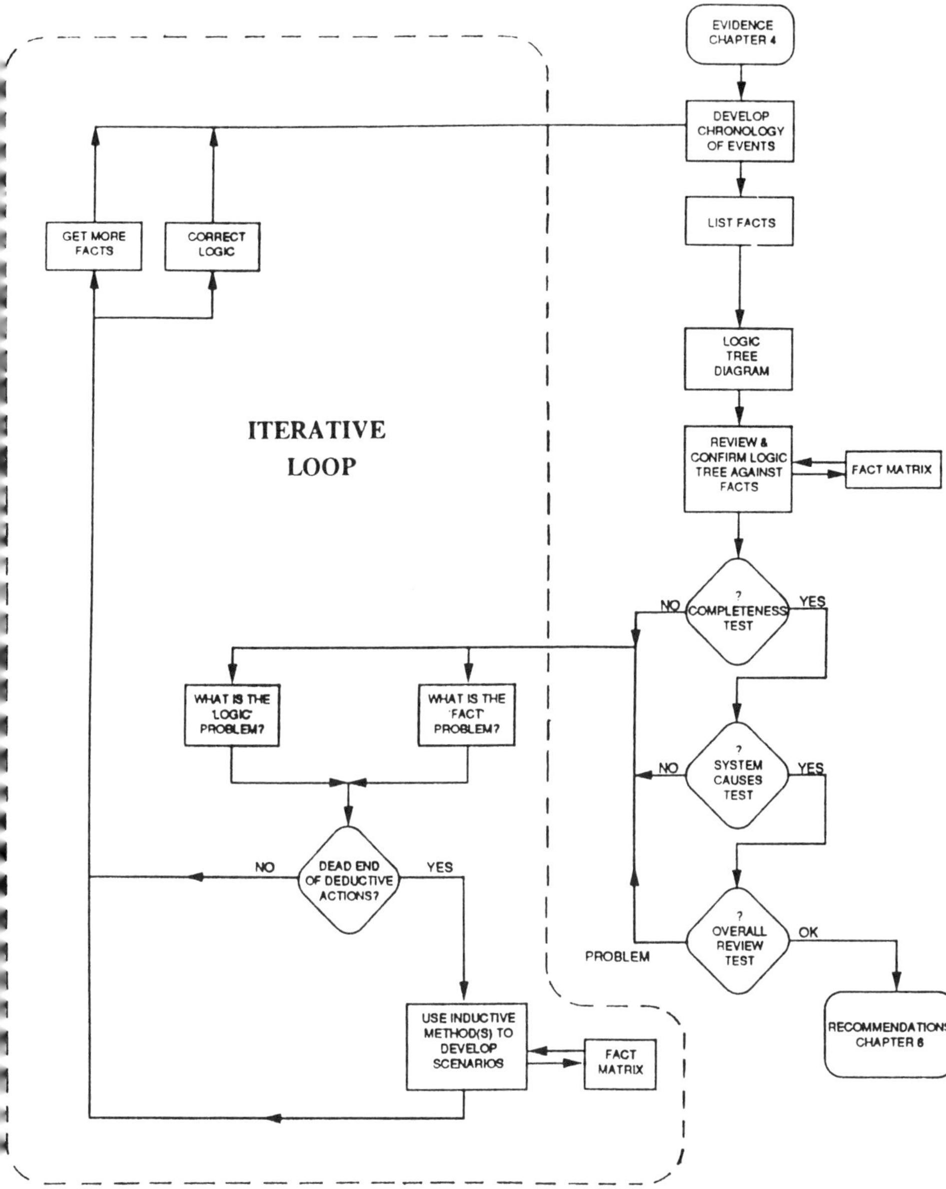

Figure 5-8: Iterative loop.

The next item in the loop is a decision point for possibly introducing the use of inductive methods into the deliberations. If the deductive process has not stalled and continues to indicate progress, then the additional facts are procured, or the logic tree is restructured. An example of this activity would be the case where one witness stated a particular valve was open, yet the postincident inspection found it to be chained and locked in the closed position. The position of this particular valve may be a critical item in determining which of two scenarios is the more probable case. The PSII team would then initiate a short-term action item to conduct a mini-investigation to resolve this small-scale question.

If on the other hand, the deductive process has reached an impasse, where no further progress seems possible or likely, then the iterative loop calls for application of inductive investigation methods. Sections 2.5.2 and 2.5.3 describe some of the more popular techniques for *inductive* or morphological (blended) methods. The inductive methods may also benefit from use of the fact/hypothesis matrix tool as described in Section 5.2.5.

5.4. CASE HISTORY, EXAMPLE APPLICATIONS

5.4.1. Logic Tree Development

Consider the following typical incident, which appears in diagram form in Figure 5-9.

Just after a moderate rain shower, employee A was driving a forklift truck. He was pulling a small trailer that was heavily loaded with boxes. Used metal parts destined for the recycle scrap metal dealer were inside the boxes.

The road sloped downward toward the factory entrance where the driver had to execute a right angle turn to reach the storeroom to unload the trailer. Due to the downward slope, the forklift and trailer build up extra speed. The driver attempted to brake, but the worn out brakes were inadequate to slow down the vehicle. The driver reached the corner at approximately 15 mph and attempted to make the turn. Most of the unsecured load fell off, hit the pavement, and broke apart.

At this moment, employee B entered the gate driving a motor scooter. He saw the debris in the road and applied his brakes hard. The scooter began to skid on the wet road and employee B fell to the ground and was injured.

This relatively simple incident can be used to illustrate several logic tree and root cause principles. The "top event" would be the injury. It is the result of many precursor events, the first two of which are the fall and the skid. The skid has two causes, the wet road and the hard braking. The two events of entering the plant and seeing the obstructed road led to the act of hard braking. Using this systematic analysis of event sequences and causes, Figure 5-9 can be developed, and a more complete understanding of the incident can be gained.

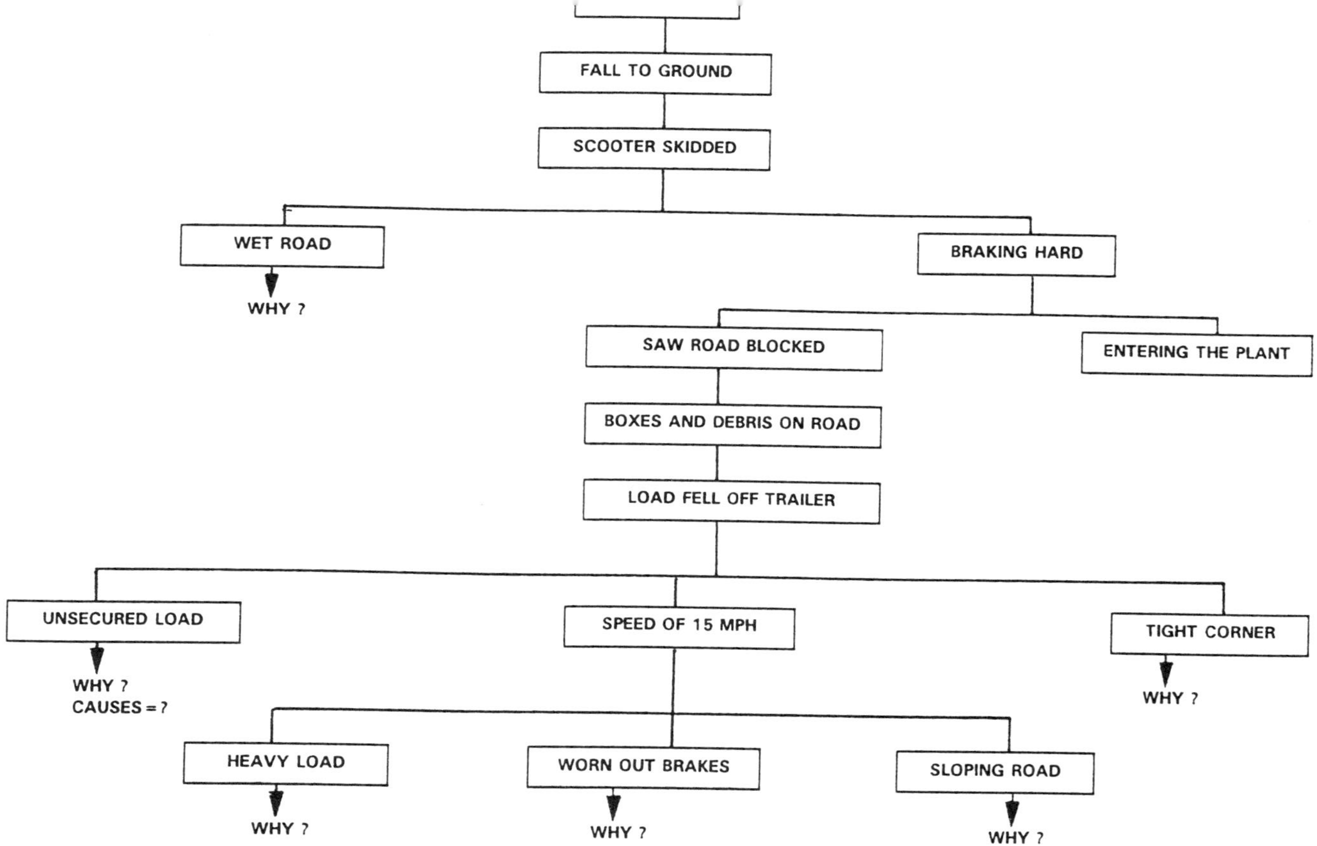

Figure 5-9: Logic tree scooter/forklift incident.

Figure 5-9 is a simplified tree. Most of the branches can be developed in greater detail by repeatedly asking "why?" What act, conditions, systems, or combination of circumstances caused the particular event to occur? Most of the logic gates represent AND-gate conditions, but for the sake of simplicity, the type of gate is not indicated.

After the logic tree diagram as shown in Figure 5-9 is completely developed, then a Type 3 PSII approach would begin a search for the various system-related causes. Some obvious possible candidates would include

- the management system for training and enforcing forklift driver operation
- design, arrangement, and approval practices (management systems) for laying out traffic flow patterns within the plan
- forklift inspection, preventive maintenance, and repair programs (management systems).

By contrast, traditional, Type 1 or Type 2, investigation approaches may often stop before evaluating such items as the program for inspecting and maintaining forklift brakes, procedures and training for securing loads on trailers, procedures for establishing and periodically reviewing employee traffic patterns, and job safety analysis and training programs for forklift operation.

5.4.2. Three-Truck Incident

Figure 5-10 illustrates the layout diagram for a three vehicle incident.

Truck 1 was trying to maneuver to avoid Truck 2, and ended up colliding with both Truck 3 and Truck 2. Truck 1 was moving north. Truck 2 was parked halfway on and halfway off of the roadway. Truck 3 was moving toward the east and making a turn to the south. Truck 1 started the action sequence by swerving to the left across the center line in order to avoid hitting the parked Truck 2. At about the same time Truck 3 made a turn at the intersection. Truck 1 saw Truck 3 and then turned back to the right in order to avoid a head-on impact. The two vehicles collided in a glancing fashion, then Truck 1 proceeded to crash into Truck 2.

Figure 5-11 shows the logic tree diagram developed in the investigation. Branch F appears three times on the diagram, but is only shown fully developed in one place. Most of the logic gates shown are AND-gate conditions. For the sake of simplicity, the type of gate is not indicated on Figure 5-11.

5.4.3. Fire and Explosion Incident—Fault Tree

The fictitious process safety incident contained in Appendix F can be used to illustrate the application of logic tree and multiple cause concepts. Extensive details appear in the appendix but a basic summary would be:

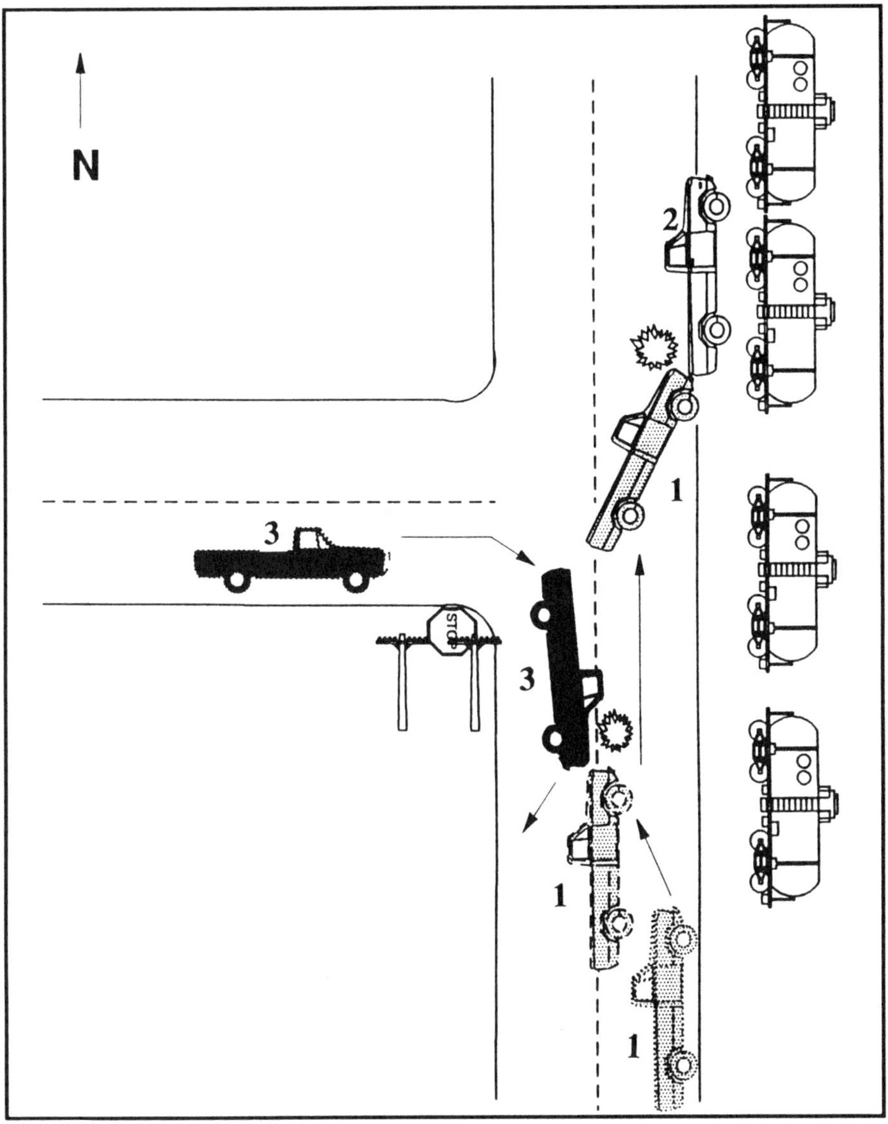

Figure 5-10: Three truck incident—layout.

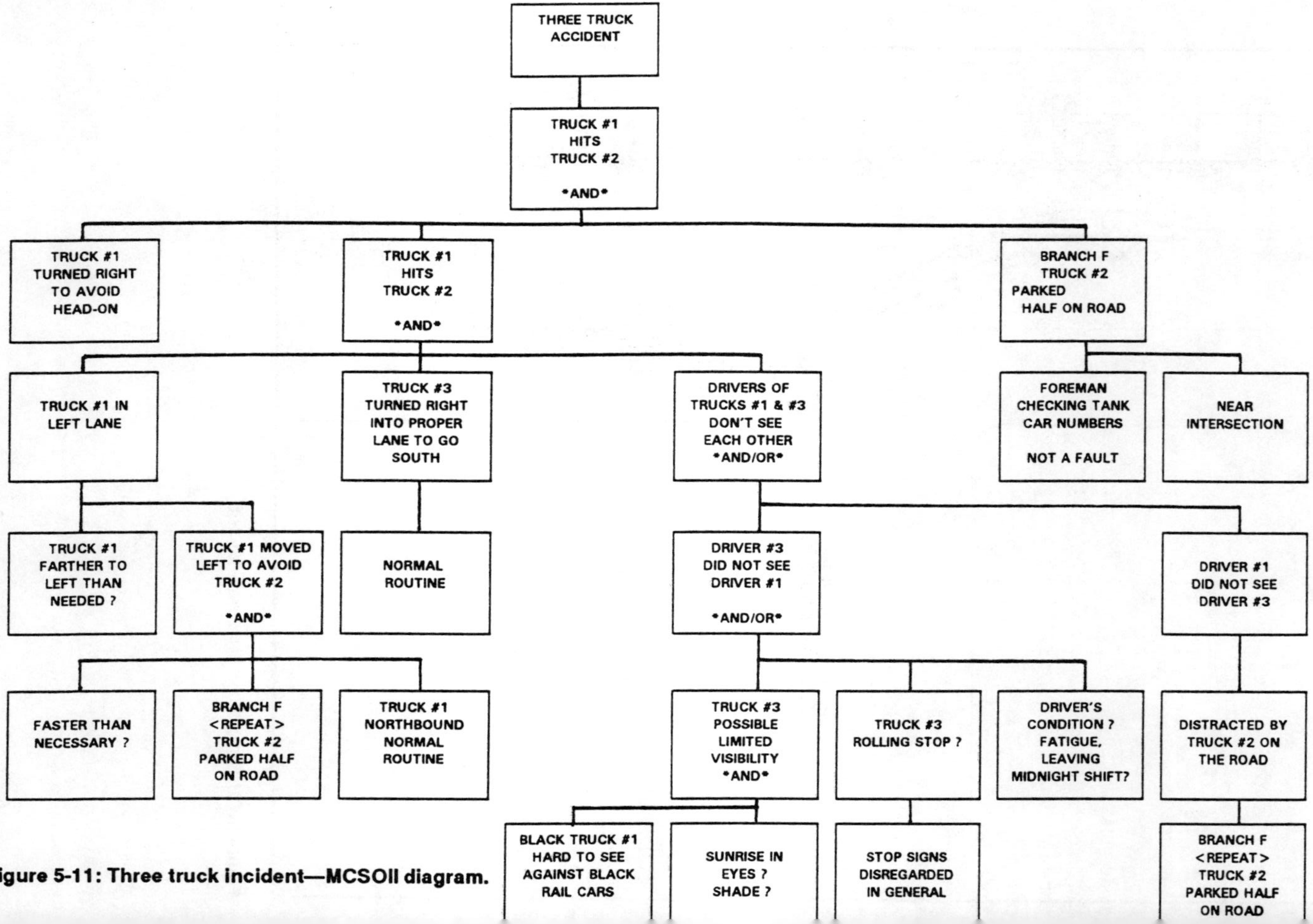

Figure 5-11: Three truck incident—MCSOII diagram.

A major fire and explosion occurred in a polyethylene manufacturing facility resulting in five fatalities and extensive damage. The fire originated when a vessel was overfilled and pyrophoric material escaped. Emergency response was impaired, which contributed to the severity of the consequences.

After collecting and analyzing the available evidence, the PSII team constructed the logic tree diagram shown in Figure 5-12. This diagram presents in a logical and systematic format, the sequence of events and conditions that ultimately resulted in the major incident. The simplified qualitative fault-tree indicates various events and conditions that could have contributed to the incident causation and progression. Some of these sequences acted with direct impact on the trigger event, the overfill and initial fire, while others acted to increase the severity.

Three faulty management systems were found to be underlying root causes of the incident.

- A breakdown of the management system for preventive maintenance on critical instrumentation allowed the vessel to become overfilled.
- A breakdown of the management system for operator training led to errors in the initial response to the high pressure alarm and to the electrical power interruption.
- Deficiencies in emergency preparedness programs (management systems) caused major increases in the severity of the consequences. Some of these deficiencies include deferring repairs to fire protection systems, incorrect response by plant fire brigade, and failure to maintain readiness by failing to execute required routine run-tests of fire pumps.

Other possible underlying causes could be argued, depending on how the data from this fictitious case are interpreted. For example, the PSII team at the facility should carefully evaluate the management systems for process hazard analysis. The absence of instrumentation interlocks and redundant devices may be an indication of deficiencies in design standards, modification standards, or process hazard review techniques.

5.4.4. Data Driven Cause Analysis

A specialized approach is to use historical data to infer or identify potential causes. In this case, the investigators use past experience to look for patterns consistent with failure hypotheses. The technique is only as good as the records, and if data have not been put in the files, or are in error, then misleading inferences may result. Failure data for the system under investigation are presented in a time line that can be correlated with overall plant history. Two things are sought: (1) evidence for correlation with plant state, plant condition, or external environmental effects and (2) evidence that indicates a failure pattern that may correlate with maintenance activities.

Figure 5-12: Simplified fault tree example.

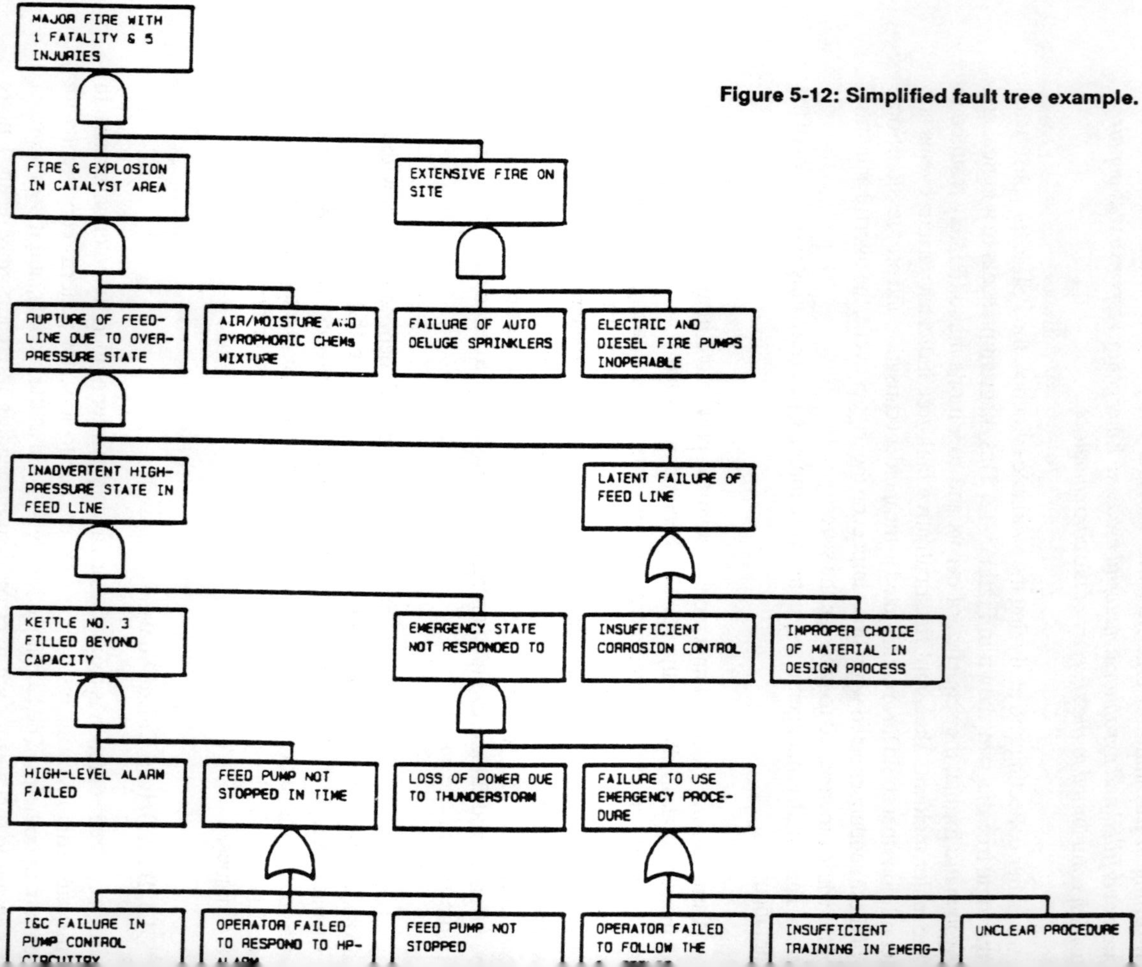

CASE STUDY

In a plant with a shaft-driven boiler feedwater pump, problems had historically occurred with failure of the bearing in the hydraulic coupling. There was no apparent cause, but throughout the 12 year life of the equipment, the failure occurred about once every 1 or 2 years and resulted in an outage of about 3 weeks.

Plant data did not indicate a cause, other than bearing failure—repaired/replaced. A detailed root cause investigation had never been performed. At the time of the investigation, the equipment was operable and detailed evidence from the last failure was lost during the repairs.

A time line for the failures was developed and patterns sought. The first thing that became clear was that failures seemed to occur predominantly following an outage in the winter. This immediately led to the thought that temperature was an important influence. The equipment is in a heated building so all components *should* have been at room temperature. If winter temperature was contributing to the problem, it was most likely a result of overcooling by one of the cooling systems, or normal lubricating oil systems operating at too low a temperature. The written reports of the previous failures stated that "bearing wipe" was the cause. This fact indicated that lubrication failure was a likely candidate.

When operational characteristics of the oil systems were examined in detail, it was found that the oil supply came from the main turbine lube oil system. The operators said that after a start in cold weather they had trouble maintaining anything but the minimum lube oil temperature) of 120°F (49°C) until the turbine was at power. The feed pump hydraulic coupling specifications indicated that a minimum temperature of 140–160°F (60–71°C) was required for proper operation. A reasonable failure hypothesis was that, during a start, oil temperature was too low (and therefore viscosity too high) to provide adequate flow and lubrication of the pilot bearings. This allowed excessive frictional contact and resulted in a "wiped bearing." The corrective action was to heat the oil feed to the coupling; and indeed the number of failures was dramatically reduced.

This example is intended to show that all of the elements of the cause determination process were used, but not quite so formally as perhaps that the process implies. This is important, because different techniques achieve the intent of the process via specific but different approaches. The investigator must understand the functional objectives that provide the foundation of the multiple cause determination. Without this understanding, a "shotgun approach" is often used, there is neither rigor nor a search for completeness, and the first identified potential cause often becomes "the cause." This is one reason that failures recur even though remedial action was taken after an earlier failure. There is also a tendency to stop the process at the intermediate causes level. In the case study provided above, the general cause of bearing wiping was lubrication failure. Suggested cures were proposed for bearing redesign, new materials, vibration monitoring, etc. Even modified bearings would be prone to continued failure following winter outages until the underlying cause, low temperature, was identified and corrected.

5.5. CONCLUSION

By following the flowchart sequence as shown in Figure 5-1, that is, using the iterative loop, the fact/hypothesis matrix, and systematically applying quality control tests, the steps all work together to produce the underlying multiple causes which are present in every process safety incident.

The success of the cause analysis is a direct function of the quality of the information available and the perceptiveness of the PSII team. *The goal of the cause analysis is not to unlock every secret of the system, but to have enough information to make reasonable judgments on how to implement a cost-effective fix.*

5.6. REFERENCES

1. Kletz, T. A. 1983. "Accident Investigation: How Far Should We Go?" Paper 11d presented at the American Institute of Chemical Engineers Loss Prevention Symposium.
2. Feynman, R. P. 1988. *What Do You Care What Other People Think?* New York: Norton.
3. Winsor, D. A. 1989. Challenger: A Case of Failure to Communicate. *Chemtech*, September
4. Hon. Lord Cullen. 1990. "The Public Inquiry into the Piper Alpha Disaster." London: UK Department of Energy, HMSO.
5. Sanders and McCormic. 1987. *Human Factors in Engineering and Design*, 6th ed. New York: McGraw-Hill.
6. Stern, A. and R. Keller. 1991. Human Error and Equipment Design in the Chemical Industry. *Professional Safety*, May.
7. Lucas, D. A. and D. E. Embrey. 1989. Human Reliability Data Collection for Qualitative Modelling and Quantitative Assessment. In Colombari, V. (Ed.), *Reliability Data Collection and Use in Availability Assessment.* New York: Springer Verlag. Pp. 358–370.
8. Paradies, M. 1991. Root Cause Analysis and Human Factors. *Human Factors* 34(8):1–5.
9. Norman, D. A. 1988. *The Psychology of Everyday Things.New York: Basic Books.*

6

RECOMMENDATIONS AND FOLLOW-THROUGH

Older investigation approaches to PSII, Types 1 and 2, stopped before the actual implementation of the preventive action. The responsibility of the investigator was considered complete once the recommendations were submitted. A major change in the Type 3 approach is the *increased emphasis on follow-through implementation.* Eliminating identified hazards is the *only* part of the PSII that actually prevents repeat incidents. All earlier phases of the investigation are devoted to what should be done and how best to do it.

This chapter then focuses on the second and third cornerstones of process safety incident investigation (PSII):

- Identifying changes in management systems that will eliminate the multiple system-related causes of the incident.
- Implementing and following through with the recommendations.

If these two steps are ignored or are only partially completed, much or possibly all of the benefits of a PSII will be lost. This chapter develops characteristics of high quality recommendations and presents practical guidelines for achieving successful implementation. The first section of the chapter is a discussion of the major concepts involved in PSII recommendations and follow through: developing effective recommendations, management of change, and inherent safety. The last section presents an step-by-step discussion of the flowchart for recommendations and follow-through.

6.1. MAJOR CONCEPTS

Figure 6-1 presents an overview of the activities in this chapter, beginning with the multiple root causes identified in the preceding chapter. Each cause is examined individually. Proposed preventive actions are evaluated first for technical merit and then from a management-of-change aspect.

The PSII team develops recommended criteria for resumption of operations and recommended preventive actions, then presents these recommendations to the

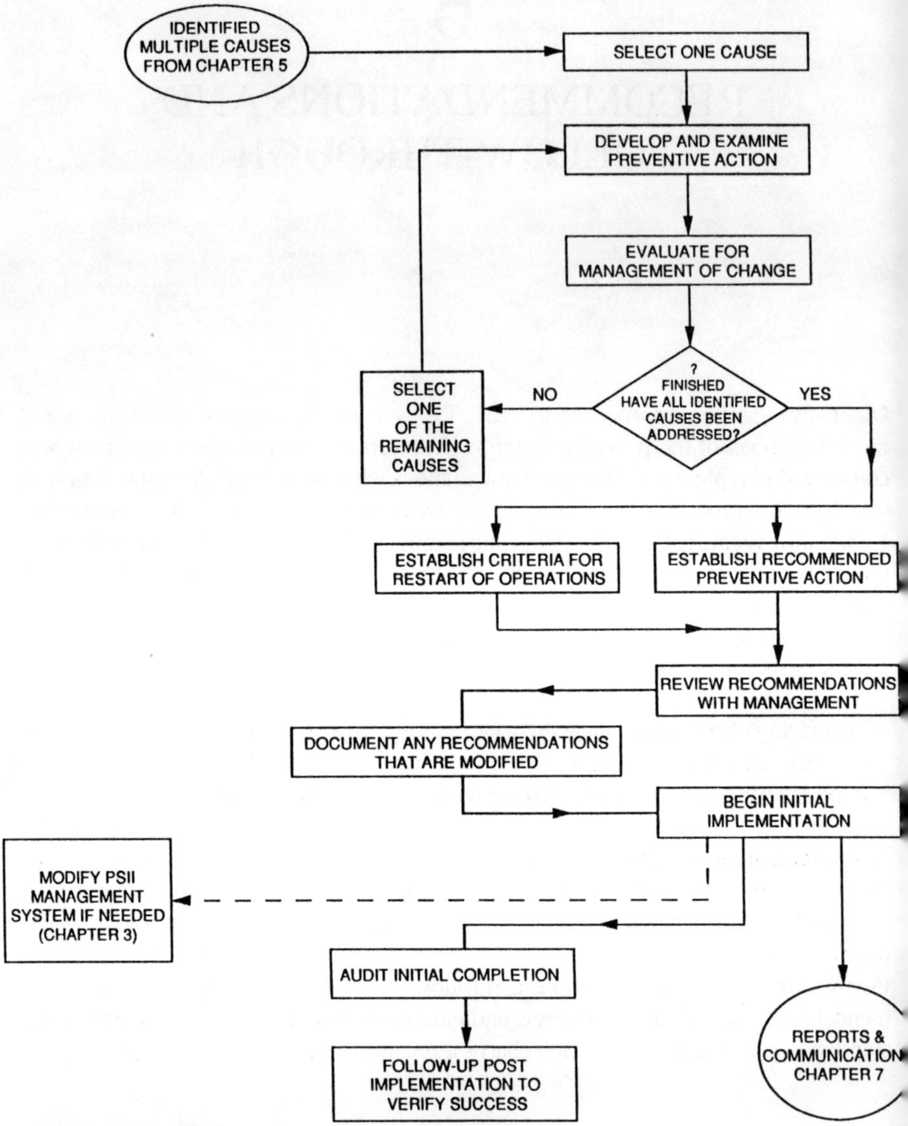

Figure 6-1: Flowchart—recommendations and follow-through.

management team. The follow-through phase begins with the review and acceptance by the line management team of the recommendations and the assignment of implementation responsibilities. Auditing is an integral portion of the follow-through phase. The flowchart concludes by leading into Chapter 7 ("Formal Reports and Communications Issues").

6.2. DEVELOPMENT OF RECOMMENDATIONS

6.2.1. Responsibilities

Each system failure that was identified as a cause should be addressed by a recommended preventive action item or comment. A formal management system must be in place to follow-up and track each recommendation until completion or resolution. The PSII team has the responsibility to develop practical recommendations and submit them to management. Then management must review, approve, resolve, and follow-through on the recommendations, including (1) allocation of sufficient resources, personnel and capital, for timely completion, (2) implementation of procedural changes and (3) follow-up with those affected by the changes to assure measures are working as expected.

Each employee affected by the recommendations has the responsibility to use altered equipment properly, abide by procedural improvements, and provide feedback to management when something is not working as expected or when the employee finds a better, safer way to address the problems identified in the recommendation.

Some pertinent management responsibilities are as follows:

1. Address the technology deficiencies identified as causing the incident.
2. Examine possible mitigation measures to: (*a*) reduce potential consequences, (*b*) improve emergency response, and (*c*) improve the initial detection, diagnosis, alert, and alarm systems.
3. Conduct a post-audit to ensure that the intent of the recommendation was actually achieved.
4. Review the PSII management system for opportunities to improve the investigation procedures.
5. Share the results of the investigation with all departments in the facility that could benefit (see Chapter 7).[1]
6. Seek out any similar situations in the company to capitalize on the lessons learned.[1]
7. Share pertinent information and lessons learned with other companies and organizations.[1]
8. Ensure that necessary resources are available for full resolution of the recommendations in a timely manner.
9. Monitor the status of the action items and periodically review the target completion dates.

6.2.2. Attributes of Good Recommendations

A well-written recommendation specifically describes the action to be taken and defines successful completion in clear and measurable terms, so that completion should be easy to recognize. Vague or ambiguous terms do not belong in the written recommendation. Terms such as "appropriate safeguards" or "improve the quality of training" should be avoided or else they should be specifically defined in performance terms. Each recommendation should have a suggested target completion date that is reasonable and reflects practical time frames. Complex actions that require several steps or an extended time to complete should contain intermediate milestones so that the progress can be monitored.

An individual, named by management, should be responsible for each recommendation. Responsibilities should include implementing, monitoring the status, resolving any problems, and finally verifying and documenting that the intended preventive action has indeed been completed.

If the original recommendation is changed, postponed, or rejected, then this decision should be fully documented. The basis for the decision should be specified, along with any new information or new options that were considered.

Recommendations concerning restart of operations are often developed before the final report is published. It is imperative that these recommendations be clearly written, understood by all, and addressed by the management organization responsible for operation of the facility. Restart criteria deserve special attention and are addressed in further detail in Section 6.3.5. Appendix F contains a report on a fictitious fire and explosion incident. The nine recommendations contained in this report are typical of the range of detail that can be found in recommendations that address changes in management systems.

Attributes of a successful recommendation are shown in Figure 6-2.

- Addresses a root system cause that will fix the problem
- Clearly states intended action
- Is practical, feasible, and achievable
- Adds an AND-gate to the tree structure
- Eliminates or decreases risks or consequences
- Includes target completion date
- Designates a person responsible for implementation
- Has been analyzed using management of change procedures
- Is compatible with other objectives of the organization

Figure 6-2: Attributes of a successful recommendation.

6.2.3. Types of Recommendations

There are different approaches to categorizing recommendations, for example:

- Recommendations targeted at *reducing the probability* of a given incident by adding AND-gates to the failure scenarios (e.g., increasing preventive maintenance inspection programs to reduce the probability of simultaneous failure of critical circulating pumps, installing back-up pumps, adding redundant control instrumentation).

- Recommendations for minimizing *personnel exposures* (e.g., minimizing duration of exposure or relocating noncritical workers to areas remote from potential blast zones).
- Recommendations intended to *lessen the consequences* should the incident occur again (e.g., dump tanks, dikes, scrubbers, fixed extinguishing systems, reducing inventories of toxic or flammable materials).

6.2.4. Inherent Safety

Recommended improvements that target inherently safe design[2] are preferred to improvements that are limited to adding-on extra protection. Inherently safe designs lessen the reliance on human performance, equipment reliability, or preventive maintenance programs for successful prevention of an incident. When they are incorporated during the early design phases of a project, they will yield greater economic benefits. Nevertheless, inherently safe design should be considered by the PSII team when developing recommended preventive actions.

Intrinsic and passive safety design features are by nature more reliable than design features that depend on the performance of a equipment, systems and human action.[3] Passive designs reduce both the probability of an event occurring and the severity or consequence of an incident. Some examples of general strategies[4] for increasing inherent safety follow:

- *Reduction of Inventories:* Advancements in process control and changing acceptable risk standards may remove the initial justification for large inventories of toxic intermediate products. For example, tight quality control of on-time deliveries of hazardous raw materials may allow for a 1 or 2 day supply on hand versus a 1- or 2-week supply.
- *Substitution:* It may be possible to substitute a less hazardous material for a hazardous one. For example, many chlorination systems for water purification have recently converted from pressurized cylinders of liquid chlorine to a pelletized hypochlorite salt.
- *Intensification:* Sometimes it is possible to achieve significant reductions in reactor size and inventory by improved mixing technology. Another example of intensification is changing a batch operation to a smaller scale or to a continuous operation.
- *Change:* Change is here defined as the use of a totally different process or method to accomplish the same objectives.

The PSII team should evaluate the inherent safety features of the recommendations being considered. Since changes can be either beneficial or detrimental, investigators *should be alert for inherently unsafe* features in any recommendations being considered. Two common examples of design changes that can *increase* overall risks are the use of flexible joints and the use of glass (rotometers, bull's-eyes, sight glasses, additional control room windows).[5] Sealless pumps are generally considered to be inherently safer than mechanical seal design pumps for seal leaks. Motor control valves should be designed to fail to a safe position when there is loss of instrument air or electric power.

6.2.5. Hierarchies and Layers of Recommendations

T. Kletz identifies three categories or "layers" of recommendations.[6] First-layer remedies use *immediate technical recommendations* that are targeted to prevent a particular incident. Consider the case in which an employee is injured by inhalation exposure while taking a liquid chlorine process sample. First-layer recommendations would address such items as changes to the sampling procedure as well as refresher training and use of personal protective respiratory equipment.

Second-layer recommendations focus on *avoiding the hazard.* A deeper and broader perspective is used for this second layer, and often the focus is on improving the normal barrier measures placed between the person and the hazard. Typical remedies for the above chlorine incident might include modifications to the sampling apparatus, sampling at a different location, or perhaps an in-line analyzer that would eliminate the need for manual sampling.

Root causes are addressed in the third layer by *identifying changes in the management systems.* These third-layer recommendations act to prevent not only this particular incident, but similar ones. Preventive measures that result in changes in management systems are, in theory, more consistent and enduring. In the chlorine exposure case, the investigators would consider such items as:

1. Improvements in the methods in which process sampling is established. (Who participates in the decision? What are criteria for determining location, method, devices? Who authorizes? Is there a periodic audit or reevaluation?)
2. Improvements in the management system for establishing, evaluating, and monitoring standard operating procedures. (Are the procedures adequate, understood, and consistently performed? Is the task still necessary?)
3. Is there a routine mechanism such as Job Safety Analysis in which tasks are systematically reviewed for potential hazards? (JSA systematically identifies (1) job steps, (2) specific hazards associated with each job step, and (3) safe job procedures associated with each step)

Multiple layers of protection is another useful concept. Chemical Manufacturers Association calls for "sufficient layers of protection through technology, facilities, and personnel to prevent escalation from a single failure to a catastrophic event."[1] This approach can be applied to multiple root-system causes when the PSII team evaluates potential remedies. The layers offer guidance in selecting practical recommendations. Shell Chemical Corporation identified a general sequence of safety layers at the 25th AIChE Loss Prevention Symposium in 1991 (see Figure 6-3).[7]

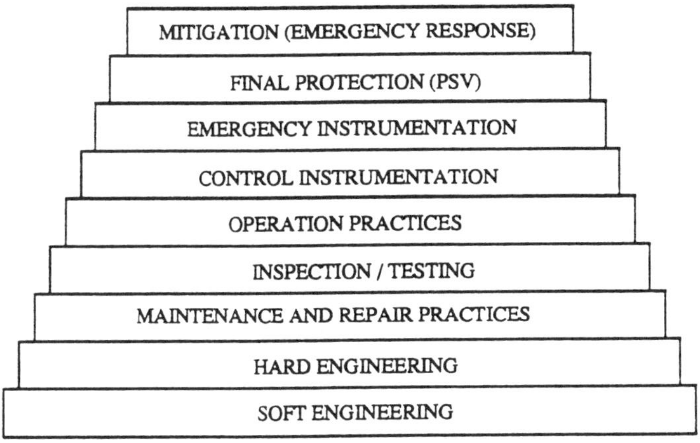

Figure 6-3: Layers of safety. [From Csengery, L. V. "The Time For Process Hazard Analysis Has Arrived." Paper 68d presented at the 1991 AIChE Loss Prevention Symposium, Pittsburgh, PA, August 18–21, 1991.]

Rhone-Poulenc's Causal Tree, Appendix D, draws on total quality principles and asks that recommendations be grouped in the categories of Organizational (Management), Human (Individual), and Material (Environment).

The key concepts are that recommendations must address system improvements and must address correction of all of an incident's multiple causes, which the PSII has looked for and found.

6.2.6. Disciplinary Action/Commendation

Recommendations for specific disciplinary action for employees involved in the incident are usually outside the scope of the PSII team. This type activity is best handled by the employees' manager. If the team determines that some disciplinary action should be considered, this decision should be worded in a recommendation. The recommendation would be included as a regular recommendation, and would be evaluated and acted upon by management.

Whenever an investigation reveals employee action worthy of commendation, the PSII team should also point this out in their comments. Cool rational actions in the middle of an emergency often limit the consequences of an incident. Those employees who demonstrate this type response should be recognized and commended.

6.2.7. The "No-Action" Recommendation

There may be rare occasions where a particular cause is identified and the PSII team decides not to issue a recommendation addressing it. This decision may be based on a valid and documented quantitative probability analysis. The risk of recurrence may be too low to warrant further action, or the cause may be outside of the control of the organization (e.g., a part falls off a flying aircraft and strikes an employee on the head).

In such cases, the cause and the decision to take no action should be documented. The logic of how the decision was arrived at should be included in the documentation, along with any specific facts and reference documents.

There may be some causes or items discovered by the PSII team that are better addressed in the form of observations or conclusions rather than specific recommendations. Again, as in the falling aircraft part, the remedy may be beyond the capability of the organization. Sometimes several specific causes or recommendations related to each other will be consolidated into a general statement. The preventive action items would appear as individual distinct recommendations, yet a general description may appear as an observation or conclusion. Some investigation guidelines[8] make a strong distinction between findings and conclusions. *Findings are restricted to known facts, factual information and data. Conclusions state judgments of the investigators.*

6.3. EXPANDED FLOWCHART DISCUSSION

6.3.1. Select One Cause

The process of developing preventive recommendations is summarized in Figure 6-1. Starting with the set of multiple causes determined previously in Chapter 5, each cause is evaluated individually to consider actions that would prevent or adequately mitigate a recurrence. Ferry, in Chapter 17 of his publication *Modern Accident Investigation and Analysis*[9] states that each recommendation should cover just one item, spelling out precisely what action is recommended.

6.3.2. Develop and Examine Preventive Action

Attributes of successful preventive action recommendations are detailed in Section 6.1.3. The PSII team should evaluate their recommendations to ensure they:

- prevent a recurrence (actually fix the problem)
- are reasonably achievable
- are compatible with other objectives of the organization such as producing product at a satisfactory level of financial return, protect the community and environment
- are measurable and clearly worded, describing specific outcomes

Recommendations can focus on changes to improve physical systems (hardware, equipment, tools), administrative systems (procedures, methods, training) or overall management systems. A hierarchical perspective as discussed in Section 6.2.5 can be applied. Increasing inherent safety, Section 6.2.4 is generally considered the most effective approach.

6.3.3. Management of Change

In addition to a management system for recommendation tracking and following-up, there should also be a system for managing the changes created by the recommendations. More often than not, these two management systems are handled as separate activities.

Management-of-change is a concept recognized by several organizations and professionals as one of the fundamental elements of successful process safety management.[1,10.] Evaluation of possible impacts of a recommendation should be done by the PSII team *before* they issue the recommendation. The management-of-change system can help the PSII team identify and analyze potential recommendations and evaluate their consequences, both positive and negative. Furthermore, the management-of-change system helps achieve a thorough follow-through for the action item.

Returning to the earlier example of the employee injured while sampling chlorine (Section 6-2.5), one typical root cause might be an inadequate standard operating procedure (SOP) for sampling. A management-of-change system will provide a mechanism to identify those publications and procedures that may be affected by changing the sampling technique. Those affected could be

- the training manual, qualification criteria, and lesson plan agenda in the operator training program;
- reference manuals in the quality control laboratory;
- specifications in purchasing and stores for ordering and stocking sample containers;
- respiratory protection program;
- preventive maintenance program instructions and records;
- engineering design standards for sampling stations

One system root cause of the *Challenger* disaster (January 1986) was inadequate management of change. In 1984, a change was made in pressure-testing procedures of the seal to prevent failures. The change actually resulted in greater risk of failure rather than the intended decease.[11] A more thorough analysis of the proposed recommendation might have identified and corrected this problem before the disaster.

If a recommendation asks for a change in process, the action must undergo a formal process hazards analysis (PHA), such as a HAZOP or other method prior to implementation. This systematic and formal approach should identify and evaluate hazards associated with the proposed revisions. The study may uncover failure scenarios, adverse consequences, and obscure relationships that are not immediately apparent. The CCPS book, *Guidelines for Hazard Evaluation Procedures, Second Edition with Worked Examples*[12] is an excellent guide to selection and proper application of PHA methodologies.

6.3.4. Completeness Test

The next activity in the sequence is to check for completeness. *Have all the identified causes been addressed?* The PSII team should remember that all of the multiple causes are not necessarily located at the bottom of the logic tree structure. Sometimes causes may be identified from events, combinations of events from upper levels of the logic tree, or by potential changes/restructures of the logic tree resulting from addition of AND-gates.

In many cases, it is appropriate at this point to group the identified preventive action items by category such as priorities, topics, systems, areas of responsibility, or general time frames.

6.3.5. Restart/Resumption of Operations

A critical responsibility of the PSII team is to recommend criteria for resumption of operations. For most process safety related incidents, the remaining or adjacent sections of the facility will be in operable condition. Thus, the question of restart criteria becomes an early task for the PSII team. The topic is often addressed in stages. Initially there may be many restraints on starting up, including as yet unknown causes, which may result in a repeat incident. The restraints may be gradually lifted as information to clear the restraint becomes available. Some restrictions on operating parameters, such as flow rates, pressures, or temperatures, may continue for extended periods.

The authority and responsibility to make a restart decision rests with the management team, which may consist of operating, engineering, research, environmental, safety, employee health, legal and communications departments. The PSII team is responsible for identifying criteria and submitting recommendations to the management team. The PSII team should clearly specify the minimum acceptable criteria that is recommended for safe resumption of operations. This list should be in writing, and it often will contain a special check list of items to be verified and completed prior to attempted restart. If a specific waiver of a restriction is needed, this fact should be clearly communicated and documented.

There will often be occasions where restart authorization, prior notification, or coordination with outside organizations is required. Regulatory agencies such as OSHA, U.S. EPA, state environmental regulators, and municipal agencies (e.g., fire departments, HAZMAT teams, building officials) are examples of organizations that may have specific jurisdiction and authority over restart. These situations are usually sensitive, and restart may require more time than originally expected. It is a good practice to verify and document communications of this nature. It is also a good practice to develop a specific check list of outside parties that should be notified regarding the restart activities. The cooperation and coordination is worth the extra effort.

If the PSII team identifies a specific change that must be made prior to restart, then the recommended change should be evaluated for potential hazards and impacts on the system before restart begins. This concept is addressed in Section 6.1. However, if most of the facility is intact and apparently ready to restart, the PSII team may come under considerable pressure to cut corners on restart recommendations and criteria.

Proposals may be suggested to the PSII team to hasten restart, such as considering resuming operations "just until the next planned outage in the near future." When these pressures arise, the PSII team should maintain standards and consistency to avoid a repeat incident.

Restart criteria recommendations should receive the same degree of scrutiny as the final and formal recommendations. Each restart recommendation should be reviewed for management-of-change and evaluated for possible adverse consequences. Some common changes likely to be found in restart criteria recommendations include

- changes in operating procedures or instructions, which should be in writing and specific;
- changes in instrument alarm set points;
- changes in emergency response actions by on-duty personnel.

For many incidents, especially major ones, it may be worthwhile to have the PSII team participate in restart activities. If the investigation is incomplete, the PSII team could develop a better understanding of actual operating practices and conditions, and they could better interpret and analyze the available information. If the investigation is complete, the PSII team would have the opportunity to validate some of the determinations and decisions made during the investigation, to verify completion of the recommended action, and to determine if the changes made were understood by employees operating the unit.

6.3.6. Establish and Prepare to Present Recommendations for Preventive Action

Section 6.2 discusses the establishment of recommendations. In preparation for presenting the recommendations to the management team, some analysis should be done by the PSII team. Related preventive action items can be grouped by priority, by systems affected, by time frame for implementation, by cost or level of approval required, or by the possible need for outside resources, such as further research or special expertise.

The impact of each recommendation should have been identified during the management of change review. Potential objections to recommendations and their implementation should be identified and answered. Expected questions and concerns of the line management team should be researched and resolved by the PSII team to the degree possible. If recommendations from similar incidents are available, they should be compared with those of the present incident. All of the above information should be taken into consideration when preparing to present the recommendations to management.

Recommendations that were dropped by the PSII team should be well-documented as to the basis for rejection.

6.3.7. Review Recommendations with Management

The next activity, as shown in Figure 6-1, is a presentation and review of the recommendations with the members of line management who have responsibility for the operations of the unit that experienced the incident. The specific responsibilities of management are detailed in Section 6.2.1 and will not be repeated here.

If the cause of an incident and its corrective recommendation are significant, the company may incur additional responsibilities to deal with a hazard. Therefore, it is important that companies resolve causes and remedial recommendations that deal with significant hazards and risks in a reasonable and timely manner.

6.3.8. Documentation of Recommendation Decisions

Once a recommendation has been accepted for implementation, a clear, auditable documentation trail should be established and maintained. If a recommendation is accepted, modified in scope or time of implementation, or is not implemented, then the basis for each decision should be documented.

6.3.9. Implementation of Recommendations and Follow-Up Action

As previously discussed, each recommendation should have a person assigned to be responsible for monitoring its implementation through completion. Initial completion dates should be set. The implementation should be monitored, documented and checked to ensure that the preventive action is indeed achieving the intended results and that the management-of-change analysis was thorough and accurate.

A follow-up audit should be conducted after an appropriate period to verify that recommended actions remain in place, are still working as intended and that the lessons learned were communicated as appropriate throughout the company and to others in the CPI. This audit may uncover that some recommended action was ineffective. Engineers, designers or person responsible for the implementation may find a reason why the original recommendation will not work or will not be effective. It may be appropriate to reconvene the PSII team to ensure that the final planned action addresses the original issues in an acceptable manner.

6.3.10. Management System for Follow-Through

Another follow-through item is the possible change to the PSII management system itself. The PSII team should critique the investigation and identify any changes that would enhance the quality of the next PSII. Any recommended action item relating to improving the PSII system should be treated in the same way as recommendations related to the incident. Chapter 3 and Chapter 8 give guidelines and options for the PSII system.

6.3.11. Reports and Communications

The recommendations as accepted for implementation are now ready to be documented in formal written reports and communicated as addressed in Chapter 7 ("Formal Reports and Communications").

A single document containing evidence, analysis, causes and recommendations may better communicate the story, causes of the incident and remedial action. However, there may valid reasons by top management and other company departments to present the results of a PSII in a different format. The PSII team should seek guidance from their company management.

6.4. REFERENCES

1. *Resource Guide for Implementing the Process Safety Code of Management Practices.* 1990. Washington, DC: Chemical Manufacturers Association.
2. Kletz, T.A. 1985. Make Plants Inherently Safe. *Hydrocarbon Processing*, September. Gulf Publishing Company, Houston, TX.
3. Hendershot, D. C. 1991. "Design of Inherently Safer Chemical Processing Facilities." Paper presented at Texas Chemical Council Safety Seminar, Process Safety Management Program
4. Knowlton, E. R. 1989. *An Introduction to Hazard and Operability Studies—A Guideword Approach.* Vancouver, British Columbia: Chemetics International Co.
5. Englund, S. M. 1991. Design and Operate Plants for Inherent Safety. *Chemical Engineering Progress* (Part 1, March 1991; Part 2, May 1991).
6. Kletz, T. A. 1988. *Learning from Accidents in Industry.* Stoneham, MA: Butterworths.
7. Csengery, L. V. "The Time For Process Hazard Analysis Has Arrived." Paper 68d presented at the 1991 AIChE Loss Prevention Symposium, Pittsburgh, PA, August 18–21, 1991.
8. NUREG-1303, "Incident Investigation Manual." U.S. Nuclear Regulatory Commission, Washington D.C., 1988.
9. Ferry, T. S. 1988. *Modern Accident Investigation and Analysis*, 2nd ed. New York: John Wiley & Sons.
10. CCPS. 1989. *Guidelines for Technical Management of Chemical Process Safety.* New York: American Institute of Chemical Engineers.
11. Winsor, D. A. 1989. Challenger: A Case of Failure to Communicate. *Chemtech*, September.
12. CCPS. 1992. *Guidelines for Hazard Evaluation Procedures, Second Edition with Worked Examples.* New York: American Institute of Chemical Engineers.

7

FORMAL REPORTS AND COMMUNICATIONS

This chapter describes practical considerations for formal written incident reports. Attributes of outstanding reports are presented. Special focus is placed on the reader/user of the report. Internal and external communications issues are addressed in Section 7.4. A generic report format is presented along with a discussion of avoidable common mistakes. This chapter assumes that the information gathering, multiple root-cause analysis, and recommendation phases have been completed. Figure 7-1 presents a flowchart of the activities and concepts addressed in this chapter.

7.1. INITIAL NOTIFICATION

In the practical world, it is easy to develop confusion about the term "report." Sometimes the term is used to represent the final, formal, written report. At other times the term could mean a verbal notification to initially alert the organization that an incident has occurred. Even after 20 years, the term "report" causes confusion when discussing the U.S. Department of Labor Occupational Health and Safety Administration (OSHA) regulations. OSHA regulations require a verbal "report" for certain incidents such as a fatality or hospitalization of five or more employees. OSHA regulations further require a written "report" be prepared for each work-related injury that is severe enough to be classified as a "recordable injury."

The required verbal notification to OSHA must be made within 48 hours following the incident, but does not require the use of a specific form. The reporter, however, should make a written documentation of this verbal communication, noting the time, person involved, extent of information disclosed, and any special instructions or requests made by OSHA at the time of notice.

Regulatory agencies are not consistent in the application of the term "immediate notification." For example, the State of California requires formal notification for dismemberment or disfigurement injury incidents. The State of New Jersey requires "immediate" notice when certain quantities of hazardous materials are released. Time periods longer than 15 minutes after the incident have not been considered "immediate" by New Jersey regulators. The U.S. Coast Guard and the Environmental Protection Agency have specific notification requirements.

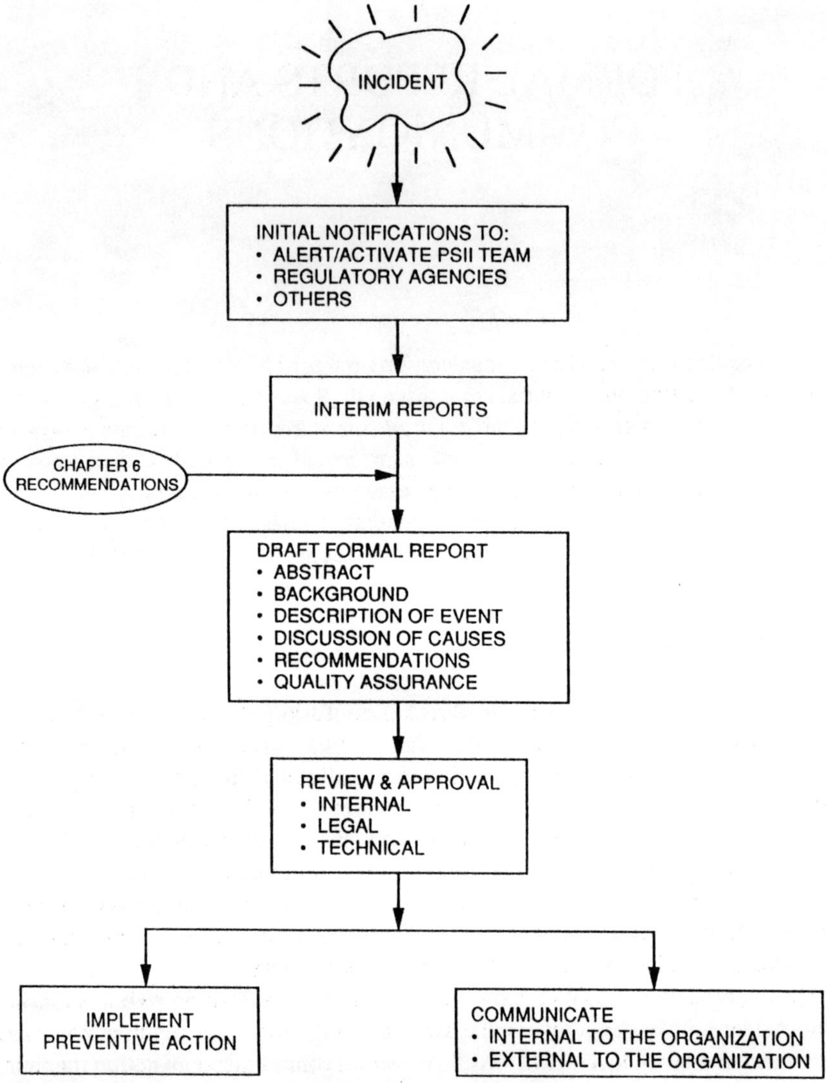

Figure 7-1. Flowchart—formal reports and communications.

The format and timing of all external notifications should be identified and incorporated into the PSII management system prior to an incident. With this information readily at hand, the proper reports may be made quickly and accurately when an incident occurs.

Internal notifications, sometimes called alerts or flash-reports, are trigger mechanisms for starting specific portions of the PSII management system and for decisions. Obviously, medical treatment of injured personnel and stabilization of the incident site must always take priority over other activities if there is a conflict regarding the use of available resources during an incident.

Initial communications, which should be part of the company's emergency response plan, may include

- internal within the facility to summon emergency responders
- internal within the site to start administrative response
- external to call-out resources
- external for mutual aid emergency response
- external to regulatory agencies, as required
- internal to company headquarters and administrative departments
- external to family members and/or next-of-kin
- external to neighboring facilities
- external to news media where appropriate
- external to insurance carriers

Making these initial alert/notification communications in a timely manner can present a serious challenge to the resources available immediately after an incident. Planning to handle these communications should be incorporated into the PSII management system and coordinated with facility emergency response plans. A check list with prearranged names, titles, and phone numbers is most helpful.

7.2. INTERIM REPORTS

Some process safety investigations will be extensive in duration. In these situations, some form of interim report may be necessary. The report content must be as accurate and thorough as possible, yet should remain flexible and responsive to new information. Each report issued by the PSII team should be retained and its contained information and distribution documented. A single member of the PSII team should coordinate all such interim reporting activity and serve as the appointed liaison between the PSII team and other departments and organizations. A single communications channel is especially helpful when team members must deal with an external regulatory agency.

For complex incidents or causes, confirmation of all scenarios or causes may require a lengthy period of time, perhaps years. Rather than waiting for the final confirmation, the team should write a complete report, indicating open research action points. As the open research items become resolved, their status should be documented. If new information indicates that conclusions or recommendations should be changed, the report document should be updated or annotated as necessary.

7.3. FORMAL WRITTEN REPORT

7.3.1. General

The formal written report is the vehicle for communicating the investigation results. It can be extremely useful, leading to process safety improvements and enhancing, summarizing, and extending the PSII team's investigation. Likewise, the report can be poorly prepared and nearly useless, negating weeks or months of productive investigation.

A mechanism for capturing and applying the results of the investigation should be an integral part of the management system for process incident investigation. *Guidelines for Technical Management of Chemical Process Safety,*[1] page 118, states that "The lessons learned from an incident investigation are limited in usefulness unless they are reported in an appropriate manner." The Chemical Manufacturer's Association (CMA) also recognizes this need by including it as one of the twenty-two management practices in the Responsible Care®, Process Safety Code of Management Practices.[2] The formal written report should convey the results of the investigation clearly and succinctly.

One key to success is to focus on the intended reader/user of the report. The expected reader should be identified and understood by the report writers. It is unreasonable to expect that all the needs of all potential audiences will be met. The large variation in the reader's technical background, the need to include technical information, and the need to be reasonably concise limits the usefulness of a single report. Every final report represents a balanced trade-off between content, details, quantity of information contained, and expected needs of the reader/user. It is reasonable to expect the reader/user has some general knowledge of chemical process technology and hazards. It is also reasonable to expect that the reader/user has some genuine interest and a desire to gain from understanding and applying lessons available for learning. The report should not be a motivational or inspirational tool.

Carper, in Chapter 11 of his book *Forensic Engineering,*[3] recognizes a primary and a secondary audience and acknowledges that the report should not be expected to reach all audiences and satisfy all questions. *Professional Accident Investigation,* by Kuhlman[4] develops the concept that different levels of management have different needs and priorities. The report should anticipate and address questions the intended reader might be expected to ask.

Formal recommendations are often excluded from investigation reports prepared by U.S. federal government agencies. For instance, the OSHA investigation often does a thorough job of determining and analyzing causes yet goes no further because the experts used to gather and analyze evidence are usually not involved in establishing recommendations.

The American National Standards Institute (ANSI) has established a voluntary consensus standard for recording basic facts relating to the nature and occurrence of work injuries, ANSI Z16.2.[5] This standard has been in use for more than thirty years and provides a consistent baseline for many report formats. The standard focuses on injury to personnel and presents standard classification categories. If alternate codes are used in incident reports, special effort and notation must be made to avoid confusing the reader.

Although it is the most important single document, the final published report is only a portion of the overall record of the investigation. A full and complete set of documents should be maintained for future reference. This systematic documentation package is sometimes referred to as the audit trail. It provides subsequent reviewers and investigators with the opportunity to understand more completely the decisions and analysis done by the original team. The set should contain lists of relevant files. All documents associated with the investigation should be preserved according to company document retention plan.

An exceptional investigation report will fully explain the technical elements and issues associated with the incident. It will describe the management systems that should have prevented the event, and will detail the system root causes associated with the human errors and other system deficiencies involved with the incident. The PSII team should constantly perform some kind of self-examination to help ensure objectivity and independence. Sometimes after being immersed in the details for a period of time, the team can lose its sense of perspective.

Incident reports will often include information that may be sensitive or controversial. The report should include relevant information even if it is not yet completely understood. If there is a reasonable doubt as to the certainty of an event sequence, this information should be addressed in the report.

As discussed, the entire purpose of the investigation is prevention. The formal report should reflect the attitude of preventing a repeat incident rather than affixing blame. This approach should be reflected in the tone and choice of words used in the formal report.

ABSTRACT: Summary of event, consequences, causes and recommendations, 1 page maximum

BACKGROUND: Process description, purpose and scope of investigation, conditions preceding the incident.

NARRATIVE: Description of the event scenario, sequence, consequences

ROOT CAUSES: Identification and discussion of the system-related root causes of the incident

FINDINGS AND RECOMMENDATIONS: Two separate sections, identifying factual findings, and recommended preventive action.

OTHER: Miscellaneous back-up information, discussion of rejected or less-probable scenarios, documents of special interest or value, method of investigation and team membership, photographs, diagrams, calculations, lab reports.

Figure 7-2. Formal report outline.

Figure 7-2 offers a suggested outline for a typical PSII report. It should be recognized that incidents vary considerably in circumstances. Consequently, all sections are not necessary for every incident report.

7.3.2. Abstract

This is a *single* page summary of the event, consequences, root causes, and recommendations. It is usually very helpful to present a highly simplified summary in the first one or two sentences. The purpose is to project a mental image of the event. For most formal reports, this synopsis is written after completing the other sections.

7.3.3. Background

This section presents an overview of the process and events leading up to the incident. It should reconfirm the purpose of the investigation and clarify any limitations on the scope of the PSII team activities. Background information for the facility and unit includes such items as history, age, size, expansions, major events, and technical sophistication. If a particular program such as a periodic inspection program or job safety analysis is involved in the incident, it is first referenced here in the background section. Information about the existing management systems, procedures, and policies is normally included in this segment, as are any unusual external events such as labor relations issues, personnel turnover rate, maintenance shutdowns or turnarounds, and interruptions (e.g., power dips).

The background of the individuals involved should be addressed, such as experience level, qualifications, and experience with the particular task involved, time in the position, years of experience, time spent at that task that day, whether working overtime or rotating shift. The environmental conditions at the time can be particularly significant (time of day, temperature, lighting, rain, fog, ice, snow, or wind conditions).

Significant process conditions preceding the incident should be identified, especially if the process is a batch operation or if there was any known deviation from normal conditions, sequences, flows, pressures, concentrations, temperatures, pH, or other process parameters. Often it is helpful to separate the background conditions into several distinct time periods. One category may be normal conditions, a second category may be the time period from 48 hours up to 1 hour before the event, and a third section may address the background immediately (1–20 minutes) before the event.

7.3.4. Narrative Description of the Incident

In this section of the report, the scenario is described, usually in chronological order, and the results are identified. This is the WHO–WHAT–WHEN–WHERE–WHY–HOW portion of the report. It should give precise and specific information using identification numbers and location of equipment. The military 24 hour clock method of recording time is especially applicable to this section. Many chemical processes operate using this format already, as it is less ambiguous. When this section is done successfully, the reader has a sense of witnessing the event as it unfolds. The extent of injury and damage is included in this section. Anticipated questions and items of special interest should be clearly addressed.

7.3.5. Root Causes

All of the system root causes of the incident are identified, analyzed, and discussed in this section of the report. Process safety incidents are the result of many factors, and therefore singling out one cause is rarely the proper approach. The underlying causes identified by the PSII team are determined by a systematic analysis. The causes should not be limited to the conclusions and opinions of the witnesses. If the PSII team merely parrots the statements and opinions of the witnesses, then the team has failed in its responsibility. The PSII team has the responsibility to analyze the facts and reach a consensus decision as to the most likely root causes.

7.3.6. Recommendations

Recommendations for preventive action are the result of the PSII investigation. The attributes of successful recommendations are addressed in detail in Chapter 6 and are shown in Figure 6-2. Each recommendation should be accompanied by a suggested target completion date and suggested assignment of responsibility. The PSII team has the responsibility to *develop and submit* the recommendation. It is management's responsibility to act on and resolve the recommendation.

7.3.7. Other

The remaining contents of a formal written incident report can vary significantly depending on circumstances. Often included as an appendix is a collection of data and additional reference information that some, but not all, readers may need. Typical of such supplemental information is maps, flow sheets, diagrams, photos, materials safety data sheets (MSDSs), a full list of reference materials consulted, a list of members of the PSII team, a description of investigative methods and approaches used, a glossary of terms and acronyms, a bibliography, log sheets, computer printouts, and pertinent extracts from witness interviews. If a map is used, it should focus on the area of interest, and show only the minimum amount of nonessential information.

Medical evidence is usually omitted from formal incident reports due to the need to respect doctor–patient confidentiality. Names of injured and other participants are also frequently omitted for privacy reasons. Descriptions such as Operator 1, 2, or 3 can be substituted.

Although not required by existing regulations, it is a good practice to include the reasons for eliminating other possible causes and alternate scenarios. This can be extremely useful and enlightening to subsequent investigators or analysts who may follow 5 or 10 years later.

All members of the PSII team should sign the final report. This is an indication of personal endorsement of the team consensus.

7.3.8. Criteria for Restart

If conditions or restrictions were imposed on restart of operations, these items should be included in the report (see Section 6.3). The discussion should include the basis for the restriction as well as the reasons for removing it.

7.4. CAPTURING LESSONS LEARNED

7.4.1. Internal

Lessons learned from one facility's incident often have applicability to other facilities within the same organization.[1] A management system should be in place to ensure that the understanding of the lessons learned is not isolated to one single location. Another way to express these thoughts was presented in Trevor Kletz's paper "Organizations Have No Memory."[6] In actual practice, organizations may find it extremely difficult to maintain continuity of the lessons learned from an incident. This challenge remains regardless of the quality of the initial investigation. A well-designed and well-operated PSII system should set up a mechanism to "communicate lessons learned to all appropriate company groups."[2] This includes maintaining an incident log and ensuring that incident reports become a part of the process safety information document package.

Organizations have no memory.

Only people have memory.

An active and sustained effort is needed so that lessons learned once will not have to be relearned.

There should be a plan for issuing the information from the investigation. Specific responsibilities and target dates should be established. Not all groups have the same information needs, so it may be practical at times to prepare more than one information release. The personnel who work directly in the unit that experienced the incident have a need to know what happened, why, and what direct specific changes are to be made. Personnel in adjacent units may not be exposed to the same specific hazards, and therefore may need a more generic presentation of the lessons learned. Workers in similar facilities within the same parent organization may be exposed to the same hazard. Unless the company has an active communication program as part of its PSII system, these workers may remain uninformed.

As discussed in Section 7.3, each formal written report actually represents a trade-off between quantity and quality of information. The information contained in the outgoing communication should be general enough to ensure that an incident is not regarded as an isolated phenomenon, and yet specific enough to ensure that the information is not regarded as too vague or too general to be useful.

Some companies have found success with a periodic publication of incident abstracts. Each incident may appear as a one or two paragraph summary in a quarterly bulletin. This information is circulated widely within the corporation. If a site has a special interest in one particular incident, full details are then requested by direct contact between the two sites. The highly abbreviated summary has other uses, such as material for employee safety training meetings or bulletin board postings. This is another example of the practical trade-off between quantity of incidents publicized and the amount of detail presented for each incident.

Historical incident recording and communicating in useful form has several beneficial results. The information suggests precautions for other facilities, allows lessons learned to be taken into account in future design, and helps identify trends not apparent from single incidents. Because incidents have many causes, some causes may not be identified in the investigation of a single incident. For example, if an incident occurs on a Saturday, it may simply be coincidence or it may be a symptom of deficiencies in management systems on weekend shifts. If a pattern of weekend incidents develops, then management can take appropriate action. Without incident recording and analysis of the records, such patterns may go unnoticed and result in even more incidents. Figures 7-3 and 7-4 show two examples of summary historical analyses.

Common cause and trend identification analysis give the opportunity to apply deductive hindsight to past incidents. This process allows a more productive allocation of resources and can maximize incident prevention and control. However, establishing relevant categories as the basis for analysis is not as easy as it might appear. There will be hard choices between having too many small categories and too few very broad and therefore somewhat nonspecific categories. Searchers should be able to focus clearly on commonalities. The categories should include specific system deficiencies/breakdowns such as design, training, process mechanical integrity, and equipment specifications. Other categories may be by specific hazard exposure.

Trend analysis can be confused or invalidated by too small a sample. If the charting or analysis is limited only to major incidents, there will often be too few within a time period to draw meaningful conclusions. For example, a facility with one thousand employees may experience only one or two serious incidents per year, and several years worth of data would be needed to make any meaningful statistical analysis. Minor incidents and near-misses can be as useful in trend analysis and preventive prediction as major incidents. All process incidents should be reported

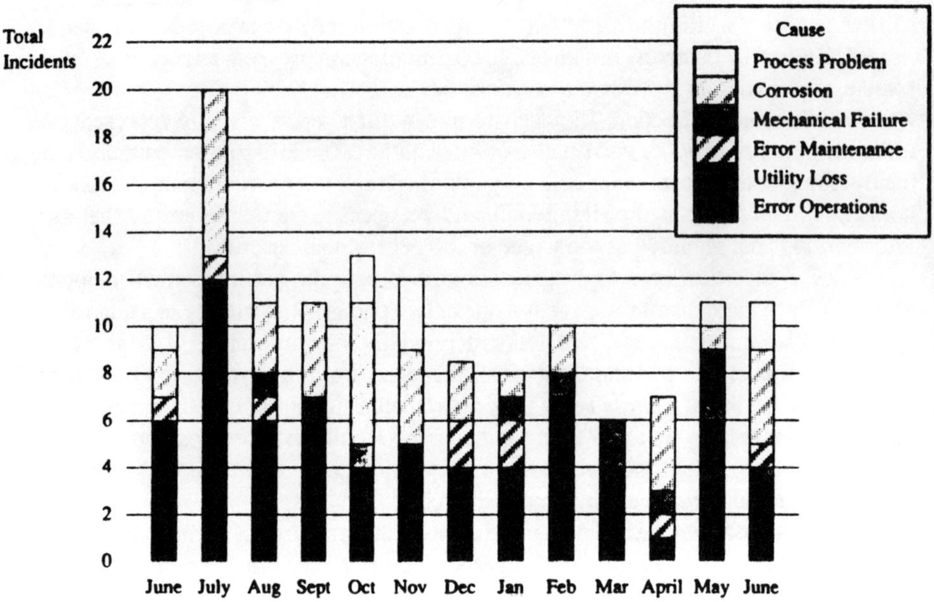

Figure 7-3. Representative incident trend data. [From CCPS. 1991. ***Plant Guidelines for Technical Management of Chemical Process Safety.*** **New York: American Institute of Chemical Engineers.]**

classified and investigated as appropriate. The severity of an incident is frequently more a function of chance than actual fundamental system differences among incidents.

Computer-aided trend identification offers potential benefits, but is dependent on the quality of the input information. Expert systems and artificial intelligence are tools being tested. When successful, they may give improved insight into identifying common causes and trend analysis.

Although the focus of this book is on the episodic process-related event with catastrophic potential, some discussion of the incident reporting form is in order. A standard form is a common and useful tool for the nonprocess incident (such as a minor sprained ankle from tripping over an unused hose). Forms tend to steer the investigators' thoughts within narrow limited channels. Forms, therefore, may not be as useful for investigating process-related events as they are for nonprocess incidents. Some companies have increased the effectiveness of reporting forms by printing memory jogging information and questions on the back of the form. Forms can be helpful for capturing cause data in a uniform manner so it can be coded for computer analysis.

Each investigation is unique and can be used as an opportunity to improve the PSII system. A critique should be conducted (see Chapter 6) and should include everyone who participated on the investigation team. It should, of course, identify

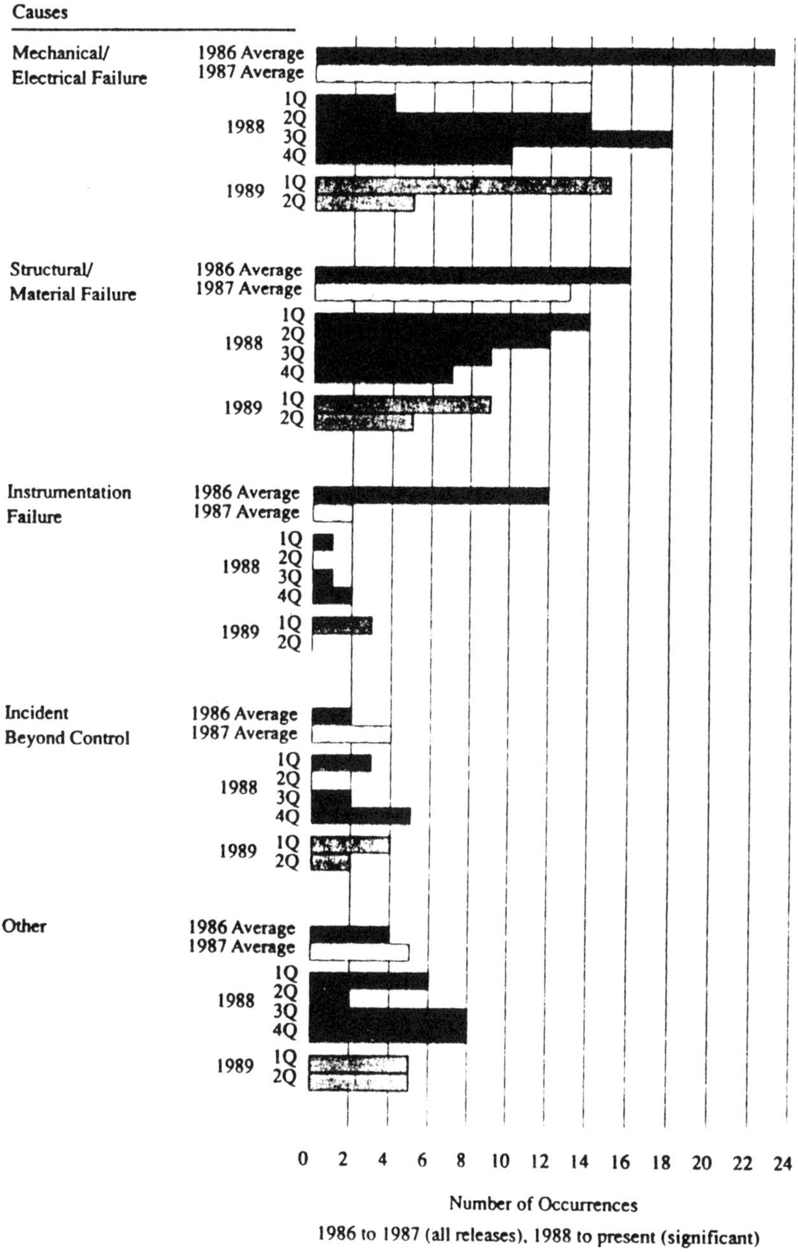

Figure 7-4. Representative incident analysis data. [From CCPS. 1991. ***Plant Guidelines for Technical Management of Chemical Process Safety.*** **New York: American Institute of Chemical Engineers.]**

potential changes that would make the next investigation more successful. It should also identify those items that were successful and do not need change. Evaluation of the planning, team supplies, coordination, and communication issues often will show areas for improvement. Proposed changes to the PSII system should be evaluated and executed using the management of change system. Changes adopted should be implemented and tracked as any other recommended action item. Modifications to the PSII team training program should be kept up to date.

7.4.2. External

Process safety is a dynamic field. Enhancing process safety knowledge is one of the twelve key elements recognized by CCPS for successfully managing process safety. "Management commitment to using all available resources for enhancing process safety knowledge at all levels in the organization is a key difference in having a minimum, adequate, or outstanding process safety program." (*Guidelines for Technical Management of Chemical Process Safety,*[1] page 137.)

One method of enhancing process safety knowledge is to learn from the experience of others. Industry data bases, which contain information about accidents and incidents, are presented in Table 2-2. This gives an overview of some 21 separate data bases with varying degrees of accessibility. The AIChE has for years sponsored public presentation of actual incidents with accompanying lessons learned. Some of these case histories are contained in the AIChE publications, *Ammonia Safety Symposium, Loss Prevention, Chemical Engineering Progress,* and *Plant Operations Progress.* The American Petroleum Institute also publishes a series of booklets on specific "Lessons Learned." In the UK, the Institution of Chemical Engineers[7] publishes the *Loss Prevention Bulletin,* which contains specific case histories.

Valuable, although unofficial, case history information can often be exchanged verbally during conferences and seminars. This is especially true for those incidents in which litigation is not expected.

Other avenues for increasing process safety knowledge exist. Previously unrecognized potential hazards and latent properties of materials are written about in industry and technical journals. Peer-reviewed research work in the area of process safety is published in several international scientific journals. Previously unrecognized failure modes are often publicized by manufacturers and suppliers of process equipment.

7.5. SAMPLE REPORTS

A representative sampling of process safety incident reports is contained in the appendices. Because there is no single universal report that simultaneously satisfies all needs of all potential readers/users, a variety in degree of detail and circumstance has been included to give readers the opportunity to select the format best suited to their needs.

Most of the sample reports answer these basic questions:

- What happened?
- How did it happen?
- Why did it happen?
- What were the multiple system-related root causes?
- What can be done to prevent a repeat?

7.6. QUALITY ASSURANCE

7.6.1. Check List

The PSII team should review the investigation and final draft of the formal written report to ensure the intended result was achieved. An example check list is shown in Figure 7-5.

Reports should have technical review for clarity and accuracy, and, where appropriate, legal review.

7.6.2. Good Practices to Avoid Common Mistakes

For improved quality of formal written incident reports, the PSII team should follow these guidelines:

1. Avoid jargon specific to the process that the intended reader may not understand. One good guide is to try to make the written report intelligible to the technically minded lay person.

- ☐ Intended reader/user identified and technical competence level chosen
- ☐ Purpose of report identified
- ☐ Scope of investigation specified
- ☐ Summary/abstract, no longer than one page
- ☐ Summary/abstract answers what happened, why, and general recommendations
- ☐ Background—describes process, investigation scope
- ☐ Narrative—clearly describes what happened
- ☐ Root Causes—identifies multiple and underlying causes
- ☐ Recommendations—describes specific action for follow-up, target dates, tracking
- ☐ Other—necessary charts, exhibits, information
- ☐ Signed by team members
- ☐ Distribution identified
- ☐ Plan for disseminating the information

Figure 7-5. Example check list for formal written reports.

2. For increased readability and comprehension, reduce the use of abbreviations and acronyms. Most of these can be avoided.
3. Decide on the selected reader's level of technical competence and then be consistent in writing to that level. Assume the reader has a certain minimum knowledge of chemical processing safety.
4. Avoid intermixing conclusions when presenting the factual findings.
5. Be sure to include a complete list of reference materials used during the investigation. Subsequent investigators or analysts who subsequently review the report several years later should be able to substantiate the conclusions reached by the PSII team.
6. Identify multiple system-related root causes determined by the PSII *team* after a systematic analysis. Root causes reported should not be limited to the opinion or judgment of a participant or witness of the incident.
7. Include specific equipment identification, because omission can cause problems for readers in other units or facilities who may have the same equipment and remain unaware of it hazards.
8. Avoid downplaying human performance factors when drafting the report. There is a natural hesitancy to criticize others or to address normally encountered performance limitations or errors. Effects of fatigue from working excessive overtime are not always addressed in the written report. If these human performance factors are neglected, the error may be repeated. All facts of the incident must be considered relevant.
9. Publish only one official version of the report. Sometimes the PSII team may release a preliminary draft copy that differs from the final version. This can cause unnecessary and avoidable confusion. If a preliminary draft is published, the team should make every effort to ensure that all copies of the preliminary version are replaced with the final edition. The preliminary report should be conspicuously identified as "Draft, not a final report and as such is subject to change."
10. Delay writing the abstract–summary until after the main body of the report has been drafted.

In summary, the report is the vehicle for transmitting and documenting the investigation. It is a direct reflection of the quality and professionalism of the PSII team. The report should be reviewed by the entire team prior to release.

7.7. REFERENCES

1. CCPS. 1989. *Guidelines for Technical Management of Chemical Process Safety.* New York: American Institute of Chemical Engineers.
2. CMA. 1990. *Responsible Care: A Resource Guide for the Process Safety Code of Management Practices.* Washington, DC: Chemical Manufacturers Association.
3. Carper, K. 1989. *Forensic Engineering.* New York: Elsevier.

4. Kuhlman, R. *Professional Accident Investigation.* Loganville, GA: Institute Press, International Loss Control Institute.
5. American National Standards Institute. "ANSI Z16.2—Method of Recording Basic Facts Relating to the Nature and Occurrence of Work Injuries." New York: American National Standards Institute.
6. Kletz, T.A. "Organizations Have No Memory." Paper presented at the AIChE Loss Prevention Symposium, April 1979.
7. Institution of Chemical Engineers. "Loss Prevention Bulletin 061." February 1985, Institution of Chemical Engineers, Rugby, England.

8

MANAGEMENT SYSTEM DEVELOPMENT AND IMPLEMENTATION

This chapter presents guidelines for initial development and implementation of a process safety incident investigation (PSII) management system. It focuses on one-time nonroutine and nonrecurring activities concerned with establishing such a system. The chapter is intended mainly to be used by the technical professional who is charged with the responsibility to establish a formal PSII program where none currently exists. The principles enunciated in this chapter, however, can also be used to review or reestablish a program that has become dormant or out-of-date.

This chapter includes insights, challenges, and opportunities for establishing or improving a systematic approach to investigations. Special emphasis is given to training issues. Some planning concerns from previous chapters are addressed for use in periodic refresher training. The key concepts of this chapter are shown in Figure 8-1.

8.1. DEVELOPING THE INITIAL MANAGEMENT SYSTEM

In developing a PSII management system, several parts of the investigative and remedial process need to be considered and addressed. These elements are covered in this section.

8.1.1. Commitment by Management

Before significant progress can be made, top management should first recognize the necessity for and the benefits of a systematic incident investigation program and endorse the formation of a PSII program. To achieve a consistent and effective PSII, management should provide resources for an ongoing program, understand the responsibilities of each level of the organization, and hold managers accountable for achieving results. Management should also endorse the reporting of all near misses, investigation of significant near-miss incidents, and persistent follow-up of PSII recommendations until they have been resolved.

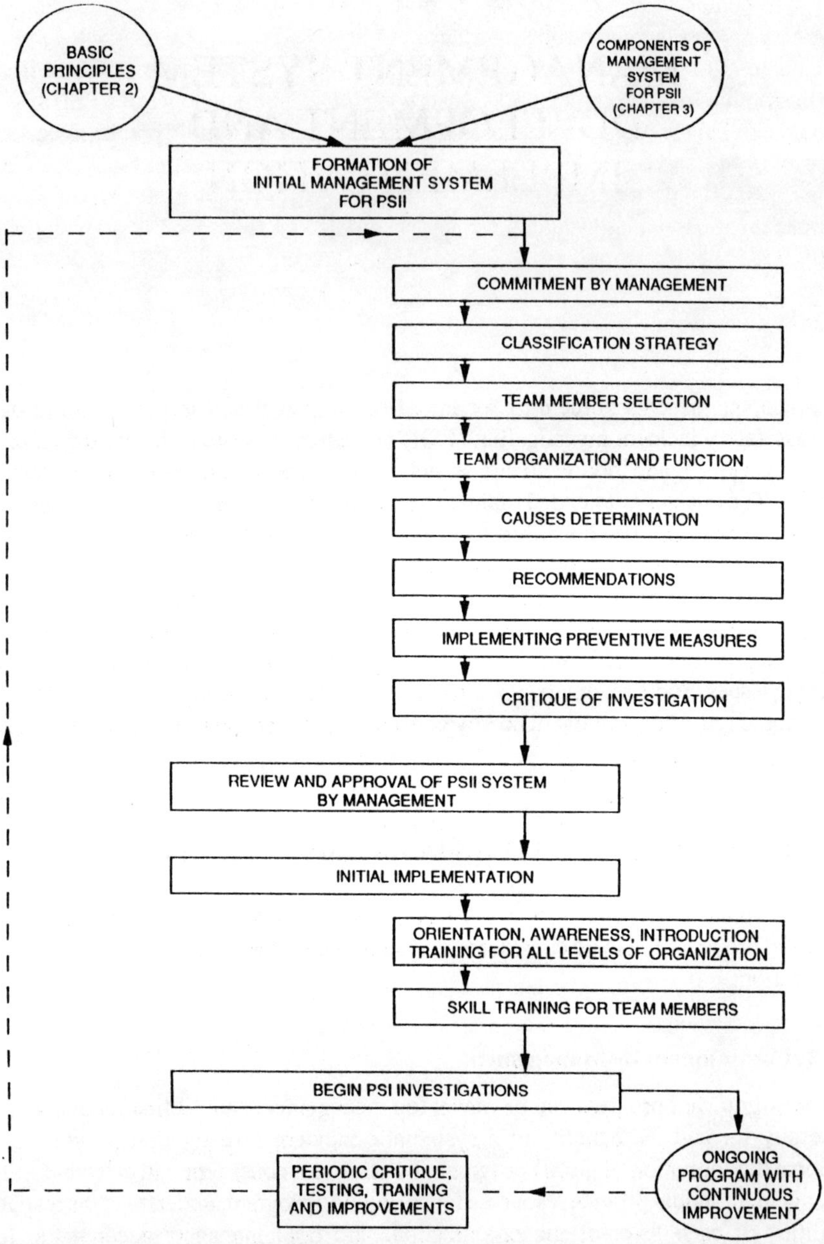

Figure 8-1. Flowchart—development and implementation of initial management system for process safety incident investigation.

The person who is drafting the proposal for a PSII management system should begin by researching the basic principles in Chapter 2 and the elements of the system in Chapter 3 to determine which of the methodologies and concepts will best fit the particular culture and perspective of the organization. The developer of a PSII system should explain the proposed system to managers at the appropriate levels, since some may not fully appreciate the structure, function, requirements, and benefits of systematic multiple root-cause incident investigations. Moreover, members of top management should be provided the opportunity to participate in the development activities. Such participation will demonstrate to the organization their endorsement of the program and help establish incident investigation as a normal line management responsibility. Management also should periodically reaffirm its endorsement and understanding of the PSII concepts.

Due to changes in company leadership, the awareness of and emphasis on PSII at all levels of management may diminish. Consequently, periodic refresher training should also be included in the original proposed system. Formal management training is addressed in Section 8.3.

8.1.2. Incident Reporting System

Although some accidents *must* be reported, incidents and near misses *should be* reported if a PSII system is to operate effectively. A discussion of incident reporting can be found in Section 7.1. The CCPS publication, *Plant Guidelines for Technical Management of Chemical Process Safety,*[5] contains two sample incident notification/reporting procedures. Appendix IIA of that book presents an example of a typical procedure for notifying, investigating, and reporting of incidents from a corporate perspective; and Appendix IID gives a sample facility level procedure for reporting incidents.

8.1.3. Incident Classification System

When establishing incident reporting procedures, a classification system appropriate to the organization should be set in place to categorize the incidents. Classification systems are a necessity for some reports, but they are also extremely useful in measuring the effectiveness of safety management programs and in ensuring that information is properly captured, which can be used to identify common causes and hard-to-find incident trends. There is no perfect generic classification system, and systems will vary depending on organizational structures and company programs. Section 3.3 presents accepted definitions for some of the common classification categories used.

In practice, every classification system has gray areas, due in part to honest differences of technical opinion, especially regarding estimates of reasonable probabilities and consequences of near-miss events. Occasionally, new information will necessitate a change in category after the initial classification. The PSII management system must allow for some flexibility while providing guidance in classification.

Another difficulty in classification involves areas that are gray by nature, for example, employee back injury. Consistency in classifying back injuries has been traditionally difficult to achieve. The American National Standards Institute ANSI Z16 standard[1] has addressed this problem with a list of questions and answers for commonly encountered cases that are difficult to classify. The National Fire Protection Association has taken a similar approach to the life safety code (NFPA 101)[2] and the National Electric Code (NFPA 70).[3] OSHA[4] includes examples in its record keeping guide. By consulting a tabulation of common questions and answers, the users of the system can achieve increased consistency. These questions are not regulations, but are intended to shed light on cases that may require further scrutiny in order to achieve consistent interpretation.

The developer of the PSII system should consider a similar approach when formulating the initial classification scheme. One technique would be to conduct some test classifications on a data bank of past company incidents and on a series of fictitious gray area cases.

During plant audits, it is common to conduct some type of emergency drill. The drill and audit provide an opportunity to test general knowledge and recognition of near-miss incident reporting and classification.

8.1.4. Formation of the Team

Team member attributes are detailed in Chapter 3. The initial members should be recruited on a strictly voluntary basis. One successful technique is for the team member to be contacted initially by a member of management who is above the level of the immediate supervisor of the team member. This higher level management involvement sends a clear signal of the team's importance. Some publicity and special recognition will help the team gain respect and motivation. A personal letter from top management or even the chief executive officer or phone calls from them are other options.

All PSII team recruits should be identified and selected based on their experience and personal interest. Service on the team should be regarded as a desirable assignment in which the individual will have an opportunity to establish or influence corporate standards and direction. Membership on the team should have specific written endorsement from the immediate supervisor and should have an identified finite ending date. Recognition should be given for service on the PSII team. Consideration should be given to conducting the formation and training meetings at a recognized desirable location. Participation on the team should be considered on performance review. Collectively, efforts such as these will help recognize the PSII team as an important function.

8.1.5. Team Organization

The actual functions and composition of the team are detailed in previous chapters. However, the effect of PSII objectives and priorities on composition of the team must be kept in mind as the proposed management system is developed. It is important to emphasize that team composition and organization, assignment of team duties, and actual operations must be structured by the requirements of the particular incident. Actual team composition may vary significantly based on the nature of the process, the degree of technical sophistication, time required, and expertise needed. It is important to remember that the team members are not full-time professional investigators of process-related incidents and may only serve once in their entire work careers. The team leader's responsibilities, Section 3.5.2, need to be clearly expressed. The management system should recognize that flexibility of team composition is a very important feature of a well-designed PSII management system.

8.1.6. PSII Team Operations

The plan for PSII team operations and communications should be integrated into the organization's crisis management program to permit the PSII team to focus on the investigation. Notification or activation of the team should be practiced repeatedly with critique and feedback sessions to discover and resolve hidden problems. "Communications only" drills are an inexpensive exercise that often yield highly positive results. A plan should also be developed to locate and to transport experts, consultants, and other contract personnel who may be required for various types of incidents.

The PSII system should provide for an investigation process that generally follows the problem-solving sequence highlighted in Chapters 4 and 5. After handling actions dictated by the priorities of the actual emergency, investigation objectives, plans, and type of investigative approach most suited to the specific incident are established. Then, usually in a series of team meetings, evidence is gathered and analyzed; information is exchanged; immediate tasks are identified; and reports are generated. The need for communication and coordination skills should be identified during the development stages.

8.1.7. Identifying Root Causes

Identifying causes is one of the three primary objectives of the entire investigation process irrespective of which investigative approach is used. Initial formation of the PSII management system will most likely require some special attention to the concept of multiple causes and to underlying system-related causes. This will be especially true in organizations that have an existing investigation program in place, which uses an older approach. Many supervisors may feel uncomfortable with the newer methods. Since members of the initial PSII team will be part of the implementation process, they will need a good grounding in the concepts of systems-related multiple root causes.

8.1.8. Recommendations and Findings

Identifying and evaluating practical recommendations are critical team activities. These activities are covered in Chapter 6. In the initial formation of the PSII management system, special attention must be given to the need for thoroughly evaluating proposed recommendations for all causes identified. In some unsatisfactory investigations, the recommended remedy only serves to *transfer* the hazard or to *create an additional* hazard that was not present before the initial incident. The management system for PSII needs a built-in mechanism to ensure that a safety analyses are completed for proposed recommendations.

8.1.9. Formal Reports

Formal reports of incidents are a complete record of the incident, its causes, recommended remedies, plan for remedial action, and decisions made. Frequently, only specific sections of the document are important to the many parties, each of which may have a different concern. Thought must be given as to how the information may be best presented in the report to serve the various interested groups. Chapter 7 addresses the elements of reports and communication.

The intended distribution of reports and required approval levels should be addressed in the planning stages. These should be included in the written management system description. Since most incidents have legal implications and some have regulatory reporting requirements, the PSII system should include a legal department review of reports required by regulatory groups and of other reports for format and content.

A topic of increasing attention is the desire to share common data regarding incident causes and types. Second-generation computer software has opened new opportunities for tracking and recognizing trends and comparing performance against other groups. The management system for incident investigation should include provisions for computer coding of data, if the report is to be used as part of a data base.

8.1.10. Implementation of Recommendations

Follow-up and resolution of recommendations has become one of the cornerstones of incident investigation. To reduce the probability of a repeat incident, the recommendations must be actually implemented and changes maintained. For lasting results, it is wise to audit the implemented recommendations periodically to ensure that they are achieving the intended objectives. This follow-up objective represents a commitment additional time and effort on the part of the team members.

During final development of recommendations, management should be involved in assigning responsibility for implementation of recommendations and schedule of their implementation.

8.1.11. Process Safety Incident Investigation Documentation

Documentation of the PSII is another important part of the PSII management system procedures, and should be reviewed with management as part of the management system ratification. As discussed in Chapter 3 and 7, all evidence gathered, analyses, deliberations, conclusions, recommendations, and *resolution of all recommendations* should be documented to create an "auditable trail." If a team recommendation is rejected or modified, the basis for the change should be thoroughly documented. Documentation of changes to recommendations has a parallel application in the process hazard analysis segment of a process safety management program.

In a similar fashion, it is important to *verify* and *document* the actual *completion* of a recommendation. Findings and observations included in the team's formal written report should be followed-up and receive some type of *written response documentation* from the management unit to whom the report is addressed. In some cases, this response will be limited to a simple acknowledgment. In other cases, the response may comment on coincidental measures related to the recommendations that are being implemented. Chapters 6 and 7 address additional details regarding follow-up recommendations.

8.1.12. Integration with Other Functions and Teams

The actual execution of the PSII will touch many other functions within the corporation. Planning for this interaction begins during the formation of the management system by identifying areas of potential interest. The developer should review existing management systems for such activities as:

- emergency response
- environmental protection
- industrial hygiene
- security
- insurance interactions
- external media communications
- external agency procedures (OSHA, EPA, state and local authorities)
- corporate legal policies and procedures
- engineering design reviews (process hazard analysis and review)
- accounting and purchasing practices
- quality assurance procedures

There should be an eventual blending of the process safety incident investigation management system with the above related functions and activities. The systems should be compatible in order to avoid redundancy and conflicting responsibility, authority, or priorities. There should also be a mechanism built into the investigation management system to resolve conflicts.

8.1.13. Process Safety Incident Investigation Critique Mechanism

Continuous improvement should be an element of the management system, and the concept should be incorporated during the design and formulation stage. As addressed in Chapter 3, the successful investigation program has progressively fewer incidents to investigate and fewer opportunities to improve. Therefore, each team investigation should be critiqued to identify lessons learned that can be applied to future investigations. This mechanism needs to be designed and incorporated as a part of the initial system procedures. The designer could, for example, include a critique/evaluation form to help guide the team leader and the corporate-level administrator who will be responsible for continuous functioning of this management system.

8.2. REVIEW AND APPROVAL

As discussed in Section 8.1.12., the investigation will interact with a multitude of other company functions. Each of these groups should be given the opportunity to participate in the development of the initial PSII system. It is quite normal for such a review cycle to be slow and tedious and require resolution of conflicts and inconsistencies. The developer should recognize these challenges as necessary and actually beneficial in most cases.

After the management system has been approved, its partial implementation, selective adoption, or inconsistent follow-through will result in the system being ineffective and failing to prevent future incidents. Therefore, when establishing the approved PSII management system procedures, there are two options available; option one is to follow the procedure rigorously; and option two is to modify or drop the procedure. If a procedure is not being enforced, then it should be changed or eliminated.

The actual approval process may take longer than the formative process. Constructive suggestions and unforeseen problems in proposed system procedures, which arise from the review process, should be resolved and incorporated where appropriate. The developer must anticipate people's reluctance to embrace automatically any new management system. It is sometimes helpful to document and retain approval copies, signatures, and distribution list.

8.3. IMPLEMENTATION

8.3.1. Initial Training

Actual implementation normally begins with a formal training program for all employees, supervision, and management. Initial training can be achieved in five segments:

- Management—corporate, division, and facility
- Workers and line supervision
- Nonmanufacturing staff groups such as accounting
- The investigation team itself
- Other teams and functions that might be expected to interact with the process safety incident investigation team

All segments of the corporation should receive a minimum amount of orientation and awareness training to introduce the new PSII system. This will also provide the opportunity to explain the philosophy behind the emphasis on near-misses, multiple causes, and systems-related root causes, and on fact-finding rather than fault-finding.

Some groups should receive *additional* training on responsibilities and function of the PSII team. A smaller group of supervisors who are designated to serve as possible PSII team members should receive a more intensive training session that deals with actual case histories.

Management should initially receive a custom-tailored training and orientation session that includes special focus on the implementation follow-up responsibilities and on near-miss concepts. The actual management system for investigating incidents as developed in Chapter 3 should provide the core for this session. It would be helpful to address the major accident cause models and types, legal implications, and regulatory requirements. Typical contents of the management training are shown in Figure 8-2.

- What is an incident?—definition
- What is an investigation?—three major objectives
- Theory of multiple causes
- Specific methodology to be used
- Management's role—specific responsibilities
- Incident investigation as part of an overall process safety management program
- The PSII management system for this corporation
- Classification criteria
  —Initial notification/alerts
  —Responsibilities
  —Process safety incident investigation team organization
  —Evidence acquisition
  —Evidence analysis
  —Cause determination and analysis
  —Formation of preventive recommendations
  —Formal report
  —Follow-up and implementation
  —Case studies—examples

Figure 8-2. Suggested initial training outline for management.

Workers and line supervision will be the first group to work directly with the incident investigation team. Initial training for this group would concentrate on the management system as described in Chapter 1, along with a summary of the evidence-gathering techniques from Chapter 4. This group needs to understand the classification and initial incident reporting procedures.

Nonmanufacturing staff groups, for example the purchasing or accounting departments, are less frequently involved with process safety incident investigation; however, they have a need to *recognize near-miss* incidents and know when to *generate the initial alert* notification. Typical training agendas for these groups are abbreviated and should require only 1–2 hours.

Special training is needed for those employees who would be expected to *interact* with the PSII team *during an investigation*. They are likely to be part of organizational groups such as emergency response teams, fire brigades, maintenance, security, site safety, site industrial hygiene, public relations, legal, and environmental. A representative training outline for these groups, workers and line supervision, and auxiliary staff groups is shown in Figure 8-3.

Definition of terms
- Near-miss
- Incident
- Accident

Need for and benefit of investigations

Three objectives of the incident investigation team
- Discover root cause
- Identify recommendations
- ensure follow-up implementation

Overall Process Safety Management Program

The management system for Investigating Process Safety Incidents
- Classification criteria
- Initial notification/alerts
- Responsibilities
- Team organization
- Evidence acquisition
- Evidence analysis
- Cause determination and analysis
- Formation of preventive recommendations
- Formal report
- Follow-up and implementation

Individual responsibilities of
- Worker
- First line supervisor

Case studies and examples

Figure 8-3. Suggested initial training outline for workers and first line supervision.

8.3.2. Team Training

The PSII team training needs will vary considerably. Each incident will present unique demands to the team. However, there is a core of common or generic training that will be beneficial to all PSII teams. It is shown in Figure 8-4.

- What is an incident?—definitions
- What is an investigation?—three major objectives
- Theory of multiple causes
- Management's role—specific responsibilities
- Process safety incident investigation as part of an overall process safety management program
- The PSII management system for this corporation
  —Classification criteria
  —Initial notification/alerts
  —Responsibilities
  —Process safety incident investigation team organization
- Attributes of a good team member
- Team leader responsibilities
- Evidence preservation
- Witness interview techniques
- Photography—videotaping
- Evidence identification
- Evidence analysis and interpretation
- Documentation
- Root cause determination
- Identifying and forming recommendations
- Case study workshops—containing witness interviews, multiple causes, and requiring evaluation of proposed recommendation
- Crisis communications with the news media
- Report writing
- Implementation and follow-up responsibilities

Figure 8-4. Suggested initial training outline for process safety incident investigation team.

8.4. REFERENCES

1. American National Standards Institute. 1967. *American National Standard of Recording Basic Facts Relating to the Nature and Occurrence of Work Injuries*, ANSI Z16.1. New York: American National Standards Institute.
2. *Life Safety Code, Standard No. 101*. Boston: National Fire Protection Association.
3. *National Electrical Code, Standard No. 70*. Boston: National Fire Protection Association.

4. U.S. Department of Labor. 1989. "A Brief Guide to Recordkeeping Requirements for Occupational Injuries and Illnesses." OSHA, Publication OMB No. 1220-0029, Apr 89. Washington: U.S. Government Printing Office.
5. CCPS. *Plant Guidelines for Technical Management of Chemical Process Safety*, Chapter 11. New York: American Institute of Chemical Engineers.
6. "The Silent Safety Program." Excerpt from Presidential Commission Report on the Space Shuttle *Challenger* Accident. *ASSE American Society of Safety Engineers, Professional Safety Magazine*. Nov. 1986, pp. 10a–10g.
7. Winsor, D. A. 1989. *Challenger:* A Case of Failure to Communicate. *Chemtech Magazine*, Sept. New York: American Chemical Society.

APPENDIXES

A
RELEVANT ORGANIZATIONS

ACGIH
American Conference of Governmental Industrial Hygienists
6500 Glenway Avenue
Cincinnati, OH 45211-4438
513–661–7881

ACS
American Chemical Society
1155 16th Street, N. W.
Washington, DC 20036
202–872–4600

AIChE
American Institute of Chemical Engineers
345 East 47th Street
New York, NY 10017
212–705–7526

AIHA
American Industrial Hygiene Association
345 White Pond Dr.
Akron, OH 44320
216–873–2442

ANSI
American National Standards Institute
11 West 42nd Street, 13th Floor
New York, NY 10036
212–642–4900

API
American Petroleum Institute
1220 L. Street, N.W.
Washington, DC 20005
202–682–8000

ASME
American Society of Mechanical Engineers
345 E. 47th Street
New York, NY 10017
212–705–7722

ASSE
American Society of Safety Engineers
1800 E. Oakton Street
Des Plaines, IL 60018
708–692–4121

ASTM
American Society for Testing and Materials
1916 Race Street
Philadelphia, PA 19103-1187
215–299–5400

CCPS
Center for Chemical Process Safety
American Institute of Chemical Engineers
345 East 47th Street
New York, NY 10017
212–705–7319

CMA
Chemical Manufacturers Association
2501 M Street, N.W.
Washington, DC 20037
202–887–1100

EPA
U.S. Environmental Protection Agency
401 M Street S.W.
Washington, DC 20460
202–260–8600

FEMA
Federal Emergency Management Agency
500 C Street, S. W.
Washington, D. C. 20472
202–646–3923

Human Factors Society
P. O. Box 1369
Santa Monica, CA 90406
213–394–1811

IChemE
The Institution of Chemical Engineers (U.K.)
165-171 Railway Terrace
Rugby, England
Warks CV 21 3HQ
Phone: 0–11–44 788 78214

NFPA
National Fire Protection Association
1 Batterymarch Park
Quincy, MA 02269
617–770–3000

NSC
National Safety Council
444 N. Michigan Avenue
Chicago, IL 60611
312–527–4800

NTSB
National Transportation Safety Board
490 Lenfant Plaza East, S.W.
Washington, DC 20594
202–382–6600

OSHA
US Occupational Safety and Health Administration
US Department of Labor
Washington, DC 20210
202–523–8148

SSS
System Safety Society
5 Export Drive, Suite A
Sterling, VA 22170
703–450–0310

B

ANNOTATED BIBLIOGRAPHY

Accident/Incident Investigation Manual, Second Edition. 1985. United States Department of Energy. Washington: U.S. Government Printing Office.

The primary purpose of this manual is to train readers to perform and report results from thorough investigations of major accidents. The main objective of the accident investigation is to try to prevent similar occurrences and detect potential hazards. The emphasis of the investigative methods should be placed on the discovery of all cause–effect relationships from which practical corrective actions can be derived. The material in this manual demonstrates useful guidelines for both accident investigation and accident management. The first chapter addresses the concepts and principles of MORT (Management Oversight and Risk Tree). A key to remember is that accidents are rarely simple and almost never result from a single cause. The conventional simplistic approach of finding the unsafe act or condition only leads the investigator to the identification of symptoms. Usually, observed deficiencies in work activities reflect management oversights and omissions.

In the second through fourth chapters, extremely detailed explanations of the preparation, initiation, and conduct of an accident investigation are given. In the final chapter, the written accident report and corrective actions are discussed. The appendixes contain worthwhile reference information about the contents of an investigator kit (Appendix C), medical evaluations (Appendix D), and witnesses (Appendix E).

Accident Investigation A New Approach. 1983. Chicago: National Safety Council.

This easily read manual explains an approach to accident (injury) investigations that emphasizes the identification of causal factors and the recommendation of corrective actions. The described investigative procedure demonstrates with good examples how to complete an accident investigation report and a suggested check list and comment form called a "Guide for Identifying Causal Factors and Corrective Actions." The conclusions from these documents are tabulated further on a form referred to as a "Summary of Causal Factors." This task compares the causes of incidents over a chosen duration. The results from this investigative technique can help management to discover underlying problems.

Accident Prevention Manual for Industrial Operations, Seventh Edition. 1974. Chicago: National Safety Council.

This National Safety Council handbook is widely used and accepted by safety professionals for the development of employee accident prevention programs. Chapter 7 addresses a statistical procedure for accident (injury) investigation that is based on ANSI

Standard Z16.2. The main focus is toward an analysis technique that identifies trends and common causes of incidents. This method relies heavily on the ability to determine important information from an accident report. Several good examples and a chart aid in the explanation of how to identify the key facts. The results of this analysis assist management in the prevention of accident recurrences. Further reference material on accident reports, ANSI Standard Z16.1, and OSHA recordkeeping is available in Chapter 6.

Carper, K. L. 1989. *Forensic Engineering*. New York: Elsevier Science Publishing Co.

Forensic engineering involves the determination of the physical or technical causes of an incident or failure, the preparation of reports, and the presentation of testimony or advisory opinions. An overview of the functions and obligations of a forensic engineer is presented in this technical book. The key topics include investigative techniques for fire losses, industrial accidents, and civil engineering-related incidents. Most useful for safety professionals and managers who are participating in accident investigations are the explanations about on-site evidence collection procedures.

Kletz, T. 1988. *Learning from Accidents in Industry*. Stomeham, MA: Butterworths.

This technical book is written for persons in design, operations, or loss prevention in the chemical industry. Worthwhile information is provided in a short introduction that discusses such topics as finding the facts, avoiding the word "cause," the irrelevance of blame, encouraging people to look for underlying causes, recording all facts, and other information to include in accident reports. The majority of the presented material illustrates results from investigations of incident scenarios of various magnitudes. The developed recommendations for prevention/mitigation of an accident are suggested to be divided into three layers: (*1*) immediate technical recommendations, (*2*) avoiding the hazard, and (*3*) improving the management system. The final chapter displays several learned key ways for incident prevention that include the following:

1. Control of Plant Modifications
2. Testing and Inspection of Protective Equipment
3. User-Friendly Designs
4. Methods to Carry Out Hazard and Operability Studies
5. Better Management

The appendix lists some good questions to ask during an accident investigation.

Ferry, T. S. 1988. *Modern Accident Investigation and Analysis*, Second Edition. New York: John Wiley and Sons.

This reference book reviews numerous methods available to perform accident investigations or ways to evaluate those studies already conducted. The purpose of this book is to provide enough material to aid in investigation of a mishap that will lead to the identification of the causal factors and corrective actions that will prevent recurrences. A mishap is defined as any one of those unexpected, undesired events that could cause a loss of resources, time, lives, money, etc. This textbook presents individual discussions of investigative techniques that involve power, electrical, hydraulic, lubricating, and computer systems. Several incident analysis procedures are reviewed.

National Fire Codes, 1991 Edition. Quincy, MA: National Fire Protection Association.

The National Fire Codes hold numerous standards that pertain to fire protection and life safety in the manufacturing and servicing industries. The reference material is detailed, constantly updated, and typically well written. The focus of the information is on how to protect and install fire protection equipment for various occupancies. With a little patience and ingenuity, an incident investigative team member especially involved with a fire or explosion could be assisted by these codes. For example, a person could discover after using the index that NFC Standard 422M, "Aircraft Fire and Explosion Investigator's Manual" has a section that discusses the temperature limits of selected materials. NFC Standard 902M, "Fire Reporting Field Incident Manual," NFC Standard 904M, "Incident Follow-up Manual," and NFC Standard 906M, "Fire Incident Field Notes" cover the full range of fire investigation from evidence collection, report writing, to follow-up procedures. Special insights on electrical fires are conveyed in NFC Standard 907M, "Investigation of Fires of Electrical Origin." As a complement to the information provided in the National Fire Codes, the seventeenth edition of the *Fire Protection Handbook* by NFPA, which is considered to be the encyclopedia of fire protection, contains more resource information that can aid an incident investigator.

Kuhlman, R. 1977. *Professional Accident Investigation*. Loganville, GA: Institute Press.

Although this reference book is aging, it is still a good choice for primary use in a several-day training seminar or self-learning course about the important aspects of industrial accident investigation for safety professionals and executive managers. In a theoretical manner, with examples and pertinent charts, the writer presents a picture of the requirements for good investigative procedures, especially pertaining to personal injuries. The Domino Sequence, the role and duties of an accident investigator, and eleven incident analysis techniques are explained in detail. In addition, other key topics such as witness interviews, evidence collection, accident reconstruction, response, photography, and accident reports are discussed. With this available information, management can begin to develop its own written incident investigation program.

Kharbanda, O. P., and Stallworthy, E. A. 1988. *Safety in the Chemical Industry: Lessons from Major Disasters*. Columbia MD: GP Publishing.

As expressed by these authors, the best way to increase safety is both to learn and then apply the lessons from accidents that already have occurred. The central theme of this reference book is the study and analysis of past major disasters. Several previous vapor cloud explosions and toxic chemical releases are examined in detail. Table 2 on page 22 displays an accepted evaluation procedure for the investigation of incidents caused by explosions. The rest of this book contains educational material for personnel who are responsible for a facility with a potential for high-consequence–low-probability events.

Peterson, D. 1989. *Techniques of Safety Management,* Third Edition. New York: Aloray, Inc.

This technical book is designed for educating practicing safety professionals involved in industry, government, or insurance. This reference material could be worthwhile to a production line manager who has an interest in loss control. The objective of the material is to extend learning beyond the normal safety textbook. Part IV, "Reactive System Elements," addresses techniques for attaining knowledge from incidents. The author believes that the slogan for safety at a plant should be SAFE PRODUCTION. An in-depth discussion is given on the weaknesses of following exclusively ANSI Standard Z16.2 procedures for accident investigations. The ANSI system is based on getting a detailed description of the circumstances around an incident instead of identifying the contributing causes. The most useful segment of this book is an examination of the positive and negative aspects of utilizing computers for accident recordkeeping and analysis. The book also contains a good section on statistical safety control methods.

Kletz, T. A. 1985. *What Went Wrong? Case Histories of Process Plant Disasters.* Houston: Gulf Publishing Company.

Unfortunately, the history of the chemical industry demonstrates that many incidents are repeated after an interval of a few years. This book was written with the objective of keeping the memories alive. The supplied information is a good source for demonstrations of why accidents happen. Readers can learn numerous accident prevention techniques. In incident investigations, this reference can aid in conclusions and corrective actions through comparisons with previous occurrences.

C

SELECTED SAMPLING OF TYPE 3 DEDUCTIVE INVESTIGATION METHODS

This appendix includes examples of two of the Type 3 deductive investigation methods which may not be readily available in other published materials. In preparing the book, the Subcommittee polled member CCPS companies for internal guidelines dealing with incident investigation. These were the only Type 3 deductive methods that were made available. Certainly, other such methods exist.

C.1. CTM: CAUSAL TREE METHOD

Rhône-Poulenc Causal Tree Method
Corporate Safety Director
Rhône-Poulenc Inc., CN5266
Princeton, NJ 08543-5266

C.2. MCSOII: MULTIPLE CAUSE, SYSTEM ORIENTED INCIDENT INVESTIGATION

Rohm and Haas Texas Incorporated
Incident Investigation Guidelines
Risk Analysis Department
Rohm and Haas Texas Incorporated,
P.O. Box 672, Deer Park, TX 77536

OTHER TYPE 3 METHODS

The following Type 3 deductive methods are readily available from public sources and many other easily obtained references.

1. MORT

Department of Energy. 1985. *Accident/Incident Investigation Manual*, Second Edition. DOE/SSDC 76-45/27. System Safety Development Center, Idaho National Engineering Laboratory, Idaho Falls, ID.

2. FTA: Fault Tree Analysis

Vesely, W. E., et al. 1981. *Fault Tree Handbook*, NUREG-0492. Washington, DC: U.S. Government Printing Office.

C.1. CTM: THE RHONE POULENC CAUSAL TREE METHOD

DESCRIPTION OF THE CAUSAL TREE METHOD

I. INTRODUCTION

An accident has occurred.....

Here is a method to prevent the same accident from happening again.

But the benefits will be even greater !

by
* selecting targets for action
* deciding measures to be taken
* fully implementing them
* and assuring effective follow up

. other similar accidents will be prevented

. the risk of accidents will be decreased

. the overall safety level will be improved.

We suggest, before working on the accident case study using the "Sectra module" training package, that you explain the method in detail, developing each step and using the examples given to emphasize the key points.

This is a simple method, based on simple rules.

The result is guaranteed provided that the rules are adhered to without any deviation.

II. MAIN STEPS OF THE METHOD

The putting into action of the method must be done carefully following the sequence shown below

a) data collection

b) accident reconstruction

c) formulation of facts

d) drawing up the causal tree

e) prevention proposals

f) decision

g) follow up

III. EXPLAINING THE STEPS

The "Causal Tree Method" does not use questions. Its originality is to find the facts connected with the accident by looking at what was unusual about what happened.

It is important to take in the situation carefully without interpreting and without making value judgements.

The Causal Tree is a comprehensive plan of the event. It is also an excellent means of communication.

After an accident, an incident or a malfunction in SAFETY, ENVIRONMENT, QUALITY, ... it may be decided to analyse the event using the causal tree method. This decision implies the setting up of a working group. To analyse an accident for example the working group should include the injured person (if possible) the supervisor, witnesses, one representative of the "Health and Safety Committee", one safety officer, ... At least one participant must be experienced in the method.

III - 1 DATA COLLECTION

We will now explain the steps to be taken when studying an accident.

The working group must listen to the injured person and anyone who witnessed the accident in order to collect all the available information connected with the event, that means :

* particular facts about the situation which are exceptional (the working group must find out why)

* and others which are permanent and have played a direct role.

This phase is usually in the form of an inquiry and direct interviews.

The greater the amount of information collected at this step, the more complete and usefull will the causal tree be.

III - 2 ACCIDENT RECONSTRUCTION

All the information should now be taken and used to reconstruct the strory of the accident in writing.

The understanding of the accident is increased by the participation of the members of the group in this reconstruction.

Why is necessary ? .....

BECAUSE EACH ACCIDENT HAS ITS OWN SOLUTION.

If an accident occurs it is a failure. But if the same accident occurs again it is simply unacceptable.

III - 3 FORMULATION OF FACTS

The working group makes a simple list of the facts and <u>only the facts</u> that it has seen, read or heard during the previous phases.

This is made without interpretation and without making value judgement.

Only one thing at a time is taken into consideration.

<u>Example</u> :
* lights left on
* the starter doesn't work
* the horn doesn't work
* flat battery

III - 4 DRAWING-UP THE CAUSAL TREE

From the list of facts which has been compiled, the working group must now put them in order and try to find the relationship between the facts which resulted in the accident.

The construction of the dynamic diagram must strictly follow a set of rules with no deviations.

The starting point of the causal tree is the end result (the accident). From this point the working group must work its way backwards stopping at each stage to ask the following key questions :

WHAT IS THE CAUSE OF THIS FACT ? (1)

WAS IT NECESSARY ? (2)

WAS IT SUFFICIENT ? (3)

This means that the working group must find the fact (s) from the list which has been already compiled, which answers the first question. Before being added to the causal tree this fact (s) must be subjected to further questions (2 and 3) and in each case the answer must be affirmative. Then the same process is followed asking the same questions about each of the last facts added to the causal tree.

Example :

List of facts : * lights left on
* the starter doesn't work
* the horn doesn't work
* flat battery

End result : * the starter doesn't work
* the horn doesn't work

What is the cause of these facts :

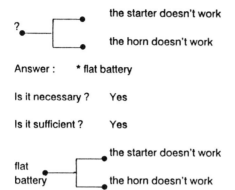

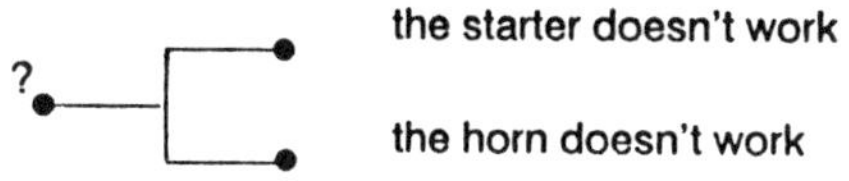

Answer : * flat battery

Is it necessary ? Yes

Is it sufficient ? Yes

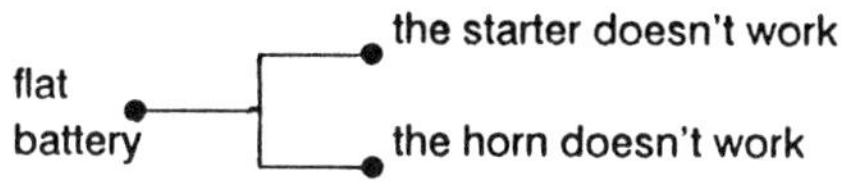

What is the cause of "Flat battery" ?

Answer : * lights left on

Is it necessary ? Yes

Is it sufficient ? Yes

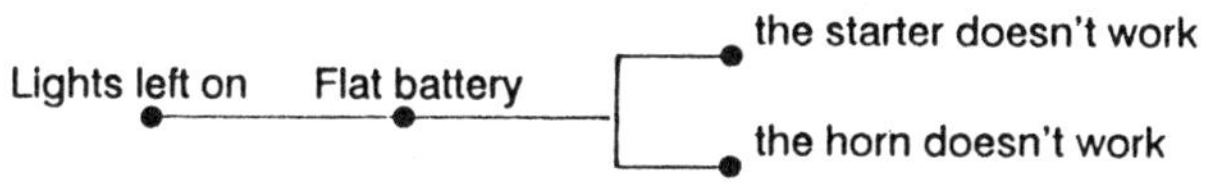

<u>What are the different types of links</u> ?

* SIMPLE PROGRESSION

1 fact has only one cause

Ex : Slipping •——• Falling

* CONJUNCTION

1 fact has 2 or more causes

Ex :

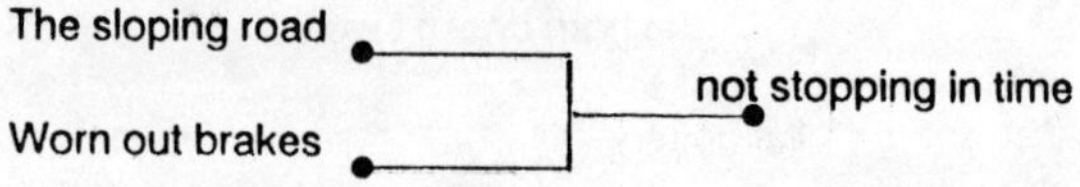

* DISJUNCTION

2 or more facts have only one cause

Ex :

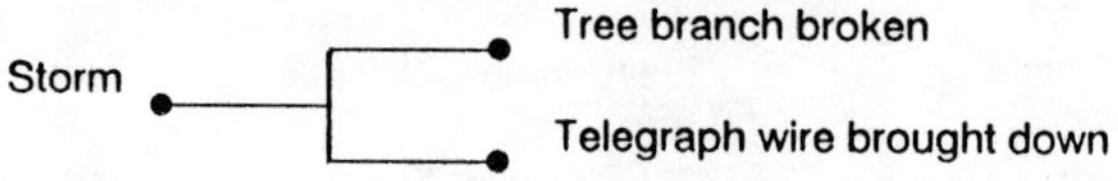

IMPORTANT

Each choice made by the group in selecting facts to add to the causal tree must be UNANIMOUS.

III - 5 PREVENTION PROPOSALS

When the causal tree has been completed the working group should begin to find methods of prevention.

Each of the facts must be carefully looked into to investigate the possibility of finding preventive actions, bearing in mind that by eliminating only one of the causes from the causal tree the accident can be prevented from recurring.

The working group tries to find what has to be done (modifications, material improvement, operating procedure, ...) so that it is possible to eliminate the greatest number of causes of the accident.

The working group must take into account the following points when proposing preventive measures :

* will the measure continue to be effective ?
* will it entail additional work for the operators ?
* will the risk simply be shifted elsewhere ?

* can it be widely applied ?

* will the measure be introduced early enough to be effective ? The further back you go, the more effective the measures become.

* how quickly can it be applied ?

* will it comply with existing regulation ?

The working group must select the most suitable preventive measures to propose to the person responsible for taking the decision.

III - 6 DECISION

After receiving the conclusions of the working group, the plant Manager or his representative has to decide which measure (s) he takes into account and explains his decision.

III - 7 FOLLOW UP

It is recommended that a table be drawn up to enable the progress of the solution to be followed.

FACT TARGETTED	PREVENTIVE SOLUTION	WHOSE JOB	TARGET DATE

IV. CONCLUSION

a) CAUSAL TREE METHOD

It is a method of analysis :

- participative
- logical

b) CAUSAL TREE METHOD

Basic principle

. An accident results from a combination of several causes.

. We do not want to judge anyone but to find means of prevention.

c) CAUSAL TREE METHOD

Working group :

- victim
- supervisor
- witnesses
- safety officer
- person experienced in the method
- decision maker
- representative of health and safety committee

to have a common view of the circumstances of the accident.

d) CAUSAL TREE METHOD

Method in 4 stages :

1. Discover the facts
2. Drawing up of the causal tree
3. Finding solutions
4. Choosing the most effective solutions.

e) CAUSAL TREE METHOD

1. List of facts

One at a time
Without value judgement
Without interpretation
Without negativity

in order to have a common view of the circumstances of the accident.

2. Drawing up of the causal tree

Starting with the end result

go back in time
asking three questions

What is the cause of this fact ?

Is it necessary ?

Is it sufficient ?

3. Finding solutions

The putting of heads together over each fact of the causal tree

How it can be avoided .... ?

4. Choice of effective solutions

Accordance with the regulation,
No risk shifting,
permanence,
possibility of evolution,
simplicity for the operator.

f) CAUSAL TREE METHOD

Creation of a plan of action.

FACT TARGETTED	PREVENTIVE SOLUTION	WHOSE JOB	TARGET DATE

J. BOISSIERAS
RHONE POULENC SAFETY DELEGATION
MARCH 1991

C.2. MCSOII: ROHM AND HAAS TEXAS INC. INCIDENT INVESTIGATION GUIDELINES

Guidelines for Systems Oriented Multiple Cause Incident Investigations ROHM AND HAAS TEXAS INCORPORATED

Version 3.009
February 19, 1990

PURPOSE: To assist unit personnel in conducting Systems Oriented, Multiple Cause Incident Investigations (MCSOII) and to provide consistency in those investigations.

APPLICATION: The multiple cause, system oriented incident investigation method can be used to investigate all types of incidents including injuries, fires, explosions, "near misses," environmental, and operational problems.

PRE-WORK: Prepare background information and documentation.
- Injury Report Form
- Chronology of events (time line)
- Schematic diagram of the process involved.
- Schematic diagram of the physical layout, plot plan, elevations, as needed to show location and events.
- Flowsheets, loop sheets, operating instructions, Job Safety Analyses.
- Photographs of the incident or incident location.

Note: The available documentation and level of detail desired will vary with the incident.

CALL THE MCSOII TREE MEETING: A sample is shown in Attachment 1.
Include unit personnel, witnesses, supervision, management, and the injured (if available).

For "lost time injuries," include the Accident Investigation Committee. (Contact the Safety Department to set up.)

For training in multiple cause concepts, include the Risk Analysis or Safety Departments.

MEETING TO DEVELOP MCSOII TREE: A flip chart is very helpful.

Agenda

1. Review written documentation.
2. Develop/confirm sequence of events.
3. Develop MCSOII tree.
   See the Generic Top Level MCSOII Tree (Attachment 2). Start with the injury as the top event. Fill in the next rows of events as applicable.
   Keep asking "why?" until all the fundamental system problems have been uncovered.

4. Make recommendations.
   Make SYSTEM IMPROVEMENT recommendations for each of the fundamental system problems.

For example, "Revised training manual to include training and testing for recognition of this hazard." IS a system recommendation.

Advised employee to be more careful." is NOT a system recommendation.

"Implemented periodic inspection and preventive maintenance program to detect and repair mechanical problems with this equipment." IS a system recommendation.

"Repaired broken equipment." is NOT a system recommendation.

---

5. Critique of meeting.
   1. What worked well?
   2. What could have worked better?
3. Was there good participation from everyone?
4. Was the pre-work appropriate?
5. Did we find system causes?
6. Did we make system recommendations?

WRITE-UP: Document the multiple cause investigation.

(Do not reveal the name of the injured or witnesses. Use terms like Operator A, Pipefitter B, etc. Cover up the injured's name and clock number when photocopying the Injury Report Form.)

The write-up should include:

1. Pre-work documentation
   - Injury Report Form
   - Chronology of events (time line)
   - Schematic diagram of the process involved.
   - Schematic diagram of the physical layout, plot plan, elevations, as needed to show location and events.
   - Flowsheets, loop sheets, operating instructions, Job Safety Analyses.
   - Photographs of the incident or incident location.
2. The MCSOII tree.

   The MCSOII tree can drawn by hand, typed out in a word processor, or drawn in a flowchart software package. (Easyflow by Haventree, used by many departments, is one of the easiest to learn and use.)
3. Summary of the incident.
4. Recommendations.

The write-up should be copied to area management, Safety, and Risk Analysis, and those who participated in the investigation. Safety will distribute selected investigations to all supervision for plant wide learning and training opportunities.

5. Critique of meeting.

Feedback on These Guidelines: Please include feedback on these guidelines in your critique, or call Risk Analysis. Give feedback on how well these guidelines work, as well as ways that the guidelines could be improved.

Attachment I: Sample Call for An Incident Investigation

RISK ANALYSIS
RISK

MEMORANDUM

ROHM AND HAAS
TEXAS INCORPORATED

TO:

FROM:

DATE: Memo #

SUBJECT: <u>**Multiple Cause, System Oriented Incident Investigation**</u>

Please come to a Multiple Cause, System Oriented Incident Investigation meeting:
at _time__________
on _date______________________________
at __location______________________________
for__incident______________________________

(Person designated) will invite appropriate personnel from operations, supervision, engineering,and labs. (Person designated) will be responsible for having the pre-meeting documentation prepared:

- Injury Report Form
- Chronology of events
- Schematic of the process involved
- Schematic of physical layout, plot plan, elevations, as needed to show location
- Material Safety Data Sheets

Agenda

1. Review written documentation.
2. Develop/confirm sequence of events.
3. Develop MCSOII tree.
4. Make recommendations.
5. Critique of incident investigation meeting.

Attachment II: Generic Top Level MCSOII Tree for Investigations

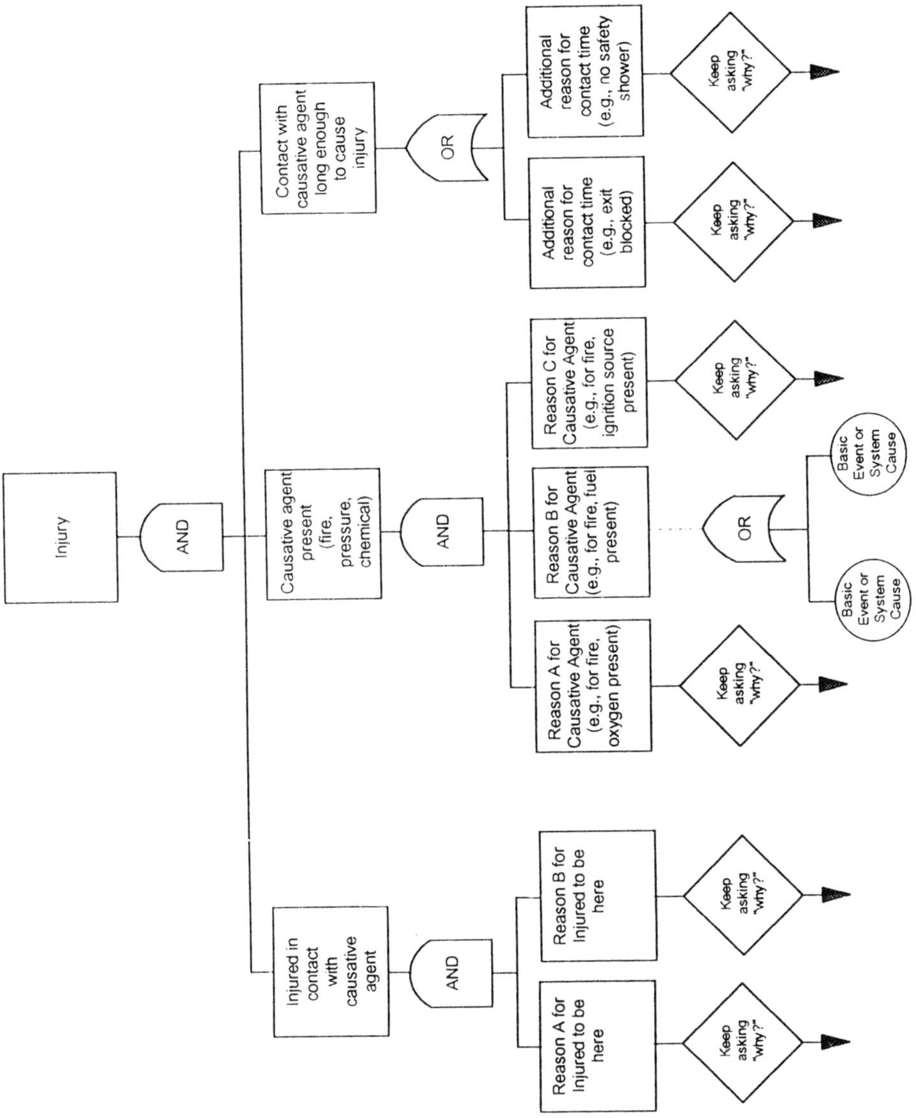

Attachment III: Training Syllabus

OUTLINE FOR TRAINING IN MULTIPLE CAUSE, SYSTEMS-ORIENTED, INCIDENT INVESTIGATIONS

1. **Bring together a small group with an incident to investigate.**

2. **Why do we investigate accidents?**
   To find the root causes of the incident so that other incidents may be prevented in the future.

3. **What do the terms in the title mean?**
   a. What is *Multiple-Cause*?
      It means all of the causes we can identify for any incident.
      Don't stop with the easiest or most obvious.

   b. What is *Systems-Oriented*?
   It means that we want to focus on the System(s) failures involved in the incident.

   Don't focus on the people mistakes -- look beyond the mistakes to find out why they happened.

4. **Why *Multiple-Cause?***
   There is almost never one simple cause for an incident.

   Most serious incidents have at least three causes. (Present-day design practices are such that at least three failures have to occur simultaneously for a serious incident to occur.) If we find many causes and fix them all, we have a much better chance of preventing recurrence than if we only worked on the one obvious cause.

   Give examples from your plant or unit to illustrate multiple-cause.

5. **Why *Systems-oriented*?**
   The Plant and every subdivision of it are systems.
   Systems exist for a reason, and each system produces something.

   What does the plant system produce?
      List: Products, etc. / Accidents, etc.

   We wish to maximize the positive products of the system and minimize the negative. It is very difficult and very slow to change a system as massive and as complex as the entire plant; however, we can bring about the desired changes by changing each subsystem, one at a time. Each incident investigation is an opportunity to do this. When we focus on the systems, we begin to try to improve them, and we stop trying to find fault with people. Systems improvements are much more lasting and far-reaching than the normal corrective action is likely to be.

Give examples from your plant to illustrate systems:

Fall from hopper car. System problem was so few cars were loaded that it wasn't economical to put fall protection around the top of the hopper car, yet loading continued on a hardship basis. Solution was to stop shipping in hopper cars.

6. **Explain and demonstrate how to do the investigation:**
   Conduct the incident investigation according to the agenda in the guidelines.
   - Insist that the trainees do the work. Don't give them the answers at each step, but ask questions to lead them to state the answers. Be sure they understand.
   - Explain MCSOII tree concepts in brief: AND gates, OR gates, events that are not a cause.
   - Watch out for taking steps in the tree that are too large. It is better to take very small steps initially to understand the logic process.
   - Have the group test to see that their recommendations are system oriented.

[end]

D

ACTUAL INCIDENTS

This appendix contains summaries of selected incidents that are significant to CPI investigators. Much of this information has previously been published. It is repeated in this guidebook because it represents a core of critical knowledge that should be available to PSII team members. The incidents represent classic examples of multiple system root cause events, and as such, demonstrate many of the principles advocated in this guidebook. **These summaries are based on available published information and are not necessarily considered to be complete or final.**

PHILLIPS 66 COMPANY HOUSTON CHEMICAL COMPLEX

During maintenance operations on a polyethylene reactor in Plant V of the Phillips 66 Houston Chemical Complex, a massive release of process gas, a mixture of isobutane, ethylene, hexene, and hydrogen, formed an unconfined vapor cloud, traveled to an unidentified ignition source, and exploded with the force of 2.4 tons of TNT. This tragic incident happened at approximately 1:00 P.M. on October 23, 1989 in Pasadena, Texas. Ensuing fires swept through this chemical plant. A total of 23 workers were killed. More than 130 people were injured. Two production plants covering an area of 16 acres on this site were completely demolished, causing nearly $750 million of property damage. Debris from the explosion was tossed as far as 6 miles into a neighboring community.

At Plant IV and V, high-density polyethylene was manufactured from ethylene gas that is dissolved in isobutane. The chemical reaction took place in long pipes under elevated temperatures and pressures. During this process, various chemicals were added to alter the polyethylene to meet desired product specifications. The dissolved ethylene combined with other similar particles to develop polyethylene. The solid product was gathered in settling legs and removed through valves in their bottoms. The settling legs could be isolated from reactor pipes with a single DEMCO ball valve. The DEMCO valve was kept open during production to allow the polyethylene to enter the settling legs.

In the reactor, plastic material frequently clogged the settling leg. When this happened, the DEMCO valve was shut, the leg was disassembled, and any blockage was removed. If the DEMCO valve was left open during a clean-out operation, process gas would be able to escape to the air.

The OSHA incident investigation concluded that the primary cause of this disaster was a sudden release of more than 85,000 pounds of highly flammable gas through an open DEMCO valve. In less than 2 minutes, the gas rapidly found an ignition source and exploded. Ensuing fires happened. Approximately 15 minutes later, a second explosion occurred involving two isobutane storage tanks. Each blast damaged nearby units and created further explosions.

At the time of this event, a settling leg was undergoing a regular maintenance procedure: the removal of a solidified polyethylene blockage. Normally, this function was performed by a contractor. Phillips' operations personnel were required to prepare the product settling leg for the maintenance procedure by isolating the leg from the main reactor loop. This task was supposed to be performed before turning the project over to a contractor.

On Sunday, October 22, 1989, a Fish Engineering crew started work to unplug three of the six settling legs on Reactor No. 6. According to witnesses, all three legs were prepared by an operator and were ready for maintenance. The DEMCO valves on each one were in the closed position. Number One Leg was disassembled and unplugged without problems. At approximately 8:00 A.M. on Monday, activities began on the Number Four Leg. The contractor team partially dismantled this leg and managed to extract a polyethylene blockage from a portion of this leg. However, another section of polyethylene was lodged 12 to 18 inches away from the DEMCO valve. After lunch, a contractor employee was sent to the Reactor Control Room to ask for assistance from an operator. A short time later, the release happened.

A physical examination of the actuator mechanism and laboratory tests confirmed that the DEMCO valve for the Number Four Leg was open when the process gas was freed. The tests indicated that the air hoses that supplied the air pressure for the actuator mechanism were connected in reverse sequence. In this arrangement, the hoses would open a closed DEMCO valve even when the actuator switch was in the closed position. In case of failure of the DEMCO valve, no backup protection in the form of a double valve or blind flange insert was required by local management in this special maintenance procedure.

Additionally, the following unsafe conditions existed:

- The DEMCO valve actuator mechanism did not have its "lockout" device in place.
- The hoses that supplied air to the valve actuator mechanism could be connected at any time, although Phillips' operating procedures stipulated that the hoses should never be connected during maintenance.
- The air hose connectors for the "open" and "closed" sides of the valve were identical which could allow the hoses to be cross-connected and permit the valve to open when the operator intended to close it.
- The air supply valves for the actuator mechanism air hoses were open which would enable flow that would have caused the actuator to rotate the DEMCO valve when the hoses were connected.

- The DEMCO valve was capable of being locked in the open as well as the closed position.

The main contributing causes that enabled this incident to escalate beyond the initial disaster pertain to the fire fighting system at this complex. This facility had no dedicated fire water system. Water for fire fighting came from the same water system that was used in production. Consequently, when the process water system was seriously harmed by the vapor cloud explosion, the plant's fire water supply was disrupted. The actual blast sheared off fire hydrants. These breakages also significantly reduced the available fire water capacity. Water for this emergency had to be transported via hoses from remote sources such as settling ponds, a cooling tower, a water treatment plant, and nearby public water mains. Of the three diesel backup fire pumps, one had to be removed from service due to mechanical problems. Another diesel fire pump promptly ran out of fuel. The electric cables supplying power to the regular service fire pumps were destroyed by the fire, rendering these pumps inoperable.

Another contributing cause that increased the severity of this incident involved the site layout, which had high-occupancy structures such as the control room and finishing building in close proximity to the large-capacity reactors and hydrocarbon storage vessels.

The following list is a brief summary of the major findings of the OSHA's incident investigation:

- A process hazard analysis or other equivalent method had not been utilized in the polyethylene plants to identify the process hazards, the potential for malfunction or human error, and ways to reduce or eliminate such hazards.
- Phillips' existing safe operating procedures for opening lines in hydrocarbon service, which could have prevented the flammable gas release, were not required for maintenance of the polyethylene plant settling legs. The alternate procedure devised for opening settling legs was inadequate. Deficiencies included no provisions for redundancy on the DEMCO valves, inadequate lockout/tagout procedures, and improper design of the valve actuator mechanism and its air hose connections.
- An effective safety permit system was not enforced with respect to both Phillips' personnel and contractor employees to ensure that proper safety precautions were observed during maintenance operations.
- No permanent combustible gas detection and associated alarm system were provided in the reactor units or in strategic adjacent locations to monitor hydrocarbon levels and give an early warning of gas leakage or releases.
- Ignition sources stood near or downwind (based on prevailing winds) of large hydrocarbon inventories. Also, ignition sources were brought into high hazard areas without appropriate flammable gas testing.
- Buildings that held personnel or vital control equipment were not properly detached from the process units or designed with enough resistance to withstand the expected consequence from a fire and explosion.

- Ventilation systems for buildings around or downwind of the process units or storage areas were not designed or configured to prevent the intake of gases in the event of a release.
- The fire protection system was not maintained in a state of readiness as required to provide effective fire fighting capability.

PIPER ALPHA

An initial explosion occurred on the production deck of the Piper Alpha Offshore Platform in the North Sea on the about 10:00 P.M. of July 6, 1988. The incident escalated into a tragedy that cost the lives of 165 of the 225 persons on the platform. Two additional fatalities occurred on a rescue boat. The Piper Alpha Platform was totally devastated.

Immediately after this blast, a fire originated at the west end of B Module and erupted into a fireball along the west face. The fire spread quickly to neighboring portions of the platform. Approximately 20 minutes later, a major explosion happened due to the rupture of the Tartan gas riser. This occurrence caused a massive and prolonged high pressure jet of flames that generated intense heat. At about 10:50 P.M., another immense blast occurred that was believed to be a result of the rupture of the MCP-01 gas riser. Debris from this explosion was projected up to 800 m away from the platform. Structural deterioration at the level below Module B had begun. This failure was accelerated by a series of additional explosions. One of these eruptions was caused by the fracture of the Claymore gas riser. Eventually, the vast majority of the platform collapsed.

After intensive incident investigations of this catastrophe, the root causes of the initial fire were believed to be a combination of poor shift turnover procedures, improper isolation practices, and an unsuitable permit to work system. Many factors contributed to the escalation of this event into a major disaster. The main lessons grasped from this incident are:

- The first priority in handling a fire is to contain the blaze by shutting off the supply of fuel. Properly located and protected emergency shutdown valves will provide a secure defense against the freeing of flammable gases into a fire that results in a major acceleration of fire propagation. Access to emergency shutdown valves is critical to ensure that proper inspections, testing, and maintenance is completed.
- Subsea isolation systems are less accessible, but they can be used effectively as double protection on large-diameter flammable gas risers. These emergency isolation valves can protect against the failures of platform emergency shutdown valves or pipelines.
- Fire protection systems should be maintained in a state of readiness and shielded from the dangers of an explosion and fire. Appropriate fireproofing of main load-bearing supports can help sustain the integrity of structures during the intense heat from a fire.

- Smoke became a severe problem as the Piper Alpha incident developed. The intense smoke hindered personnel evacuation and, eventually, migrated into the accommodation module. Many methods are being evaluated to mitigate the effects of smoke during an emergency.
- A reliable means of evacuation must be present. Improvements that are being completed by industry include area heat shields, better lighting, and secondary evacuation systems.
- The permit to work system and good communication is one foundation for a safe working atmosphere. More emphasis is being placed on these critical procedures by industry.

BHOPAL, INDIA

The incident at Bhopal, India, in December 1984, is by far the worst chemical disaster on record, resulting in several thousand known fatalities. A methyl isocyanate (MIC) gas cloud drifted several kilometers downwind into heavily populated areas. This incident, like most others, had multiple root causes associated with management and equipment systems, which affected both the probability of an incident (prevention) as well as the severity of consequences (mitigation). Some of the information is still incomplete; however, the following points are generally accepted:

- Water contamination entered the storage tank by some means.
- For a variety of reasons, clearly established operating procedures were not followed regarding the operating conditions on the MIC storage tanks.
- Emergency response equipment systems were inadequate to contain the vent from the overpressured storage tank.
- Recommendations for improvement of MIC safeguarding were submitted from an internal audit prior to the incident, but had not been adequately addressed.
- Offsite emergency response plans, procedures, and actions were less than adequate and contributed to the severity of the consequences.

PEMEX

On Monday, November 19, 1984, a major incident occurred at a liquified petroleum gas (LPG) storage and distribution center that was operated by Pemex (Petroleos Mexicanos), a state-owned oil company. This facility was located in San Juan Ixhuatepec, a northeastern suburb of Mexico City, Mexico. This disaster caused 542 fatalities, injured more than 4000 people, and resulted in extensive property damage.

On the previous Sunday, the distribution and storage facility was almost empty. The employees on the afternoon shift started to fill storage tanks via a 30-cm pipeline that came from a refinery that is located about 500 km from this site. The nearest pump station on this pipeline stood 40 km from the depot. Several persons were monitoring the progress of the filling operations at both the pump station and refinery. The depot contained 54 above-ground storage vessels. By early Monday morning, the two largest spheres and 48 horizontal (bullet) storage tanks were full and segregated from these operations. The remaining four spherical tanks were 40% full. A sudden drop of pressure was observed at the pump station. Apparently, a leak had occurred in the 20-cm pipeline loading these spheres. The liquified petroleum gas escaped from the piping with a deafening noise and vaporized.

With a slight wind, the freed gas moved southwest in the form of a cloud that spread over an area of 200 m x 150 m. One edge of the unconfined vapor cloud reached a residential area while another section approached a flare on this property. The cloud was estimated to be approximately 2 m deep by eyewitnesses just before it found an ignition source, the flare, at 5:40 A.M. Immediately fire and flames were noticed everywhere in the vicinity. The conflagrations affected portions of this depot and the local community. The inferno propagated rapidly through the facility and caused many secondary explosions. Within minutes, one of the smaller LPG spheres was engulfed with flames and detonated. A fireball with a diameter of about 300 m and a temperature of 1200°C developed and rained cooled gas droplets from a cloud all over the neighboring houses. This precipitation made all that it touched highly flammable. Shortly after this explosion, several of the horizontal storage tanks had BLEVEs that sent red-hot metal projectiles in all directions. Some of these metal fragments totally destroyed homes.

The holocaust continued throughout the residential area. Within this plant, 4 smaller spheres and 12 bullet tanks exploded and launched more metal pieces that flew up to 600 m in distance. A total of nine explosions occurred within the initial 2 hours of this incident. Near total devastation was evident for a distance of 300 m from the depot site. Some 200 homes were totally gutted and 1800 other homes received severe damage. Strangely, the two largest spheres did not BLEVE.

Little evidence was available to help determine the proximate root cause of this disaster. As early as 3:00 A.M., a witness stated that he smelled gas, heard a hissing noise, and noticed the pilot flame for the flare out. Many of the other survivors confirmed that they smelled gas well before the first explosion. The indications are that the leak initiated from the pipeline that was filling the last four spheres, and somehow this pipe eventually ruptured. The failure of the pipe would explain the sudden pressure drop at the pump station.

Several other root causes enabled the primary incident to intensify into a catastrophe. The Pemex depot was built in the 1930s on a site that was severely restricted in area. This insufficient space resulted in the bullet and spherical storage tanks being placed too close together. In addition, preventive and routine maintenance at this site was regarded as poor. Repair work was often postponed and seldom recorded. The adjacent residential community was much too near this hazardous installation. Only a distance of 130 m existed between the nearest houses and the tank farm areas.

Contributing causes of this event included a wide range of safety and fire protection deficiencies. Also, the emergency response plan, including outside communications, was insufficient to handle this crisis.

The news coverage of this incident was short lived because the Bhopal tragedy occurred two weeks later.

THREE MILE ISLAND

On March 28, 1979, the Unit 2 nuclear power station at Three Mile Island in Pennsylvania overheated and let a small quantity of radioactivity escape to the atmosphere. Even though no one has been harmed, this incident annihilated public confidence in the nuclear industry and initiated widespread demands for suspension of the growth of the nuclear industry.

A pressurized water reactor is used in the process at Three Mile Island. Heat is generated in the core of the reactor by nuclear fission and removed by circulating primary water around the core. This water is kept under pressure to prevent boiling. The primary water transfers energy to a secondary water stream that boils. The steam drives a turbine and then is condensed. The condensate is recycled. All radioactive materials including the primary water are enclosed in a containment building to prevent their escape to the open atmosphere.

Problems started when the secondary water was passed through a resin polisher to extract traces of impurities. One of the paths to perform this function choked. The operators made an attempt to clear the choke using instrument air. The pressure of the air was less than that of the water, which enabled water to enter the instrument air lines. A nonreturn line existed in the air but it was defective. The water in the instrument air line caused instruments to fail, which initiated a turbine trip. This occurrence stopped the heat removal from the radioactive core. The production of heat by fission was halted automatically within a few minutes. This fission shutdown is done by dropping metal rods that absorb neutrons down into the core.

However, some heat continued to be developed by radioactive decay. This energy source caused the primary water to boil. The pilot-operated relief valve (PORV) on the primary circuit lifted and the pumps engaged automatically to replace the evaporated water. Unfortunately, the PORV stuck open. The operators did not realize this situation, because the control panel indicated that the PORV was closed. Although other readings suggested that this valve was open, the operators decided to believe the PORV position light. Since their training had emphasized that too much water is wrong, they shutdown the water pumps. With the make-up water off, the water level in the primary circuit decreased and exposed the top of the radioactive core to steam. The zirconium alloy cans that protect the uranium reacted with the steam and formed hydrogen gas. During this time, the contaminated steam was discharged through the PORV, condensed in a drain tank, overflowed into the containment building sump, and was automatically transferred to the exterior of this building.

The root causes of this incident included the following items:

- The packaged units, ancillary units, off-plots, etc. did not recieve sufficient attention in their design and review. These auxiliary items can be just as important as the mainstream components, especially when their failure can cause a shutdown of the operations or safety problems.
- A service line such as instrument air should never be connected to process equipment that is under higher pressure.
- The use of instrument air lines for line blowing is a poor practice. If ordinary compressed air is used, the results of any contamination would be less serious.
- A preventive maintenance schedule should have been used for regular inspection of nonreturn valves. These valves have a substandard reputation in many plants, but they are seldom maintained correctly.
- The position of the PORV should have been measured directly. If a direct measurement was impossible, the label on the control panel should display exactly what is indicated.
- The operators exhibited their lack of knowledge and understanding of this plant during this incident. Their training should be increased to review the processes, address diagnosis skills, and give them diagnostic aids. Also, emergency response procedures for minor failures as well as the major ones should be taught to them.

A contributing cause that helped intensify this occurrence in the public eye was that the management of this facility was not prepared to handle the news media. The emergency procedures for this site should have included specific methods on how to brief the press, with simple explanations of what occurred and the extent of the risk.

The main lesson learned from this event or any other disaster is that we should try to design, whenever possible, inherently safe plants instead attempting to make them safe by adding protective equipment that may fail or be neglected.

SEVESO

On July 10, 1976, a discharge of highly toxic dioxin from a bursting disk polluted a neighboring village, Seveso near Milan, Italy, that had a population of 17,000 people. Approximately 250 people developed chloracne, a skin disease. From this incident, a large portion of land nearby was contaminated and declared uninhabitable. This event occurred at the Icmesa Chemical Company which manufactures 2,4,5-trichlorophenol (TCP) from 1,2,4,5-tetrachlorobenzene and caustic soda in the presence of ethylene glycol through a batch process. As an intermediate product, the TCP is used to produce bactericides and herbicides. Dioxin (2,3,7,8-tetrachlorodibensodioxin) is not normally formed, except in minute amounts. In this case, the reactor got too hot, which caused the interior chemical reaction to become uncontrollable. Dioxin was produced as well as other materials. The reactor's internal pressure rose drastically, causing the emergency relief valve to open to the atmosphere. The contents of the reactor, about 6 tonnes, including 1 kg of dioxin, was freed and distributed over the surrounding area.

Even if production was in the middle of making a batch of TCP, the Italian law required this chemical plant to shut down for weekends. On July 9, 1976, an operator shut down the reactor at an abnormal stage. The reaction had concluded, but the removal of ethylene glycol was not done. This situation had never occurred in the past. He had no reason to envision that this point of shutdown would be hazardous. The reaction mixture was at a temperature of 158°C, which is well below the required temperature for an exothermic reaction to begin (around 180°C).

This reactor was heated by an external steam coil that uses exhaust steam at 12 bar and approximately 190°C from a turbine on another unit. Because of the weekend shutdown, this turbine was placed on a reduced load that allowed the steam temperature to escalate to 300°C. When this exhaust steam was isolated at the reactor, the steam at the liquid level fell to an equilibrium temperature with the interior liquid. After the stirrer for the reactor was disengaged, the upper few centimeters of the liquid climbed in temperature to about 190°C. At this temperature, a slow exothermic reaction began. Seven hours later, the reaction reached a runaway state that eventually caused the reactor's contents to be relieved to the open air at 7:30 A.M. on July 10, 1976. The temperature rise was probably caused by direct heat transfer and/or the presence of catalyzed material along the upper wall that degraded from the heat and fell into the liquid.

Numerous root causes combined to start this occurrence. The laws passed by legislators left management of the facility no freedom to finish a batch before shutting down for the weekend. This law resulted in production being ceased at an unusual phase. The decision to shut down the reaction at this point demonstrated the operators' lack of knowledge about the process. The plant personnel's lack of understanding of the operations was also exemplified by not realizing that the reduced load on the turbine would substantially raise the temperature of its exhaust steam. Management was oblivious to the consequences that could result from a runaway reaction and lacked suitable knowledge about previous incidents that involved Dioxin at other facilities. They may have believed that this chemical reaction could never become intractable. This ignorance lead to the decision not to provide a catchpot that would gather any hazardous materials released from the reactor relief device.

The aftermath from this event was escalated by poor communication between the local community and this plant. A lack of information about the seriousness of the incident was evidenced by the fact that 17 days elapsed before the first evacuation from this town began. An estimated $200 million was spent to try to restore the affected land, without success.

FEYZIN

On January 4, 1966, multiple explosions and a conflagration occurred at the Feyzin refinery in France. The incident resulted in 18 fatalities and 81 injuries. On this day, a spillage of liquified propane through a 2 inch line happened when an operator was draining water from a 1200 m^3 pressurized propane spherical storage vessel. One valve handle had broken during its operation while a secondary valve froze open. The liberated liquified gas began to evaporate quickly and developed into an approximately 1-m-deep visible vapor cloud that spread in all directions. After 25 minutes of a continuous release, the gaseous cloud was ignited by an automobile 150 m away from the sphere. The fire propagated back to the release source within a minute and initiated a blaze with flame heights up to 60 m. Even though the existing water-spray sprinkler protection that was insufficiently designed was actuated, the fire caused this spherical storage tank to overheat. The drastic increase in internal pressure within this vessel resulted in a Boiling Liquid Expanding Vapor Cloud Explosion (BLEVE). The ensuing fireball caused several fatalities and injuries. Flying projectiles resulting from this BLEVE broke the legs of an adjacent spherical storage tank that later evolved into another BLEVE. The conflagration caused the legs of three other spheres that were inadequately fireproofed to collapse due to the extreme heat impinging on them. The fire propagated to the nearby gasoline and fuel oil tanks and took almost 48 hours to bring under control.

Extensive but minor structural damage from this incident occurred in the neighboring village of Feyzin that was centered about 500 m away from the affected storage area. Two thousand people were evacuated from this community. Property damage to the refinery was estimated at $4.6 million. The property damage to the surrounding areas outside the refinery totaled $2 million.

One of the multiple system root causes that led to the explosion was an operational error by the plant operator. He failed to follow proper sampling instructions. The written technique for sampling is as follows:

1. Put an operating lever (valve spanner) on either of both valves.
2. Open fully the upper valve closer to the sphere
3. Adjust the small draw-off rate, as necessary, by using the lower sample valve.

The employee operated the upper and lower valves in reverse sequence. This mistake was made easier by the insufficient access space to these valves and the unavailability of permanent valve spanners. Also, a solid plug of ice or propane hydrate that could have been restricting the draw-off line above the upper valve may have prompted the operator's error. This blockage was probably freed when the upper valve was fully opened.

The main contributing cause that generated this release of propane involved the design of the drain line. The spout for the drain line was directed downward in the immediate vicinity of and under the two valves, instead of to the side, which enabled a powerful jet of liquified propane to frost burn the operator and lead him to break the valve lever by accident. This drain line position also aided in the formation of a gaseous cloud that made the recovery and repositioning of the broken lever impossible.

The escalation of the incident resulted from the following contributing causes:

- Darkness and poor lighting around the incident scene added to the difficulties of replacing the detached lever.
- A long delay occurred between the initial propane leak and the actuation of the facility's emergency alarm.
- The emergency response time by the refinery firemen was excessively slow.
- The personnel for this facility failed to keep motor vehicles and thus ignition sources safely away from the scene of this incident.
- The design of the fixed water-spray sprinkler system for the affected propane spherical storage sphere was deficient.
- The available fire water supply capacity was insufficient to handle both the total water demand for the fixed water-spray sprinkler systems for the eight spherical storage tanks at this tank farm and for any necessary hose streams for manual fire fighting efforts.
- The refinery and other personnel did not foresee the potential consequences of a fire surrounding Sphere No. 443.
- The supporting legs for the spherical storage tanks were inadequately fireproofed.

The Feyzin disaster has led to a better understanding of the hazards involved with liquified flammable gases that are stored in spherical storage tanks. Liquified gas spheres are now being protected from fire engulfment by fire protection of improved design. Due to the severe hazard, firemen and other emergency personnel have a more cautious philosophy for fighting large fires affecting spheres. Evacuation of personnel and giving them safe shelter is a necessity during these type of incidents.

OTHER RECENT MAJOR INCIDENTS

Albright and Wilson America's Chemical Plant, Charleston, SC: An explosion and ensuing fire resulted in 6 fatalities and 23 injuries including two firemen on June 17, 1991. The incident occurred one day after a week-long shutdown while employees where mixing chemicals to produce a fire retardant used in the textile industry.

Pioneer Chlor Alkali Plant, Henderson, NV: During the middle of the night of May 5, 1991, a pipe from a storage tank leaked thousands of gallons of chlorine. This release initiated the evacuation and shutdown of this town, A total of 55 people were sent to the hospital for treatment of injuries, mainly respiratory problems.

Angus Chemical Company, Sterlington, LA: A fire in or near a compressor on May 1, 1991 detonated nitro methane at this plant. The resultant blast killed 8 workers and injured a total of 128 people including both workers and residents of the neighboring community. Most of the town's main business district was destroyed. About 300 families were left temporarily homeless. The economic loss has been estimated at more than $110 million.

Union Carbide Seadrift Plant, Port Lavaca, TX: An explosion within the ethylene oxide unit at this facility caused one death and injuries to 19 people on March 12, 1991. The economic loss has been calculated to be between $50 million and $75 million.

Kerr-McGee Southwestern Refinery, Corpus Christi, TX: On March 5, 1991, two workers died and five others were injured by escaping hydrofluoric acid vapors from a gasoline blending unit.

Citgo Petroleum Refinery, Lake Charles, LA: A fire and explosion on March 3, 1991 killed 6 employees, injured 12 others, and caused extensive property damage at this site.

BASF Coatings and Ink Plant, Cincinnati, OH: On July 19, 1990, a fire and explosion that resulted from the cleaning of a chemical reactor with volatile solvents killed 2 workers and injured 80 people. A large portion of the plant was ruined and 162 other buildings were damaged.

Atlantic Richfield Owned Plant, Channelview, TX: An explosion in a waste water tank on July 5, 1990 resulted in 17 deaths. This incident caused an economic loss of $90 million.

Exxon U.S.A. Refinery, Baton Rouge, LA: On December 24, 1989, a pipeline operating at high pressure ruptured. A gaseous cloud of ethane and propane was released from the break. The vapor cloud exploded. The blast killed 2 workers, injured 7 people, and damaged property up to 6 miles from this site. The economic loss from the explosion was $44.7 million.

Shell Oil Refinery, Norco, LA: At this refinery, an eight inch pipe ruptured on May 5, 1988 and released vapors that formed a gaseous cloud. The unconfined vapor cloud ignited into an explosion that killed 7 workers and injured 42 people. The blast caused property damage that resulted in 5200 claims. The total economic loss from this incident was $327 million.

Pacific Engineering and Production Company Plant, Henderson, NV.: On May 4, 1988, a fire and explosion occurred in this plant that manufactured ammonium perchlorate, a component for rocket fuel. Two employees including the plant manager died. A total of 350 people were injured. The facility received extensive property damage from the blast. Approximately 17,000 residents were evacuated from their homes and property damage to community was found to a distance of 12 miles from the plant. The economic loss from this occurrence was $75 million.

Hoechst Celanese Corporation Chemical Plant, Pampa, TX: On November 14, 1987, a ruptured tank leaked butane and acetic acid. These hydrocarbon vapors formed in a cloud that ignited and exploded. The majority of the plant was destroyed. Three fatalities and 35 injuries resulted from the incident. This event resulted in an economic loss of $241 million that included property damage, business interruption, legal expenses, and fines.

Marathon Oil Refinery, Texas City, TX: On October 30, 1987, a worker operating a crane at this facility dropped a heater onto a storage tank. The collision caused a rupture within the storage tank that allowed a release of approximately 30,000 pounds of hydrogen fluoride, About 3000 residents were evacuated from the local community for three days. An estimated 800 people received treatment for various breathing disorders and skin problems.

E

EXCERPTS FROM REGULATIONS ON INVESTIGATION OF PROCESS SAFETY INCIDENTS

FED. REGISTER 24-FEB-92, PART II

Excerpt from Federal Register, 24-Feb-92, Part II, Department of Labor, Occupational Safety and Health Administration, 29 CFR Part 1910.119, Process Safety Management of Highly Hazardous Chemicals, Part m....

(m) *Incident investigation.*

(1) The employer shall investigate each incident which resulted in, or could reasonably have resulted in a catastrophic release of highly hazardous chemical in the workplace.

(2) An incident investigation shall be initiated as promptly as possible, but not later than 48 hours following the incident.

(3) An incident investigation team shall be established and consist of at least one person knowledgeable in the process involved, including a contract employee if the incident involved work of the contractor, and other persons with appropriate knowledge and experience to thoroughly investigate and analyze the incident.

(4) A report shall be prepared at the conclusion of the investigation which includes at a minimum:

(i) Date of incident;

(ii) Date investigation began;

(iii) A description of the incident;

(iv) The factors that contributed to the incident; and,

(v) Any recommendations resulting from the investigation.

(5) The employer shall establish a system to promptly address and resolve the incident report findings and recommendations. Resolutions and corrective actions shall be documented.

(6) The report shall be reviewed with all affected personnel whose job tasks are relevant to the incident findings including contract employees where applicable.

(7) Incident investigation reports shall be retained for five years.

Excerpt from 29 CFR 1910.119, Process Safety Management of Highly Hazardous Chemicals, Appendix C (Nonmandatory Guideline).

12. *Investigation of Incidents.* Incident investigation is the process of identifying the underlying causes of incidents and implementing steps to prevent similar events from occurring. The intent of an incident investigation is for employers to learn from past experiences and thus avoid repeating past mistakes. The incidents for which OSHA expects employers to become aware and to investigate are the types of events which result in or could reasonably have resulted in a catastrophic release. Some of the events are sometimes referred to as "near misses," meaning that a serious consequence did not occur, but could have.

Employers need to develop in-house capability to investigate incidents that occur in their facilities. A team needs to be assembled by the employer and trained in the techniques of investigation including how to conduct interviews of witnesses, needed documentation and report writing. A multi- disciplinary team is better able to gather the facts of the event and to analyze them and develop plausible scenarios as to what happened, and why. Team members should be selected on the basis of their training, knowledge and ability to contribute to a team effort to fully investigate the incident. Employees in the process area where the incident occurred should be consulted, interviewed or made a member of the team. Their knowledge of the events form a significant set of facts about the incident which occurred. The report, its findings and recommendations are to be shared with those who can benefit from the information. The cooperation of employees is essential to an effective incident investigation. The focus of the investigation should be to obtain facts, and not to place blame. The team and the investigation process should clearly deal with all involved individuals in a fair, open and consistent manner.

F

EXAMPLE CASE STUDY: FICTITIOUS NDF INCIDENT

The following information demonstrates the investigation procedure for a hypothetical occurrence, using a Type 3 multiple root-cause systems approach, and displays an example incident investigation report by a assigned team of plant personnel.

At the NDF Company in Georgetown, South Carolina, a major fire occurred in the catalyst preparation area on August 1, 1991. The fire originated at Kettle No. 3 and was discovered by an outside operator at 11:10 A.M. Final extinguishment of the fire was accomplished by the local fire department and plant fire brigade at 12:10 P.M. One fatality and five personnel injuries happened during this event.

On resolution of this incident, the catalyst preparation area was secured against unauthorized entry, and plant management assembled for a meeting to discuss immediate actions. A process safety incident investigation team was assigned. The process engineering supervisor was designated as the team leader. The rest of this team included the safety supervisor, the catalyst preparation supervisor, an outside operator, a Polyethylene Process Unit No. 1 foreman, and a maintenance foreman. Representatives from OSHA, the local fire department, and the property insurance carrier were invited to participate in the incident investigation.

The selected team initially established a specific plan of investigation procedures for this occurrence. This strategy session listed priorities and necessary actions to ensure that all required information was obtained in a prompt manner. Needless delays in evidence collection were avoided by the use of this plan which helped to accelerate the rebuilding/restarting of the catalyst preparation area.

The investigation team visited the scene of this incident before the physical evidence could be disturbed. The maintenance foreman was given the duty of taking photographs of the damaged area with a simple 35 mm camera. He was careful to obtain overall views of the scene and individual equipment. All team members were provided with a field investigative kit and appropriate safety protective gear. Important evidence was gathered, preserved, and identified using a written log and tagging system.

On completion of this task, preparatory work was performed by the team members for preliminary witness interviews. Emphasis before the actual interviews was placed on the downplay of blame and the need for confidentiality. One team member, the safety supervisor, was chosen to meet with the witnesses. A conference room in the Administration Building was allocated for this project. The setting was arranged informally to allow the person involved to feel at ease. After considerable debate within the team, a conclusion was reached to not use a tape recorder during the witness interviews. The interview process was started early the evening of incident and was continued throughout the next two days. At the end of each day, the investigation team met to discuss the information obtained from the interviews and other activities.

The catalyst preparation area supervisor, on-duty control room operator for the catalyst operation, and maintenance superintendent were key sources of information. Their written records and logs were examined in detail. Other personnel that were interviewed included two outside operators, fire brigade members, and associated maintenance employees. During these conversations, special attention was paid to nonverbal signals and screening out inappropriate information. The interview process generated several unanswered questions about operational and maintenance procedures that required further study.

On August 2, 1991, the other incident investigation team members were assigned the responsibility of coordinating visits from the outside agencies. Meaningful facts and concepts that were learned from these external organizations were used as resource material to aid in the incident investigation.

Second interviews, further evidence collection and examination, and thorough evaluations of operational and maintenance records were conducted to try to find explanations for the questions created by the preliminary witness interviews. Due to a high pressure alarm occurring at Kettle No. 3 in the catalyst preparation area prior to the fire, an analysis of the software and hardware for the control panel that oversees this process was deemed essential for this study.

The team conducted a series of fact finding and evidence analyzing meetings. During each of these meetings, specific action item assignments were made in order to further understand the events, systems functions, systems interrelationships, and failure modes.

Using a deductive approach, a logic tree diagram was constructed to systematically identify the multiple root causes that related to system (hardware and software) involved in the incident.

On completion of the investigative work, the team convened to discuss their findings. During the discussions, important recommendations for corrective actions were developed. Special attention was allotted toward determining the potential effects of these suggested alterations on the efficiency of the plant operations. After long deliberations, responsibilities and desired completion dates were designated for each recommendation.

After completion of the incident investigation, the report below was developed by the investigation team and was been reviewed by important personnel within plant management.

CHRONOLOGICAL ORDER OF EVENTS

Incident at Catalyst Preparation Area on August 1, 1991

Time	*Occurrence*
10:56 A.M.	Control room operator initiates filling of Kettle No. 3
11:00 A.M.	Severe thunderstorm began
11:03 A.M.	High pressure alarm for Kettle No. 3 acknowledged by control room operator
11:05 A.M.	Plantwide electrical power outage. Diesel driven generator actuated to supply electricity to critical equipment.
11:07 A.M.	High temperature alarm at Kettle No. 3 sounds in the control room. The control room operator requested the lead outside operator to visually investigate Kettle No. 3.
11:10 A.M.	The thunderstorm had passed overhead. The lead outside operator discovered an incipient fire at Kettle No. 3 and notified the control room.
11:11 A.M.	A heat detector for the catalyst preparation area alarmed at the annunciator in the control room. Noise from an explosion was heard. communications with the lead operator were lost.
11:12 A.M.	The catalyst preparation supervisor notified the plant's fire brigade and the local volunteer fire department.
11:15 A.M.	The plant's fire brigade reached the emergency location to find the fire raging, the fire protection system impaired, the lead outside operator dead, and an injured contractor. The commander of the fire brigade sent a team member to the fire pump house.
11:20 A.M.	A second explosion occurred at the catalyst preparation area. Four fire brigade members were injured by the blast.
11:22 A.M.	Arrival of local fire department to the emergency location.
11:30 A.M.	Repairs on one diesel fire pump were completed and this fire pump was engaged.
11:58 A.M.	The Fire was considered under control.
12:10 P.M.	Final extinguishment of the fire at the catalyst preparation area.

INCIDENT INVESTIGATION REPORT

ABSTRACT

On August 1, 1991, a major fire occurred in the catalyst preparation area at the NDF Company in Georgetown, South Carolina. The fire originated at Kettle No. 3 and was discovered by an outside operator at 11:10 A.M. Due to a power outage and other circumstances, the fire water supply system faltered. The fire intensified to a serious state and caused substantial property damage. Several fireballs/explosions during the incident caused one fatality and five personnel injuries. One of the diesel fire pumps was finally engaged and supplied sufficient water capacity for fire fighting efforts. Extinguishment of the fire was accomplished by the local fire department and plant fire brigade at 12:10 P.M.

BACKGROUND

In 1979, the NDF Company opened a facility in Georgetown, South Carolina to produce low density polyethylene. Manufacturing of the polyethylene is done in two 50 ton reactors that are encased individually within their own 8 story high process unit. The main raw materials for the manufacturing operations include ethylene, hexane, and butene. The polymerization is completed in the presence of a catalyst. The base chemicals for the catalyst are aluminum alkyl and isopentane. Aluminum alkyl is a pyrophoric material. The desired composition of the catalyst is developed in another process unit through a batch blending operation in three 8000-gallon kettles. The flow rates of components are regulated by an operator at the control room. Temperature, pressure, and liquid level within the kettles are monitored by the control room operator. The formulated catalyst is stored in four 12,000-gallon vertical storage tanks within this process unit.

The isopentane for the catalyst preparation unit is stored as a liquid in a 60-ton horizontal (bullet) storage tank. The aluminum alkyls and other required chemicals for this process are received in small truck trailers and kept beneath a metal canopy.

Due to the size limitations of this property site, the placement of catalyst preparation area was difficult. For strategic purposes, this operation was positioned between the two polyethylene production units with 60 feet separating each one. The aluminum alkyls storage canopy and isopentane horizontal storage tank are located at a remote area at an approximate distance of 150 feet away from the production and utility areas. The isopentane is transported to the catalyst preparation area through a 3-inch pipeline. An remote actuated isolation valve on this supply line that fails closed is located at the isopentane storage tank. This control valve and an associated isopentane feed pump are managed by the operator in the control room.

The catalyst preparation area is protected by an automatic water-spray sprinkler system including in-web sprinkler coverage for the load bearing structural members that is actuated by associated heat detectors. Fixed fire water monitors surround this process area. The water for these fire protection systems is supplied through 8-inch underground water mains by three (two diesel and one electric) horizontal, centrifugal, 2500 gpm rated, 125 psi automatic fire pumps that take suction from a 750,000 gallon above-ground storage tank. The electric fire pump's power source is from an independent electrical feed. The water supply for this facility was designed to meet the highest water demand within the facility when one fire pump is out of service.

DESCRIPTION OF THE INCIDENT

On August 1, 1991 at 10:56 A.M., a control room operator remotely started the feed lines for Kettle No. 3 at the catalyst preparation area. A high-pressure alarm for this vessel was acknowledged at 11:03 A.M. by the control room operator for this process. At 11:00 A.M., a severe thunderstorm had started and within 5 minutes caused a power outage throughout the immediate vicinity. The ambient temperatures were around 85°F. With the assistance of the available diesel emergency generator, the production operations automatically began shutdown. The control room operators immediately addressed crucial shutdown procedures for the two reactor areas. At 11:07 A.M., a high-temperature alarm for Kettle No. 3 sounded at the control room. The lead outside operator was sent through radio communications to investigate the problem. The control room operator noticed that during the confusion of the power outage that the remote actuated valve for the isopentane feed line from the storage tank was closed. At 11:10 A.M., the outside operator discovered a fire developing from Kettle No. 3 and warned the control room operator. The thunderstorm had passed overhead and the rain was diminishing. At about 11:11 A.M., a heat detector for the automatic water-spray sprinkler coverage in this area alarmed at the control room. Suddenly, vapors released from both sides of a cracked isopentane supply line to Kettle No. 3 ignited into a fireball and instantaneously killed the lead outside operator. The noise roared throughout the facility.

The local volunteer fire department and fire brigade were notified by the supervisor of the catalyst preparation area at 11:12 A.M. On their arrival to the scene of the fire at 11:15 A.M., the fire brigade found the dead outside operator and a seriously injured unknown person. (This person was eventually determined to be a service contractor who entered the premises at 9:30 A.M. with the objective of replacing malfunctioning gas detectors around Polyethylene Reactor No. 1.) An ambulance was summoned via radio communications and a telephone call. Also, the automatic deluge sprinkler coverage for this area had actuated, but no water was available. The fire was raging. As piping and vessels failed from the extreme heat, released flammable vapors of isopentane served as fuel to continue fire propagation. The fire brigade tried to activate a fixed monitor, but again got no water flow.

The commander of the fire brigade sent a team member to the fire pump house. The electric fire pump was inoperable due to the power outage. One diesel fire pump was known to be impaired due to mechanical problems and other diesel fire pump had failed to start because its batteries were dead. Several maintenance personnel were sent immediately to repair this diesel fire pump.

Another explosion occurred at 11:20 A.M. as the fire spread to the formulated catalyst vertical storage tanks. Hot metal fragments from this blast severely injured four fire brigade members. The local fire department arrived at 11:22 A.M. With the limited water supply on two of the fire trucks and the utilization of another fire truck to pump water directly from a nearby cooling water tower basin, the firemen were able to slow the fire spread. By 11:30 A.M., the Maintenance Department was able to transfer the set of batteries from the impaired diesel fire pump to the other diesel fire pump. On completion of this task, this diesel fire pump was started. The automatic deluge sprinkler protection was severely damaged by the fire/explosions and had to be valved into the off position. Three fixed monitors were turned onto full flow and directed at the fire. Also, the firemen and fire brigade used two hose streams off nearby fire hydrants for fire fighting purposes. At 11:58 A.M., the fire was under control. Final fire extinguishment was accomplished by 12:10 P.M.

The consequences of this incident were one death and five personnel injuries. The catalyst preparation area received extensive property damage. The production operations at this facility are estimated to be suspended for 2 months until this area including associated pipelines can be rebuilt.

DISCUSSION OF CAUSES AND ROOT CAUSES

The incident investigation team concluded that the fire occurred due to failure of the isopentane feed line to Kettle No. 3 in the catalyst preparation area. The failure opening allowed air containing moisture to mix with pyrophoric chemicals in the vessel, which initiated an ignition of the contents. The ensuing fire propagated at a rapid rate due to the presence of isopentane.

Four root causes contributed to this incident. Initially, (1) the malfunctioning of the high-level alarm for Kettle No. 3 allowed this vessel to be filled beyond capacity by the control room operator. This situation overpressurized both the isopentane supply pipeline and the kettle. (2) The control room operator did not follow standard operating procedures during the loading of Kettle No. 3 and reacted inappropriately when the high-pressure alarm signaled in the control room and the power outage happened. (3) The loss of electricity automatically deactivated the isopentane supply pump and initiated the main control valve for the isopentane storage tank to fail closed as designed. The shutting of this valve trapped excess pressure within the isopentane feed line and Kettle No. 3. The continuous force from the excessive pressure caused a defective portion of the isopentane feed line to crack near Kettle No. 3. (4) The weakness in this pipe was believed to caused by corrosion. The resulting break in the pipe permitted wet air to enter Kettle No. 3.

Two contributing factors that allowed the fire to escalate were related to deficiencies in the fire protection system. (1) An unjustified delay in the performance of repairs to the diesel fire pump that was overheating due to mechanical problems generated a prolonged impairment within the fire water supply. (2) Indications were given during an annual performance test that the two sets of batteries for the second diesel pump were weak. Further investigation by the team discovered that maintenance checks of this fire pump are inadequate. The last time the fire pump was started was July 3, 1991.

RECOMMENDATIONS AND FINDINGS

The following recommended corrective action items are submitted in respect to the findings of this incident investigation. This items are presented to help prevent future accident recurrences and to improve the overall safety throughout this facility.

Findings

1. Plant management was aware of the existing corrosion problems throughout this facility. In February 1990, the maintenance superintendent proposed a project to address this serious situation. Areas of concern for corrosion failures were noted especially for process and sprinkler piping at both polyethylene production units and the catalyst preparation area. Because of the facility's financial misfortunes in 1989, only a limited portion of the proposal was executed by the plant management. Replacement of critical piping and equipment affected by substantial corrosion defects within the process areas was arranged to be done on a program basis. By July 1991, only the vicinity around Polyethylene Reactor No. 1 had progressed through this maintenance program.
2. Due to the engine seriously overheating, one of the diesel fire pumps was taken out of service on May 1, 1991. This mechanical problem was discovered during an annual performance test that was conducted by an outside agency. The other diesel fire pump failed to start automatically during this annual testing procedure. The two sets of batteries for this diesel fire pump were recharged by the Maintenance Department.
3. Further investigation by the team discovered that only monthly starts and checks of the fire pumps are conducted by the Maintenance Department. During this procedure, the diesel fire pumps are started automatically and manually on each set of batteries. The diesel fire pumps are run a total of 5 minutes. The last time the two operable fire pumps were started was July 3, 1991.
4. Information obtained from the witness interviews indicated that the *Standard Operating Procedures* for the catalyst preparation area are not frequently utilized by employees.

5. Research by the investigation team determined that a service contractor was admitted onto the plant's boundary without an employee escort. This procedure left him vulnerable to an accident during any emergency.
6A. The fire brigade members did not respect the potential hazards that existed during this incident. They stood unnecessarily to close to the fire when fire fighting capabilities were nonexistent.
6B. The pre-emergency plan was not followed by the fire brigade. Immediately on notification of fire, one member is suppose to report directly to the fire pump house. This procedure was not followed.
7. The critical instruments for Kettle No. 3 had not been checked for over one year. The preventive maintenance records for this program are poorly kept.

Recommendations for Corrective Actions

1. The problem of corrosion at this facility is an immediate concern. Prompt actions to correct this situation should be taken by upper management to prevent future failures, breaks, or ruptures of pipelines, equipment, or vessels. The existing corrosion replacement schedule should be revised to allow completion of the project by February 1992. Hydrocarbon releases as displayed by this incident can lead to serious losses.
2. The impairment of one of the diesel fire pumps for 2 months is unjustifiable. Punctual attention should be given to the execution of repairs to both safety and fire protection equipment. A document with authorization signatures should be established by the Maintenance Department with the assistance of a safety engineer to initiate prompt actions toward repairing critical safety equipment. A draft of this form should be presented to plant management by September 1, 1991. The diesel fire pump was finally repaired by an outside contractor on August 15, 1991.
3. The existing fire pump starts and check program should be done on a weekly schedule to ensure that this crucial equipment remains operable. This procedure should be revised to require the diesel fire pumps to be run for a minimum of 30 minutes. A preventive maintenance program should be established to oversee the maintenance on all the fire pumps. These items should be immediately corrected by the Maintenance Department, which is responsible for the proper operation of this equipment.
4. The insufficient actions by the control room operator for the catalyst preparation area signified that personnel needs further training in response to emergencies. Their use of *Standard Operating Procedures* and the *Emergency Procedure Manual* should be a starting place to improve their education. The obligation of initiating a better training program belongs to the operations manager. Formal education procedures for the control room and outside operators should be in place by November 1991. Promotion should be based on an employee demonstrating consistent knowledge of the processes and emergency procedures.

5. Emphasis should be placed immediately by the area supervisors to their subordinates on the importance of the using of the *Standard Operating Procedures*.
6. Any visitor, new employee, or contractor who is allowed on the property site should be given a safety orientation that describes the plant hazards, required protective equipment, and emergency procedures for this facility. This information should be displayed through either a formal presentation or videotape by the Safety Department. This new program should also stress that visitors and contractors should be accompanied by plant personnel at all times. The implementation of the safety orientation should be done by August 15, 1991. With time, the presentation can be revised to be efficient and more suited to meet the particular needs of this plant.
7. Further training should be given to the fire brigade members to educate them in safe methods of fire fighting. This training should be conducted by the Safety Department and/or outside institutions. This educational process should begin during the next monthly fire brigade meeting.
8. The malfunctioning high-level alarm for Kettle No. 3 at the catalyst preparation area identified that the preventive maintenance on critical instrumentation is insufficient. This program should reevaluated by both the Maintenance and Operations Departments before the restart of the production operations. Special consideration should be given to increasing the frequencies of checking these important devices and improving the recordkeeping.
9. Due to the potential for active fire protection such as in-web automatic water-spray sprinkler protection being inoperative, the major load-bearing supports for the catalyst preparation area should be provided with adequate fireproofing to prevent their rapid collapse during a fire.
10. Review and revise as necessary the emergency relief systems for Kettle No. 3 and the isopentane feed line. This should also include the instrumentation systems for reliability and redundancy.

OTHER

Refer to the attached photographs and drawings for further details of the incident.

CRITERIA FOR RESTART

Before the production operations are restarted, a thorough study should be performed throughout the facility to address the corrosion problem. Also, critical instrumentation for the polyethylene reactors and the catalyst kettles should be tested. Any problems found should be corrected prior to restart of the manufacturing operations. The rest of the above-listed recommendations should be completed by the indicated dates. Start-up should be only done on the authorization of the operations manager, maintenance superintendent, and safety supervisor (all three signatures required).

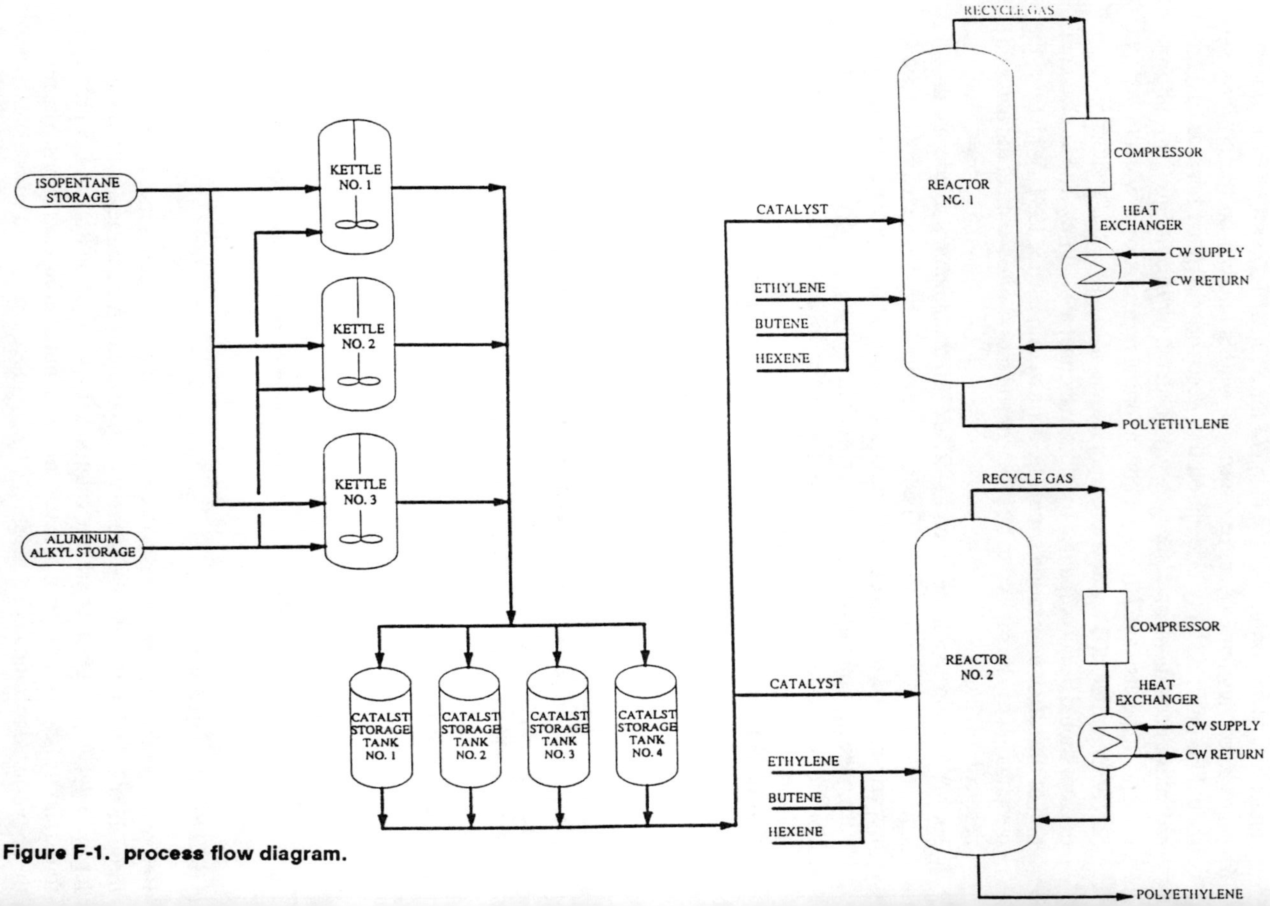

Figure F-1. process flow diagram.

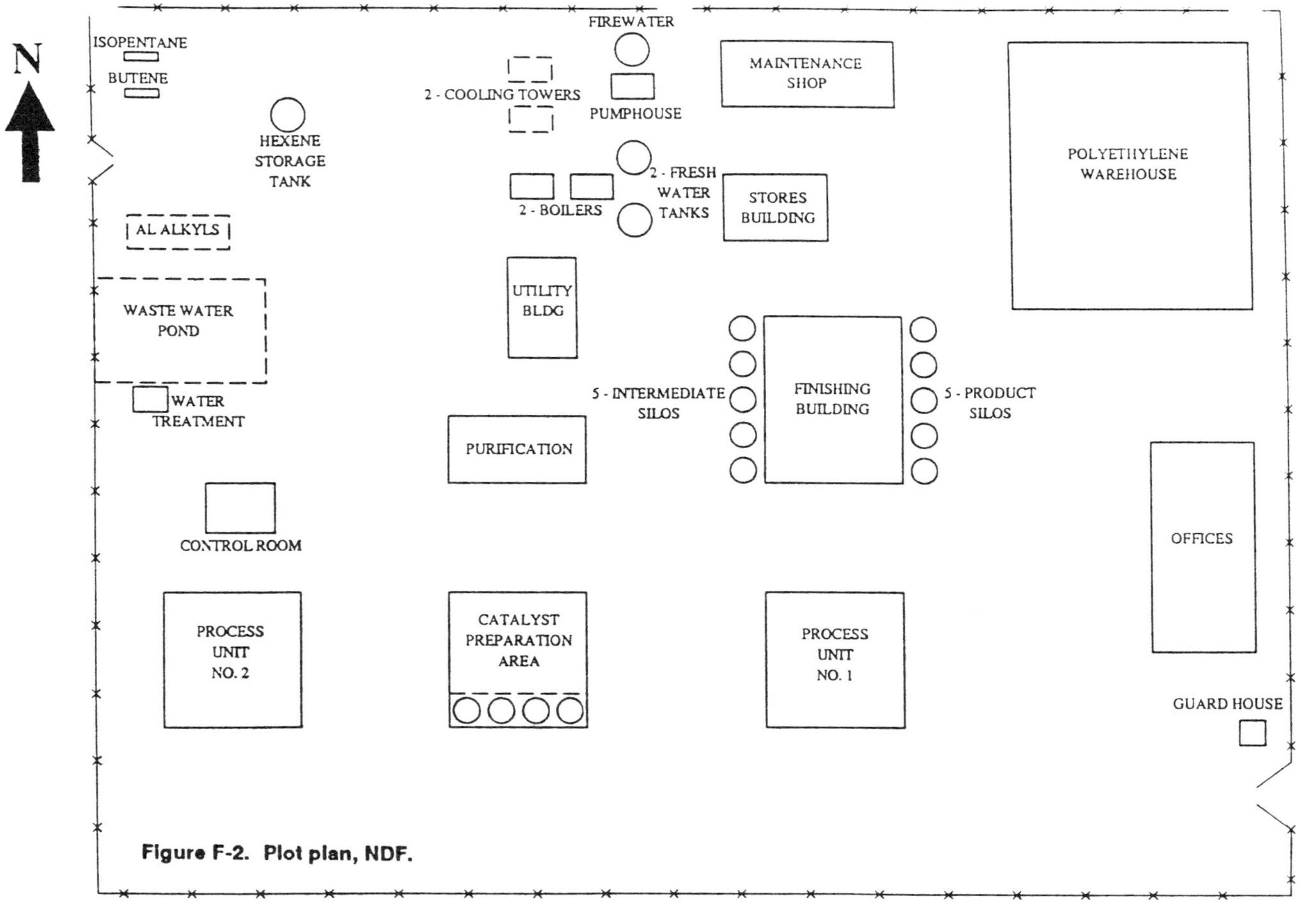

Figure F-2. Plot plan, NDF.

SIGNATURES

Team Leader	Date
Safety Supervisor	Date
Operations Manager	Date
Plant Manager	Date

G

SAMPLE APPLICATIONS OF VARIOUS ROOT CAUSES DETERMINATIONS

MULTIPLE-CAUSE SYSTEMS-ORIENTED INCIDENT INVESTIGATION METHOD APPLIED TO NDF HYPOTHETICAL INCIDENT IN APPENDIX F

See Appendix F for the incident description, flowsheets, plot plan, and evidence gathering. On August 1, 1991, management selected the incident investigation team:

- Process Engineering Supervisor, Team leader
- Safety Supervisor (trained and expert in the multiple-cause systems-oriented incident investigation methodology)
- Catalyst Production Supervisor
- Outside Operator
- Polyethylene Process Unit No. 1 Foreman
- Maintenance Foreman
- Representatives from OSHA, the local fire department, and the property insurance carrier were also invited to participate in the incident investigation.

In the incident investigation team's daily meetings, they began a chronicle of the key times and events preceding and during the incident, using flip charts and "stick-on" paper note pads for easy modification as new information became available.

On completion of the preparatory exploratory work, the team met in a multiple cause, systems-oriented incident investigation session to review the data and the sequence of events, to prepare an event tree with root causes, to make recommendations for **system** improvements to prevent reoccurrence, and to assign action points and target completion dates.

SEQUENCE OF EVENTS

(Developed by the team before the multiple cause meeting, and modified during the meeting.)

DATE	TIME	EVENT
2/90		Corrosion control project proposed.
Before 8/90		Last critical instrument check for No. 3 kettle.
5/91		No. 1 diesel fire pump taken out of service due to overheating during annual performance check by outside agency. No. 2 diesel pump fails to start automatically. No. 2 diesel pump batteries recharged by maintenance.
7/91		Corrosion control work completed around Polyethylene Reactor No. 1 only.
7/3/91		Last maintenance check of No. 2 diesel and the electric fire pumps: 5 minute test run.
8/1/91	9:30 A.M.	Service contractor enters area to replace malfunctioning gas detectors around Polyethylene Reactor No. 1.
	10:56 A.M.	Control operator initiates filling of Kettle No. 3 (started remotely).
	11:00 A.M.	Severe thunderstorm starts, ambient temperature 85°F. Kettle No. 3 overfilled by control room operator, high level alarm does not sound. [Concluded from the data.]
	11:03 A.M.	Kettle No. 3 high pressure alarm acknowledged by control operator.
	11:05 A.M.	Plantwide electrical power outage. Diesel emergency generator actuated and supplied electricity to critical equipment. Shutdown begins, control operators work on crucial shutdowns. Isopentane supply trips off: no power. Main control valve for isopentane storage tank failed closed (as designed) on electrical failure. Excess pressure trapped in isopentane line and Kettle No. 3. [Concluded from the data.] Isopentane line cracks near Kettle No. 3. Wet air enters Kettle No. 3. [Concluded from the data]

DATE	TIME	EVENT
8/1/91	11:07 A.M.	Kettle No. 3 high temperature alarm sounded. Control room operator requests (by radio) for the lead outside operator to visually inspect Kettle No. 3.
		Control operator notices remote-actuated valve for isopentane feed line from storage was closed in the confusion.
	11:10 A.M.	Thunderstorm has passed overhead; rain diminishing.
		Outside operator discovers fire at Kettle No. 3 and notifies the control room.
	11:11 A.M.	Heat detector alarms for catalyst preparation area (Kettle No. 3 area), annunciated in control room.
		Noise is heard from an explosion. Communications from lead outside operator lost.
		Fireball: vapors ignite, released from both sides of cracked isopentane supply line to Kettle No. 3. **Lead outside operator killed.**
	11:12 A.M.	Catalyst preparation supervisor notifies plant fire brigade and local volunteer fire department.
	11:15 A.M.	Plant fire brigade reaches emergency location and finds the fire raging, the fire protection system impaired, the lead outside operator dead, and an injured (unidentified, at that time) service contractor.
		Automatic deluge sprinkler had actuated, but no water available. Fire is raging.
		Ambulance called by phone and radio.
		Isopentane vapors continue to be released as piping and vessels fail from extreme heat.
		Fire brigade tries to activate a fixed monitor, but no water flows.

DATE	TIME	EVENT
08/1/91	11:15 A.M.	Fire brigade member sent to fire pump house. Electric fire pump inoperable: no power. One diesel pump down due to mechanical problems (known). Second diesel pump down: dead batteries.
		Several maintenance employees dispatched to repair diesel pump No. 2.
	11:20 A.M.	Fire spreads to formulated catalyst vertical storage tanks. Another **explosion** occurs. **Four fire brigade members injured by metal fragments.**
	11:22 A.M.	Local fire department arrives. Spread of fire is slowed using water on fire department trucks.
	11:30 A.M.	Maintenance moves batteries from No. 1 diesel fire pump to No. 2 diesel fire pump. No. 2 diesel fire pump started.
		Automatic deluge sprinkler system found to be severely damaged by fire/explosions and is now valved into OFF position.
		Three fixed fire monitors directed on fire at full flow. Two hose streams from hydrants directed on fire.
	11:58 A.M.	Fire under control.
	12:10 P.M.	Final extinguishment of fire
8/15/91		No. 1 diesel fire pump repaired.

Cause Determination

After the team completed the preliminary sequence of events, they began to develop a MCSOII tree to describe the events. As the top event, they choose the last injuries in time, those to the four fire brigade members. They asked, "Why did these injuries occur?" Two events are required and are sufficient: the explosion at the storage tanks AND the presence of the fire brigade members. The team added these events to the tree and continued to ask "Why?" until system-level root causes were determined (Tree A, pages 1–4, Figures G-1 through G-4). To reduce the complexity of the tree, the team chose to treat the injury, fatality, and first fireball as a separate tree (Tree B, pages 1–2, Figures G-5 and G-6). Since explosion at the vertical storage tanks resulted from the spread of the fire from Kettle No. 3, Tree B is shown as one of the branches of Tree A.

Some events were personnel or equipment doing what they were supposed to be doing at that time; these events are depicted as a "house" symbol. For many events at the bottom of the tree, the team did not have enough information in their possession to answer the "Why?" question. Such events are shown as a diamond, indicating a team decision to stop the tree at that point. For many of the diamonds, the team recommended further study or investigation by other groups.

Root Causes

The team looked at the bottom events on the tree for the root causes and prepared this summary:

The fire at Kettle No. 3 was caused by isopentane release from the cracked isopentane feed line; ignition was from wet air contacting the aluminum alkyl in Kettle No. 3. The fire could not be controlled because the fire water pumps were down, and the fire spread to the vertical catalyst storage tanks.

The root causes are:

- The isopentane line was weakened by corrosion:
  —Was it correctly specified?
  —Was the line the specified material of construction?
  —Is the observed corrosion normal for the material?
  —Was the material consistent with "good practice" for this service?
- The corrosion repair program (proposed in February 1990) was delayed by the 1989 budget crunch.
- The plant shutdown (which distracted the operators and made the electric fire water pump unavailable) was caused by a thunderstorm that tripped the primary feeder and no backup feeder was installed.
- The No. 1 diesel fire water pump was down because it overheated in the outside agency annual performance test on May 1, 1991. Further investigation is needed to determine why it was not repaired quickly. Also, mild overheating may not be detected in monthly maintenance tests because the 5 minute run time may not sufficient to find the overheating.
- The No. 2 diesel fire water pump was down because its batteries were dead. The dead batteries were detected and recharged in the 7/3/91 monthly check, but they were not replaced or rechecked. There may a cultural issue here of "make do" due to the budget crunch.
- There were several causes for the high pressure in the isopentane feed line:
  —The control room operator did not stop filling Kettle No. 3.
  —The high-level alarm did not sound (it failed; cause and timing not yet determined).

—It had been over a year since the last critical instrument check. The preventive maintenance records are poorly kept.
—There was no redundant back-up level alarm or shutdown for this critical service.
—There was no emergency relief for Kettle No. 3 and the isopentane feed line (a code violation, since it could be blocked in).
—The isopentane feed isolation valve closed during the power failure as designed.
—The outside operator failed to checked the isopentane feed isolation valve.
He may have been unaware of the emergency procedure, or
The control room operator did not send the outside operator:
–Because the control room operator was not drilled in the emergency procedures, or
–The control operator was distracted by the shutdown needs during the power failure (should more of the system shut itself down automatically?)
–Also the time for manually opening the isopentane feed isolation valve to be effective was fairly short (4–8 minutes).
–The source of the high pressure in the overfilled Kettle No. 3 could have been continuing reaction or thermal expansion; the team did not have the expertise to determine which.

- No fire brigade member reported to the fire pump house, a violation of the emergency procedure. This may be a training or drill issue.
- The fire brigade approached Kettle No. 3 unnecessarily closely while fire fighting capabilities were nonexistent, exposing themselves to injury from the later explosion. While the fire brigade did not respect the potential hazards of this incident, further investigation is needed to determine if it is a training problem or if the emergency response plan is deficient in this area.
- The presence of the injured contractor was not known to unit personnel and there was only limited time to notify the contractor to evacuate. Further investigation is needed to determine why the escort policy was not followed; it could have a training issue, or it could have been ignored due to workload, culture, or lack of management audit.
- The contractor was repairing malfunctioning gas analyzers; further investigation is needed to determine if these repairs are a high frequency occurrence and if more reliable analyzers are needed.
- Witnesses reported that the *Standard Operating Procedures* for the catalyst preparation area are frequently not used by employees. Further investigation is needed to determine if the lack of use is caused by training issues, lack of management audits and feedback, or deficiencies in the procedures themselves (cumbersome, incomplete, or out-of-date).

As the team developed the tree and this list of causes, their initial reaction was to focus on the operator errors in responding to the power failure and the high pressure alarm. However, as they considered the situation, they recognized that emergency relief should have been provided for the system.

The operations people pointed out several factors affecting operator response:

- the short time between the alarms and the fireball (8 and 4 minutes),
- the press of the shutdown duties following the power outage,
- the distance from the control room to the isopentane line isolation valve, and
- the presence of the thunderstorm.

Therefore, they consulted a human factors expert for additional analysis. Based on the facts of the incident, the time for diagnosis and action was less than 4 minutes from the high-temperature alarm and less than 8 minutes from the high-pressure alarm (without allowance for the system response to opening the isopentane feed isolation valve). Using Table 20-1 from NUREG/CR-1278, the human factors expert reported that the human error probability (HEP) is 0.5 for correctly diagnosing the first event within 10 minutes (that is, half the time the operator will make the correct diagnosis). If the thunderstorm and power failure are considered to be first events, then the HEP for correctly diagnosing the high alarms within 10 minutes is 1.0; the operator is guaranteed to mess up!

With this information, the team incorporated recommendations for emergency relief and automatic redundant interlocks on the catalyst kettle fill systems.

Recommendations

The team looked at the structure of the trees and the bottom events on the trees to develop the following list of recommendations and timing. They also assigned each action to the appropriate individual in the plant.

- Isopentane line integrity:
  —Replace the corroded lines with new lines before startup.
  —Confirm the correct specification for the isopentane lines. Are we using the best material for this service? Are there abnormal conditions that give high corrosion, can we avoid those conditions, or should we design for them? (before startup)
  —Review the rest of the corrosion repair program (proposed in February 1990, delayed by the 1989 budget crunch) to be sure other critical systems have acceptable integrity. (Review complete before startup. Replacement complete by February, 1992.)
- Consider a backup electric feeder to reduce the frequency of shutdown in thunderstorm. Review electric power system design for protection against thunderstorms. (By August, 1992.)
- Establish a weekly fire pump start and check program to be sure that this equipment works as intended. Revise the procedure to run the diesel pumps for a minimum of 30 minutes to detect overheating problems. Establish a preventive maintenance program to oversee all the maintenance on all the fire water pumps. Establish a high priority (Priority 1) for repairs on the fire equipment. (Before startup.)

- Establish criteria for finding the cause of dead batteries on the diesel fire water pumps and for checking that recharged batteries retain the charge. Establish criteria for replacing dead batteries. Management should work to change the cultural mindset of "make do." (Before startup.)
- Isopentane feed line:
  —Before startup, design and install emergency relief for Kettle No. 3 and the isopentane feed line. Hold a PHA (Process Hazards Analysis) on the routing of the emergency relief. Determine the source of the high pressure in the overfilled Kettle No.3. Was it continuing reaction or thermal expansion? Include in the emergency relief design.
  —Design and install redundant back-up level alarms and automatic feed shut downs for all catalyst preparation kettles (a critical service). (Before startup.)
  —Review (if possible) the cause of the high level alarm failure and modify the design. (Before startup.)
  —Establish a strong preventive maintenance testing program for the critical instruments in the plant. Determine testing frequency based on experience of problem instruments. (One year is too long. Consider starting at 60 days, and lengthening the interval if experience is favorable.) Develop a good record keeping system for the testing program. (Test all critical instruments before startup. Program established within 60 days after startup.)
  —Review the design criteria for the isopentane feed isolation valve. Should it fail closed on power failure as currently designed? What is the best way to accomplish isolation and to provide relief for the Kettles? (Before startup.)
- Procedures:
  —Review Standard and Emergency Operating Procedures for ease of use, up-to-date, and accuracy. (By November 1991.)
  —Review and improve the operator training system to emphasize the use of procedures. Develop drills and talk-throughs for emergency procedures. Set priorities for emergency actions and have the personnel memorize and the most important actions. (By November 1991.)
  —Review the emergency procedures for the allowable time to diagnose and act and the required response time for the system to recover after corrective action. Do a Human Reliability Analysis on the actions, including the time for an operator to walk to the remote location. For critical actions (high consequence potential) with a required short time period for diagnosis and action, automatic interlocks should be installed. Consider a fault tree analysis to determine the reliability of the interlock designs. (By November 1991.)
- Improve training and drill for the fire brigade members to ensure that someone reports to the fire pump house. (Before startup.)
- Improve the emergency response procedures, training, and drills, to help the fire brigade members respect the potential hazards of an incident and avoid unnecessary exposure, particularly when fire fighting capabilities are below par. (Plans complete by November 1991.)

- Any person (visitor, new employee, or contractor) allowed on the property site should be given a safety orientation that describes the plant hazards, required protective equipment, evacuation and emergency procedures for the facility. This orientation should be given by the safety department by either a formal (with syllabus) presentation or by video tape. The program should stress that visitors and contractors should be accompanied by plant personnel at all times. A list should be maintained of those who have taken the orientation (wallet cards can be issued also) and the orientation must be taken again annually. Over time, the presentation can be revised to be efficient and to meet better the needs of the plant. (First presentation and record keeping in place by August 15, 1991.)
- Consider an evacuation horn and/or public address system to warn visitors, maintenance workers, and contractors to leave the area. (Not all visitors will have radio communication.) Establish criteria to pull the evacuation horn. Drill in evacuation once per quarter on each shift (one drill per quarter must be on days). (By November 1991.)
- Since an incident can deactivate the active fire protection (such as in-web automatic water spray sprinkler), the major load bearing supports for the catalyst preparation area should be provided with adequate fireproofing to prevent their rapid collapse during a fire. (By March 1992.)

Criteria for Restart

The team then developed the conditions that must be met before the plant could be restarted.

1. All recommendations required for restart must be completed.
2. All changes introduced during repair and installation of the recommendations must go through a PHA (Process Hazards Analysis).
3. A walk-through safety, health, and environmental review must be completed after construction and before introduction of chemicals to ensure that repairs and additions have been made as intended.
4. Startup must be authorized by the signatures of the Operations Manager, Maintenance Manager, and Safety Supervisor (all three signatures required).

REPORTING

The team presented their findings to the plant management and to the corporate safety department orally and handed out lists of the causes, the trees, the recommendations, and the criteria for restart. Management accepted the oral report and appointed the Operations Manager to be responsible for seeing that the action points were completed.

Over the next two weeks, the investigation team compiled and published a detailed report using the following outline and incorporating the lists given to management. The team leader appointed one member to edit the report; the editor used the criteria that the report would be understandable to a new operations or engineering person two years in the future. It was assumed that the new person would be experienced in polyethylene technology and NDF culture, but would not have any knowledge of the incident.

Report Outline

- Abstract
- Executive Summary
- Background
- Description of the Incident
- Chronology of Events
- List of Root Causes
- Discussion of Causes
- Recommendations
- Criteria for Restart
- Critique of the Investigation
    - Features That Worked Well
    - Opportunities for Improvement in Future Investigations
- Appendices
    - Photographs
    - Drawings
    - P&IDs
    - Supporting Reports from Internal and External Consultants
    - Acknowledgments

The investigation team members were consulted frequently during the design and installation of the repairs for restart and several team members participated in the pre-startup safety review.

To reduce risk in the industry as a whole, NDF endeavored to share the lessons learned from the incident with others in the same or similar industries.

- In October 1991, the site manager gave an oral summary of the incident to the local manufacturers' association.
- In December 1991, the NDF representative on the co-producers' safety committee informally discussed the causes and corrective actions with the other co-producers.
- In July 1992, the safety supervisor presented an overview of the incident, causes, and corrective actions to a safety meeting sponsored by the regional chemical industry council.
- In March 1993, the process engineering supervisor gave a paper on the incident at a Loss Prevention Symposium of the American Institute of Chemical Engineers. The paper was published later in *Plant Operations Progress*.

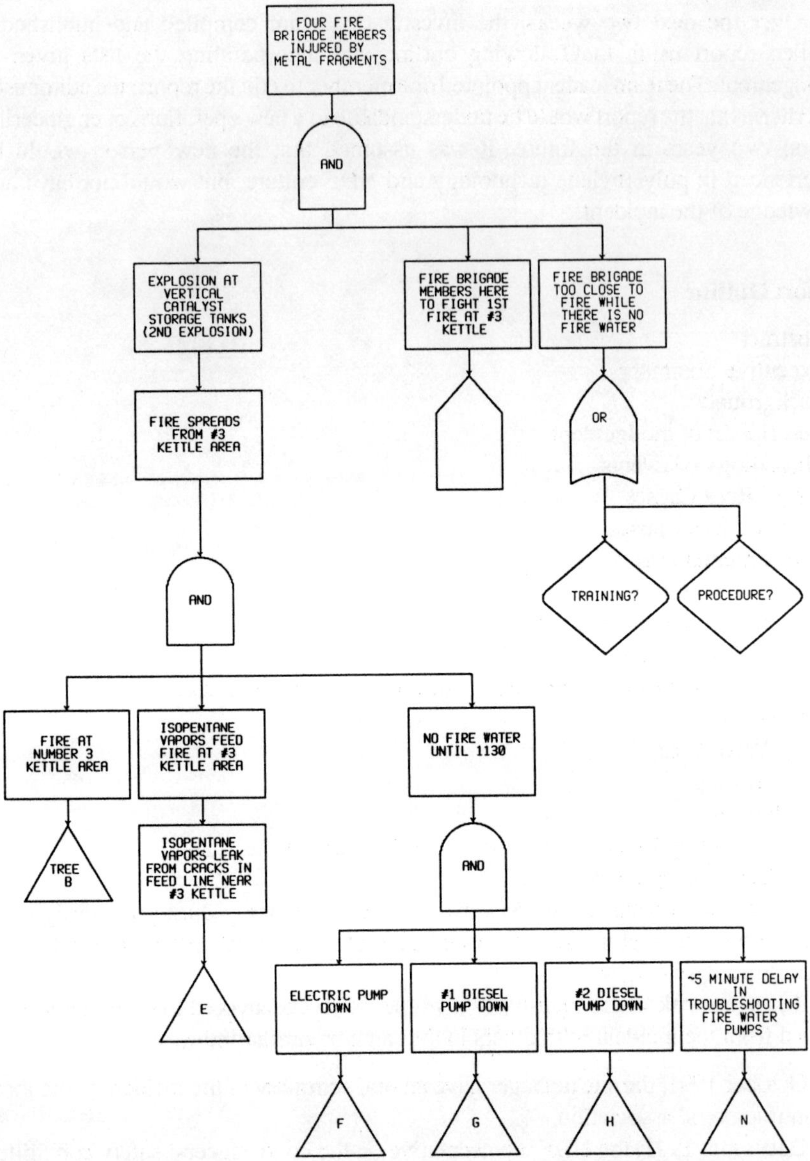

Figure G-1. Tree A, Page 1. Second explosion and four fire brigade injuries.

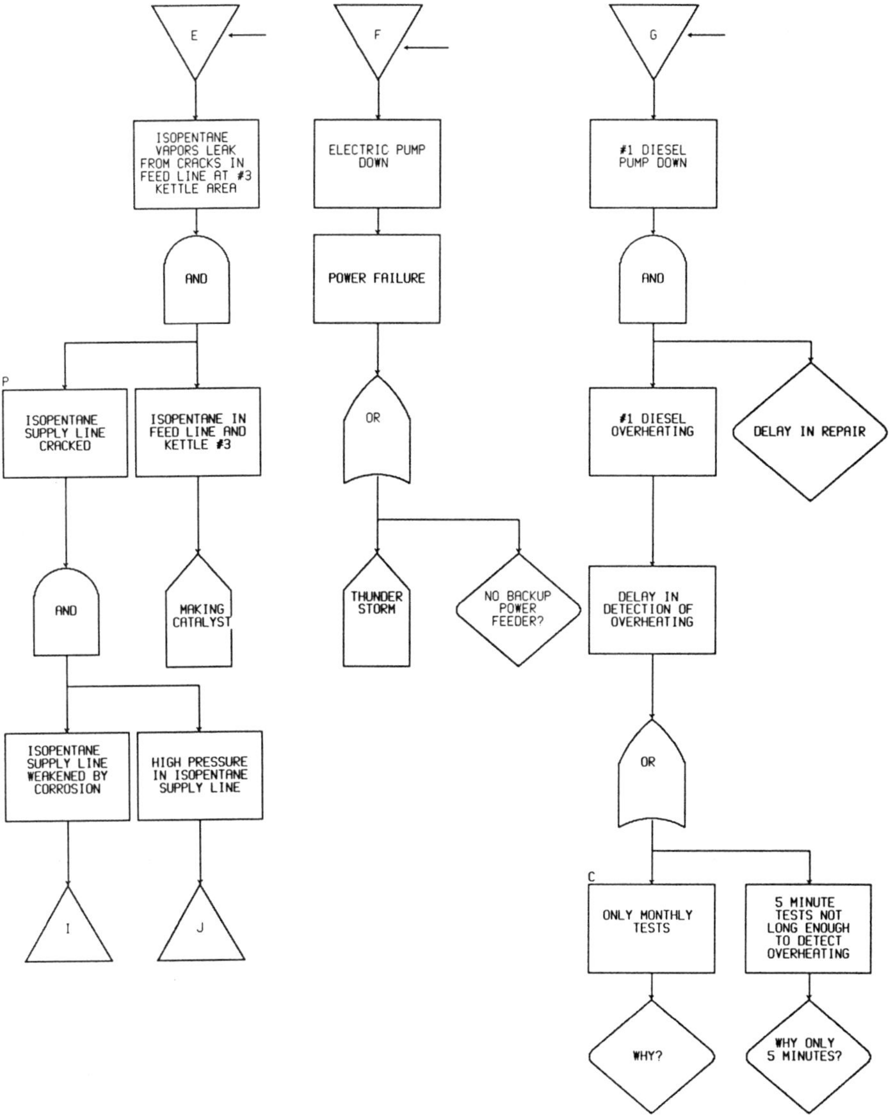

Figure G-2. Tree A, Page 2 (left). Second explosion and four fire brigade injuries.

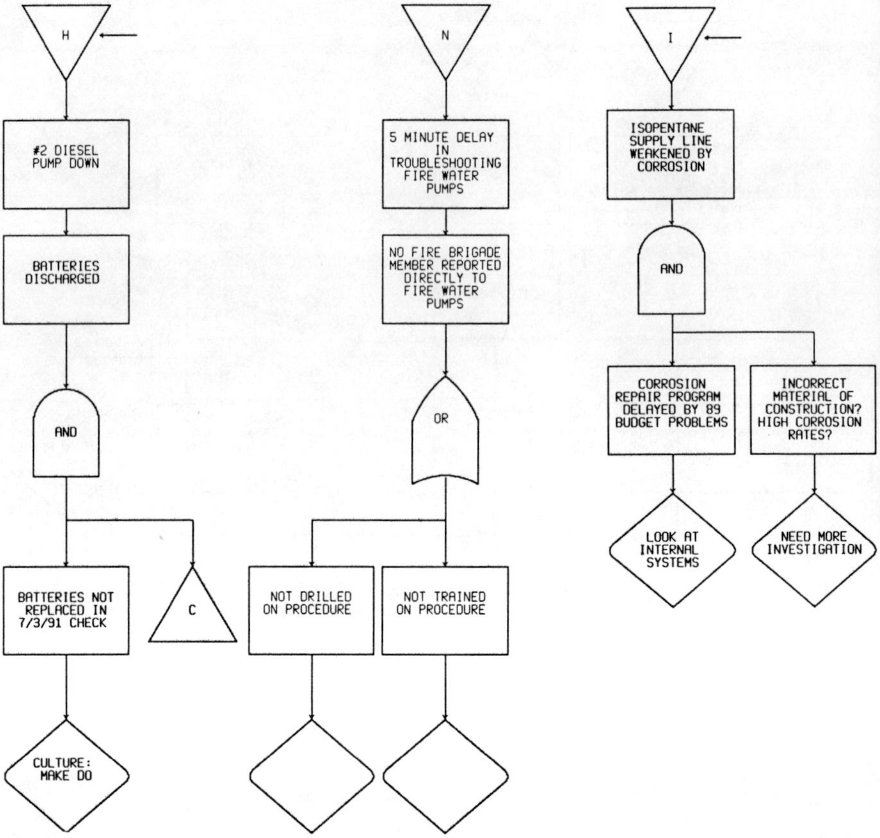

Figure G-2. *(Cont'd)* **Tree A, Page 2 (right). Second explosion and four fire brigade injuries.**

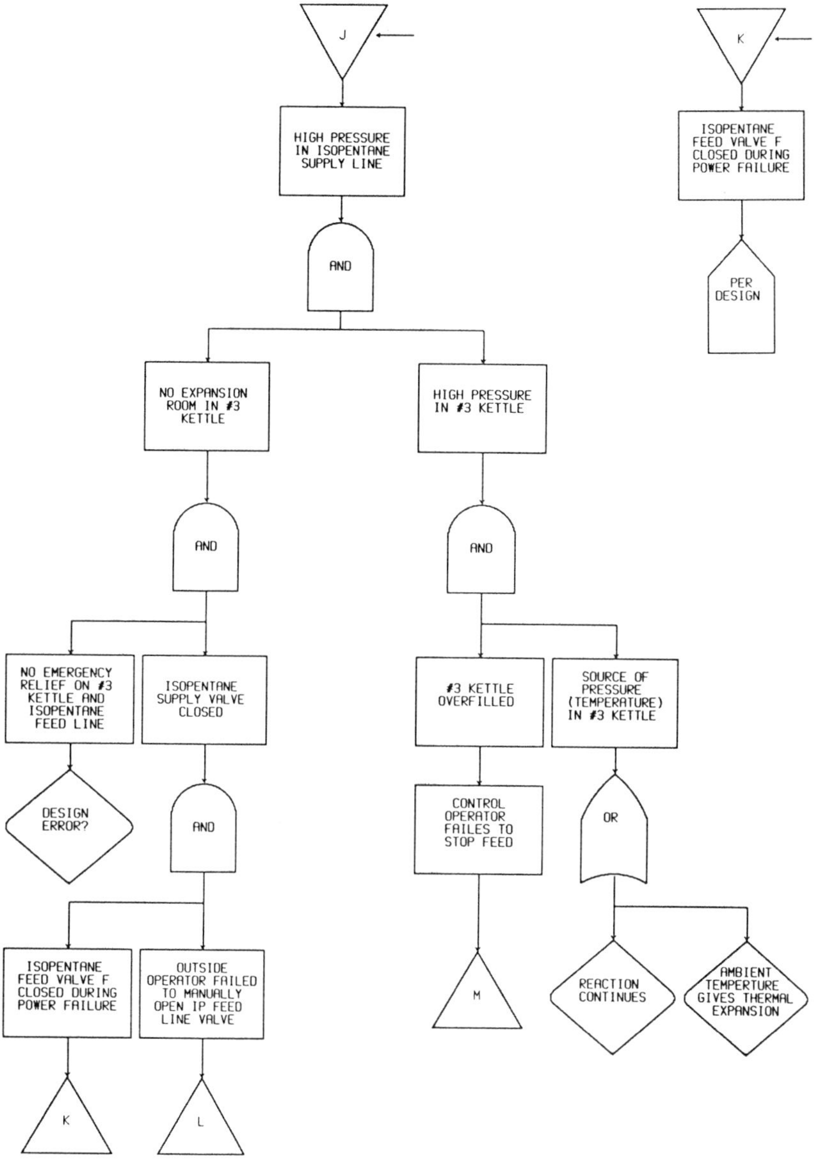

Figure G-3. Tree A, Page 3. Second explosion and four fire brigade injuries.

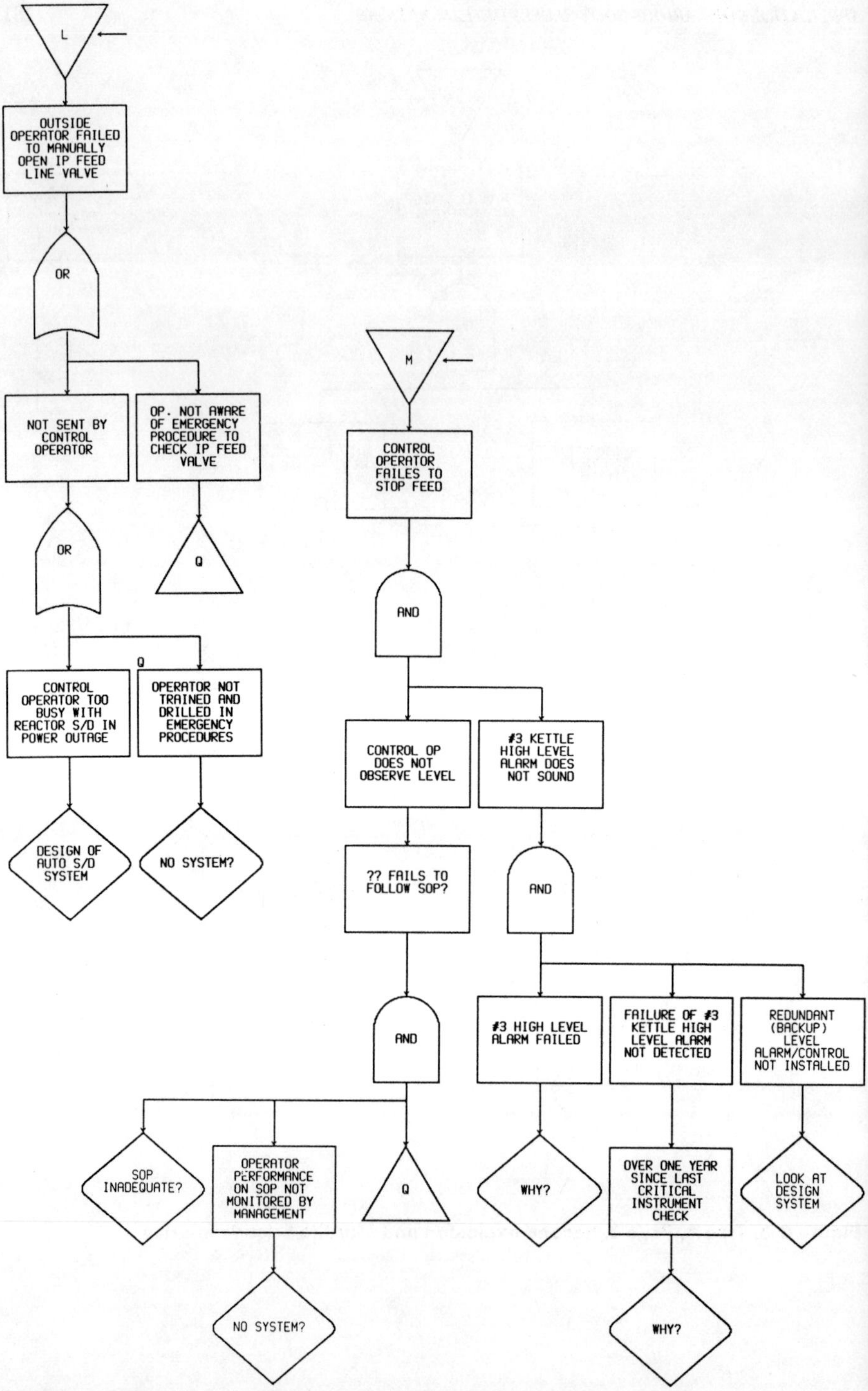

Figure G-4. Tree A, Page 4. Second explosion and four fire brigade injuries.

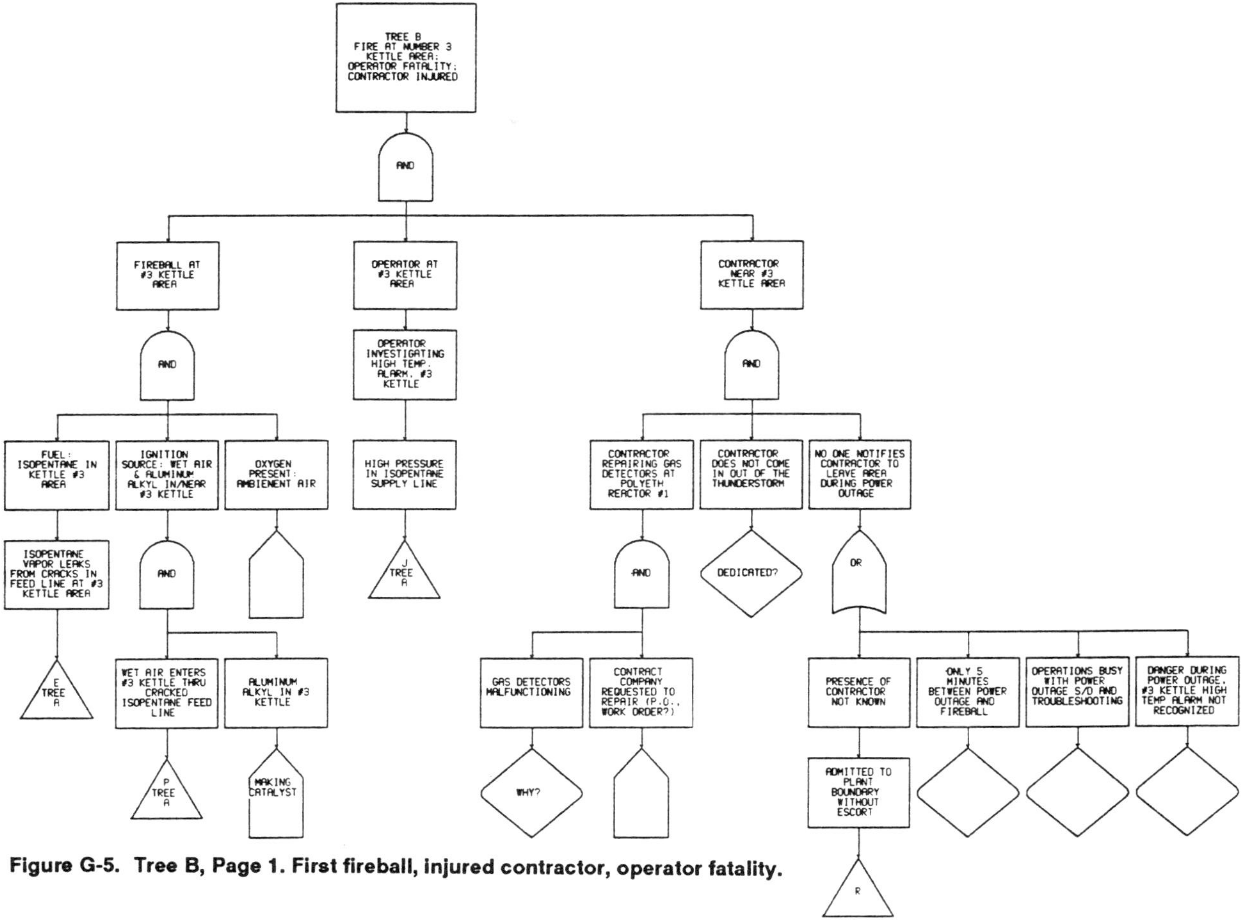

Figure G-5. Tree B, Page 1. First fireball, injured contractor, operator fatality.

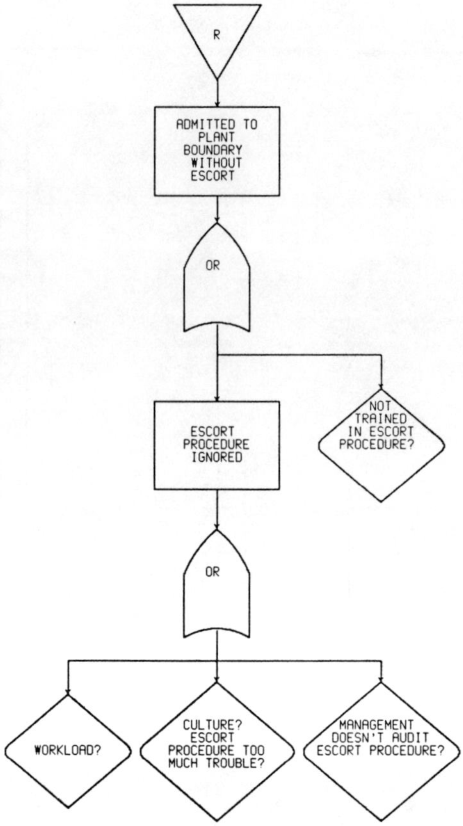

Figure G-6. Tree B, Page 2. First fireball, injured contractor, operator fatality.

FLASHBACK FROM WASTE GAS INCINERATOR INTO AIR SUPPLY PIPING

S. E. Anderson, A. M. Dowell, III, P.E.,
and J. B. Mynaugh

Rohm and Haas Texas Incorporated

P.O. Box 672

Deer Park, TX 77536

Presented at the 25th Annual Loss Prevention Symposium, August 22, 1991

Session: Case Histories, Paper 73c

Rohm and Haas presents this paper as part of our commitment to the Chemical Manufacturers Association (CMA) Responsible Care® Process Safety Code of Management Practices. The code includes Management Leadership in "Sharing of relevant safety knowledge and lessons learned from . . . incidents with industry, government and community."

SUMMARY

A waste gas incinerator experienced a flashback with a pressure wave in the Suction Vent Gas (SVG) system. Extensive damage resulted to the SVG flame arrestor, SVG fan, SVG valves, and incinerator piping. There were no injuries.

The primary cause of the incident is believed to be a fuel rich SVG stream that was rapidly introduced into the incinerator creating a "puff." This "puff" allowed flame from the natural gas ring burner to blow back into the windbox igniting the fuel rich SVG. The combustion of gas in the ducting then created a pressure wave that blew apart the flame arrestor and caused the remainder of the damage.

BACKGROUND

The Waste Gas Incinerator uses natural gas as its primary fuel and is designed to incinerate waste gases (called AOG) from a plant unit as well as the minor organic constituents found in the SVG (suction vent gas). A sketch of the incinerator system is shown in Figure 1.

The SVG is the primary source of combustion air. It flows into the incinerator wind box (D) to provide air for the main natural gas burner (E). Some SVG also provides quench air (I) to the firebox (J), entering the AOG nozzles. Combustion air also can be supplied by a running combustion air fan (C).

The SVG system is a vacuum collection system that picks up volatile compounds from tank working losses and distillation system vents from all areas within two units. Analyzers continuously sample each major branch of the SVG for combustibles. The SVG system design is to run at less than 10% of the lower explosion limit (LEL). The analyzers sound an alarm when the fuel content of the gas reaches 25% of the LEL. The analyzers activate controls that switch the SVG to the flare when the fuel content reaches 50% of the LEL.

A large fan (A)—located in the incinerator area—provides the motive force for the SVG system. A crimped metal ribbon type flame arrestor (B)—located just downstream of the fan—protects the SVG system from a flashback from the incinerator or flare. Downstream of the flame arrestor, the SVG can be routed either to the flare or to the incinerator via two 30 inch (76 cm) butterfly switching valves. These valves are normally operated remotely from the control room but are also equipped with hand wheels for manual operation.

INCIDENT SEQUENCE

At the time of the incident, the reactor system feeding waste gas to the incinerator tripped off line. The reactor system shut down safely and the operator began preparations for a restart by switching the waste gas (AOG) to its dedicated flare. Once the

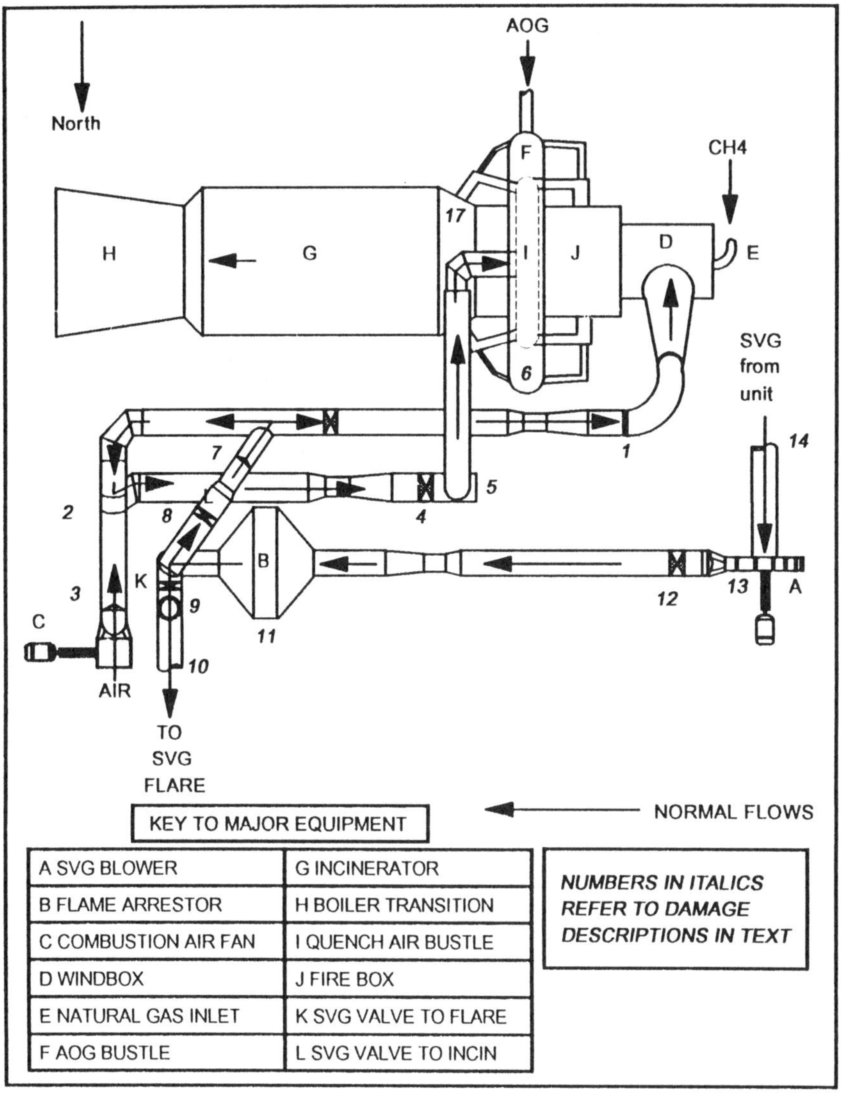

Figure 1. Waste gas incinerator schematic.

valves were switched, the control room operator noted that the indicator lights on both valves were showing open, and he instructed the outside operator by radio to "Close the 'A' train AOG valve to the incinerator."

Either through mis-communication or because the outside operator was in a high noise area, the outside operator thought he was instructed to close *the SVG valve to the incinerator*. Working now with a second person, he climbed up to the platform to access the SVG valves and they proceeded first to close manually the valve to the incinerator (L) and then to begin opening the valve to the flare (K).

When the SVG flow was blocked in, a low SVG flow alarm sounded in the controlroom. The control operator, responding to the alarm and recognizing what was occurring, radioed to the outside operators that they had closed the wrong valve and instructed them to reopen the SVG valve to the incinerator.

One operator began closing the valve to the flare (and the other operator reopened the SVG valve to the incinerator). Since the automatic controls still commanded the SVG valve to the incinerator to be open, the operator simply disconnected the manual wheel from the actuator and assisted the valve movement by pushing on the actuator piston. The valve rapidly reopened.

Once the SVG valve to the incinerator was 100% opened, or nearly so, an explosion occurred.

DAMAGE DESCRIPTION

Listed below is a detailed list of the damage. The numbers shown show the location of the damage as shown on Figure 1.

Number	*Description*
1	The elbow in the combustion air line feeding the windbox was pushed west 1 to 2 inches (3 to 5 cm). The expansion joint connecting this elbow to the piping run was stretched and deformed.
2	The check valve at the combustion air fan was broken from its supports and blown back toward the fan casing.
3	The piping supports (concrete bases) for the combustion air piping were cracked and broken.
4	The quench air control valve (butterfly valve) was sheared from its mounting pins and blown west into the quench air bustle.
5	Two holes, approximately 1 inch (2.5 cm) in diameter, were found in the end plate of the bustle that connects to the quench air duct. Our belief is that parts of the quench air valve caused this damage.
6	The entire quench air bustle was moved off its pipe supports approximately 14 inches (36 cm) west. The expansion joint in the quench air duct was stretched and distorted.
7	The counterweight on the check valve in the SVG line feeding the combustion and quench air header was broken from its mounting bracket.

Number	*Description*
8	The SVG switching valve to the flare was broken from its supports and the manual valve wheel was broken off at the gear box casing (note: an operator was holding onto the manual wheel for this valve when the explosion occurred).
9	The rupture disk (polyethylene sheet) in the SVG line to the flare was blown. The rain hat covering the plastic was also snapped from its fasteners and was found laying below on the ground.
10	The duct work directing SVG gas to the flare was badly wrinkled.
11	The SVG flame arrestor was broken free from its mounting bolts and sheared into two pieces. Several arrestor elements were severely distorted and pushed west toward the fan. The tubesheet supporting the arrestor elements was bowed—again indicating a pressure wave coming from the incinerator.
12	The piping connecting the SVG flame arrestor to the SVG fan was broken free from its supports. The piping came to rest partially on top of the SVG fan. The butterfly damper in the SVG discharge was bent into the shape of a pipe saddle and was torn loose from its mounting bracket.
13	The SVG fan was broken from its base. The fan housing was pushed approximately 3 inches (8 cm) west and 1 inch (3 cm) south. The bearing housings on the fan shaft were also snapped.
14	Piping connected to the suction side of the SVG fan was sheared and broken from its supports (note: all suction piping in the SVG system is fiberglass reinforced plastic (FRP); all piping after the fan discharge is stainless steel).
15	A "S" in the SVG piping in the reactor rack fell from the third level to the ground—damaging a safety shower, some insulation, and a pump oiler during its fall (not shown in Figure 1).
16	Many piping supports for the FRP piping in the reactor rack were found broken or stretched (not shown in Figure 1).
17	The incinerator had several radial cracks in the refractory brick—indicating an overpressure in the firebox.

INCIDENT ANALYSIS:

With the unit personnel and the plant safety director, the incident investigation team conducted a multiple cause, system-oriented incident investigation. We developed a chronology (sequence of events), we listed the facts, and then we generated a logic tree based on Fault Tree Analysis methodology.

Early in the logic tree development, we hit a dead end in explaining the source of a combustible mixture in the combustion air. We brainstormed 17 scenarios of timing, actions, and equipment failures. We tested each scenario against 20 established facts, using a matrix decision analysis system[1] (Figure 3).

After we agreed on the scenario described below as the only one satisfying all of the facts, we further tested and verified it by showing that it explained all the observed damage. Pressures generated were not high; estimates were, for the most part, in the 15–20 psig (200–240 kPa) range.

INCIDENT CAUSES

We concluded that the incident cause was a rapid introduction of a fuel rich SVG stream that initially ignited in the incinerator firebox. The sudden shock of fuel—along with sufficient air—caused the incinerator to "puff," momentarily stopping or reversing the flow of SVG, and allowing a flame front to proceed into the windbox and back into the combustion air header. (See Figure 2.)

This flame front generated or sustained a pressure wave that caused the damage in the combustion air header, the quench air header, the SVG piping, the SVG flame arrestor, and the SVG fan.

Damage shows that the flame continued to propagate past the SVG fan and up into the Reactor Rack SVG header piping until the fuel content of the gas dropped below flammable limits. The ignition source for this segment is not positively known. Although the flame arrestor was blown into two sections, the section of the arrestor containing the crimped metal ribbons was intact and we believe it should have been capable of halting the flame front. We feel it is more likely that movement of the SVG fan—possibly the fan wheel contacting the housing—generated sparks or a hot spot that again ignited the fuel-laden SVG.

The source of the fuel in the SVG was the routine collection of tank working losses and system vents. Organics built up in the system while the SVG was deadheaded and while it was slowly bled to the flare. This built up a "bullet" of fuel in the SVG that zipped through the piping into the incinerator when the operator reopened the SVG valve to the incinerator.

We concluded that the normal incinerator controls, interlocks, and shut downs acted normally and were not a contributor to this event. Although there was evidence of water in the instrument air system, we conclude that wet instrument air did not affect the performance of the instruments or controls on the night this incident occurred.

---

1 *The Rational Manager* by C. H. Kepner and B. B. Tregoe (1976) describes this type of analysis.

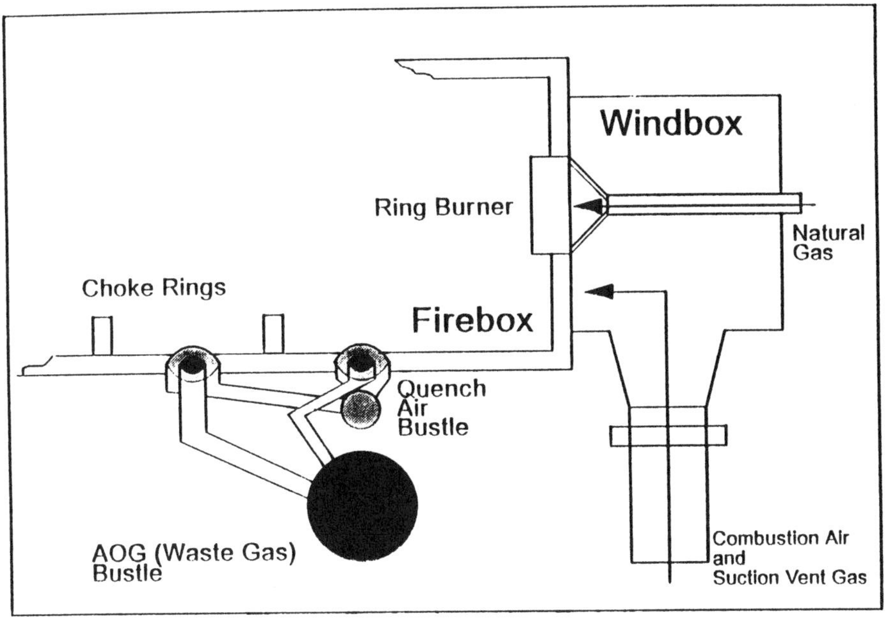

Figure 2. Incinerator detail.

Fact -- Scenario Matrix

Does the Scenario Explain the Facts?

Scenerios

Facts	1	2	3	. . .	16	17
1	y	y	y		o	o
2	y	y	x		o	o
3	y	y	x		o	y
. . .						
19	x	o	x		o	y?
20	y	o	x		o	y

Y=Yes
X=No
o=Neutral

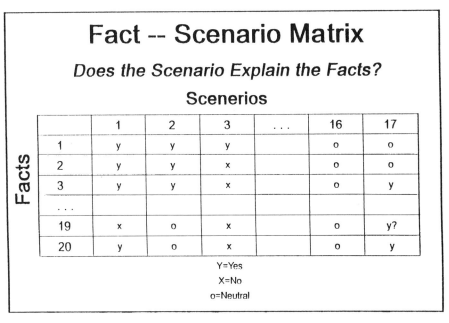

Figure 3. Testing the scenarios against the facts.

We felt strongly that timing of the various actions was in itself a cause of the explosion. Had the operator opened the valve to the flare fully, and left it open long enough, the fuel rich "bullet" would have passed out the unlit flare and would have dissipated safely. In addition, a longer period at the low flow condition would have given the LEL analyzer at the SVG fan sufficient time to detect the high fuel content of the stream; then automatic controls would have prevented reintroduction of the SVG into the incinerator. The LEL analyzer response time was 20 seconds (10 seconds for the sample loop and 10 seconds for the analyzer itself). Also, had the operator reopened the SVG valve to the incinerator slowly, the fuel rich combustion air would have burned normally instead of causing the "puff" that allowed flame to enter back into the windbox.

This is a complex scenario. It is complex because the incinerator is a well-designed system. For a well-designed system to fail, a number of unforeseen failures must occur at the right time to defeat the safeguards that were already in place. Thus, determining the actual failure mode was difficult; it was difficult to come up with additional safeguards.

ADDITIONAL CAUSES

We identified some additional causes:

- A LEL analyzer on an SVG branch header upstream of the SVG fan was out of service, waiting for repair. An operating unit fed SVG into that branch header. This analyzer could possibly have warned of the buildup of flammable vapors in the SVG header while the flow was stopped.
- The operators thought they should have corrected the blocked in SVG valves quickly. The production culture is to correct mistakes quickly and the training system had not addressed education in what could go wrong with the SVG system.
- There was a history of sticking valves in the SVG system. Thus, it was easy to think "same problem again." Efforts were underway to repair the sticking valves, but had not been successful at the time of the incident.

CORRECTIVE ACTIONS

The incident investigation team along with unit personnel developed the following corrective actions intended to prevent future incidents and/or to mitigate the damage caused by any future recurrence of this incident. We grouped the corrective actions by mechanical, operational, and training categories. While it may seem that there are many actions, they are system oriented and are aimed at the multiple causes identified by the incident investigation. We believe it is important to make improvements, where practical, in <u>all</u> the areas that contributed to the incident cause and its severity.

Mechanical

- Consider pressure relief on the combustion air line and SVG line (both sides of the arrestor). (It was installed.)
- Critique flame arrestor design. (It is acceptable.)
- Improve SVG valves and actuators. These valves were relatively flimsy and have been a maintenance headache at times over the years. The Instrument Shop replaced these valves with a better design as part of the incinerator rebuild.
- Improve AOG valves/actuators. Failure of an AOG valve was an indirect initiator of this event. We recommend these valves be inspected and repaired or replaced. (Improved valve being identified.)
- Design/install facilities to ensure dry instrument air. Water in the instrument air system will disrupt controls and may prevent them from performing their function. While we do not believe that water (or ice) in the instrument air was a factor in this incident, we found evidence of liquid in several lines and suggest prompt action to eliminate this potential hazard.
- Consider removing a 1.5 second delay in the low low combustion air flow shutdown. This shutdown was originally intended to prevent the incinerator from shutting down when the SVG is switched to the flare.
- Improve the mechanical integrity of failed components. A structural assessment of the damage shows that much of the serious damage was the result of poor construction. We suggest the following:
  —Add tie-rods on the expansion joints to prevent future stretching/distortion.
  —Dye-penetrant check or x-ray the old and repaired welds on the SVG flame arrestor.
  —Upgrade the quench air flow control valve with stronger components.
  —Consider additional support or better construction of the check valve in the combustion air line.
- Consider faster response LEL analyzers. Analyzers are now available with less than five seconds total response time (sample loop and analyzer).
- Consider reviewing the mechanical integrity of systems that didn't fail. Other areas of the incinerator could have been stressed by the pressure wave but damage may not be visible to the naked eye. Additional failures (accompanied by additional downtime) may pop up in the future if these are not identified.

Operational

- Consider rebalancing the SVG air flows in the unit. Considerable changes and additions have been made to the suction vent system over the years and it is not clear that operations are at the design basis of 30 ft/s (9 m/s).
- Consider revising the controls to divert the SVG to the flare automatically on low flow.
- Develop operating strategy for lower explosion limit (LEL) analyzers that ensures that all of the SVG passes an analyzer (e.g., if the SVG fan LEL analyzer is out of

service, SVG must be flared). The LEL analyzers are the first defense against generating a flammable mixture in the SVG, if flows are disrupted. Some LEL analyzers need to be added. Develop a plan that addresses how many LEL analyzers are required for operation.

- Consider a review to establish a list of all components in the SVG / Incinerator / Flare system. From this, develop a "Minimum Equipment List." This task could require a fault tree. Train operators, foremen, maintenance personnel, and engineers on what is critical for safe operations of the system. Institute such training as part of the ongoing unit training.
- Consider adding LEL alarm status to the logs, and instituting a program for reducing the frequency of trouble.
- Correct the documentation to show that there is a low flow shutdown for SVG to flare.
- Consider alternate technology to handle the SVG stream.
- Consider means of exercising standby equipment regularly (e.g., combustion air fan damper).
- Consider air–fuel ratio controllers to compensate automatically for changes in composition and/or flow.

Training

- Consider additional operator training to emphasize the importance of not blocking in both SVG valves (i.e., to flare *and* to incinerator) simultaneously, and to review procedures for introducing SVG into the incinerator (i.e., slowly, using automatic controls).
- Consider application of these Corrective Actions to construction of similar systems in the future.
- Consider adding a data acquisition system to the incinerator. (Strip charts recorded some variables, but more detailed operating data would have been helpful to the investigation.)

LESSONS LEARNED

- At the end of the investigation we identified the following learnings that may be helpful in future investigations:
- Interview *all* the involved personnel as soon as possible.
- Include instrumentation expertise on the investigation team, or have it available as a resource.
- The damage analysis was critical in developing the correct scenario.
- The technique of listing facts and then testing each fact against each scenario in a matrix was very helpful.
- Early arrival of investigation team was very helpful (within 10 hours of the event).

- The videotape, photographs, and description of the damage (made on the first day) were very helpful to investigators who arrived later.
- Write the report as soon as possible after the investigation is completed.

Acknowledgments

The authors would like to express our appreciation to everyone who assisted us in the investigation of this incident. We could not have done the investigation without the help of each listed person and group: the production unit operators, the Plant Protection Officers, the structural and mechanical experts from Rohm and Haas Corporate Engineering Division, the power specialist from Bechtel (T. McLean), W. C. Stone of Stone Engineering, the production unit Management Team, and the Maintenance Teams.

MORE BANG FOR THE BUCK: GETTING THE MOST FROM ACCIDENT INVESTIGATIONS

E. Anderson and R. W. Skloss

Rohm and Haas Texas Incorporated

Deer Park, Texas

Presented at the 25th Annual Loss Prevention Symposium, August 22, 1991

Session: Case Histories

ABSTRACT

An incident investigation system based on a combination of Fault Tree Analysis logic and the Deming Principles of Systems and Quality was developed during a 3-year period. The system was given an excellent test in the investigation of the explosion of a tank car filled with methacrylic acid. In this case, the event tree constructed during the investigation was easily converted into a fault tree. The fault tree so constructed was then used to evaluate the effectiveness of proposed corrective changes to the production, loading, and analytical systems before the changes were actually implemented. By making use of these tools to guide the inclusion of feedback loops (AND-gates in fault tree terminology), the intrinsic safety of the methacrylic acid production and shipping system was greatly enhanced at a relatively low cost.

INTRODUCTION

Obtaining the best results from supervisors' investigations of incidents that occur in the plant environment has been a goal of many safety professionals for many years, and the goal has often been quite elusive. In 1983, plant management became convinced of the merits of the accident causation theory of Dan Petersen[1] and decided to create a task group to attempt once more to develop an accident investigation technique that would achieve the following improvements:

1. Improve quality of investigations
   —Force the investigator to go beneath the surface to the underlying causes
   —Foster attempts to find as many of the causes as practicable
   —Improve documentation of the investigations
   —Increase utility for training and information sharing
2. Increase uniformity of investigations
3. Improve utility of recommended corrective actions

Toward this end, the task group (called the Accident Investigation Committee, or AIC) was put together from a group of carefully chosen individuals to bring together the desired mix of skills and expertise. The chosen individuals contributed a broad range of experiences:

1. Safety professionals
2. A unit manager
3. A day foremen (second line manager)
4. An experienced process engineer skilled in hazard analysis

During about 3 years of development and testing, the AIC tried and screened a number of different approaches. The one that met most of the performance requirements was based on the marriage of Fault Tree Analysis technology and Deming's concepts of Quality and Systems; we called it the multiple-cause, systems-oriented incident investigation (MCSOII) technique. From Fault Tree Analysis we obtained a semi-rigorous technique that forces the participants to look more deeply into the layers of accident causation than they otherwise would, and from Deming came the idea that a failure in the plant "system" can produce a failure in "safety," and that all such failures are amenable to the same kinds of systems analysis and correction.

As a result of the AIC's efforts, we now have a process for investigating accidents in which we construct an event tree for each incident. The tree is quite similar to a fault tree from the quantitative risk analysis discipline, except that in the investigations we often sacrifice some structural rigor to get the most results in a reasonable time. Basically, the process uses a team to reconstruct the chronology of the incident and to construct the event tree. We try to include those who are most familiar with what actually happened, including the injured person(s) if any. We use the same basic method to investigate process failures, spills, injuries, or any other system failures. Emphasizing the system aspects of the failure removes much of the confrontational aspects of such proceedings, and facilitates achieving comprehensive results. The event trees that are obtained contain much information, communicate it in an easily understood form, are very useful in training, and can easily be converted to fault trees if desired.

After the investigation process described above had been in use for several years, an incident occurred that afforded an unique opportunity to use the system to its fullest, and demonstrate the great potential of the process.

THE INCIDENT

Chronology

At 4:30 A.M. on July 21, 1988, a plant protection officer making rounds saw and heard vapors emitting from the relief valve on tank car UTLX 647014. This report indicated that the contents of the car, technical methacrylic acid (TMAA) were reacting, and that we had a serious situation. The car was in a marshalling yard awaiting transfer to a terminal. Cars filled with hazardous materials that were near the reacting car were removed, and empty cars were moved into position on its south side and west end. Remote fire monitors were placed into position on the north side and directed at the relief valve and the dome in an effort to control vapor emissions during the remainder of the reaction. The east end of the car could not be reached. Fortunately, the car at that end was empty. Personnel were kept away from the car as much as possible from the time vapor emissions were noticed. At about 12:25 A.M. on July 22 (about 20 hours after the problem became known), the car ruptured.

Effects

The forces released when the tank car skin ruptured were quite impressive. Parts of the car were found 250–300 yards (228–274 m) away from the skin. The wheels of the car were driven into the ground about two feet (61 cm) while the wheels were still on the rails. The skin of the car was essentially flattened, with the impressions of the two rails clearly seen through the skin. The sound of the explosion was heard about 10 miles away. The overhead 138,000-volt electrical lines were severed, and the arcs resulted in two small grass fires. Plants connected to these electrical lines were shut down. There was no fire from the polymerization. In addition to the car that was destroyed, the nearby cars were also damaged. Foam-like polymer covered an area about 200 by 50 yards (182 by 46 m). Because of the precautions we had taken, there were no injuries.

THE INVESTIGATION

On-the-spot photographs and videotapes were taken as soon as light permitted. Samples of polymer from different areas of the car were also collected. Records of loading and lab results for production and loading were also assembled. File samples were retrieved for testing. A 13-person team was formed to investigate the incident. The team was made up of persons from the AIC as well as from each group involved in producing, loading, analyzing, and shipping TMAA.

The Facts and Findings

- The car had been loaded on July 11, 1988, and the temperature had been in the 90–98°F range (30–33°C) between loading and the explosion.
- The car was one of six that were being accumulated for combination in a ship's deep tank for subsequent export.
- These cars were stainless steel. This was the first time TMAA was loaded in cars that were not internally coated.
- File samples from the destroyed car indicated low levels of inhibitor (at the process rundown levels, not shipping levels). Other cars were sampled and found to be normal.
- Some of the polymer was found to contain about 300 ppm iron.
- The polymer was dehydrated to a significant degree. There was also almost no odor of MAA in the area covered with the polymer, indicating virtually complete conversion.

The Event Tree

The team developed the event tree from the facts in hand. It was clear that the car had exploded because of a polymerization. The first layer of significant causation we reached for the polymerization was as follows (see also Figure 1):

- The MAA in the car had ineffective inhibitor. Either the inhibitor had not been added or it was ineffective.
- The car had been held at moderately high temperature for several days.
- The polymer showed evidence of iron contamination at levels high enough to promote polymerization. (Iron is a known promoter of polymerization.)

Each of these causes was followed to an end point by repeatedly asking "why" something happened. Branches are ended when no more questions about "why" something happened can be asked, or when we reach a reason like "It is naturally hot in Southeast Texas in the summer." These are called "primal events" in fault tree terminology. In our system, possible causes are followed, even though we may not think they apply to a particular incident. This makes the incident investigation event tree more valuable for future applications, such as in training, because more than one

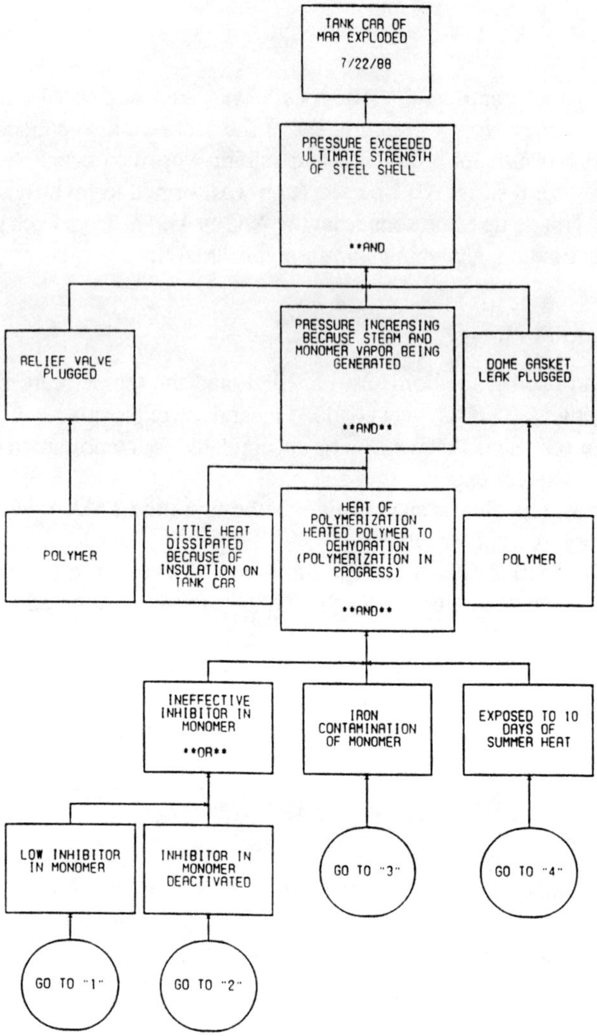

Figure 1. Event tree for a MAA tank car explosion.

scenario is included in the result. Thus we followed the branch dealing with contamination causing inhibitor deactivation to its conclusion; even though we did not think contamination was a cause in this case, it could have been. The detailed trees are shown as Figures 2 through 5.

THE CAUSES IDENTIFIED

The primary causes of this event were a direct result of systems that resulted in a low level of TMAA stability. We had enjoyed freedom from accidents for years because

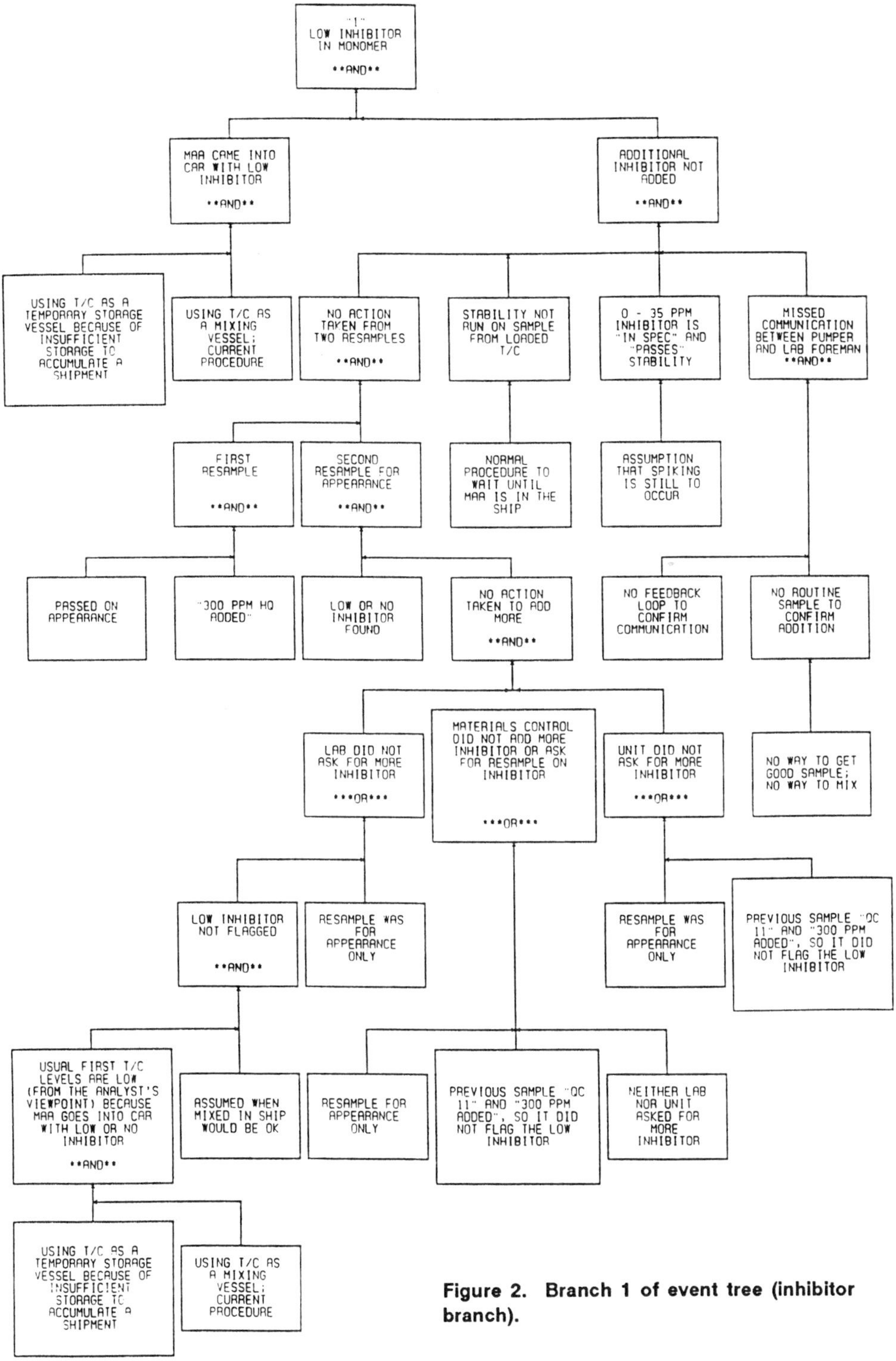

Figure 2. Branch 1 of event tree (inhibitor branch).

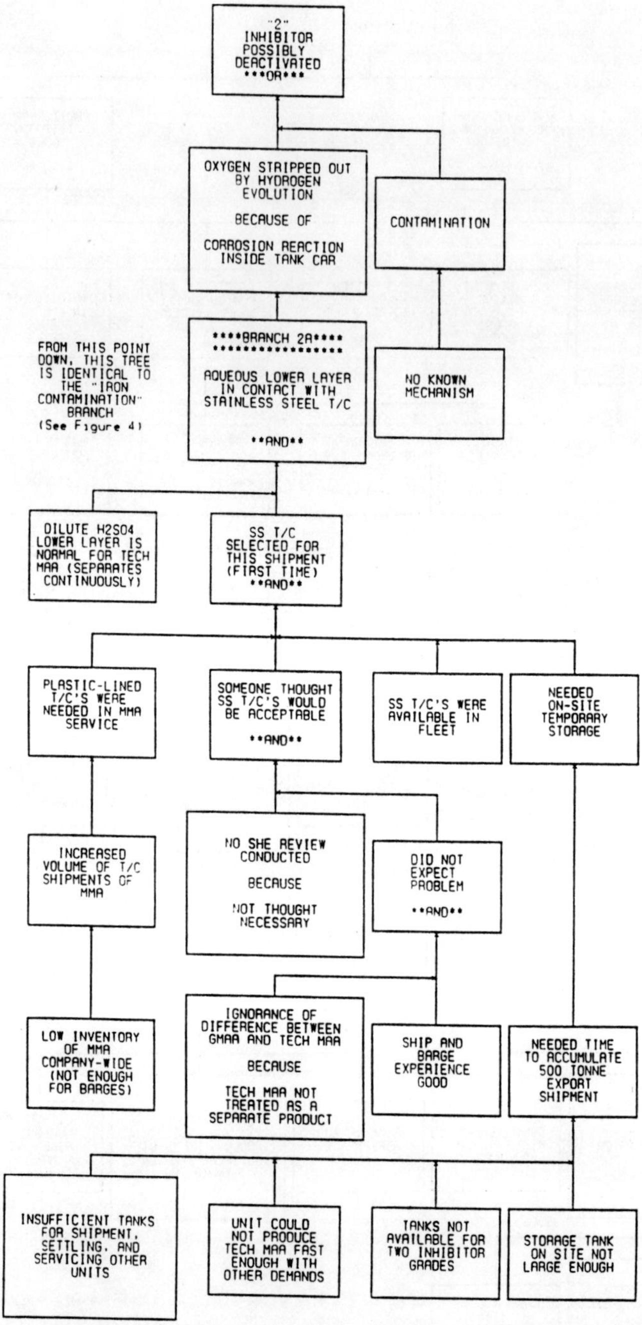

Figure 3. Branch 2 of event tree (inhibitor deactivated branch).

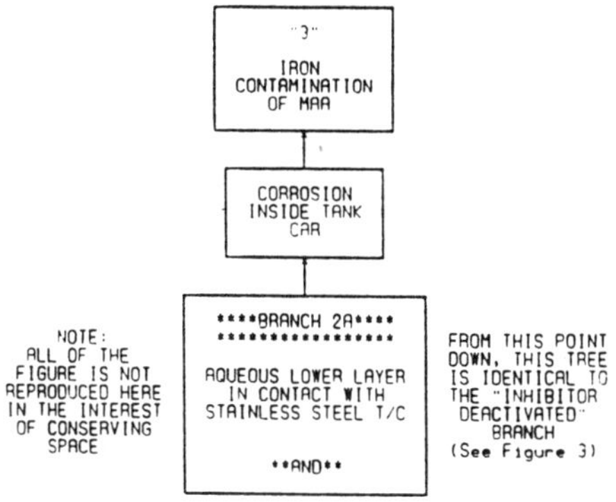

Figure 4. Branch 3 of event tree (iron contamination branch).

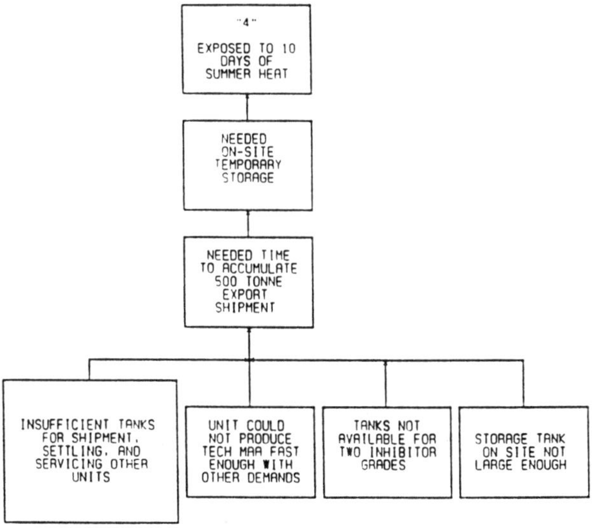

Figure 5. Branch 4 of event tree (warm storage branch).

a great many people worked very hard to see that everything was in order; however, there were not enough systems with built-in safeguards to ensure that the probability of failure was as low as we really wanted. This analysis pointed out the need for systems studies and subsequent improvements if we were to be satisfied with future performance. Space will not allow detailed discussion of all problems found and their ramifications; however, key deficiencies are listed below without comment:

1. Technical methacrylic acid was not a product we sold outside the Company. It had largely been considered analogous to Glacial MAA, but it had important differences.

—TMAA had a layer of dilute sulfuric acid that separated out on standing. This dilute acid layer was very corrosive to ferrous materials.
—No product code had been assigned to this material. No unique specifications for stability and inhibitor content had been established. (Again, handled by analogy.)

2. GMAA was routinely shipped in stainless steel cars; when lined cars became scarce, TMAA was loaded into stainless steel cars without hesitation or review.
—The corrosion of the stainless steel by the acid layer was thought to have *promoted* the polymerization, but the *cause* was the low level of inhibitor; if the inhibitor level had been correct, the presence of the iron would not have mattered.
3. The MAA was loaded into tank cars containing only the rundown inhibitor levels from the process.
—There were no tanks in which inhibitor levels could be adjusted prior to loading the material.
4. After the inhibitor was added to the loaded tank car, there was no way to obtain analytical feedback to verify that the correct level had been achieved.
—The car could not be mixed well enough to obtain a representative sample for feedback.
5. Responsibility for and ownership of the tank into which product was run down, and from which tank cars were loaded, were not clear.
—Handing off from production to shipping allowed for missed communications.
6. In the laboratory system, samples of TMAA were not tested for stability unless analysis showed that the inhibitor was in specification. Neither was stability run on material for which no inhibitor results were available.
—These procedures removed a possible feedback loop from the overall system.
7. Ship schedules and overseas requirements sometimes placed unrealistic demands on the production and shipping systems.
—This meant that results of all analyses (in particular, the stability test took 24 hours) were sometimes not available before cars were transferred to the terminal.

Other shortcomings were identified, but these should be enough to show the nature of the findings about the causes of the event.

It was highly unlikely that only one of the causes above would have resulted in a polymerization. Properly inhibited TMAA is stable in stainless steel for long periods. On the other hand, TMAA having the amount of inhibitor contained in this tank car is also stable for long periods if iron is not present.

THE RECOMMENDATIONS

As implied in the causes identified, the recommendations were to take a serious look at all the systems we used to handle monomers of all kinds. We deemed it especially critical to ensure that our systems had mechanisms to ensure feedback on important variables, such as inhibitor concentration, and that the results of analyses were reliable. (One cause for inaction after receipt of a bad inhibitor analysis was that the reputation of the analysis was so bad.) The investigation team recommended the formation of a team to work these systems issues in depth, and to make recommendations for sweeping changes in our operations where needed.

THE IMPLEMENTATION OF RECOMMENDATIONS

The Shipping Stability Team (SST) was formed to implement the recommendations of the investigation. Our mission was as follows:

- To recommend changes that increase the reliability of the system that stores, prepares, loads, and approves monomers for shipment.
- To develop a quantitative measurement system of improvement over the current system.

The desired outcomes of the team's efforts were

1. to have an understanding of the systems we have now
2. to reduce the risk of a polymerization during shipment
3. to have an assessment of the risk to the public
4. to implement longer term system changes to manage the public risk at acceptable levels

The SST was empowered by plant management and had members from every discipline involved in the shipping and handling of monomers at the plant; shipping, pumping, production, quality assurance, process chemistry, chemical engineering, and safety/risk analysis. Consequently, it was not difficult to obtain cooperation when requests were made of various entities.

We started the work by analyzing the event tree from the investigation (Figures 1–5) and pinpointed the areas in the system where the most benefit could be obtained with the least effort. To fulfill the first part of the mission, we essentially produced, or had produced, top-down flow charts (TDFCs) for all operations in the system. Only after the systems were completely defined could we confidently look for the most beneficial improvements.

To provide a baseline, a vehicle to monitor the effects of proposed changes, and to be able to fulfill the second part of the mission, we took the event trees and refined them into more rigorous (but still imperfect) fault trees that were capable of being analyzed using existing computer programs. The first generation fault tree corresponding most closely to the original event tree included all of the "challenges" (items identified by the AIC as having potential adverse effects on TMAA stability, such as "iron contamination," "exposed to 10 days of summer heat," and "inhibitor possibly deactivated").

However, this tree was unwieldy, and the SST had reached consensus early in its investigations that none of the visualized "challenges" would have caused the polymerization if there had been sufficient inhibitor in the material to start with. In order to expedite tree analysis, the subcommittee decided to concentrate only on the inhibitor system branch of the tree. This also allowed us to concentrate on the effects of changes in the system without the unnecessary complications of second-order effects that were not well-quantified and that could not be controlled. (The weather in Houston is going to be hot in July, and there isn't much we can do about it.) The top events in all subsequent versions of the trees was "insufficient inhibitor to meet stability specifications."

A subcommittee of the SST met to agree on the probabilities to assign to the various primal events. It was recognized that these probabilities were not necessarily correct; however, the same probabilities would be used in all versions of the trees, or changes would be assigned by the same people. This meant that there would be internal consistency, and comparisons between systems to evaluate the effects of incorporated improvements would be valid. This is an important point; no fault tree is perfect, and nobody should expect them to be. Nevertheless, the value of fault trees for comparisons remains excellent. The inhibitor branch of the original tree was designated "Old Inhibitor System—No Challenges." The complete trees are quite large and are not amenable to reproduction in this paper in readable format. Therefore, the trees have been reduced to the include only the primal events from the minimal cut sets. The reduction of "Old Inhibitor System—No Challenges" is shown as Figure 6. The calculated probability indicated that 4 out of 10 cars would not meet inhibitor specifications! The overriding primal events were loading the car with low inhibitor in the monomeric acid (always true) analytical difficulties, and inhibitor addition mechanics.

The first improvement to the system was that the unit took on the responsibility for ensuring that the material was properly inhibited before releasing it for loading and shipping. More accurate scales were also added at the same time. This improved the accuracy of weighing inhibitor and added one feedback loop to the system, but no other changes were made at that time. These changes reduced the probability of error in weighing the inhibitor and added one AND-gate to the tree. (AND-Gates are the best way to reduce the probability of an undesirable event.) The tree for that system was designated "New Inhibitor System—No Challenges" (Figure 7). In this system, probability calculations from the fault tree showed that only 8 cars out of 1000 would now fail specs. This is a significant improvement (almost three orders of magnitude) as a result of these relatively simple and inexpensive changes.

Extensive work by the SST and all groups related to the TMAA system resulted in several additional basic systems changes that were implemented in the final version of the tree that was analyzed. These included the following:

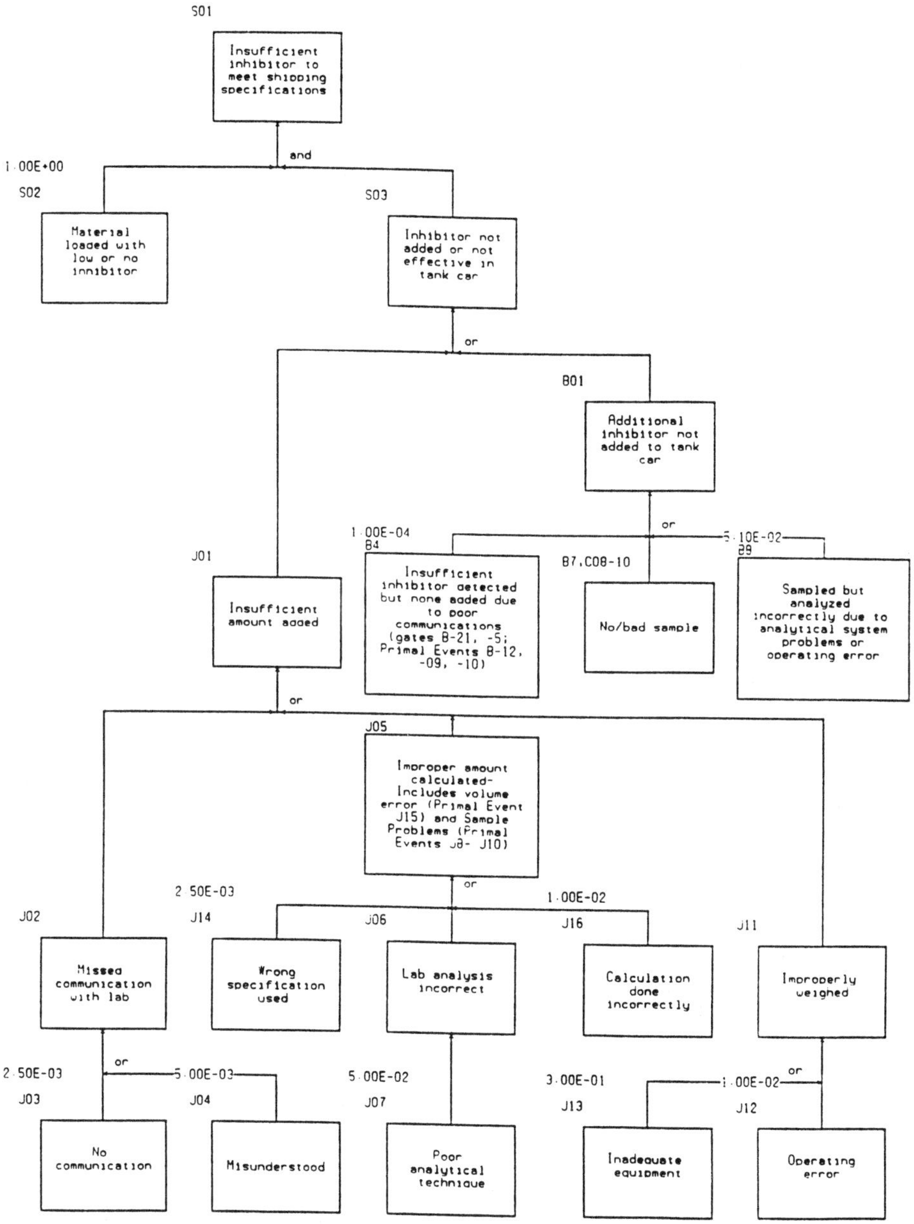

Figure 6. Old Inhibitor System—No Challenges.

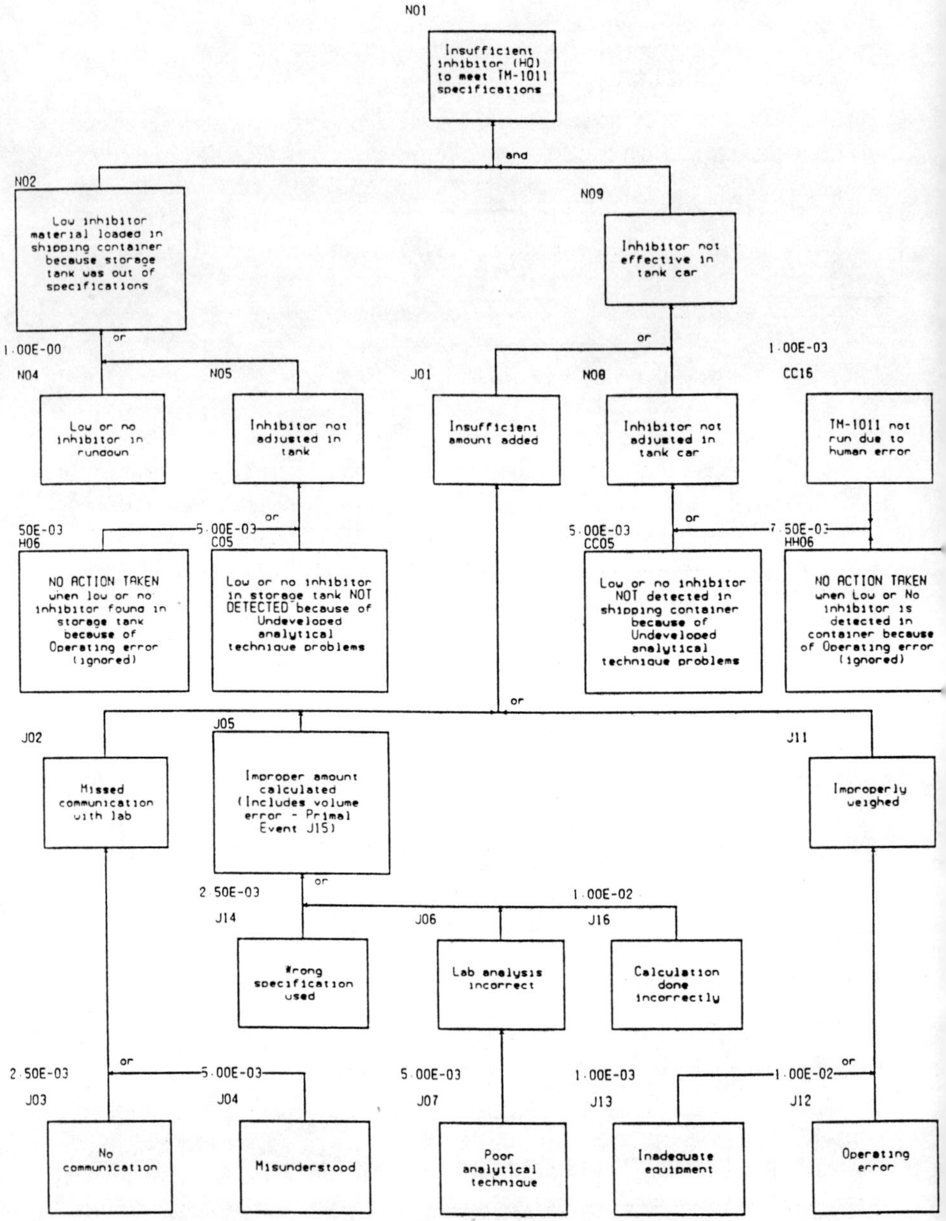

Figure 7. New Inhibitor System for TMAA—No Challenges.

1. The method for analyzing for inhibitor in TMAA was improved dramatically. This reduced the probability of error in that area and also increased the likelihood of appropriate action based on analytical results.
2. The inhibitor content of the rundown was increased to a level that was sufficient to ensure that the product could pass stability even if no additional inhibitor were added to the tank. This, in effect, added another AND-gate to the system.
3. Lab procedures were changed to assure that stability was always run on every sample regardless of inhibitor content. This added still more AND-gates to the tree.
4. Procedures for releasing shipments were improved, and a feedback loop was added to ensure that the surveyors did not accept tank cars for export without proper documentation. (Another AND-gate.)

The tree for this system was designated "Improved Inhibitor System—No Challenges" (Figure 8). Probability calculated from this fault tree indicated that fewer than 3 out of 10,000,000 cars would fail with this system. Again, these changes were relatively simple, and cost very little to implement. I should mention again that we do not claim that these probabilities are *accurate*, but because the fault trees and the input data are consistent the comparisons remain meaningful and the results are dramatic (Figure 9).

The next generation system used an on-line analyzer to monitor the inhibitor concentration in the rundown continuously. This system would virtually have a vanishingly small probability of out of spec inhibitor.

THE RESULTS

1. This investigation/systems analysis/fault tree analysis of this incident provided an excellent opportunity to demonstrate the power of the investigation method and the ease with which it may be adapted to a systems analysis for facilitating improvements and corrective actions.
2. The power of systems-oriented thinking was clearly shown by the dramatic improvements which were obtained by relatively simple, inexpensive changes.
3. A thorough understanding of systems is necessary if basic changes are to be made. This concept is the foundation of the Rohm and Haas Texas system for process safety management: "Know what you want to do." But that is another story.[2]
4. The SST work has been the basis for a complete revision of the monomer handling systems in the plant. In particular, we have looked at all of them to make sure that there were enough feedback loops (AND-gates in fault tree terminology) to ensure adequate inhibitor levels. The more loops there are, the greater the assurance. Examples of increasing integrity are given below:
   —Sample well-mixed car contents and receive results before releasing.
   —(a) *and* load only from tank containing correct material (that has been verified by sample results).

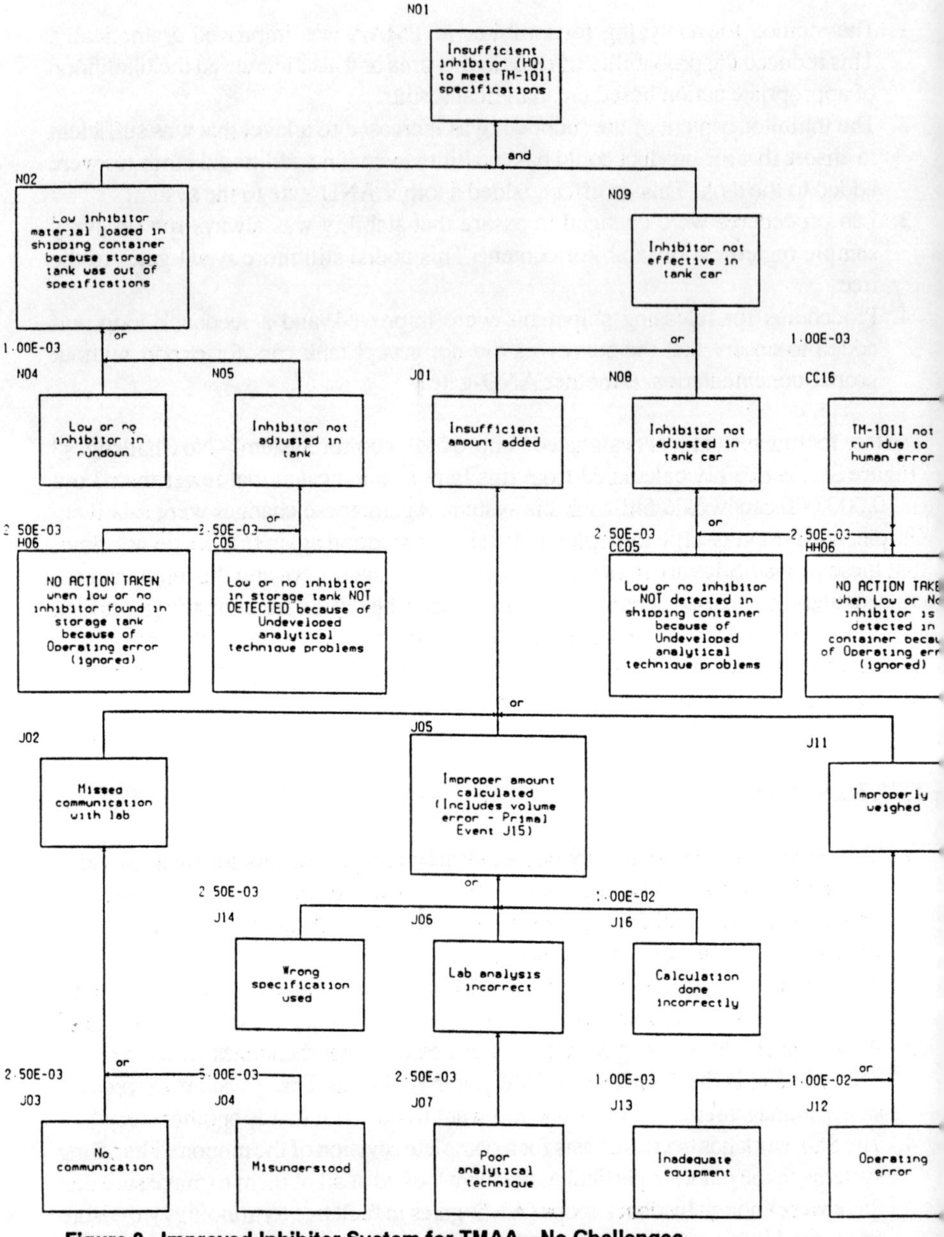

Figure 8. Improved Inhibitor System for TMAA—No Challenges.

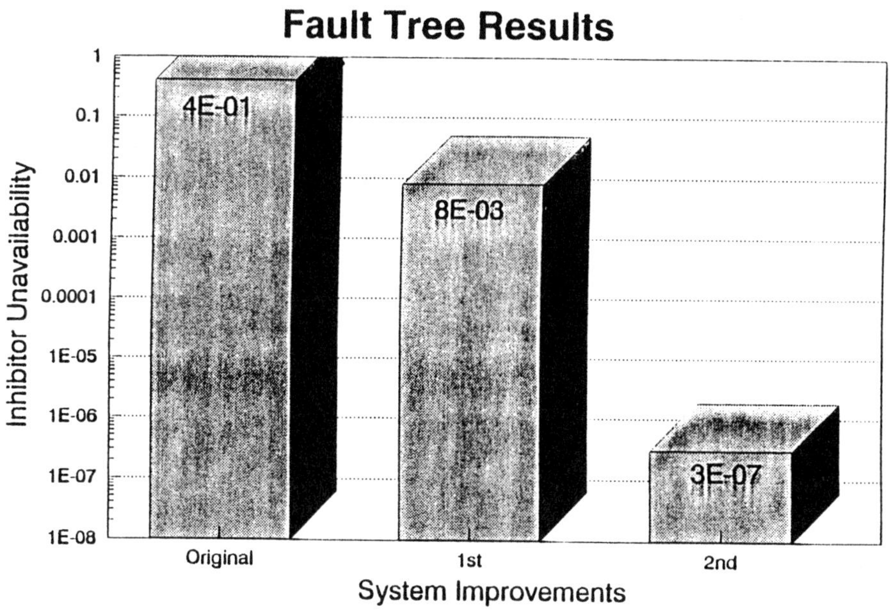

Figure 9. Basic system improvements give dramatic increase in reliability.

TABLE I

Monomer Handling Guidelines Recommended by the SST

1. No dry inhibitor should be added to any shipping container unless the container is gas-free
2. No inhibitor adjustment should be made without confirmatory feedback
3. Never assume that stability will pass
4. Analytical techniques must be statistically capable to be reliable
5. All monomers should be run down containing enough inhibitor to pass stability test
6. All monomers should be loaded at the inhibitor shipping specification to ensure a feedback loop
7. A tracking system is needed to account for all loaded containers of monomer

Acknowlegments

The Authors are grateful to the following groups and individuals for their candor, expertise, and dedication to the task of investigating this accident, analyzing the systems, and implementing the appropriate changes: A. M. Dowell; members of the AIC and the SST; Plant and Unit Management; and the terminal personnel and surveyors who work in the shipping system.

REFERENCES

1. Petersen, D. 1978. *Techniques of Safety Management*, Second Edition. New York: McGraw-Hill Book Company.
2. S. E. Anderson, A. M. Dowell, III, and D. K. Martin. "An Audit System for Process Safety." Paper presented at the Texas Chemical Council Process Safety Seminar, June 4, 1990.

FAILURE OF SYNTHESIS GAS COMPRESSOR

R. R. Marshall, H. Van praag, and J. Shaw
ICI Nitrogen Products, Courtright, Ontario NON 1HO, Canada

From *Ammonia Plant Safety,* Volume 31, pages 49–53

ICI Canada, Lambton Works is a manufacturer of ammonia and ammonia-based agricultural products.

The Ammonia II plant, rated at 1120 t/d, where the incident took place, is based on the ICI AMV Ammonia process. The process is very unusual because of its low synthesis pressure operation. As a consequence, the synthesis gas compressor consists of one casing. Circulation is achieved by a separate compressor.

All the main machines are electrically driven except the air compressor. The air machine, steam turbine drive, also drives an alternator, which supplies approximately 50% of the power required to operate the plant.

The process is controlled by a Honeywell TDC 2000 process control system, together with a supervisory computer and a computer trip system.

The plant has been in service since 1985 and has exceeded designed rate regularly. Operation of the machines has been almost trouble free.

DESCRIPTION OF MACHINE AND INCIDENT

J301, the synthesis gas compressor is a Nuovo Pignone (BCL 408) barrel type compressor operating at 12,544 RPM and driven through a Maag gearbox by a Canadian General Electric 12,500 HP, 1800 RPM motor.

Operating conditions are 30.5 barg and –9°C at inlet and 85.1 barg and 130°C at the outlet, The flow through the compressor is 4541 M^3/hr (measured at inlet conditions) or 140,000 SM^3/hr (Figure 1).

On July 27, 1989, the power to the site was interrupted due to a direct lightning strike on Ontario Hydro's Lambton Generating Station. Ammonia II continued to generate power but several pieces of electrical equipment tripped. The plant was shut down and it was decided to carry out normal shutdown repairs. During this period, J301 was also overhauled.

A week later, the Ammonia II plant was progressing through the start-up sequence. During the evening of August 3, J301 ran without problems for 6 hours at 50% speed circulating nitrogen.

At 0630 hours the next day, J301 was started up and the gas was advanced to vent HV-3109 downstream of the methanator. The methanator was being warmed up and had achieved a 3 ppm CO_2 slip. Gas was introduced to the synthesis loop drier at 0715 hours and via the HV-4120 at 0725 hours. At this time the J301 anti-surge controller was on manual and almost completely closed with HV-3109 open 43% (see Figure 1).

At 0727 hours, HV-3109 was closed. This effectively dead-ended the machine. At 0745, the problem was noticed, and HV-3109 was reopened. The machine discharge temperature immediately rose from 198°C to 290°C. Three minutes later, the machine tripped on axial displacement. An attempt to restart the machine showed that it had severe internal damage.

Figure 1

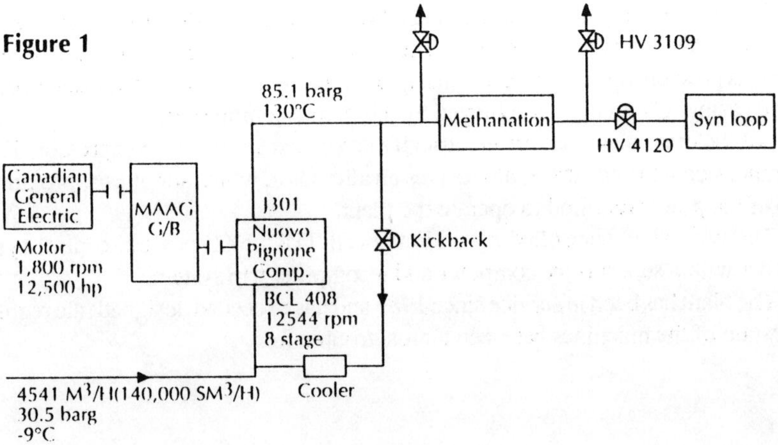

OBJECTIVES

After the incident, it was obvious that the damage to the machine was extensive. There were several objectives defined:

- Repair the machine and return it to service.
- Define the cause of the failure.
- Ensure that the failure would not be repeated.

MACHINE DAMAGE AND REPAIR

Overview

- Rotor seized in barrel
- Thrust-bearing pads wiped so that ±90% of Babbitt removed. Insignificant damage to thrust collar. (Active and inactive in similar condition.)
- Radial bearings very slight damage
- Severe electrical arcing on thrust bearing and seals.
- The machine was dismantled, inspected, repaired, and returned to service. Total plant down time was 30 days.

Rotor Damage

- The 7th impeller had rubbed against diaphragm just above labyrinth seal. Impeller was dished so that opposite side at outer area rubbed against diaphragm (see Figures 2 and 5).
- The 8th impeller had rubbed against diffuser (Figure 2).

Figure 2

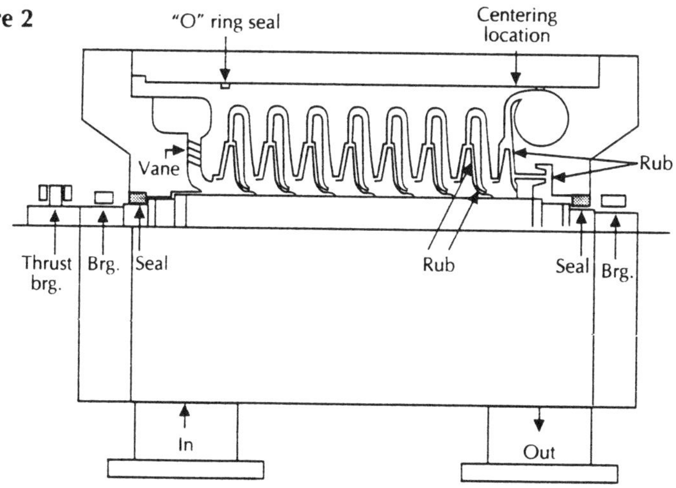

- Impellers 6, 7, and 8 were coated with aluminum material from labyrinths.
- Balance piston was severely grooved and "nose" had rubbed against head (Fig. 2)
- All sleeves had rub marks from labyrinths, seals, etc. Worst areas were from fifth wheel onward.

Diaphragm Assembly Damage

- Entire assembly had become elliptical uniformly, This required machining to 2 mm at the split line (1.2 mm from bottom; 0.8 mm from top) and line boring and installation of inserts at labyrinth location.
- Rubbing of seventh wheel on diaphragm near seal 6C deformed labyrinth retainer. The severe heat generated dished the entire diaphragm up to 4 mm (Figure 6).
- Several bolts at split line joints had stripped the threads in the diaphragm.
- One bold on diaphragm 7B had cracked the diaphragm axially.
- Two cracks were seen on diaphragm 7B at the dowel holes.

Figure 3

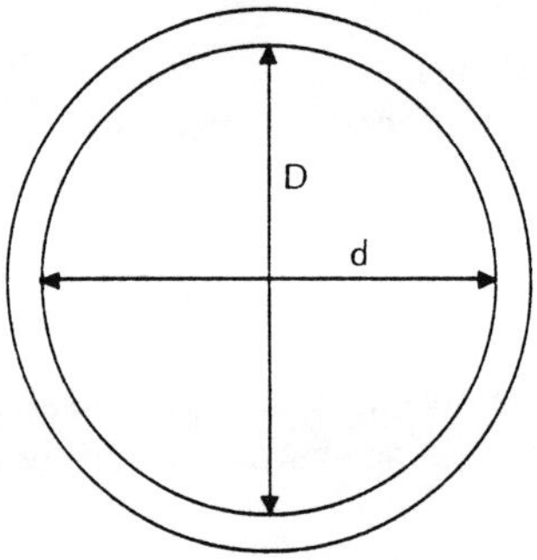

D – d = 0.15 – 0.20 mm
Casing distortion

Figure 4

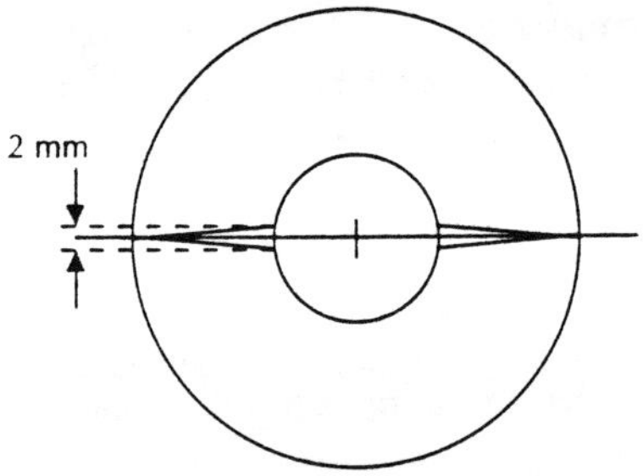

Diaphragm assembly distortion

Figure 5
Impeller distortion

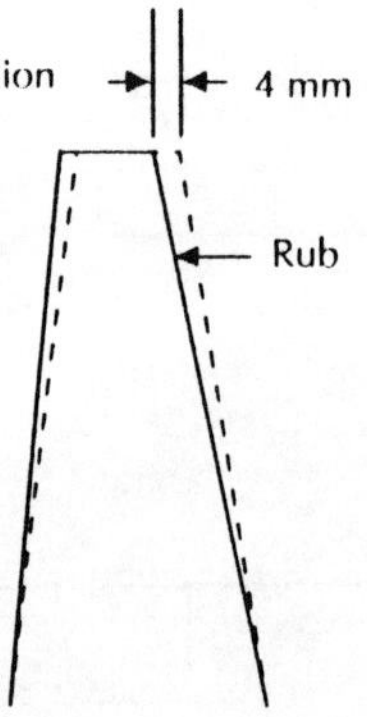

Figure 6
Diaphragm distortion

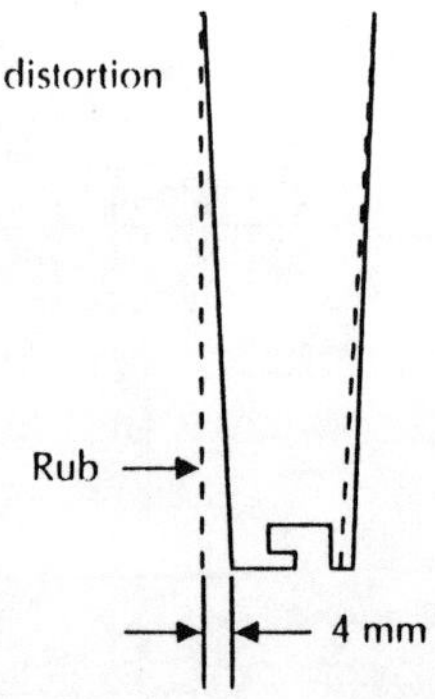

Figure 7

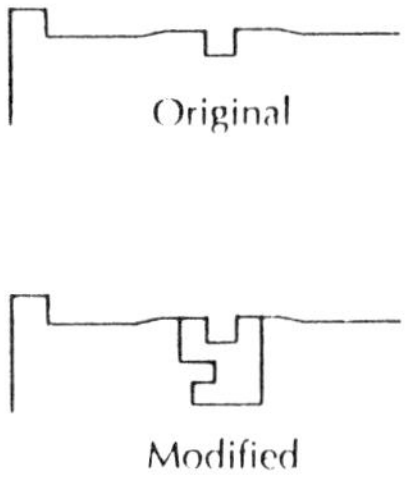

Diaphragm
"O" Ring

Figure 8

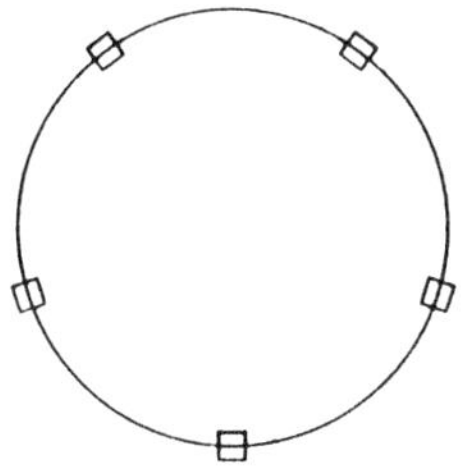

Diaphragm
Location Repair

Figure 9

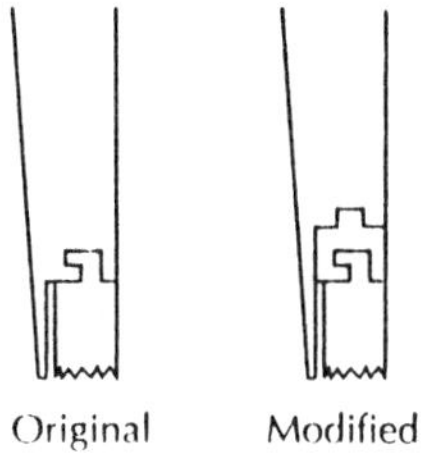

Diaphragm
Labyrinth Repair

Casing Damage

- The entire casing became elliptical by 0.15 to 0.20 mm with the larger diameter vertical. No repair necessary (Figure 3).

Repairs

- The rotor, barrel assembly, and the two heads were sent to Nuovo Pignone in Florence, Italy for repair.
- The rotor was stripped, examined, one wheel replaced, and all sleeves replaced. Repair time was 6 months.
- Diaphragm assembly
  —Split line machined.
  —"O"ring location end was machined and insert installed.
  —Diaphragm location (sliding) end 2" diameter pins installed and assembly machined (Figure 8).
  —Entire assembly line bored; inserts installed ar each labyrinth location (Fig. 9)
  —Repair to the barrel assembly required 14 days.

METHOD USED TO DETERMINE CAUSE OF FAILURE

To define the cause of failure, it was decided to use Root Cause failure analysis techniques.

A team of investigators was formed involving process instrumentation and mechanical specialists together with a specialist in Root Cause Failure Analysis.

The procedure followed was:

- Collection of facts and review.
- Root cause decision tree analysis.
- Hypothesis.
- Define root causes.
- Recommendation to prevent reoccurrence.

COLLECTION OF FACTS

Before J301 Failure

- One week previous to the J301 failure (July 27, 1989), power was lost to the site, Ammonia II continued to generate power, but several pieces of electrical equipment tripped.
- This caused the air compressor turbine, JT101, to trip on low vacuum. Ammonia II shut down for a one-week period.
- J301 was overhauled during the shutdown.
- The evening prior to the incident, J301 ran at 50% speed for 6 hours circulating nitrogen as part of the normal start-up procedure.
- Gas that is kicked back to prevent surge for J301 is warmer than feed gas to the machine.
- The anti-surge system is part of the general TDC 2000 control system and is not an independent hard-wired machine protection system. Note: The TDC System is designed as a control system, not as a machinery protection system.

During J301 Failure

- At 0630 hours, J301 was started to 100% speed.
- At 0630 hours, process of heating up methanator started.
- Shift change took place between 0705 hours and 0730.
- Field man was at the methanator 0720 hours through 0748.
- At 0725 hours, valve HV-4120 was cracked open to 10% (allowed forward flow) (Figure 10)

Conditions:	Suction	24 bar
	Discharge	60 bar
	Syn loop	51 bar

Figure 10

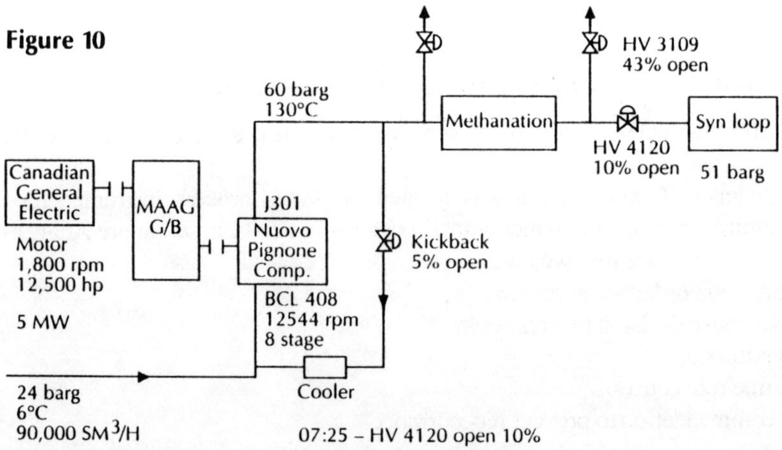

Figure 11

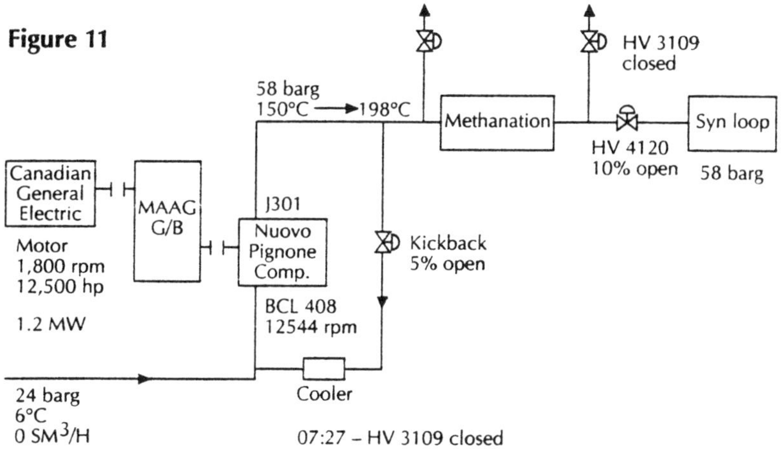

- At 0725 hours, molecular weight of gas was normal for start-up conditions (gas to air ratio of .75). During operating conditions, it is lower (.5).
- At 0727 hours, HV-3109 closed over a two-minute period. Also at that time, kick back on manual 5% open (Figure 11)
- At 0727 hours, drive motor megawatts down to 1.2 MW. Normal at this stage of start-up would be 4 MW.

Conditions:	Suction	24 BARG	0 SM^3/hr
at 0727	Discharge to	58 BARG	(90,000 SM^3/hr normal)
	Methanator	58 BARG	0 SM^3/hr
	Syn loop	58 BARG	

- Feedback signal from guide vane was not working correctly
- At 0745 hours, discharge temperature was 198°C. Suction side was 6°C.

Figure 12

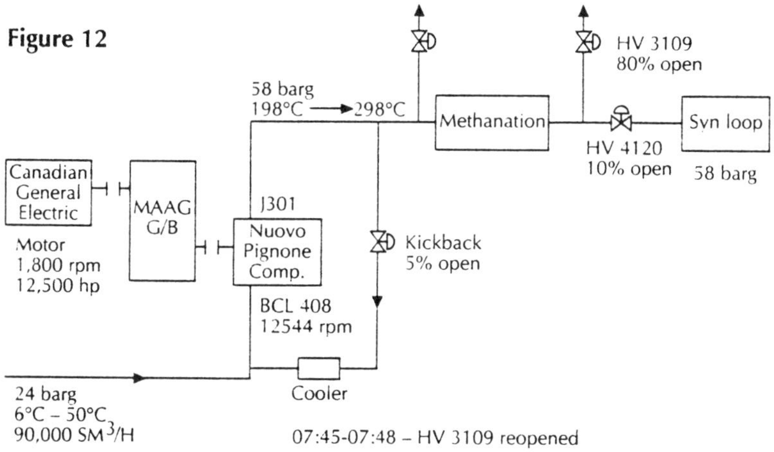

- At 0745 hours it was noticed that the machine had no forward flow. Vent HV-3109 was opened to 80% (Figure 12)
- After HV-3109 was opened, the discharge temperature rose from 198°C to 298°C.
- At 0748 hours, the machine tripped on axial displacement. Trip point is –17 mil; –18 mil was indicated.
- At 0747 hours, radial vibration arm at thrust end sounded, No other vibration alarms were recorded.
- The thrust bearing rose by approximately 10°C.

After J301 Failure

- First attempt to restart the machine was aborted because of axial displacement.
- Second restart, the machine would only turn at very low RPM. A noise was heard form the machine and it tripped on stall.
- A complete inspection of the gear box showed that it was in perfect condition.
- Mechanical damage on the compressor was evident.

ROOT CAUSE DECISION TREE ANALYSIS

- A decision tree was developed. With the known facts, it was immediately agreed that the incident was not an "Act of God" and could have been prevented (Figure 13, item 1).
- Equipment was constructed properly—it had been in service for 4 years.
- The machine had been correctly designed and manufactured (Figure 14, item 2).
- There were design errors on the protection system (Figure 14, items 3 and 4).
- There was no evidence of inadequate maintenance (Figure 15, item 5).
- The machine was not operated correctly. Operating error and procedures need review (Figure 15, items 6 and 7).

Figure 13

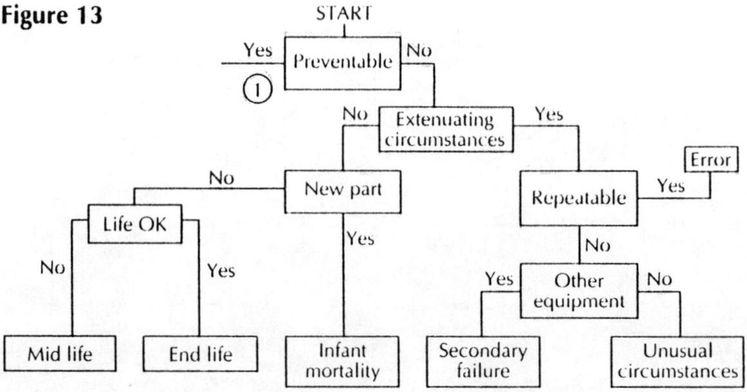

Figure 14

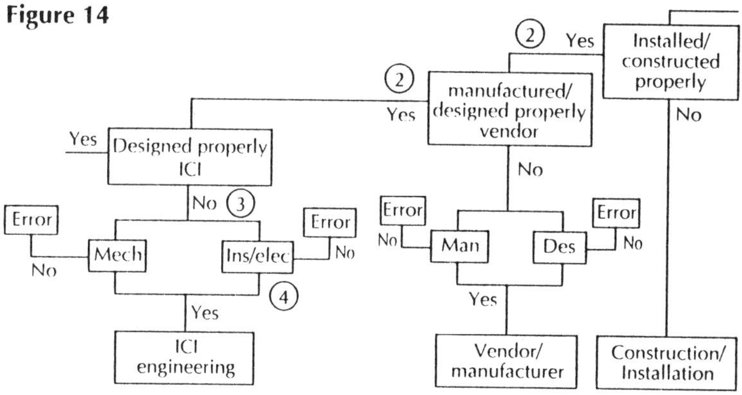

Figure 15

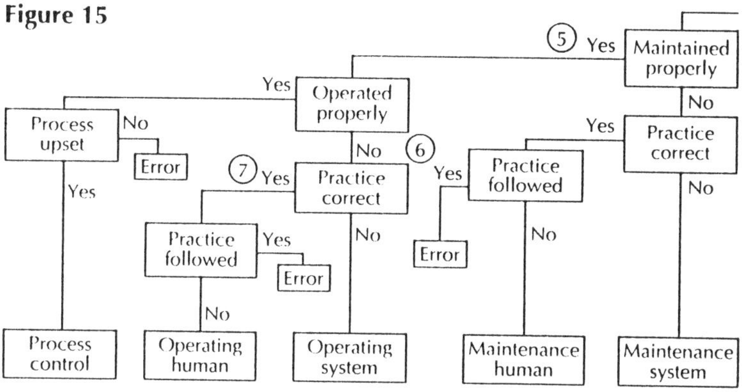

HYPOTHESIS

The machine overheated due to zero forward flow. The surge protection did not protect the machine. Damage caused internally by distortion due to overheating and/or thermal shock on reestablishment of flow or other thermal event.

Reasons for zero forward flow: (1) The anti-surge bypass was only open 5% on manual. (2) Discharge vent was closed and main loop pressure equalized with compressor discharge, which effectively dead-ended the machine.

ROOT CAUSES

There were three root causes of failure found:

- The anti-surge system was not properly designed.
- The Anti-surge controllers were not operated properly.
- Human error occurred by closing valve HV-3109 and failing to monitor the consequences.

RECOMMENDATION FOR CORRECTIVE ACTION

- Redefine operational control procedures for J301 (i.e., operator access to control mode and set points, etc.).
- Redesign process control system for J301 such as, range of setting for operator access, close loop control with no access by operator.
- Establish a procedure for transferring responsibilities at shift change during unusual conditions.
  —Manpower overlap
  —Improve logging system
- Assess surge protection for all compressors at Lambton Works and recommend actions to be taken.

CONCLUSION

Root Cause Failure Analysis is a useful tool for defining causes of failure. With multiple disciplines involved and everyone with an open mind, the true causes are found.

When designs are being done by different disciplines, it is vital that everyone has an understanding of the involvement of the other disciplines. "I know what I wanted, and I thought he knew what I wanted" is lack of understanding. In this incident, the machines engineers assumed that the process controls engineers knew that the anti-surge system must not be capable of being bypassed.

It is very easy to jump to the first obvious conclusion on the cause of failure. This may be wrong or incomplete. The initial reaction was that we had a thrust failure and there was a mechanical design error. In addition, we had just completed an overhaul. It was possible that errors had been made.

Surge protection systems are vital to prevent equipment failure. They must be designed so that on one can bypass the protection.

The axial position trip prevented more extensive damage. Without this protection, the machine would have continued running until overload tripped the motor.

Thrust bearing temperature/monitoring trips would not have saved the machine.

The sequence of events was too fast. (Note: thrust temperature rose only 10°C.)

It is sometimes dangerous to use process control systems as machinery protection. It is advisable to have the protection independent from the controls.

H

SOURCES OF INFORMATION ABOUT INCIDENT INVESTIGATION TECHNIQUES LISTED IN TABLE 2-1

Accident Anatomy Method (AAM)

Bruun, O., J. R. Taylor and A. Rasmussen, 1979. *Cause–Consequence Reporting for Accident Reduction*, Risø-M-2206. Roskilde, Denmark: Risø National Laboratory.

Keiding, J. T. and L. Skou, 1981. "Comparison of Two Methods for Analysis of Drilling Machine Accidents." SCRATCH Seminar 7. Methods for Risk and Safety Analysis, NORDFORSK, Stockholm (Sweden).

Accident Evolution and Barrier (AEB) Analysis

Svenson, O., 1991. AEB Analysis of Incidents and Accidents in the Processing Industries. In Apostolakis, G. E. (Ed.). *Probabilistic Safety Assessment and Management*. New York: Elsevier. Pp. 271–276.

Svenson, O., 1991. The Accident Evolution and Barrier Function (AEB) Model Applied to Incident Analysis in the Processing Industries. *Risk Analysis: An International Journal*, 11(3):499–507.

Action Error Analysis (AEA)

Taylor, J. R., 1979. *A Background to Risk Analysis*, Vol. IV. Roskilde, Denmark: Risø National Laboratory. Pp. 777–793.

Causal Tree Method (CTM)

Rhône-Poulenc Causal Tree Method, Corporate Safety Director, Rhône-Poulenc Inc., CN5266, Princeton, NJ 08543-5266.

Cause–Effect Logic Diagram (CELD)

Mosleh, A. et al., 1988. *Procedures for Treating Common Cause Failures in Safety and Reliability Studies*, EPRI NP-5613. Palo Alto, CA: Electric Power Research Institute.

Change Evaluation/Analysis (CE/A)

Kepner, C. H. and B. B. Tregoe, 1976. *The Rational Manager*, 2nd ed. Princeton, NJ: Kepner-Tregoe, Inc.

Kuhlman, R. L. 1977. Professional Accident Investigation. Loganville, GA: Institute Press, International Loss Control Institute.

Fault Tree Analysis (FTA)

Vesely, W. E. et al., 1981. *Fault Tree Handbook*, NUREG-0492. Washington, DC: U.S. Government Printing Office.

Hazard and Operability Study (HAZOP)

Center for Chemical Process Safety (CCPS), 1989. *Guidelines for Chemical Process Quantitative Risk Assessment*. New York: American Institute of Chemical Engineers. Pp. 509–518.

Center for Chemical Process Safety (CCPS), 1992. *Guidelines for Hazard Evaluation Procedures: Second Edition with Worked Examples*. New York: American Institute of Chemical Engineers. Sections 4.7 and 6.7.

Human Performance Enhancement System (HPES)

Bishop, J. and R. LaRhette, 1988. Managing Human Performance—INPO's Human Performance Enhancement System. Conference Record for 1988 IEEE Fourth Conference on Human Factors and Power Plants, 88CH2576-7. New York: Institute of Electrical and Electronics Engineers. Pp. 471–474.

Smith, R. G., III. 1988. Implementation of the Human Performance Evaluation System at Virginia Power. Conference Record for 1988 IEEE Fourth Conference on Human Factors and Power Plants, 88CH2576-7. New York: Institute of Electrical and Electronics Engineers. Pp. 475–478.

Human Reliability Analysis Event Tree (HRA-ET)

Bell. B. J. and A. D. Swain, 1983. *A Procedure for Conducting a Human Reliability Analysis for Nuclear Power Plants*, SAND81-1665 (NUREG/CR-2254). Albuquerque, NM: Sandia National Laboratories.

Management Oversight Risk Tree (MORT)

Department of Energy, 1985. *Accident/Incident Investigation Manual*, 2nd ed., DOE/SSDC 76-45/27. Idaho Falls, ID: System Safety Development Center, Idaho National Engineering Laboratory.

Multilinear Events Sequencing (MES)

Benner, L. Jr., 1975. Accident Investigation: Multilinear Events Sequencing Methods. *Journal of Safety Research*, 7(2):67–73.

Multiple-Cause, Systems-Oriented Incident Investigation (MCSOII)

Rohm and Haas Texas Incorporated, Incident Investigation Guidelines, Risk Analysis Department, Rohm and Haas Texas Incorporated, P.O. Box 672, Deer Park, TX 77536.

Sequentially Timed Events Plot (STEP)

Hendrick, K. and L. Benner, Jr., 1987. *Investigating Accidents with S-T-E-P.* New York: Marcel Dekker.

Systematic Cause Analysis Technique (SCAT)

International Loss Control Institute, P.O. Box 1899, Loganville, GA 30249

TapRoot™ Incident Investigation System

Systems Improvement, Inc., Suite 301, 238 Peters Road, Knoxville, TN 37920

Technique of Operations Review (TOR)

Seaver, D. A. and W. G. Stillwell, 1983. *Procedures for Using Expert Judgment to Estimate Human Error Probabilities in Nuclear Power Plant Operations*, NUREG/CR-2743 (SAND82-7054). Albuquerque, NM: Sandia National Laboratories.

Weaver, D. A., 1973. TOR Analysis: A Diagnostic Training Tool. *ASSE Journal*, June, pp. 24–29.

Work Safety Analysis (WSA)

Suokas, J., 1981. "Experiences of Work Safety Analysis" SCRATCH Seminar 7. Methods for Risk and Safety Analysis, NORDFORSK, Stockholm, Sweden.

Suokas, J. and V. Rouhiainen, 1984. *Work Safety Analysis. Method Description and User's Guide*, Research Reports No. 314. Espoo, Finland: Technical Research Centre of Finland.

GLOSSARY

(Special sources are referenced at the end of this glossary.)

Accident: An unplanned event or sequence of events that results in undesirable consequences. An incident with specific safety consequences or impacts. As used in this guidebook, the term accident is defined as any incident which is accompanied by actual negative consequences.

Accidental Chemical Release: An unintended, sudden release of chemical(s) from manufacturing, processing, handling, or on-site storage facilities to the air, water, or land.[1]

Ad Hoc Investigation: Incident investigation which is fashioned from the immediately available information and concerns. Typically, the ad hoc investigation is performed whenever there are no prior investigation procedures. A synonym to ad hoc is unsystematic.

Agency (or Agent): The principal object, substance, or material inflicting the physical harm or property damage in an accident.[1]

Amelioration: Improvement of conditions immediately after an accident; treatment of injuries and conditions which endanger people and property.[2]

Anomaly: An unusual, abnormal, or irregular set of circumstances that, left unrecognized or uncorrected, may result in an incident.

Catastrophic: A loss of extraordinary magnitude in physical harm to people, with damage and destruction to property, and/or to the environment.[2]

Cause: An event, situation, or condition which results, or could result (Potential Cause), directly or indirectly in an accident or incident.[2]

Consequence: The cumulative, undesirable result of an incident, usually measured in health/safety effects, environmental impacts, loss of property, and business interruption costs.[1]

Consequence Analysis: The analysis of the expected effects of an incident, independent of its likelihood.[1]

Contributing Cause: Physical conditions, management practices, etc. that facilitated the occurrence of an incident.

CPQRA: The acronym for Chemical Process Quantitative Risk Analysis. It is the quantitative (numerical) evaluation of incident consequences and frequencies, and their combination into an overall measure of risk when applied to the chemical process industry. It is particularly applied to episodic events. The

CPQRA process is always preceded by a qualitative systematic identification of process hazards.

Deductive Approach: Reasoning from the general to the specific. By postulating that a system/process has failed in a certain way, an attempt is made to determine what modes of system/component/operator/organization behavior contributed to the failure.

Episodic Event: An event (typically incident) of limited duration; e.g., release of hazardous materials, spill, explosion.

Forensic Engineering: The art and science of professional practice of those qualified to serve as engineering experts in matters before the courts of law or in arbitration proceedings.[3]

Failure: An unacceptable difference between expected and observed performance.[3]

Failure Mode and Effects Analysis: A hazard identification technique in which all known failure modes of components or features of a system are considered in turn and undesired outcomes are noted.[1]

Fault Tree: A method for representing the logical combinations of various system states that lead to a particular outcome (top event).[4]

Fault Tree Analysis: Estimation of the hazardous incident (top event) frequency from a logical model of the failure mechanisms of a system.[4]

Hazard: A chemical, physical, or changing condition that has the potential for causing damage to human life, property, or the environment.[1]

HAZOP: Hazard and Operability Study: A systematic qualitative technique to identify and evaluate process hazards and potential operating problems, using a series of guidewords to examine deviations from normal process conditions.[4]

Historic Incident Data: Data collected and recorded from past incidents.

Human Error: Any human action (or lack thereof) that exceeds some limit of acceptability (i.e., an out-of-tolerance action) where the limits of human performance are defined by the system. Includes actions by designers, operators, or managers that may contribute to or result in accidents.

Human Factors: A discipline concerned with designing machines, operations, and work environments so that they match human capabilities, limitations, and needs. Includes any technical work (engineering, procedure writing, worker training, worker selection, etc.) related to the human factor in operator-machine systems.

Human Reliability Analysis: A method by which the probability of a person successfully performing a task is estimated.

Incident: An unplanned event or series of events and circumstances that may result in an undesirable consequence.[1,4]

Incident Investigation: The management process by which underlying causes of undesirable events are uncovered and steps are taken to prevent similar occurrences.[4]

Incident Investigation Team: A group of qualified people that examine an incident in a manner that is timely, objective, systematic, and technically sound to determine that factual information pertaining to the event is documented, probable causes are ascertained, and complete technical understanding of such an event is achieved.[3]

Incident Stereotype: A fixed or general pattern of incident causation. From a review of historical incident data it can be possible to identify "classes of incidents," each with certain features (or typical, repeated patterns) in common; that is, incident stereotypes are defined.

Inductive Approach: Reasoning from individual cases to a general conclusion by postulating that a system element has failed in a certain way. An attempt is then made to find out what happens to the whole system or process.

Injury: Physical harm or damage to a person resulting from traumatic contact between the body and an outside agency or exposure to environmental factors.

Latent Failure: Failure in a component as a result of a hidden flaw.

Likelihood: An estimate of the expected frequency or probability of the occurrence of an event.[4]

Medical Treatment: As defined by OSHA, treatment (other than first aid) administered by a physician or by registered professional personnel under the standing orders of a physician.

Morphological Approach: A structured analysis of an incident directed by insights from historic case studies but not as rigorous as a formal hazard analysis.

Near-Miss: An extraordinary event that could reasonably have resulted in a negative consequence under slightly different circumstances, but actually did not.[4]

Occupational Incident: Incident involving injury to workers.

Organizational Error: Latent management system problem that can result in human error.

OSHA Reportable Event: An incident that causes any fatality or the hospitalization of five employees or more requires a notification report to the nearest OSHA office.

OSHA Recordable Cases: Work-related deaths, injuries and illnesses (other than minor injuries requiring only first aid treatment) which involve medical treatment, loss of consciousness, restriction of work or motion, or transfer to another job.[4]

Process Hazard Analysis: An organized effort to identify and evaluate hazards associated with chemical processes and operations to enable their control. This review normally involves the use of qualitative techniques to identify and assess the significance of hazards. Conclusions and appropriate recommendations are developed. Occasionally, quantitative methods are used to help prioritize risk reduction.[4]

Process-Related Incident: An incident with impact, or potential impact, on process, equipment, people, and/or the environment. The incident could be internal or external to the process. An occupational incident can result from a process related incident.

Process Safety: A discipline that focuses on the prevention of fires, explosions, and accidental chemical releases at chemical process facilities. Excludes classic worker health and safety issues involving working surfaces, ladders, protective equipment, etc.[1]

Process Safety Management: A program or activity that involves the application of management principles and analytical techniques to ensure process safety in chemical facilities. The focus is on preventing major accidents rather than dealing with classic worker health and safety issues.[1]

Proximate Cause: The cause factor which directly produces the effect without the intervention of any other cause. The cause nearest to the effect in time and space.[4]

Risk: A measure of economic loss or human injury in terms of both the incident likelihood and the magnitude of the injury.[1]

Risk Management: The systematic application of management policies, procedures, and practices to the tasks of analyzing, assessing, and controlling risk in order to protect employees, the general public, and the environment as well as company assets, while avoiding business interruptions. Includes decisions to use suitable engineering and administrative controls for reducing risk.[4]

Root Cause(s): A prime reason why an incident occurred. Root causes often are related to deficiencies in management systems.

Safety: A general term denoting an acceptable level of risk of, relative freedom from, and low probability of harm.

Serious Injury: The classification for an occupational injury which includes all disabling work injuries and nondisabling work injuries as follows: eye injuries requiring treatment by a physician, fractures, injuries requiring hospitalization, loss of consciousness, injuries requiring treatment by a doctor and injuries requiring restriction of motion or work, or assignment to another job.[4]

Software: The programs, procedures, and related documentation associated with a system design and system operation. The system can be a computer system or a management system.

Task Analysis: An analytical process for determining the specific behaviors required of the human components in a man-machine system. It involves determining the detailed performance required of people and equipment and the effects of environmental conditions, malfunctions, and other unexpected events on both. Within each task to be performed by people, behavioral steps are analyzed in terms of (*i*) the sensory signals and related perceptions, (*ii*) the decisions, memory storage, and other mental processes, and (*iii*) the required responses.

Taxonomy: A structure for classification of incidents.

Trigger Event: Normal event which, in combination with abnormal conditions, allows an incident to occur.

Underlying Causes: Actual root causes.

Witness: A person who has information related, directly or indirectly, to the accident or incident.[4]

REFERENCE SOURCES FOR GLOSSARY

1. Chemical Manufacturers Association. 1990. *Responsible Care: A Resource Guide for the Process Safety Code of Management Practices*. Washington, DC: Chemical Manufacturers Association
2. Kuhlman, R. 1977. *Professional Accident Investigation.* Loganville, GA: Institute Press, International Loss Control Institute.
3. Carper, K. 1989. *Forensic Engineering*. New York: Elsevier Science Publishing.
4. CCPS. *Guidelines for Technical Management of Chemical Process Safety*. New York: American Institute of Chemical Engineers.

ACRONYMS AND ABBREVIATIONS

AAM	Accident Anatomy Method
AEA	Action Error Analysis
AEB	Accident Evolution and Barrier
AI	Artificial Intelligence
AIHA	American Industrial Hygiene Association
AIM	Accident Investigation Methodology
AIChE	American Institute of Chemical Engineers
ANSI	American National Standards Institute
APAU	Accident Prevention Advisory Unit
API	American Petroleum Institute
ASME	American Society of Mechanical Engineers
ASSE	American Society of Safety Engineers
ASTM	American Society for Testing and Materials
CAER	Community Awareness and Emergency Response
CCDM	Cause Consequence Diagram Method
CCPS	Center for Chemical Process Safety
CDCIR	Community Documentation Centre on Industrial Risk
CE/A	Change Evaluation/Analysis
CELD	Cause–Effect Logic Diagram
CFA	Causal Factors Analysis
CMA	Chemical Manufacturers Association
CPI	Chemical Process Industry
CPM	Critical Path Method
CPQRA	Chemical Process Quantitative Risk Assessment
CTM	Causal Tree Method
DCS	Distributed Control System

DOE	Department of Energy
DOT	Department of Transportation
EAM	Ergonomic Accident Model
ECU	European Currency Unit
EPA	Environmental Protection Agency
ES	Expert System
ESA	European Space Agency
ETA	Event Tree Analysis
EuReDatA	European Reliability Data Association
FAA	Federal Aviation Authority
FACTS	Failure and Accident Technical Information System
FMEA	Failure Mode and Effect Analysis
FTA	Fault Tree Analysis
HAZCOM	Hazard Communication, OSHA Standard 29CFR 1910.1200
HAZOP	HAZard and OPerability Study
HAZWOPER	Hazardous Waste Operations and Emergency Response
HOE	Human and Organizational Errors
HPES	Human Performance Enhancement System
HRA	Human Reliability Analysis
HSE	Health and Safety Executive (UK)
IChE	Institution of Chemical Engineers (UK) *also* **IChemE**
IDA	Interactive Data on Accidents
IFP	Institute Fran'ais du Petrole (France)
IG	Index of Gravity
INPO	Institute for Nuclear Power Operations
ITACA	Industry and Transport Accident Catalog
JRC	Joint Research Centre (Ispra, VA, Italy, operated by the European Communities)
JSA	Job Safety Analysis
MARS	Major Accident Reporting System
MCS	Minimal Cut Set
MCSOII	Multiple-Cause, Systems-Oriented Incident Investigation
MES	Multilinear Events Sequencing
MHIDAS	Major Hazard Incident Analysis System
MMS	Minerals Management Service

MMSA	Man–Machine System Analysis
MORT	Management Oversight and Risk Tree
NDE	Non-Destructive Evaluation
NIOSH	National Institute of Occupational Safety and Health
NSC	National Safety Council
NPD	Norwegian Petroleum Directorate
NFPA	National Fire Protection Association
NPRA	National Petroleum Refiners Association
NRC	Nuclear Regulatory Commission
NTSC	National Transportation Safety Board
OARU	Occupational Accident Research Unit
OCAAR	Occupational Accidents Analysis and Reporting
OE	Organizational Error
OECD	Organization for Economic Cooperation and Development
OSHA	Occupational Safety and Health Administration
PC	Personal Computer
PFD	Process Flow Diagram
PHA	Process Hazard Analysis
P&ID	Piping and Instrumentation Diagram
PSF	Performance Shaping Factor
PSII	Process Safety Incident Investigation
PSM	Process Safety Management
PSV	Pressure Safety Valve
SONATA	Summary of Notable Accidents in Technical Activities
SRD	Safety and Reliability Directorate (UK Atomic Energy Authority)
STEP	Sequentially Timed Events Process
TNO	Netherlands Organization for Applied Scientific Research
TOR	Technique of Operations Review
TQM	Total Quality Management
VTT	Technical Research Centre of Finland
WOAD	World Offshore Accident Data
WSA	Work Safety Analysis

INDEX

Q

R